SONOMA COUNTY LIBRARY

W9-CRH-759

1000 06 261047 0 3

SONOMA COUNTY
BAUMGARTNER, FREDERIC J.
LOUIS XI
C1994
LIBRARY

OFFICIAL
DISCARD

10000626104703
CENT

LOUIS XII

Louis XII on Horseback by Jean Marot,
Bibliothèque Nationale, Paris (*Giraudon/Art Resource, NY*)

LOUIS XII

BY FREDERIC J. BAUMGARTNER

ST. MARTIN'S PRESS
NEW YORK

© Frederic J. Baumgartner 1994

All rights reserved. For information, write:
Scholarly & Reference Division,
St. Martin's Press, 175 Fifth Avenue,
New York, N.Y. 10010

First published in the United States of America in 1994

Printed in the United States of America

ISBN 0-312-12072-9

Library of Congress Cataloging-in-Publication Data

Baumgartner, Frederic J.
    Louis XII / Frederic J. Baumgartner.
        p.   cm.
    Includes bibliographical references.
    ISBN 0-312-12072-9
    1. Louis XII, King of France, 1462-1515. 2. France—Kings and
rulers—Biography. 3. France—History—Louis XII, 1498-1515.
I. Title.
    DC108.B38 1994
    944'.027—dc20   94-4477
                                                            CIP

INTERIOR DESIGN BY DIGITAL TYPE & DESIGN

▪ CONTENTS ▪

▪ PREFACE ▪

When I wrote *Henry II, King of France* (1988), I felt that it needed to be done partly because no modern English biography of that king then existed. I never expected that six years later I would be making the same case for a biography of a second French king. Upon finishing the biography of Henry, I intended to write a history of sixteenth-century France and begin it with the reign of Louis XII. Much to my surprise, I found that there was no English-language biography for him from any era nor a scholarly study of his reign in French since the nineteenth century, despite the fact that in 1506 the French Estates-general voted him the unique honor of "Father of the People." Like Henry, Louis has been overshadowed by Francis I, Louis's successor and Henry's father. As is the case for Henry also, the women in Louis's life—Jeanne of France, Anne of Brittany, and Mary Tudor—have been the subjects of far more biographies than he. A total of thirteen books has been published on the first two since 1980.

In 1985 the French historian Bernard Chevalier called Louis XII's era "this no man's land where neither the medievalists nor the modernists dare to penetrate."[1] Histories of medieval France generally end with Louis XI and those of the French Renaissance begin with Francis I, while the broader histories of France tend to move very quickly from Louis XI to Francis. Louis XII neither began nor concluded the Italian wars that were a major feature of his reign, while his successor quickly abandoned many of the policies primarily responsible for his title of "Father of the People." Francis is far more identified than is Louis with the two major movements of the era, the Renaissance and the Reformation.

Certainly I will not argue that Louis XII stands in the first rank of French kings. Acknowledging that, however, does not explain the obscurity in which Louis has languished in the twentieth century, at least until Bernard Quilliet's publication *Louis XII* (1986). Quilliet's book, however, is intended for a mass readership, lacking notes and having a limited bibliography. The large number of letters, however, to and from Louis in the manuscript collection of the Bibliothèque Nationale are not very informative about either royal decisions or their motivation because they often included simply salutations and best wishes, while the letter's courier delivered the real message by word of mouth. As a letter of Louis's from 1499 put it, "I have spoken on this at length to [his aide] who will tell you for my part." Nonetheless, the numerous diplomatic letters printed in Godefroy's *Lettres du roy Louis XII et du Cardinal d'Amboise* are useful sources. However, only the first volume warrants that title. The other volumes are largely made up of the correspondence of Margaret of Austria, regent of the Low Countries. Unfortunately, the fire that destroyed the Chambre des comptes in 1737 burned most of its records, so the fiscal accounts for the reign are very limited. A large portion of other manuscript sources has been printed. Louis's edicts are in volume 21 of *Ordonnances des roys* and also in Isambert's *Recueil des lois*, volume 5. Maulde La Clavière edited the records of the two major legal cases of Louis's reign and the pertinent letters in his massive *Procédures politiques*. Relations with the city of Paris are denoted in *Registres du bureau de l'hôtel de ville de Paris*.

A great deal of the diplomatic correspondence from Louis's reign is available in modern editions. The texts of the treaties and alliances can be found in Dumont's *Corps universel diplomatique*, volume 1. In addition to the above-mentioned *Lettres du roy Louis XII*, Habsburg diplomacy is presented in Le Glay's *Négociations diplomatiques* (2 volumes) and *Correspondance de l'Empereur Maximilien I et de Marguerite d'Autriche* (2 volumes). Relations with England are detailed in *Letters and Papers, Richard III and Henry VII; Letters and Papers, Henry VIII*, volume 1; and Champillion-Figeac's *Lettres des rois de France et d'Angleterre* (2 volumes). Spanish diplomacy is covered in *Calendar of State Papers, Spain*, and the documents printed in Boissonnade's *Les négociations entre Louis XII et Ferdinand Le Catholique*. Documents for Italian affairs are found in a large number of sources. Among them are *Calendar of State Papers, Milan; Calendar of State Papers, Venice;* and the numerous books and articles by Pélissier on Milan. Sanuto's *Il Diarii*, volume 1 to 19 for Louis's reign, is an enormous font of information drawn from the Venetian diplomatic correspondence. The Florentine point of view is found in Desjardins's *Négociations diplomatique de la France avec la Toscane;* Guicciardini's *History of Italy;* and several works by Machiavelli. All these works are also informative on the diplomacy and decision making at the papal curia, as is the diary of Burchard, the papal chamberlain in that era.

In regard to Louis himself, two of his historiographers, St-Gelais, in *Histoire de Louis XII*, and d'Auton, in *Chroniques de Louis XII*, provide extensive detail for the years they cover, but both chronicles end well before the king's death. There are several other histories of the reign by men associated with the court, such as Seyssel's, *Histoire de Louis XII*, but they lack the detail of the above. The memoirs of Floranges and the contemporary biographies of Bayard and La Trémoille, captains deeply involved in Louis's wars, provide good coverage of his campaigns, while Brantôme, whose grandmother and great-aunt were ladies-in-waiting at Louis's court, provides a good deal of gossip about Louis and his court.

There are a number of biographies of the king from the Ancien Régime; the best is Tailhé, *Histoire de Louis XII* (1755). During the Bourbon Restoration, two useful biographies were published: Masselin, *Histoire de Louis XII* (1822) and Roederer, *Mémoire pour servir à une nouvelle histoire de Louis XII* (1827). Both saw Louis as the prototype of the constitutional monarchy they hoped France was then becoming. In the late nineteenth century, Maulde La Clavière published a number of works of great value for the study of Louis XII, but he did not produce a full biography of the king. His mistitled *Histoire de Louis XII* (3 volumes) studied the House of Orléans only up to 1498. He wrote biographies of Jeanne of France and Anne of Beaujeu as well as a lengthy study of diplomatic style during Louis's era, *La Diplomatie au temps de Machiavel* (3 volumes). I do not know whether he lost interest in Louis's biography or died before writing it. In the twentieth century, there have been several popular biographies of Louis in French, of which the best is Quilliet's. The closest to an English-language biography of the "Father of the People" is Bridge's *History of France from the Death of Louis XI to 1515* (5 volumes), which is very strong on the French campaigns in Italy.

Some points of style: The French year began in Louis's time on Easter, and, therefore, new year's day moved about from year to year. (The French fiscal year went from October 1 to September 30.) The dates in this book are all in "new style": The year begins on January 1. For example, the date of February 8, 1499, as found in a document from the era, will be given as February 8, 1500. The names of kings, queens, princes, princesses, and other rulers are given in English; names of all others are in the form appropriate for their native languages. The names of French cities are in the French spelling; cities elsewhere are in the English. The money system in use in France is explained in the Appendix; but it should be noted here that all references to *livres* (*l*) are to the *livre tournois*, unless its obsolete rivals are specifically noted. References to the *écu* are to the *écu du soleil* rather than the slightly smaller *écu à la couronne*. The term "crown" will be used only when it is clear that the French *écu* is not meant.

A wide range of persons, some anonymous, contributed greatly to this book. Financial aid for the necessary research trips to France came from the American Philosophical Society and Virginia Polytechnic Institute and State University. Librarians and archivists in Paris and Blacksburg, especially the Interlibrary Loan staff at Virginia Tech, were immensely helpful. Special thanks must go to A. Lynn Martin of the University of Adelaide, who read most of the work; my students Ginette Aley, Kelly Barton, and Karen Byrne, who helped me in a wide variety of ways; and Linda Fountaine, Rhonda McDaniel, and Jan Francis of the Department of History, who put the entire manuscript on the word processor. I wish also to thank Simon Winder and his staff at St. Martin's Press, who did so much to facilitate the publication of this book.

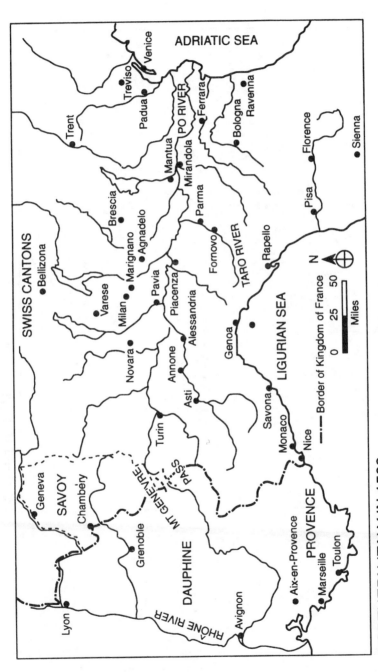

NORTHERN ITALY IN 1500

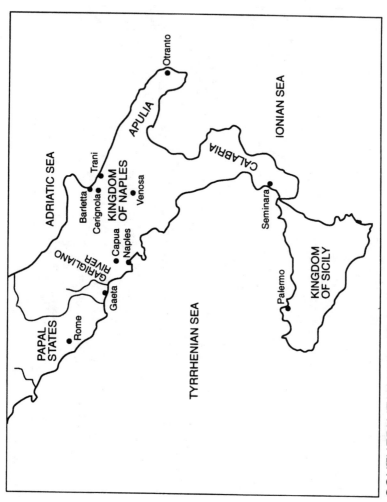

SOUTHERN ITALY IN 1500

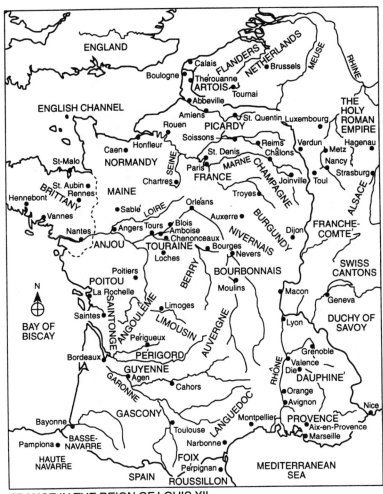

FRANCE IN THE REIGN OF LOUIS XII

LOUIS XII

1

At Last a Son

The arrival of Louis of Orléans into the world during the late hours of June 27, 1462, was an event of exceptional joy for the House of Orléans-Valois. As the only son of sixty-eight-year-old Charles of Orléans, he ensured that the family would keep its privileged position as a cadet branch of the royal family and its place high in the line of succession to the French throne. The baby's birth was widely regarded as a miracle, since his father, with good reason, had all but given up hope that he would ever have a son.

Charles of Orléans had one of the most romantic lives in French history. He was the eldest son of Louis I of Orléans, who was in turn the second son of King Charles V. Born in 1394, Charles was thirteen when his father was assassinated by agents of Duke John of Burgundy. He was too young to take revenge on Duke John as honor demanded before he was caught up in the Hundred Years War. Leading a large force of knights in the Battle of Agincourt, he was captured and taken to England to be held for a huge ransom. There he joined his younger brother, Jean of Angoulême, who had been sent as a hostage in 1413 and had not been ransomed. Their captivity, mostly in the Tower of London, was comfortable, and Louis was able to indulge in his favorite pastimes, reading works that had been brought to him from his library at Blois and writing poetry.[1] The poet-duke was able to direct the management of his estates with the help of his father-in-law, the count of Armagnac, whose daughter Bonne had become Charles's second wife after his first, a daughter of Charles VI, had died in childbirth.[2] After the Burgundians murdered Armagnac in 1418, Charles's bastard half brother Jean de Dunois, the famed companion of Jeanne d'Arc, protected his interests in France.

The chaotic state of affairs in France after Agincourt, the feebleness of both the French and the English monarchies after 1422, and the devastation of Orléanist property by war all contributed to the continued captivity of the Orléans brothers, as they were unable to raise their ransoms. Year after year they languished in the Tower, while Jeanne d'Arc rallied the French from their nadir in 1429 and began the reconquest of the country and the reestablishment of the monarchy. It was, however, Duke Philip of Burgundy, the son of the bitter enemy of the House of Orléans, who finally arranged for Charles's ransom. Having made a truce with the French king Charles VII in 1435, Philip was eager to make allies among the French nobles and began in 1439 to aid Dunois in collecting the ransom. Through his efforts, the English finally agreed to accept a sum of 200,000 *écus* for Charles—80,000 paid at his release on November 5, 1440, and 120,000 within six months. Charles had to sell several estates and mortgage other properties to raise that sum, but a portion still went unpaid. As late as 1514, his son had to agree to pay the remaining part.[3] His brother remained in England as hostage for the rest of the ransom but was finally freed in 1445. Jean soon married and in 1460, at age fifty-six, had a son, Charles, who was the father of Francis I.

Since Bonne d'Armagnac had died soon after Agincourt, Philip of Burgundy also arranged for a new bride for Charles of Orléans, who was now forty-six years old. She was Philip's fourteen-year-old niece, Mary of Cleves, the daughter of Duke Adolf IV of Cleves and Philip's sister Mary. Three weeks after Charles finally set foot again on French soil, their nuptials were celebrated. Her dowry went entirely into paying on his ransom. The new couple settled into the Château of Blois, which Charles rarely left after that. He set to work beautifying it, building new wings and establishing the famous gardens, and adding to his library. He and Charles VII were not on good terms because of his resentment at the king's failure to ransom him and the king's suspicion of the good relationship between him and Philip of Burgundy. Charles VII involved him little in the affairs of state despite the fact that he was third in line of succession after the king's two sons.

Charles and Mary had no children for seventeen years while he became crippled by gout and rheumatism. Then, to the surprise of the world, Mary gave birth to a daughter, Marie, in December 1457. After five more years Mary, now thirty-six, again became pregnant. The implausibility of Charles, approaching the age of seventy and physically quite feeble, fathering a child led to rumors that he was not the father. It is now impossible to settle such a matter, but there is no question that the family fully accepted Louis as Charles's son and heir; and in 1498 there was no effort to raise the suspicions as a way of denying him the throne.[4]

King Louis XI, the "Universal Spider," who had gained the throne in 1461, was one of those who was highly suspicious of the paternity of his new second cousin. He remarked to the ambassador from Milan: "As feeble and as poisoned as he is [referring to Charles's accusations that he was being poisoned by Francesco Sforza over his claim to Milan] he still has made his wife pregnant." He also commented to the Milanese ambassador that the duke was aged and without much sense.[5] Although he had contributed to Charles's ransom in 1440, the king, suspicious by nature, distrusted his Orléanist relatives, in part because of their continuing good relations with the duke of Burgundy. He hated to think of an Orléanist on the throne, a real possibility in 1462, for only his younger brother Charles, a sickly and rebellious young man, stood before them in the line of succession. Nonetheless, the king agreed to serve as the baby's godfather. The presence of the ill-humored king dulled the festivity of the occasion, since he clearly wished to finish the ceremony as quickly as possible. His mood became even blacker near the end of the ceremony when the baby he held in his arms wet his sleeve. He rushed out of the château without waiting for dinner. Louis took the event as a bad omen, and his dislike for his Orléanist relatives intensified.[6]

Louis XI's suspicion of the House of Orléans was said to have been the cause of the death of Duke Charles in 1465, two months after the birth of his second daughter, Anne.[7] Charles was summoned to a meeting at Tours of the princes and great nobles of the realm to deal with the revolt of the duke of Brittany at the end of 1464.[8] He spoke favorably of the rebellious duke, and Louis, enraged, chastised him before the assembly of his fellow magnates. Humiliated and exhausted, Charles set out for home but only reached Amboise, where he died in January 1465, at the advanced age of seventy-one years. His body was brought back to Blois for burial, but after his son had become king, he had his father's coffin carried to Paris in 1504 and re-buried in the Church of the Celestins, second only to the Basilica of Saint-Denis as a place of honor for burial.[9]

Duke Charles's death put two-year-old Louis under the guardianship of his mother, Mary of Cleves.[10] Her ancestors included counts of Holland and Flanders. Through her mother she was a granddaughter of John the Fearless of Burgundy, who had plotted the death of her husband's father. Blond, tall, and slim, she was said to have kept her beauty well into middle age. She had been brought up at the Burgundian court and was thoroughly imbued with the lingering—some say decadent—chivalric tradition that pervaded it.[11] Like her husband, she wrote poetry of some quality. Mary loved to dance and hunt and was fond of dogs and horses. She was well practiced in the refined manners of the era and had a taste for the fine arts. She especially liked richly illustrated books. Mary was conventionally devout in the religion of the day, which emphasized ritual and pious practices, and was generous in alms-giving as far as her limited resources permitted.

After Mary's husband died, as duchess dowager and guardian for her children, she had control of the family properties, which were extensive: the duchy of Orléans, the counties of Valois and Blois, the seigneuries of Coucy and Chauny, and the county of Asti in northern Italy. Despite the large estates, the family income was small; in 1455 its annual revenues were only 5,637 *livres* (*l*).[12] As mentioned, most of the property had been mortgaged to pay the ransoms of Charles and Jean, while Louis XI, miserly to virtually everyone, was especially tight with his Orléanist relatives. The pensions they received, 12,000 *l* for Mary and 6,000 *l* for Louis, were small in view of their high rank. Mary was forced to maintain a tight budget in order to make ends meet. While most of the time she imposed a frugal regime on her children, she did appreciate the need to keep up appearances when the public was watching. Only on feasts, for instance, was the young duke allowed to wear the scarlet satin robes indicative of his rank. Thus Louis was imbued with the frugal nature that characterized his reign, although as a young adult he did rebel against it for a time.

Like most high-born women of her era, Mary of Cleves was raised to be passive and submit quickly to the will of men in authority, such as Louis XI. The king exercised a forceful hand when it came to making decisions about his young cousin. It was he who insisted on the appointment of Guyot Pot, Comte de St-Pol, as Louis's governor. Pot came from a prominent noble family that had served the dukes of Burgundy for several generations. His brother Philippe was one of the closet confidants of Charles the Bold, whom he served until 1477, when he entered the service of the French king. Guyot Pot had made the move to France much earlier; by 1457 he was *maître d'hôtel* for Duke Charles.[13] Although he was attached to the Orléanist court, Pot, a flexible politician, gained the confidence of Louis XI while still remaining in the good graces of the duchess. He kept the king informed of happenings at Blois and on the upbringing of his young charge.

Pot's first responsibility as governor was to train Louis in the skills essential for a nobleman—war, hunting, and sports. As a young man Louis was regarded as the best jumper and tennis player in the realm, although it is not clear what sort of organized competition, if any, existed to allow such a judgment to be made. It may have simply reflected the usual practice of praising princes and kings as exemplary physical specimen. These were sports that involved vigorous physical exercise, and the training for war that they promised was the principal justification for allowing young noblemen to play them constantly. *Jeu de paume* (handball), which evolved into tennis, was Louis's favorite. The ball, made of leather and stuffed with animal hair, was hit with a gloved hand. The racket made its appearance several decades later. It is not clear from the brief descriptions of the game that come from Louis's time whether such innovations as the enclosed court and the use of a net instead of a cord strung across the court had appeared by then. The basic feature of the game was that two players or teams faced each other across the net or cord and struck the ball back and forth within a marked space.

The competition was often fierce, especially since there was heavy betting on the matches. One game before Louis became king had serious consequences. It was being played at Paris, and Anne of Beaujeu, the older daughter of Louis XI, was watching. She was asked to decide a disputed point and gave it against Louis. He became very angry and said that she lied. Anne became enraged herself and asked the duke of Lorraine if he was going to allow her to be insulted. Lorraine gave Louis a box on the ear. The others present separated them, but from then on the two were enemies, and Louis's relationship with Anne hardly became any warmer.[14]

Louis was equally well regarded as a horseman and jouster: "the best horseman and man-at-arms that I have seen," said Jean de St-Gelais, a confidant of the Orléanists,[15] although again it may have been convention to say that about royalty. Nonetheless, good horsemanship was a talent highly admired in that era, and anyone who hoped to command the respect of the warrior class had to ride well. Hunting a great stag was an opportunity to demonstrate one's riding skill. As king, Louis was not noted for playing *jeu de paume* or jousting, but he was constantly mentioned as being out hunting, often in the mountains of Dauphiné. In the last years of his life, his daughter Claude usually went with him. Hunting stag had a ritual and a procedure that were carefully followed. When the stag was finally killed, it was cut up according to a strict formula; the king was given its right hoof as a sign of honor. Stags were hunted with dogs, which were dear to the heart of every nobleman. The sport had rather little danger for hunter and dogs. Far more risky was hunting wild boar, and the hunters would not take their best dogs on a boar hunt because of the large number that would be killed. The other way to hunt was using hawks to catch birds.

The ultimate training for war for the young nobleman was the tournament. By Louis's time, the massed combat of dozens of competitors had largely given way to jousting by individuals, although a few instances of the former style did occur in his reign. Shattering a jousting lance, which was lighter than a lance used in combat, on the opponent's chestplate was the goal of the joust. Jousters carried heavier armor than in combat, since maneuvering was not needed and killing or maiming the foe was not the purpose of the event, but deaths did occur. After 1500, the standard form of jousting was to run two jousters at each other along a barrier about a yard in height that separated them; they held the lances in the right hand aiming at the left side of their foes. There were numerous other types of mock combat, such as assaults on a mock fort or battles between two galleys. Before becoming king, Louis took an active part in tournaments, but in 1498 he retired, perhaps because it was deemed inappropriate for the king to risk his life in them, or simply because he was getting too old.

Less is known of how Louis's mind was developed. He had access to the excellent library that his grandfather and father had collected, but it appears that he took little interest in it as a youth. An eighteenth-century historian wrote that Mary of Cleves spared no expense for his education, but the lack of docility in her son, who did not accept any correction, rendered her efforts futile.[16] The name of only one of his tutors is known for certain — Jean Thomas, a physician who contributed a book on medicine to the library at Blois.[17] Regardless of who Louis's tutors were, he became well versed in French literature and history and could read and write Latin. When he was in Pavia later in his life, he attended a lecture in Latin by a noted legal scholar. It is less clear whether he learned Italian as a child, but he did know something of the language as an adult. He was curious about the world of scholarship, especially ancient history, and art, but was most interested in music. The statement by a nineteenth-century biographer that he loved learning and scholars is probably too strong. While there is little firsthand evidence about the routine of his first twelve years, there is no reason to dispute the image of a happy childhood, although it comes from chroniclers who wrote after he became king. Their descriptions of his happy and studious childhood may have been tailored to his high rank.

The event that blackened Louis's life for twenty-five years, his marriage to Jeanne of France, the daughter of Louis XI and Charlotte of Savoy, had little impact on his early years since it occurred in 1476, although the marriage was first proposed within days of her birth in 1464. Historians have generally seen the betrothal as very much the idea of the king, who presented the proposal to Charles of Orléans four days after his daughter's birth in April 1464. However, the Milanese ambassador recorded Louis XI as telling him that the old duke of Orléans wanted to betroth his son Louis to the king's new daughter, but the king was reluctant to do it because the duke had so little income to leave to his heir. Regardless of whose idea it was, on May 10 an envoy from the king arrived at Blois with a marriage contract, providing a dowry of 100,000 *l* for Jeanne. Charles signed it on May 19.[18]

Louis XI is usually attributed a sinister motive for the planned marriage: As he was told that Jeanne's deformed and crippled condition probably rendered her sterile, by marrying her to the Orléanist heir the king would extinguish the House of Orléans and unite its lands to the crown. However, the very short length of time after her birth that the marriage was proposed would seem to acquit the king of such a cruel motive, since most infants appear misshapen for several days after natural childbirth. It is hard to believe that such a medical judgment could have been made within four days of Jeanne's birth. It is more probable that Louis planned well before her birth to marry a female child in the House of Orléans. Furthermore, Duke Charles had asked that Louis's daughter Louise, who died before Jeanne's birth, be betrothed to his son, so the idea of a marriage between a royal daughter and the Orléans son was in the air. Last, while Louis XI was often cruel, he always seems to have had the best interest of the monarchy at heart. Would he have consciously created a potentially very serious crisis in the line of succession to the throne when only his sickly and often rebellious brother and the aged duke of Orléans preceded young Louis in that line?

If it is possible to argue in Louis XI's behalf in respect to the betrothal of Louis and Jeanne at the time of her birth, it is far less plausible to do so in 1473, when he insisted that the marriage contract be renewed. By then he had a son, Charles, born in 1470, who was healthy and past the most dangerous period for infant death. Also by 1473 the defects of Jeanne's deformed body were obvious to all who saw her, although her father was said to have never yet seen her. He had sent her off to the Château of Linières in Berry shortly after her birth, where she lived on a pension of 1,200 *l*, tiny for a king's daughter. Jeanne was lame—one leg being shorter than the other—hunchbacked, and badly sloped-shouldered. She was very short—almost a dwarf—and extremely thin and had her father's long nose on a face that was much too small for it. Her beauty of soul, which eventually would bring the Catholic Church to canonize her a saint, and her intelligence were not the sort of qualities that have usually been appreciated in a bride-to-be. The nature of the deformity that apparently rendered her incapable of bearing children is never explained in the sources, but her sterility seems to have been unquestioned, except by Jeanne herself.

Louis XI's own words of September 1473 convict him of using Jeanne's deformity as motive for insisting on the marriage. He expressed it in a letter to his *grand maître*, Antoine de Chabannes, one of his closest confidants: "I have resolved to make the marriage of my little daughter Jeanne and the little Duke of Orléans because it seems to me that the children they will have together will cost nothing to feed. I warn you that I hope to make this marriage and those who oppose it will not be sure of their lives in my realm."[19]

Envoys of the king arrived at Blois in 1473 to demand that Mary of Cleves sign a new marriage contract. He had become aware of both her objections to the proposed match and her desire that her son marry his older daughter Anne (born 1460), who was regarded as surprisingly attractive, given the fact that both her parents were homely at best.[20] Louis XI did raise Jeanne's dowry to 100,000 *écus*, an increase of 62 percent over what had been proposed in 1464 and well above what was traditional for royal daughters.[21] The royal officers threatened to send Mary back to Cleves, force her son into the monastery of Cluny, and cut off the heads of her advisers if she refused. Her reply, that she cared "not a broken link of mail" if the king did these things, surely frightened her servants more than it bothered the king.[22] As for the young husband-to-be, he had never seen Jeanne, but he had heard a great deal about her deformed appearance and had developed a strong repulsion for her that only grew worse as time passed.

Louis XI then ordered mother and son to come to his court. The duke was threatened with being sewn in a sack and tossed into the river. His mother capitulated and signed the marriage contract on October 28, 1473. Her son signed it the next day. He would later claim that he had signed a secret protest at the same time; but if he did, it could not be produced at the annulment process in 1498. Shortly thereafter Mary decided to go see her future daughter-in-law for herself at Linières. She reportedly almost fainted when she saw her for the first time.[23]

Since the betrothed couple was still too young to be married, the wedding had to be delayed until 1476, when Louis would be fourteen. In the meantime, Louis XI's older daughter Anne was married in November 1473 to Pierre de Bourbon, Sire de Beaujeu. He was nineteen years older than she and a widower, but they had an unusually close relationship and worked exceptionally well together during their period of power, the first seven years of the reign of Charles VIII. However, their marriage was another humiliation for Mary of Cleves, since her daughter Marie had been betrothed to Beaujeu in 1461. Marie was soon wedded to Jean de Foix, Vicomte de Narbonne, a man of high status but not at the level of the Bourbons. She seems to have passed out of her brother's life once she married, but her two children would play important roles in Louis's reign. She and her husband died by 1505, when her children came to their uncle's court. Louis kept in touch with his sister Anne, soon to enter the religious life, and took refuge with her at least twice during his period as a rebel.

As Louis approached his fourteenth year, preparations for the marriage began. In February 1475 Cardinal Giuliano della Rovere arrived in France with a bull from Pope Sixtus IV, which provided a dispensation from the canon in church law that forbade marriages within five degrees of consanguinity. It was necessary because Louis and Jeanne were second cousins once removed, resulting in three degrees of consanguinity. The papal bull also contained a dispensation for the impediment of spiritual consanguinity, created because Jeanne's father was Louis's godfather.[24]

Louis had not yet seen Jeanne, but he refused to visit her. When his mother insisted that he pay a call on his intended, upon approaching the Château of Linières, he turned back to Blois. In 1475 Louis XI finally saw Jeanne for the first time at Tours—he viewed her as she crossed a courtyard. His reported words "I didn't believe she was so ugly!" sum up her life—the repulsion her appearance created; her isolation from her family, for even her mother rarely visited her; and her use as a pawn in the king's political chess. Jeanne was well aware of her appearance and circumstances. She dealt with them with a spirit of humble resignation and a deeply devout religious life. Her only desire was to be allowed to become a nun and devote her life to God. The king would hear none of that, as he would hear none of the anguished protests of the duchess dowager and her son. He again threatened to force Louis into a monastery if he did not go through with the marriage.

On September 8, 1476, in the Château of Montrichard near Tours, Louis of Orléans was dragged to the altar to be wedded to Jeanne of France. Neither Louis XI nor Mary of Cleves were present; the royal chancellor, Pierre Dorielle, watched to ensure that it was done. François de Bailhac, bishop of Orléans, officiated. He was still alive twenty-two years later and gave a deposition on the event to the commission hearing Louis XII's request for an annulment.[25] At that time he stated that when he asked the duke of Orléans the required question of whether he was acting of his own free will, the young man replied: "Alas, my friend, what can I do? I don't know how to resist. I would be dead if I refused to do this because you know with whom I'm dealing." The bishop then asked him if he wished to go on; Louis responded: "I have been forced and there is no remedy." Despite Louis's clear statement that he was being coerced and despite what church law stated about coercion in marriage, the bishop proceeded with the ceremony. He pronounced Louis and Jeanne husband and wife and hurried out of the château.

In spite of what must have been a truly gloomy atmosphere, the celebration of the wedding proceeded, and the new couple and the guests sat down to a sumptuous meal. Louis refused to look at his bride or touch his food and sobbed throughout the meal. Jeanne, who, one can presume, had expected that her marriage would free her from her isolation, quickly understood her status with her husband: "It is easy to see that he takes no account of me." Louis would later swear that the marriage was never consummated, while Jeanne would insist that it had been. It seems curious that Louis XI, given the circumstances of the marriage, had not seen to the presence of witnesses to ensure the legal requirements for consummation, but his absence from the scene probably resulted in the oversight.

Louis left Jeanne's side the next day and fled back to Blois. His mother, terrified at what the king would do when he heard that his daughter had been abandoned, ordered him to reside at Linières, where Jeanne had returned. He avoided her as much as possible and never spoke to her directly. After three days there, he rushed back to Blois. Louis XI quickly learned of it. In a rage he sent for Pierre Dupuy, one of the duke's companions, and thundered that they both would be tossed into the river if Louis did not do his duty as a husband.[26] Louis again made his way to Linières, where he found the royal physician present. The physician ordered Louis to go to his wife's room. Infuriated by this impertinence, Louis raged: "The devil take me [his usual oath]! I would prefer to have my head cut off than do that!" Instead he went out to play tennis with his companions. Then, having had time to think things over, Louis finished his game and went to Jeanne's room. It is difficult to believe that with the royal physician present to serve as an expert witness, the marriage was not consummated at this time. Yet Louis would always swear that he never had conjugal relations with Jeanne. The physician did not provide a deposition for the annulment process; presumably he was dead by 1498.

For the next seven years Louis officially resided at Linières, but frequently was absent for long periods. His cruel disregard for Jeanne's feelings was obvious to everyone who dealt with them, but there was nothing further that either the king or his mother could do to force him to be more solicitous, although he did send his wife gifts in 1478.[27] Jeanne responded with patience and forbearance. When in 1483 Louis fell seriously ill with smallpox, Jeanne devotedly nursed him back to health without receiving any sign of affection or gratitude from him. That illness was the first of many health problems to threaten his life.

Louis spent those seven years largely in the pursuit of pleasure and recreation.[28] His accounts mention only sports, pleasures, and minstrels, but despite being constantly short of funds, he did not touch Jeanne's dowry.[29] He had no real responsibilities of any sort, and whatever formal education he had been getting in his younger years ended. Jean de St-Gelais wrote that Louis's education was deficient in arts and letters and even in the practical management of estates. St-Gelais commented that too much emphasis had been given to training the young duke in hunting and riding, and his native intelligence was often betrayed by his poor education.[30]

Unrestrained by any sense of being married, Louis threw himself into numerous affairs. Brantôme, whose grandmother and great-aunt were ladies-in-waiting at Louis's court, said of him: "He was a merry gallant in his day and did love fair women." One in particular was a young commoner of unusual beauty and spirit named Amasie. Louis installed her in a house near the Château of Blois, where they carried on a very public affair for some time. His treasurer's accounts included payments to *les filles de joie*.[31] Louis was said to have had an illegitimate son around 1484, named Michel de Bucy, who was chosen archbishop of Bourges in 1505 and died in 1512.[32] Louis spent a great deal of his time in hunting, and the quality of his hounds and falcons became famous across France. Such a lifestyle was certainly common enough among the young nobles of the era, but Louis seems to have carried it well beyond the norm. Yet precisely because he lived such a lifestyle, he endeared himself to the nobility and made a number of fast friends among the young nobles, who would be loyal to him for the rest of their lives. While his elders regarded him as a frivolous young man, his age group in the French warrior class was ready to follow him even into rebellion, as happened shortly after Louis XI's death in 1483.

2

Prince of Blood

While Louis of Orléans hunted, jousted, and whored his way to manhood, momentous events were occurring in France and Europe that profoundly affected his life and reign. The most important of these was the bitter feud between the French monarchs and the dukes of Burgundy. All of the direct participants in the feud were members of the royal family, but blood ties had not kept John of Burgundy from arranging the assassination of his nephew Louis I of Orléans in 1407. The French royal house, the Valois, became involved in the resulting blood feud when the dauphin Charles (Charles VII) gave his approval to the murder of John in 1419. For well over a century, it was one of the major facts of French politics and foreign policy.

While the two assassinations added the powerful element of a blood feud to this rivalry, it would surely have erupted in some form anyway because of the growth of the Burgundian domain. Through marriage, the House of Burgundy acquired title to several of the seventeen provinces of the Low Countries, and Duke Philip II added most of the rest in 1430 when he made good his claim to them as the heir of Albert of Bavaria, their former ruler. Now the Burgundian domains, which had already included the duchy of Burgundy and the Free County of Burgundy (the Franche-Comté), an imperial fief, included the Low Countries and Artois and part of Picardy. While the geopolitical imperative of forming a unified block of land out of these two compact but separated regions may not have been as strong then as it would become later, the advantage of controlling Alsace and Lorraine was obvious to the Burgundian dukes.

Gaining the Low Countries had given the Burgundian dukes lands outside of the French cultural and political sphere, and their attention was often directed away from French politics. Duke Philip, however, was very conscious of being a member of the royal family and took an active part in French politics. For example, he gave refuge to the future Louis XI when he fled from his father in 1456. Philip's son Charles the Bold, who succeeded him in 1467, was far less oriented toward France. He viewed himself as an independent prince, and his fondest hope was of gaining a title of king for himself, perhaps even being elected Holy Roman Emperor. Charles did seek to make use of the factions among the French nobles, but his political behavior was largely that of one sovereign ruler involved in international diplomacy, intrigue, and even war against another.

Duke Charles hardly had taken his father's place when he began to work toward achieving the two major goals of his dynasty. He began to push his claims to parts of Alsace and Lorraine, and in 1473 he pressed Holy Roman Emperor Frederick III into agreeing to grant him the title of king in exchange for the promise of the hand of his only child, Mary, in marriage to the emperor's son, Maximilian. Frederick, persuaded by French gold, reneged at the last minute before the coronation, although discussion of the marriage continued. More seriously, Charles's aggression in Alsace aroused the Swiss, since western Switzerland had once been part of the early medieval realm of Burgundy that he was seeking to re-create. By liberal use of gold, Louis XI heightened those fears, and in 1474 Swiss forces attacked the Franche-Comté. It was contemporary opinion that the Swiss fought Charles as Louis's mercenaries. Caught up in occupying Lorraine, Charles did not respond to the Swiss until two years later, when he took an army of Burgundian knights and German pikemen and the best artillery train of the time into Switzerland.

Stopping to recover Grandson from the Swiss, Charles was suddenly confronted with a powerful Swiss army. Over the previous century they had developed a style of war that had made them all but invincible on the battlefields of the fifteenth century. Wielding their eighteen-foot pikes and swinging their halberds—heavy battle axes on eight-foot poles—and wearing little armor so they could move rapidly, the Swiss advanced toward their foes in their three columns already in battle order. Thus it often was only a matter of moments after "the forest of pikes" was first sighted before the lead center column crashed into the enemy line. The Battle of Grandson took place in an open field favorable to Charles's cavalry and artillery, but the speed and shock of the Swiss columns rendered both ineffective and gave victory to the men of the Alps. Charles was able to save most of his manpower and return to the attack in three months. He moved deep into Switzerland, to within fourteen miles of Bern, where he laid siege to the town of Murten. When a week passed without a Swiss attack, his men relaxed their guard. They were largely taken by surprise when the Swiss charged their camp from a neighboring forest. Charles's cannon tore huge holes in the Swiss columns, but their speed allowed them to reach the guns before they could be reloaded. The Burgundian army broke and ran, but the Swiss pursued vigorously and inflicted 8,000 casualties, in large part because their practice was to kill all prisoners and wounded.

Charles's defeat allowed Duke René of Lorraine to recover much of his duchy, including the city of Nancy. Despite the catastrophe at Murten, Charles rebuilt his army with his usual vigor and laid siege to Nancy. The duke of Lorraine called on the Swiss for help. In January 1477 they assembled an army of about 20,000 men and moved to relieve Nancy. In the bloody battle that followed, Charles, trying to rally his men, was killed by a blow from a halberd, which split his helmet and his skull. His frozen body was found on the battlefield two days later.

Their victory at Nancy had little direct consequence for the Swiss, as their internal rivalries made it impossible for them to stay unified after the foreign threat had passed. Thus they passed up the opportunity to carve out conquests in Alsace and Lorraine and instead served in larger and larger numbers as mercenaries in other armies. The death of Charles, on the other hand, had enormous consequences. His heir was his twenty-year-old daughter, Mary, who was in no position to lead Burgundian resistance to Louis XI. Louis's scheming mind immediately struck on forcing her to marry his seven-year-old son Charles, although the marriage would have had to wait until the boy was fourteen. Mary, then at Ghent where the Burgundian court had taken up residence and surrounded by advisers who had much to fear from submitting to the French king, refused the offer. She decided to wed her father's choice, Maximilian of Habsburg, in hope of gaining a protector against the French. In August 1477 nineteen-year-old Maximilian entered Ghent to claim his bride. Within a year they had a son, Philip, and a year later a daughter, Margaret.

Mary gave full power to her husband, but he could not prevent Louis XI from making deep inroads into the Burgundian lands. Louis claimed both Burgundys on the grounds that they had escheated to the crown in default of a male heir, and French troops quickly enforced his claim. The king himself led a force into Artois and Picardy. After securing them, he pushed on into Flanders but was defeated at Guinegate in August 1479. Negotiations soon began, but they stalled until Mary's accidental death in a fall from a horse in 1481. She had been much more intransigent than Maximilian toward Louis XI, and the Peace of Arras was soon agreed upon. It arranged for the betrothal of Louis's son Charles with Maximilian's three-year-old daughter Margaret; Artois and the Franche-Comté were to serve as her dowry. She was to be raised at the French court. The duchies of Flanders and Burgundy were recognized as fiefs of the French crown. Philip of Habsburg, as the heir of his mother, would do homage for Flanders at the appropriate age, but Burgundy was permanently incorporated into the French realm.

Maximilian's prospects had seemed to improve greatly in 1480 when he had signed an alliance with Edward IV of England. Edward still claimed the title of king of France, as all English monarchs did for another century, and intended to make good that claim. Continued English occupation of Calais after their evacuation of the rest of France in 1453 gave them easy access into France, while its combination of natural and manmade defenses rendered it invulnerable to French attack, at least until 1558. Many of the inhabitants of the provinces of Gascony and Guyenne, which the English had ruled for 300 years before 1453, still remembered them fondly. Also the English monarchy already had a well-established tradition of intervening in the Low Countries against French interests there. Thus the English had a clear strategic advantage over the French, but France did have a counterweight of sorts—the "Auld Alliance" with Scotland. The Scots routinely invaded northern England when the French requested it, not that they always needed French prodding. In a way Scotland was the French answer to Calais, since on several occasions French troops were transported to Scotland to attack England.

Four centuries of conflict between the French and the English monarchies had made the French keenly aware of how political events across the Channel usually had a direct impact on them. Just as the English had successfully fished in the troubled waters of France in the early fifteenth century, so Louis XI hoped to exploit the bitter rivalry between the Yorks and the Lancasters in England. Like the earlier situation in France, it was created in part by the insanity of a king, in this case, Henry VI, from the House of Lancaster. His periodic fits of madness, beginning in 1453, gave the House of York, which was descended from Edward III, its opportunity to regain the throne. The Yorkists gained the upper hand when in 1461 Duke Edward of York defeated Henry VI's troops and forced Henry and his queen to flee to Scotland. Louis was too cautious, or perhaps too shrewd, to get involved directly in English politics, but he did provide some support and encouragement to the Lancastrians to keep Edward IV busy at home. Edward for his part entered into an alliance with the duke of Burgundy.

When in 1469 civil war again erupted in England after several years of quiet, the tide turned entirely in favor of Edward IV. Two years later Henry VI was captured in battle and died soon after, and his only son was killed. With Edward's control of England now uncontested, his alliance with Charles the Bold was far more threatening to France. In 1475 they signed an agreement by which Charles recognized Edward as the true king of France while the English king recognized Charles's claims to most of northern France. Edward brought a substantial force across the Channel that summer. However, Charles had become too involved in his war with the Swiss to strike into France as planned. Abandoned by his ally, Edward was quick to accept Louis's offer to negotiate. In August 1475 they agreed to a treaty by which Louis pledged to pay Edward 75,000 *écus* to return home and an annual subsidy of 50,000 *écus* for seven years to stay there.

The death of Charles the Bold at Nancy revived Edward's interest in meddling in France, as Mary and Maximilian soon made overtures to him. Edward pledged 1,500 archers for their use. Louis took little time to demonstrate that he was capable of causing trouble for Edward. The Scots crossed the border, and several Lancastrians appeared openly at the French court. Since Mary and Maximilian were unable to muster enough forces for a credible strike against France, Edward renewed his agreement with Louis under the same terms. By 1481 rumor was circulating across Europe that Louis XI was ill and about to die. Edward advised Maximilian to wait for his imminent death before attempting a joint enterprise. But it was Edward who died first, in April 1483, at age forty-one. His ambitious brother Richard quickly pushed aside Edward's twelve-year-old son and seized the throne. Lacking popular support and widely deemed to be a usurper, Richard III presented Louis with a golden opportunity to meddle in English affairs; but before Louis could make a move, he died at Tours in late August 1483.

The removal of that powerful and energetic personality from the scene had profound consequences in France and across Europe. Most significantly for our story, the succession of thirteen-year-old Charles VIII to the throne made Louis of Orléans first in the line of succession and First Prince of Blood. Now twenty-one, Louis was ready and eager to make his mark in the affairs of state. Late in the previous year, the old king had made Louis swear his loyalty to Charles when he came to the throne, but the duke had made no objection since he fully expected to dominate the government of his young cousin.[1] Charles was not regarded as being a very bright lad, and his education both formal and political had been limited by fears that his fragile body could not take rigorous effort. While not as misshapen as his sister Jeanne, he had much the same slight frame, spindly arms and legs, and a long, narrow face, but unlike her he was plagued with frequent fevers and nagging colds.[2] His father had kept him isolated at Amboise and had not seen him for over ten years until shortly before his death.

A decree of 1374 had established the age of majority for a young king as having "attained fourteen years of his age."[3] In 1483 this was taken to mean that he had to have reached his fourteenth birthday, as opposed to being in his fourteenth year by having reached his thirteenth birthday, as the clause would be interpreted in 1563 for Charles IX. Accordingly Charles VIII needed a regent for ten months.[4] The obvious choice was the queen-mother, but she had never been involved in political affairs and was terminally ill, dying in December 1483. Louis of Orléans, the First Prince of Blood, also had a strong claim to the office, but he was inexperienced and not highly regarded. Louis XI had not made any provision for a regent but had arranged for the formation of a royal council eight days before his death. He intended it to include the queen-mother, Louis of Orléans, Duc Jean II de Bourbon, and Pierre de Beaujeu, who was named presiding officer.[5] Not only was Beaujeu to be the president of the royal council, he, along with his wife, also was given the guardianship of the young king. When Louis of Orléans had given Louis XI his pledge of obedience to his son in 1482, he had acknowledged that the guardianship of the royal person would go to the Beaujeus.[6] According to Philippe de Commynes, a royal counsellor, Louis XI several days before his death had sent Beaujeu to Amboise to take charge of his son as his governor and to keep certain unnamed persons away from him.[7] There appears to have been no written record of these appointments, but no one challenged them. While their positions gave the Beaujeus broad authority in the new government, they did not constitute the legal position of regent. The ten months to Charles's fourteenth birthday passed without anyone formally holding the title.

While Beaujeu held the official appointments, it was his wife Anne who, it quickly became clear, really held power. Her father, in his ungracious manner, had called her "the least foolish of her sex." Brantôme, writing nearly a century later, said that "she was the true image in everything of her father."[8] Anne was, everyone has agreed, a more attractive version of her father, combining the same iron will, political sagacity, and tightfistedness[9] with greater tact, better humor, and a more gentle nature. She had great control over her brother while he was a teenager. The story was told of how Charles, celebrating his coronation, fell into a dumbfounded silence when she entered the room "to see how the king was behaving." When Louis complained to the Estates-general in 1484 about his exclusion from power, his complaint was directed against the "government of Madame de Beaujeu."[10]

Louis was badly overmatched in political acumen in his competition with Madame de Beaujeu for control of the government, but he did have some strengths. He was the highest-ranking prince in a society where that meant a great deal, and he represented the large part of the French people who had reason to hate Louis XI and were eager to undo his government, while the Beaujeus stood for the detested old regime. However, Anne and Pierre moved quickly to appease those who had the greatest grievances against the dead king. They confirmed all of the old king's officers in their positions and gave high offices to the great nobility. Louis received the governorship of the Ile-de-France and the command of a company of 100 lances, and his pensions and salaries came to 44,000 *l.* Beaujeu also gave up the presidency of the royal council to him on the same day in October 1483 that he did homage to the new king for his fiefs. Louis's cousin, François I de Dunois, who was as loyal to him as François's father had been to his father, gained the governorship of Dauphiné. Beaujeu's older brother, Duc Jean II de Bourbon. became lieutenant-general of the realm and constable, the major office open in 1483.

It may well be a measure of the insecurity of their position in late 1483 that the Beaujeus gave out all of these offices without taking any for themselves.[11] The new government moved to gain the support of the other classes by reducing taxes by a fourth, disbanding the companies of Swiss mercenaries, and rehabilitating the great number of persons and families exiled, imprisoned, or ruined by Louis XI. Although the new order recognized the preeminent status of Louis of Orléans, it hardly satisfied him. Even before Louis XI's death, his son-in-law had been preparing the way to take over the government. Despite having sworn in September 1482 to the old king that he would not deal with the duke of Brittany, three months later he sent an envoy to Nantes to discuss the policy they would follow after Louis XI was gone.[12]

After 1477 the duke of Brittany replaced the Burgundian dukes as the major internal foe of the French monarchy.[13] Brittany had long behaved as an independent state, even if its duke did do homage to the French king, but he did it standing, not kneeling. The Bretons, distinct from the French by language and culture, were strongly opposed to union with France. They refused to send delegates to the French Estates-general, despite always being requested, although the dukes did send envoys to the meetings. They paid no taxes to the royal treasury and allowed no royal judges into the duchy. The dukes had an agreement with the papacy dating from 1411 by which the pope named bishops for the Breton dioceses, who had to be acceptable to the duke. Efforts by Louis XI to appoint prelates in Brittany were successfully resisted. John Bridge, an early twentieth-century historian, nicely defined the relationship between Brittany and France: "The Breton was instinctively the friend of every foe of France. Every French malcontent subject could count upon his sympathy; . . . from Saint-Malo to Roscoff, from Brest to Nantes, his ports stood open to welcome every foe of France who might brave the perils of his coast."[14]

Thus Louis of Orléans had a sympathetic ear at the court of Duke Francis II. Francis was not a strong leader, however; he was sickly and not very bright and hardly up to the task he faced: maintaining his dynasty and the autonomy of his duchy with two daughters as offspring. The problem of the Breton succession would be a major theme of the reigns of Charles VIII and Louis XII. Louis's relationship with Francis blossomed in the last months of Louis XI's reign. It was aided by Orléans's sister Anne, who provided Guillaume Chaumart, a member of a Dominican house that she governed, as a messenger for his clandestine diplomacy. Louis proposed to the Breton duke that once he obtained an annulment from Jeanne, he would betroth Francis's older daughter Anne. He would then be named as the duke's heir to Brittany and give up his duchy of Orléans to the French crown in order to gain royal approval. Francis received the proposal enthusiastically.[15]

Louis made contact with other princes and great nobles, including Jean de Bourbon; Jean de Châlons, the prince of Orange; Alain d'Albret, who held extensive estates in the southwest of France; and the two d'Aydie brothers, both named Odet, who also were influential there.[16] They were prepared to listen to intrigue, especially when it was presented to them by Dunois, a highly respected leader of the nobility. A number of men who had been in authority at the court of Louis XI, among them Guyot Pot and Commynes, came over to the Orléanist camp. A major recruit was Georges d'Amboise, the twenty-three-year-old bishop of Montauban. One of the eighteen children of Pierre d'Amboise, a chamberlain for Louis XI, Georges was a subtle politician at an early age, and he gave Louis valuable advice from the beginning of their relationship.

The princes and great nobles, of whom Louis was the leader in rank but not in experience and talent, won numerous concessions from the Beaujeus in the first months of the new reign. The most notable was the disgrace of two of Louis XI's closest confidants, Jean de Doyat and Olivier Le Daim, who had notorious reputations as harsh enforcers of the royal will. Their disregard for the privileges and presumptions of the nobility, the clergy, and the bourgeoisie had earned them a broad range of enemies. Doyat avoided the ultimate penalty by forfeiting lands, offices, and wealth to his most implacable foe, Jean de Bourbon; Le Daim, who had made far more enemies, was convicted in a quick trial and executed. His confiscated wealth was given to Louis of Orléans, which did much to relieve Louis's financial embarrassment.[17]

Despite the many concessions the Beaujeus made to the dissident nobles, they remained in control of the government because they controlled the person of the king and had the political astuteness largely absent in their adversaries. They agreed to enlarge the royal council as demanded by their opponents, yet took advantage of the move to increase the number of their supporters on it. As the princes on the council found themselves outmaneuvered, they began to miss meetings, and the Beaujeus' influence increased apace.[18]

Nonetheless, in the first two months of Charles's reign, it was unclear where the balance of power would swing. In the hope of winning the favor of the populace, either faction may have suggested at the first meeting of the new royal council that the Estates be convened.[19] In late January 1484 the spokesman for the Orléanist camp, Philippe de Luxembourg, bishop of LeMans, declared before the deputies that his party had been responsible for summoning them, but that may have been simply an attempt to identify his party with the popular enthusiasm for the Estates. In a letter to the duke of Bourbon from May 1486, Louis claimed credit for the meeting, saying that he had asked the king to assemble the Estates of the realm.[20]

On October 24, 1483, letters convoking the Estates at Orléans for January were sent out; in December the site was changed to Tours because of a plague.[21] The letters contained a major innovation in the manner of selecting the deputies. The traditional procedure had the king summoning selected members of the clergy and nobility to attend and ordering the cities to select delegates in their urban assemblies. The new procedure called for the *sénéshaux* and the *baillis*, the local royal officials, to assemble the churchmen, nobles, bourgeoisie, and inhabitants of their districts in order to elect one deputy for each estate, although several of the heavily populated districts were allowed two delegates per estate.[22] The major royal officials were summoned to sit with the Estates; but when the bishops claimed the same right as a body, they were refused on the grounds that the Estates were a political body and did not require the consent of all the prelates. Some bishops did win election as deputies. Factionalism probably was not involved in this decision since the bishops were fairly evenly split between the parties. The new procedure for selection of deputies had the consequence of involving all three estates in the choice of all the deputies from their districts and perhaps gave each deputy a greater sense of speaking for all the people of his district.[23]

In early January the 221 deputies began to arrive in Tours.[24] On January 14 Charles VIII made his formal entry into Tours, and on the next day he opened the assembly. The royal chancellor, Guillaume de Rochefort, a former member of the Burgundian court, delivered the opening address, a brilliant piece of oratory in which he praised the French people for their loyalty to their monarch; thus he said, their young king could trust them to deal with the grave matters of the realm.[25] Rochefort set the tone for the meeting; everyone present found ample support for his viewpoint, ranging from those who had an activist agenda for establishing for the Estates a major role in governing to those who were quick to defer to the monarchy.

After the opening ceremonies, the deputies divided themselves into six groups to prepare their *cahiers,* the lists of grievances and suggested corrections. The First Estate requested a return to the Pragmatic Sanction of Bourges, which had been drawn up by Charles VII in 1438. It had eliminated the papacy from the process of appointing bishops and abbots by placing the power of election to those offices in the cathedral and monastery chapters, but Louis XI had taken over the appointment of prelates without conceding anything to the pope. The Second Estate demanded that military command be prohibited to foreigners. The Third Estate asked that taxes be drastically reduced, and the revenue needs of the crown be met by decreasing royal pensions and offices. All three Estates called for the reform of justice and especially the elimination of the sale of offices.[26] There is no suggestion that Orléans was involved in drawing up the *cahiers,* but he clearly was aware of their content. Once he became king, he implemented much of their program.

The duke of Orléans was primarily interested in the meeting of the Estates as a way to curb the Beaujeus and elevate his power by pressing the deputies to support him on the issue of the membership of the royal council. On January 17 his spokesman delivered an attack on the "disorders of the state and the government of Madame de Beaujeu."[27] After three weeks in which the factions calculated their support, the issue came before the Estates in early February. The bishop of LeMans attacked the oppressive members of the council and urged that they be replaced. He attempted to identify the Beaujeus with the hated policies of Louis XI and turn deputy sentiment in favor of Orléans. However, the effort to promote Louis for the office of protector of the young king had one major problem—the duke himself. He had scandalized the deputies by his behavior in Tours with his lavish entertainments and his visits to *filles de joie.* On February 7, after the Beaujeus had submitted a list of members for the council for ratification, Jehan Masselin, the leader of the Norman delegation, was sent to Louis to hear his views. The duke, however, was about to go to dinner "with many others" and gave only a curt reply.[28] Although the Estates declined to accept the Beaujeus' list as presented, Orléans gave the impression that he was too frivolous a playboy to be given a leading role in government.

By February 9 it had became clear to Louis that he would not receive the position of royal guardian; in a fit of pique he then demanded that his name be withdrawn from consideration for the council as well because of the failure of the Estates to recognize his rank as First Prince of Blood. It is not clear whether Louis's request actually ended discussion of his being named Charles's guardian; but in his famous address to the Estates, Philippe Pot, an advocate of a powerful Estates, stated why many objected to giving him that authority. "In so important a circumstance there would be an inducement to act against the ward."[29] Pot's powerful speech is remarkable for its advocacy of an effective representative assembly in the French state. Nonetheless, the impact was negligible, since the deputies moved to accept the status quo in government. They agreed to include on the royal council those who were already on it plus twelve or more "learned men of good respect" chosen by the king and the council. Orléans, as "the second person of the realm," was to preside in the absence of the king, followed by Jean de Bourbon and Pierre de Beaujeu. The question of the guardianship of the young king was left to the council, but that solution favored the Beaujeus since Anne was left in charge of his education. In short, the Estates gave no satisfaction to Louis's claim to control the government.

Once the deputies began to touch on such sensitive matters as the size of royal pensions and the army, the chancellor moved to close the meeting. On March 7 it was announced that the king was leaving Tours because of poor health, and five days later the deputies were told that their salaries would end the next day. Thus the Estates-general of 1484 meekly concluded its business with a pledge from the king that it would reassemble in two years.[30] Its place in history as the greatest Estates until 1789 was firmly established, but yet it had accomplished rather little. Only in 1498, when Louis XII began to put into effect much of what it had advocated, could the meeting be deemed a success.

Louis emerged from the Estates a disappointed man. With the Beaujeus rapidly consolidating their power, his hope for an annulment was fading. Charles and Anne were strongly protective of their sister. Louis had found Jeanne at her brother's side when he went to Amboise in September 1483 to make his *obéissance* to the new king, and Charles informed him that they were expected to occupy the same suite in the château.[31] It was obvious that Jeanne's brother was as unlikely to agree to an annulment as her father had been.

Nonetheless, as First Prince of Blood, Louis had every right to remain close to the king, and after the Estates he remained at court. The duke and the king soon developed a close relationship, as Louis's exuberance and athletic skills appealed to the teenage king, who had little of either. After Charles was crowned at Reims in May 1484, the court returned to Amboise, where Louis spent several happy months despite the presence of his wife, jousting, hunting, and playing sports. In June the king sent Louis to Honfleur, at the mouth of the Seine, to speak to the admiral about coastal defenses against a possible English invasion. In his letter to Charles, Louis wrote that he was eager to serve him the best he knew how. His natural concern for the common people, so much more obvious after he had become king, came through in the letter, as he told the king that he found the people in great despair because of the pillaging of the men of arms. He said he also recognized that the soldiers were made to "come and go three or four times without giving them what they need."[32]

Soon the situation changed for the worse. Louis had expected that his presidency of the council would lead to increased power, but Anne saw to it that her brother usually was present. Louis had little interest in attending the meetings over which he did not preside, and his attendance became erratic. More seriously, Anne became alarmed at his influence over her brother. She took the king to the Château of Montargis near Orléans, which was too small to accommodate the full court. Louis responded by filing suit in the Parlement of Paris, charging Anne with keeping sole control over the king contrary to the will of the Estates. His chancellor argued his case in early January 1485, presenting Louis as the true protector of the laws and customs of the realm against Anne, who was violating them. The parlementaires refused to see things Louis's way, and they urged him not to disrupt the unity of the royal house. A similar appeal to the faculty of theology of the University of Paris had the same result.[33]

The Parlement also forwarded Louis's request to the king. Charles responded with a long letter in which he praised his sister's administration of his affairs and supervision of his person and rejected Louis's contention that she was holding him against his will.[34] The king wrote that he hoped Louis would conduct himself in accordance with his professed respect for the monarchy; if he did not, Charles would respond appropriately. The clear threat in the letter set Louis's nerves on edge. When he was informed that Anne was coming to Paris with the intention of arresting him, he, Dunois, and Guyot Pot fled.[35] They dashed off so quickly that they had only mules to ride and were not dressed in riding clothes. After riding all night they reached Mantes, where they changed clothes and mounts and continued on to Verneuil, west of Dreux, which was held by the duke of Alençon, Louis's ally.

From there couriers scurried in all directions calling on Orléans's allies to put into action the conspiracy that they had been planning since the previous spring. The center of the conspiracy was Francis of Brittany. Since he was increasingly feeble in health, the question of his succession was looming ever larger. He had taken on a "grey eminence" in the person of

Pierre Landais, his treasurer. The son of a tailor, he had come to the duke's attention while tailoring his clothes and had soon gained a commanding confidence over him. Truly talented at political intrigue, he had made a great number of enemies among the Breton nobles. On the other hand, while serving as the Breton envoy to the Estates, Landais had developed a close relationship with Louis. He had come up with the scheme that Louis would marry the duke's daughter and be named his heir and transfer Orléans to Charles VIII in exchange for his approval. Since Brittany had the separate arrangement with the papacy, the schemers felt that an annulment could be obtained for Louis when he was in the duchy. In the meantime Landais committed Francis to supporting Louis and the other princes in any showdown with the Beaujeus. Dunois signed the agreement for Louis in which they agreed to take the king "out of the hands of those by whom he is presently detained as a prisoner in subjugation."[36]

Before the plan could be implemented, the situation in Brittany changed drastically. In April 1484 a group of prominent Breton nobles, fed up with Landais's arrogance and slights, had attempted to abduct him. Through gross incompetence they failed to apprehend him and were forced to flee to France. The Beaujeus invited them to the court, where they served to further French designs on Brittany. For the moment this aided Louis, because Duke Francis had to commit himself more fully to the dissident French nobles. They made contact with Maximilian of Habsburg and Richard III, both of whom promised help.[37] One result of the English alliance was that Henry Tudor, who was keeping alive the hopes of the House of Lancaster despite being only a distant relative, had to flee Brittany, where he had lived in exile. The duke had promised to turn him over to Richard. Tudor, perhaps warned in advance by Francis, made his way to the French court, where he was warmly welcomed.

The alliance that Louis and Francis had crafted was a potent one, but it had the serious defects of not having a clear plan of action or a dominant leader. The Beaujeus on the other hand had reacted quickly and firmly to Louis's flight from Paris. They removed him from the governorship of the Ile-de-France and gave it to his old nemesis, Antoine de Chabannes. Dunois was stripped of his government of Dauphiné, which went to Beaujeu's brother-in-law. More important, they rushed royal forces into Normandy to cut off communication between Louis and Francis and prevent them from joining their forces. Lacking a strong army of his own and becoming convinced that his allies would not be able to help him anytime soon, Louis was forced to capitulate. He obeyed an order to meet the Beaujeus at Evreux and submitted to them on March 23, 1485.

3

Rebel Prince

ouis of Orléans's first excursion into rebellion, the *Guerre folle* in 1485, ended with only some embarrassment for him. It had not cost him the goodwill of his young cousin, Charles VIII, since at about the same time as he had fled from Paris, the king had whispered to Georges d'Amboise that he wanted to be on good terms with Louis. Although agents of Anne of Beaujeu arrested d'Amboise after his letter detailing the conversation had fallen into her hands, word reached Louis, and he felt encouraged to return to the court.

In March 1485 the duke attended a meeting of the royal council at Evreux, and he was prominent in Charles's first entry into Rouen several days later. Nonetheless, Louis had not given up his intrigues. He dispatched the monk Chaumart with letters to Rome to prepare the groundwork for an annulment of his marriage. Anne of Beaujeu, however, learned of the mission and effectively countered Louis's influence in Rome. When he heard that secrecy had been breached, he ordered Chaumart to burn all the documents he had, "Lest we both be lost."[1] Despite the fright this caused, Louis did not halt his plotting. Shortly thereafter, in May, another Orléanist messenger arrived in Rome and spent over a year there before returning in late 1486. In the annulment process of 1498, the messenger affirmed that he had been sent to persuade the pope to free Louis from his marriage.[2]

In Brittany affairs were not going well for Orléans. Aided by the French government, Breton nobles hostile to Duke Francis's confidant Pierre Landais returned in force to the duchy in June 1485. The forces the duke assembled defected to the rebels, and they entered Nantes and arrested Landais. Without informing Francis of their intentions, they tried, convicted, and executed Landais in a single day. For a time the removal of Landais dramatically changed the relationship between France and Brittany. In August the Treaty of Bourges was hammered out; in it both sides agreed to perpetual peace and the suppression of any plots against the other.[3]

For the moment Louis was deprived of Breton support for his schemes, but he continued intriguing with several French nobles, Richard III, and Maximilian. To disguise his activity he published a manifesto in which he professed his loyalty to the king but denounced the fiscal and political policy of the Beaujeus.[4] In late August 1485 Louis's cause received another hard blow when Richard III was killed in the Battle of Bosworth. The victor, Henry Tudor, had resided at the French court for the previous year and received French financial and military aid for his campaign against Richard. Although the victorious Tudor took the titles of king of England and France and soon began scheming how to make good his claim to the French throne, for the moment Louis could expect no help from England. He made a second submission to the Beaujeus, and his arch coconspirator, Dunois, was exiled to Asti in Italy.

Despite these setbacks, Louis never ceased his plotting to remove Anne and her husband from power. More quickly than could have been predicted, the situation in Brittany turned in his favor. With Landais dead, Duke Francis asserted himself and again took an active part in the affairs of state. He procured from the duchy's Estates a confirmation of his daughter Anne's right to succeed him, and he let Louis and the other French malcontents know that he was still in sympathy with them.[5] Orléans also renewed contact with Maximilian, who had just been chosen King of the Romans by the seven electors of the empire, making him heir to the imperial title. Maximilian was angry at the French for trying to deny him the election and was eager to tear up the Peace of Arras and reclaim lost Burgundian lands. Several of the French nobles, such as the dukes of Bourbon and Lorraine, who wavered almost weekly between Beaujeu and Orléans, were now back on Louis's side. Last, Dunois had quietly slipped back into France in November 1486 and ensconced himself in a fortress in Poitou.

Anne of Beaujeu soon learned of the new feudal league. In early January 1487 she sent Marshal Pierre de Gié to summon Louis to the court at Amboise. Well aware of the meaning of the summons, Louis slipped away by pretending to be going hunting. He made his way to his sister Anne's convent at Fontevrault, where he received money and fresh horses. On January 13, 1487, he crossed into Brittany. The young king's sense of betrayal at Louis's action is clear in a letter he wrote a few days later lamenting that the duke of Orléans, instead of obeying the royal will, had ridden "at full speed day and night west to Brittany without our knowledge and approval and in breach of the promises he had given us."[6] When intercepted correspondence revealed that several men at court, including Commynes, were involved, they were arrested. The others were released without a trial seven months later, but Commynes was confined in one of Louis XI's notorious iron cages at Loches. Perhaps Anne felt his betrayal more keenly because of his closeness to her father.[7]

On February 10 Louis wrote to Charles of his grievances and his reasons for fleeing to Brittany. He denounced Madame de Beaujeu's violation of the decisions of the Estates in 1484 and her subjugation of the king, and he called for a new meeting of the Estates.[8] Two weeks after Louis arrived at Nantes, Francis felt obliged to bring him before an assembly of nobles, clerics, and bourgeoisie. There Orléans swore that he had not come with the intention of marrying the duke's daughter. According to Brantôme, that eager gossipmonger, Louis, then twenty-four, was deeply smitten by nine-year-old Anne and was determined to wed her despite his oath. Most historians have discounted this story.[9]

Be that as it may, Anne of Beaujeu moved quickly to recover the initiative from Louis. She had the Parlement declare Dunois guilty of lèse-majesté, which was made easy by his refusal to answer the summons to appear.[10] At the same time, she moved against Louis's supporters in France. The most dangerous among them were in the southwestern part of the realm: the Sire de Lescun, from a cadet line of the House of Armagnac, and the two brothers d'Aydie. Their defection to Orléans threatened royal control of the southwest, still a very sensitive matter because it had been recovered from the English only three decades before. Anne and Charles personally led a royal force south from Tours in February 1487 and quickly captured the rebel strongholds of Saintes and Blaye. St-Gelais remarked how the presence of the young king was a major factor in the easy victories, for the rebels felt that their quarrel was with the Beaujeus and not the monarch. The captains of the rebel garrisons immediately surrendered when they heard the king was at their gates. Charles immensely enjoyed his first military experience, in which he was victorious with almost no bloodshed.[11] He would soon seek to repeat it on a grander scale. The expedition also marked Anne of Beaujeu's final emergence as the dominant influence on her brother, as her husband had remained in the north: "Madame de Beaujeu his sister was with the king all the time . . . nor was anything touching the king and the kingdom done except with her knowledge, approval, and consent."[12]

The schemes of the rebel nobles collapsed like a house of cards. A few—Dunois, Orange, Lescun, and the elder Aydie—fled to Brittany, but the rest submitted to the king. Louis tried once more to negotiate with Anne before his situation grew worse. He again proposed that he give up the duchy of Orléans to the king and Coucy and Blois to her in exchange for their support of his marriage to Anne of Brittany. He pledged to render homage for Brittany in the same manner as he had for Orléans. But Louis also sent his herald to Rome for another attempt at gaining an annulment from the papacy.[13]

The irritating presence of so many French nobles at the Breton court and their influence over the duke led many Bretons to make contact again with the French government. In March 1487 they met with French envoys at Châteaubriand and came to an agreement calling for 6,000 French troops and a sum of money to aid in expelling the French rebels. The pact was hedged with numerous restrictions in order to prevent the French from occupying Brittany; in particular, the French government agreed not to attack any place where the duke was present.[14]

Command of the French forces was given to Louis de La Trémoille, who was from one of the most important noble families in France. He was only twenty-seven, but his qualities as a commander were already known. The 15,000-man army he led into Brittany was much larger than the pact called for. He headed for the fortified town of Ploërmel between Vannes and Rennes, near the midpoint of the duchy. Louis rushed there with the small band of French fighting men he had with him and a large number of ill-disciplined and poorly trained Bretons. The better Breton troops were in the French camp.[15] On June 1, 1487, Ploërmel fell, and Louis's army retreated to Vannes on the south coast. With the French army in hard pursuit, Louis and a few companions fled by boat to Nantes, while the rest of his men surrendered. La Trémoille moved on to put Nantes under siege. Duke Francis was in the city, however, and the siege was a violation of the pact with the Breton nobles. When the people of western Brittany heard that their duke was under siege, they rose en masse to go to his rescue. Dunois, returning to St-Malo from a mission to England, put himself at the head of some 10,000 men to relieve Nantes. When they approached, the French lifted their siege.

During the siege Louis had performed well in the defense of the city. He was on the walls day and night and personally led a band that repulsed an assault on a breach.[16] His valor made a strong impression on the Bretons, who always responded well to such actions. But his cause was not going well. In order to get Maximilian to invade northern France, Louis had agreed to allow him to court Anne of Brittany. Maximilian's invasion of Artois was easily turned back, and no aid was forthcoming from Henry VII, although he allowed an English nobleman to lead some 800 men to St-Malo on his own initiative. Desultory war continued through the winter of 1487-88, during which the French gained control of several castles and towns. In January 1488 the government finally made a legal move against Louis, who had not been named in any of the earlier indictments. The king ordered Louis and Francis of Brittany to appear in the Parlement the next month for trial and summoned the peers of the realm and the other princes of blood to sit with the Parlement in judgment of them. When the trial opened on February 20, neither duke was present, and the court adjourned without a verdict. It appears that Louis was never legally convicted of treason in a court of law.[17]

In early July 1488 Charles wrote to La Trémoille, "Make war as vigorously as you can and give them no leave to make repairs, get provisions, or prepare."[18] La Trémoille had about 15,000 men, 4,000 of whom were Swiss mercenaries, while Louis led some 10,500 men of several different nationalities. The usual problems of a multilingual, multinational army prevented Louis from moving fast enough to relieve the fortified town of Fougères north of Rennes. When the town fell before Louis's forces reached it, La Trémoille headed for Rennes and crossed Louis's line of march near the town of St-Aubin-du-Cormier on July 29. The Breton army was the first to become aware of the presence of its foe and prepared battlelines. The French emerged from a forest to find the Bretons in battle array about 700 yards away. Had the Bretons attacked immediately, victory should have been theirs; but as often happens in battle, a commander, in this case Alain d'Albret, waits until his men are "perfectly" deployed until attacking. Louis and the other captains deferred to d'Albret as the most experienced captain, and the French had time to form lines and bring up their artillery. Nonetheless, Louis acquitted himself well in his first true experience of military command. Advised by his fellow captains that his presence among his infantrymen would strengthen their resolve, he personally led his infantry into the fray. St-Gelais stated: "If everyone had done his duty as well as he, the day would have been theirs."[19]

The Breton attack, when it finally came, was thrown back, and a body of French cavalry quickly exploited a gap in their center. The Breton line was broken, and panic spread out from the center. In the massacre that followed, 6,000 of the Breton army fell, including virtually the entire English contingent. A story has it that many of the Bretons had dressed as Englishmen hoping that it would shake the French, who feared the English more than any others. After the battle, the French slaughtered all the "English."

As for Louis, he valiantly tried to halt the rout. St-Gelais severely criticized those who persuaded Louis to fight with the infantry, since that prevented him from escaping when the army collapsed around him. Louis was captured "sword in hand and face to the enemy with immortal honor and prowess," amid the ruins of his army, along with the prince of Orange. The French infantrymen wanted to kill him, but the nobles saved him.[20]

Louis was held briefly at St-Aubin, where La Trémoille hosted him, Orange, and two other French nobles at dinner. According to a story of questioned authenticity, two Franciscan friars entered the hall as they dined. In the pall that their presence threw over the conversation, La Trémoille told Orléans and Orange: "Messieurs, I don't have the authority to decide about you; that's the king's to do." Turning to the other nobles, he said: "As for you, you have betrayed your oath; you have been the cause of this fatal war; you must bear the punishment. Prepare yourselves for death." When Louis tried to protest, La Trémoille brusquely told him to be quiet, and the two unfortunates were led out, presumably to their deaths.[21]

Charles ordered that the two princes be brought to him, but Madame de Beaujeu, fearful that her kind-hearted brother would pardon them when he saw them, had them sent to dungeons, Louis to Sablé and Orange to Angers. La Trémoille had been told to keep a tight guard on his prisoners, and he followed orders well, confining Louis so rigorously that the duke protested. However, there was no one to ask for help. Most of his fellow rebels were dead or captive, and Francis of Brittany was in no position to come to his aid. Louis's mother had died the previous summer, and neither of his sisters could help. He would not appeal to his wife.

La Trémoille soon moved his army to St-Malo. As soon as the French artillery began to fire, the townspeople, hoping to save their lives and property, forced the garrison to surrender. By August 14, 1488, St-Malo, the place regarded as the most invincible in Brittany, was in French hands.[22] Duke Francis was compelled to seek peace. Anne of Beaujeu demanded harsh terms, but the king undermined her hardheadedness. He chose to listen to the Breton envoys' requests for pity on the poor duke and his people. Terms were agreed upon on August 20: Francis agreed to dismiss all foreigners in his service and never summon any again, not marry his daughter off without the king's consent, and recognize the jurisdiction of the Parlement of Paris in his duchy.[23] The French were allowed to garrison St-Malo and three other sites to ensure the treaty's fulfillment.

Duke Francis, broken by the terrible defeats and the harsh peace treaty, died on September 9, 1488, after gaining the pardon he had begged of the king. The hand of his daughter, Duchess Anne, now eleven, was more valuable than ever. While Orléans was no longer a suitor, the other European princes took an even stronger interest. Henry of England and the Spanish monarchs Ferdinand and Isabella were involved in extensive negotiation over a suitable husband for Anne and a possible war against

France. In December 1488, for example, Ferdinand and Isabella wrote to their ambassador in London telling him to secure Henry's support for the marriage of their son Juan to the Breton duchess. He was to tell the English monarch they were ready to pledge themselves to the English recovery of Gascony and Normandy if Henry agreed to help them win Anne for their son and regain Roussillon and Cerdagne. The latter provinces, on the north slope of the eastern Pyrenees, had been taken from Aragon by Louis XI in 1463. Their loss was a major factor in the lifelong enmity that Ferdinand bore to France.[24]

It soon became clear that the favorite for Anne's hand was Maximilian, whose one consistency was his desire to injure France.[25] Although the Habsburgs had little reason to be hostile to France, Maximilian had adopted the ill-will of his late wife's family toward the Valois. In February 1490 Henry and Maximilian came to an agreement to help each other recover lands lost to the French monarchy and offer Maximilian as Anne's groom. The three governments providing her with aid, limited as it was, pressed her into agreeing to a marriage contract with Maximilian. On December 6, 1490, Maximilian's proxy stood for his master at the wedding and consummated the marriage in a grotesque ceremony that apparently was new to western Europe: He placed a leg, naked to the knee, under the sheets of the bed where fourteen-year-old Anne lay fully clothed.[26]

Assuming that the marriage was now indissoluble, Maximilian delayed joining Anne because of business in Germany. But he was not familiar with the morass that was Breton politics. Alain d'Albret, captain of the garrison at Nantes and a disappointed suitor of the duchess, agreed to hand over that city to the French in exchange for a full pardon, the return of his confiscated lands, and a large sum of money. In February 1491 French forces entered the city. Both Maximilian and Henry VII promised aid, but neither moved fast enough to help Anne before a French army under La Trémoille had invested Rennes, where she resided. With the chances of withstanding a siege almost nil and no forces available for a relief army, the young duchess was in a desperate situation. Her advisers told her to agree to marry Charles, for there was no question that it was what the French sought. Angry at Maximilian for failing to come to her and persuaded by her confessor that she was free to marry Charles, she consented, and a marriage contract was hammered out. Her helpless position was obvious, for it required that she marry Charles's successor, should he die without a son.[27]

As for Maximilian, not only had he lost his bride and her duchy, but his daughter Margaret, who had been betrothed to Charles in 1483 and was living at the French court as the queen of France, was now repudiated. It would take two years for the girl to be sent back to her father and three more years for her dowry to be returned. Little wonder that distrust of the Valois was the keynote of the lives of both father and daughter.

For Louis of Orléans, the sumptuous wedding of Anne and Charles was a bittersweet moment. On one hand, his hopes of marrying her himself and becoming duke of Brittany were firmly dashed; on the other, he was there as a free man after three years in prison. Upon his capture in the Battle of St-Aubin in 1488, he had been harshly treated. He was a defeated rebel and traitor; and although his life was safe because he was of royal blood and still successor to the throne, there was no obligation to make his life in prison pleasant. La Trémoille, his captor, quickly received a letter from the king ordering that his prisoner not be ransomed.[28] After a month at Sablé, a large body of troops escorted Louis to Lusignan in Poitou, where he was guarded by 200 *gens d'armes* (knights), and the gates of the town were closed to all but those who had special passports. A rescue attempt by d'Albret led to Louis's transfer to Bourges. The great tower there had been turned into the most secure royal prison.[29]

Louis's jailer for the first year of his imprisonment was Philippe Guérin, an old confidant of Louis XI; his idea of how to treat rebels drew on the style of his late master. Guérin was later alleged to have refused Louis a physician and kept him on a diet of bread and water. He supposedly replied to his prisoner's complaints about his diet that he could eat the rats and spiders of his cell. He also was reported to have prevented Louis from writing letters. Louis furthermore lived in fear of poisoning.[30]

The duke soon began to feel that his health was suffering from his diet and the lack of air and exercise. He was able to persuade one of his guards to go to the court to beg for improved conditions for him. The guard presented Louis's complaint to Pierre de Bourbon (the death of his older brother earlier in 1489 had made Beaujeu the duke of Bourbon). This mission was partially successful. Guérin was replaced, and the new jailer was more sympathetic to the prisoner.

Of those who interceded on Orléans's behalf, the one who had closest contact with those who controlled his fate was his wife. Despite having been abandoned for the previous several years, Jeanne put her heart into helping her husband. She wrote to her sister: "I beg you to bear the case of my husband in mind and to write about him to our brother."[31] When Louis's physician came to ask her to intercede with the king, she asked him: "Don't you believe that I am doing all I ought or can do?" When he replied that he believed her, she expressed her fear that after his release, Louis would not love her and added: "I am not the person for such a prince."[32]

Jeanne did a great deal more than simply appeal to her sister on Louis's behalf. Shortly after he was thrown into the dungeon at Lusignan, she visited him there; but despite his terrible circumstances, he treated her rudely. When he was transferred to Bourges, she soon arrived to stay with him in his cell. Again Louis responded coldly, to the point that his *maître d'hôtel* advised him to receive her better if he wished to avoid worse treatment. Louis then allowed Jeanne to stay in the cell for a time. She acquired for him oranges from Italy and fresh fish as well as new linens and clothes. Jeanne also took an active role in managing his finances and estates, which were in terrible shape because of the forced sale of 50,000 *l* worth of property shortly after his capture. Her own income, reduced to the 10,000 *l* of her royal pension, was expended largely on her husband's case. She frequently wrote to Louis's officers and friends, asking them to intercede for him with the king.[33]

Louis spent much of his time in prison reading books; for the first time in his life, he was engaged in serious reading. The books he asked for included the *Chroniques de France*, Froissart's chronicles of the Hundred Years War, *The Golden Legend* of Jacobus de Voragine (a "Lives of the Saints"), and Boethius's *Consolation of Philosophy*, which Louis's father had translated from Latin during his captivity. Late in his life Louis quoted Cicero to the royal successor, Francis of Angoulême. He probably read him in prison.[34]

While Louis wasted three years of his early adulthood in a dungeon, events outside the tower of Bourges were moving toward his release. As the French position in Brittany improved, the threat of another *Guerre folle* waned. Charles VIII passed his twenty-first birthday in 1491, and his dependency on his sister began to decline. He surrounded himself with ambitious young men who resented Anne's tight control over the government. Among them was Georges d'Amboise, who had retrieved his credit from its low point of 1487 and now was among those closest to the king; yet he remained a true friend to Louis. When Admiral de Graville, one of the strongest supporters of the Bourbons, married his daughter to d'Amboise's nephew, it was a clear signal there had been a shift in influence at the court. After Alain d'Albret surrendered Nantes in February 1491, he recovered his position in the court, and he used it to press for his friend's release. Dunois, serving as the ambassador of Brittany to France, used his access to the king to remind him of the good times Louis and he had shared in the past.[35]

Orléans's advocates proposed to Charles that the duke's high credit at the Breton court would make him valuable for persuading the duchess to marry the king. They convinced him that Louis would be so grateful for his freedom, he would become a most loyal servant. Aware of his sister's continuing hostility toward Louis, the king decided to act without consulting her. On June 27, 1491, he left Anne at Tours, pretending to be going out hunting. Instead, he rode hard toward Bourges, sending Béraud Stuart, the captain of the Royal Scots Guard, ahead with a written order to release the prisoner. Louis met Charles outside of Bourges. Upon reaching the king, the duke threw himself in tears at his knees. Charles embraced him, and they rode together into Bourges. St-Gelais wrote: "All these things were kept secret from Monsieur and Madame de Bourbon." The reconciled friends dined together, slept in the same bed, and rode the next morning to Tours.[36]

Louis pledged his word that he would serve the king faithfully, and Charles restored his properties and gave him the governorship of Normandy, a very important office, which affirmed Charles's faith in him.[37] A month later Louis and Dunois were on their way to Rennes on a mission to convince Duchess Anne to marry the king. Meanwhile, Charles pressed Louis and the Bourbons to be reconciled. Anne's biographer suggests that the reconciliation was more difficult for her than for Louis, "who was at heart generous and without hatred."[38] In September 1491 a protocol of entente was drawn up, and the signatories swore on the Gospels that they would forgive without rancor and would serve the king loyally, despite their past differences.[39] Charles also pardoned the remaining rebels, some in prison, others still at large. By the end of 1491, it had become clear that Madame Anne's influence over her brother was waning. She quickly found herself at odds with her new sister-in-law, who despite being only fourteen had her own will and was determined not to have a rival in her influence over Charles. In early 1492 the Bourbons left the royal court for their own at Moulins in the Bourbonnais. Over the next several years they continued to be called on for advice and to attend major festivals at the court. However, they largely directed their vast talents to building up their estates. Their success at it would help bring about the last major feudal revolt in France three decades later, by Charles de Bourbon, husband of their only child, Suzanne.

As for Louis of Orléans, he cheerfully attended the king at his marriage to Anne of Brittany in December 1491. Whatever regrets he may have had were well buried beneath his relief at being free and the delight he always took in great festivals of that sort. Two months later he attended Queen Anne at her coronation in the Basilica of St-Denis. He had the task of supporting the massive royal crown on the queen's small head as she was anointed.[40]

In November 1492 Louis stood as godfather for the royal couple's son, whom they gave the strange name of Charles Orland. The duke hid well whatever dismay he might have had at being moved to second place in the line of succession.[41] During his imprisonment Louis appears to have curbed his ambition and was now ready to play his role as confidant to the king and peer of the realm. He even seems to have reconciled himself to his marital situation. Nonetheless, Louis's relationship with Jeanne of France was hardly any warmer than before. And certain traits of his youth remained with him as he reached his thirtieth birthday—a great fondness for hunting, sports of all kinds, jousting, and other martial arts, and an unquenchable thirst to gain a reputation as a great military leader. In regard to the latter, he would soon have his chance to earn such a reputation.

4

Le Roi est mort! Vive le Roi!

After having made his peace with Charles VIII upon his release from the Tower of Bourges, Louis of Orléans became one of the king's closest advisers and his boon companion in pleasure and sport. After the birth of his son, the king moved the court to Lyon in March 1494. St-Gelais reported: "Monseigneur d'Orléans always accompanied him because when he was not about, the court was greatly diminished." Surrounded by young gentlemen "who wished to be involved only in all things pleasant and agreeable," Charles sponsored tournaments and other displays of arms, and "Monseigneur d'Orléans was the first to try everything."[1]

According to St-Gelais, the king was so moved by the great feats of arms at Lyon that he decided to undertake a great enterprise. It proved to be the expedition to Naples, generally called the First French Invasion of Italy. He wrote that Louis heartily approved, because "his greatest pleasure was following arms, which he loved the best of all things. He advised the matter with all his power."[2] Commynes, however, did not put Louis on his list of supporters of the Italian adventure.[3] However, it is far more probable that Charles went to Lyon to prepare for the Italian expedition, for there is good evidence that he had it in mind well before 1494. The papal legate at the French court reported in February 1490 that the Breton war was impeding the French from making war on the king of Naples. The prince of Salerno was then at the court urging the Italian enterprise; he had furnished a map and detailed information on Naples for fighting a war there.[4] He was the leader of a band of Neapolitans whose rebellion in 1486 had been crushed and who had fled to France.

The roots of French involvement in Italy were two centuries old by 1494. The papacy before 1100 had successfully claimed Naples and Sicily as papal fiefs. When the popes found themselves caught up in a bitter dispute with Emperor Frederick II and his descendants, Pope Clement IV in 1265 granted the kingdom of Sicily and Naples to Charles of Anjou, Louis IX's brother. The next year Charles led a French force to Italy and established his rule in southern Italy and Sicily. Charles, who had hopes of carving out a wider sphere of power in the Mediterranean, purchased the rights to the defunct crusader kingdom of Jerusalem in 1277. Five years later French mistreatment of the Sicilians led to a revolt known as the Sicilian Vespers, which was aided by the king of Aragon, who claimed the island through his wife, a granddaughter of Frederick II. Twenty years of fighting left the House of Anjou in control of Naples and the House of Aragon, of Sicily. Naples remained in the House of Anjou until the death of Queen Joanna II in 1435. Alfonso of Aragon invaded southern Italy to make good his claims, driving out the last Frenchmen in 1442. Joanna's will left her titles to her kinsman René I of Anjou, Count of Provence. "Good King René" disinherited his grandson, the duke of Lorraine, and passed his titles to his nephew Charles of Maine. When Charles died in 1481, claims to Naples, Jerusalem, and Provence came to Louis XI, but Provence was the only one of those lands that he made the effort to possess. With Provence came the port of Marseille and the opportunity for France to become a player in the naval wars in the Mediterranean Sea.

When Charles VIII succeeded his father in 1483, he added the titles of king of Naples and Jerusalem to his honors. Despite the limited legal merit of his claims, Charles was convinced that he was the rightful ruler of Naples, while King Ferrante I was a usurper, despite having secured investiture from the pope, the lord of the fief in question. In January 1494, when King Ferrante died, Alexander VI immediately granted the investiture of Naples to his son Alfonso despite French appeals and threats.

Charles's focus was on Naples, but he also desired to lead a crusade against the Turks and secure his claim to the kingdom of Jerusalem. Another factor was the influence of the ruler of Milan, Ludovico Sforza. The duchy of Milan in north-central Italy was one of the most prosperous and heavily populated regions of Europe. The duke drew some 700,000 ducats in revenues from it.[5] Like most of the states of Italy in the late fifteenth century, the legitimacy of its ruler was in serious question. When the male line of the Visconti dynasty died out in 1447, the Milanese ignored the claim of Charles of Orléans through his mother, Valentina Visconti, and reestablished a republic. Bitter factionalism disrupted the Milanese republic, and in 1450 Francesco Sforza, a *condottiere* (mercenary captain) in the pay of one of the factions, seized control of the city and proclaimed himself duke. Upon his death in 1466, his son ruled the duchy until his assassination ten years later. The title then passed to Francesco's seven-year-old grandson Gian Galeazzo. Gian's uncle Ludovico became his guardian and regent for the state. Il Moro (the Moor), as Ludovico was called because of his swarthy complexion, soon arranged for the marriage of his nephew to the granddaughter of Ferrante I of Naples, which took place in 1489. By then twenty years old, the young duke, prompted by his Neapolitan in-laws, was eager to take control of the state from his uncle, but Ludovico refused to relinquish it. Restless to exercise power, Gian sought support across Italy. Allies against il Moro were easy to come by. Milan's neighbors to the east, Venice, and to the south, Florence, enlisted, as did the papacy.

The Sforzas and the French monarchy had been on good terms since 1450. In 1464 Louis XI had conferred the right to rule Genoa on Sforza. The French king's claim to be suzerain over Genoa was based on a decision of the Genoese republic in 1396 to offer rule over the city to Charles VI be-cause of internal factionalism and the threat from Milan. Charles, of course, accepted the offer and installed a French governor. By 1409 the Genoese had repented of their foolhardiness and had thrown out the French. How-ever, the French continued to claim sovereignty in Genoa, and the Sforzas had been eager to give a legal gloss to their power there by asking for investiture from the French kings.[6]

The warm relations between France and Milan continued into Charles VIII's reign.[7] Perhaps Ludovico was using the threat of calling for French intervention to stymie his enemies, since a French expedition in support of il Moro's position also would bring with it the threat of the Orléanist claim to Milan. Neither Charles of Orléans nor his son allowed it to be forgotten for a moment that they were the rightful heirs of the Visconti. The marri-age contract between Louis I of Orléans and Valentina Visconti had expressly granted the duchy of Milan to her or her descendants in default of male issue from her two brothers. Between them the two brothers had only one child, a daughter, who married Francisco Sforza, and he used her rights to support his pretensions to power in Milan.[8]

An authority on the relationship between France and Milan has written: "Nothing could have been more vague than the basis of the Orléanist claim to the Visconti inheritance."[9] That did not stop Louis from pressing his claims. He styled himself "Duke of Orléans and Milan" in his official docu-ments and issued coins at Asti that combined the arms of Milan and Orléans. He now hoped to persuade the king to divert some of his forces from the Neapolitan expedition to occupy Milan.[10] In 1492 Henry VII had written to il Moro warning him of the danger of inviting the French into Italy and declared that the king of France "threatens the duchy of Milan no less than other principalities near him and advances claim to your duchy for the Duke of Orléans."[11] Ludovico, however, forwarded the letter to Charles VIII as proof of his goodwill toward France.

In order to gain the neutrality of neighboring princes and settle disputes that might prompt them to attack France while he was in Italy, Charles negotiated a series of treaties with them. The first was with Henry VII, who was then laying siege to Boulogne in Picardy. The Treaty of Etaples, signed in November 1492, committed Charles to paying the 620,000 *écus* that Anne of Brittany owed Henry for the defense of her duchy and 150,000 in back payments from the pension Louis XI had agreed to give Edward IV. It also committed Charles to continue paying the pension regularly. A treaty of January 1493 with Ferdinand and Isabella committed them to aid France in any war with its neighbors in return for the provinces of Cerdange and Roussillon, which Louis XI had annexed in 1463. The third, with Maximilian, arranged for the return of his daughter Margaret and her dowry from the French court as well as several forts in Artois that Louis XI had occupied. Charles was to get Arras back from Maximilian.

If there still was any hesitation on Charles's part, one more event—the sudden arrival of Cardinal Giuliano della Rovere at the French court in April 1494—provided the final persuasion. The cardinal had been Alexander VI's chief rival for the papal election in 1492 and was his bitter foe. Fearing that Alexander was about to have him arrested, della Rovere fled Rome and dashed to France. There he passionately spoke of Charles's duty to free Italy of its tyrants and the ease with which it could be done.

In November 1493 Charles asked his most experienced commanders to detail the requirements for an Italian campaign. They estimated that it would take 3,500,000 *l*. A *crue* (surtax) of 800,000 *l* was placed on the *taille* (the major tax), and several new *aides* (sales taxes) were levied. Royal pensions were reduced, and the clergy agreed to a *décime*, a "gift" of a tenth of its income supposedly intended for a crusade against the Turks, which provided 700,000 *l* for the royal treasury. Loans provided much of the money for war, as the Genoese bankers agreed to lend over 100,000 *l*, while Ludovico Sforza advanced a similar sum. To meet the manpower needs, Charles sent a representative to Switzerland to recruit 6,000 pikemen. The French cavalry was based on the lance, a unit consisting of a heavily armored lancer (a knight) and five mounted troops with lighter armor; 1,500 lances, or 9,000 men, were summoned to Lyon. Some 20,000 French infantrymen were called to serve; about half were from Gascony, where the English, unlike the French nobles, had been willing to arm the peasants for infantry service. The army also included the largest artillery train that Europe had yet seen, about seventy large guns.[12]

When all was finally ready, Charles named Pierre de Bourbon as regent during his absence from the realm and in August began the trek to Italy. A month earlier Louis had crossed the Alps with a force of cavalry and entered his county of Asti for the first time. Asti had been part of Valentina Visconti's dowry for her marriage to Louis's grandfather, and her descendants' title to it was never in dispute, although it frequently had been the subject of schemes to trade or sell it.[13] St-Gelais stated that Louis was welcomed warmly to the city of Asti because its inhabitants "were good Frenchmen."[14] Ludovico Sforza felt threatened by Orléans's presence at Asti on the western border of his duchy and convinced Charles to dispatch the duke to Genoa in order to command the combined Franco-Genoese fleet. Louis would have preferred to stay in Asti with his company of 100 lances.

The situation of the French navy in the late fifteenth century was complicated. The many seaports on France's long Atlantic coast provided a large merchant fleet of sailing ships, which had to be capable of defending themselves against the constant threat of piracy. In times of war, usually against England, the king would impress these private ships, perhaps boosting their crews with men in royal service and adding guns if necessary. This "fleet of the Ponant" allowed France to go to the aid of the Scots and pose the threat of invading England, even if it never happened.[15]

In the Mediterranean the situation was entirely different. Having gained ports there only recently, France did not have as strong a maritime tradition there as it did in the Atlantic. The independent county of Provence with its port of Marseille had not been a major factor in the naval wars of the Mediterranean in the late Middle Ages. When in 1481 Provence passed to the French monarchy under the terms of the will of Count René, the fleet at Marseille consisted of about ten galleys. A few more had been added since, but so small a fleet made France at best a third-rate naval power in that sea.

Both the style of fighting and the types of ships used were so different between the Atlantic and the Mediterranean that fleets from the two seas could not be interchanged except in dire emergencies. Mediterranean fleets were based on the galley, which was more effective in that sea's light breezes from April to October and around its many islands and peninsulas. An Atlantic sailing ship of 1494 would have been becalmed and swarmed over by galleys, while the lightly built galley was not suited to the ocean's rough waters.

The small galley fleet at Marseille was not large enough to provide the naval force the French needed for the Neapolitan campaign. Although most of the French forces would go overland, a large fleet was needed to carry the heavier guns and supplies to Italy to avoid hauling them across the Alps. Galleys also would give Charles a way to return to France quickly if necessary. When il Moro offered the Genoese fleet to Charles provided Louis command it, the king quickly agreed. Although Genoa had clearly slipped behind its great rival, Venice, in sea power, its fleet still gave the French the means to control the seas off Italy if Venice remained neutral, as was expected.

Louis of Orléans had been to sea only once, when he had gone from Vannes to Nantes by boat in 1487; but in that era a fleet was regarded as largely an army at sea, and the tactics of sea battle were little different from those on land. What was important for naval command was high status to have the respect of the men abroad the fleet. The duke arrived in Genoa on August 19, 1494. The Genoese put on a brilliant pageant to welcome him, but he did not have much time to enjoy himself. Word arrived at virtually the same time that the Neapolitan fleet under Don Federigo, the brother of King Alfonso, had reached northern Italy. A group of Genoese exiles accompanied Federigo to help take control of Genoa and prevent the French from using it as a base for naval operations against Naples. He chose the small, undefended coastal village of Rapello, about twenty miles east of Genoa, to land a small force.[16]

When Louis heard of the landing, he decided to strike before Federigo could move on to Genoa.[17] A force of several thousand men—Milanese, Genoese, and Swiss—were sent by land to Rapello, while on September 5 Louis took eighteen galleys and six galleases (large, rowed merchantmen) there. Although Federigo's fleet was larger in number, its galleys were smaller and not as well armed. Federigo decided not to risk a battle and withdrew, leaving his forces on shore. Louis was able to put his men ashore without opposition and join them up with the forces coming by land. The Neapolitan troops had time to fortify a bridge across a stream outside of the village, which they stubbornly defended. The site, however, was within the range of the heavy bow guns of Louis's galleys, which were drawn up at the water's edge. Their fire broke the Neapolitan flank, and the enemy fell back into Rapello. After several more hours of fighting, Louis received reinforcements from Genoa, and with numbers now over-whelmingly in favor of the French, the Neapolitan forces broke ranks and ran. Charles VIII reported to his court that 700 to 800 of the enemy were killed or captured. St-Gelais wrote: "It was good to see Monseigneur d'Orléans in combat and see him give courage to his men and do all that is appropriate for a brave prince."[18]

After the battle, Louis returned to Genoa with the fleet while his Swiss units disgraced themselves by killing their captives and pillaging Rapello and the towns on the route back to Genoa. This kind of atrocity in war was new to the Italians, who were accustomed to the far less bloody style of warfare of the condottieri; it gave them some hint of worse things to come. At Genoa Louis became ill, most probably with malaria.[19] Soon after, Charles VIII also fell seriously ill at Asti, where he had arrived on September 8. Louis returned there two days later despite his own illness to report on his victory. For the moment the Neapolitan campaign was in doubt, and Louis's hopes of using the French army to oust il Moro were revived.[20] They received a further boost when word came in late October that the young duke of Milan, Gian Galeazzo Sforza, had died. As was always true in that era, any sudden death raised suspicions of poisoning, and in this case il Moro's reputation made him the only suspect. Suspicion only increased when he took the title of duke of Milan over the rightful heir, Gian's infant son. Most of the Frenchmen around Charles were highly indignant that they were allied with such a villain and were ready to support Louis in an attack on Milan.

The king, however, could not be distracted from Naples. Il Moro craftily played on his mind, telling him: "If you will trust me, I shall help make you mightier than Charlemagne ever was, and we shall easily drive the Turks out of Constantinople after you have obtained the Kingdom of Naples." Charles continued the march south.[21] The amazingly quick reduction of several well-regarded fortresses by the French artillery convinced the Italians that resistance was futile. The massacre of the defenders of those forts also shocked the Italians. Town after town capitulated to Charles without offering resistance. In Florence an anti-Medici faction took advantage of the passage of the French army to oust Piero de Medici and install a pro-French government, which agreed to loan Charles 120,000 ducats.

Charles reached Rome in time for Christmas. Pope Alexander VI, as a member of the Spanish Borgia family, was sympathetic to the Aragonese kings in Naples, yet he dared not try to impede the French entry into Rome. In early January the pope and the king negotiated an agreement by which the French would have safe passage through the papal states and their lines of communication to France secured. Charles took his oath of obedience to the pope, and Alexander agreed to Charles's demand that the bishop of St-Malo be named a cardinal, but he refused to invest the king with Naples.[22]

At the end of January 1495, Charles moved his army on toward Naples. As the French crossed into his realm, Alfonso in panic abdicated his throne to his son Ferrantino in the hope that his son's greater popularity would rally the populace to his cause. The move did no good, however, as towns and fortresses fell to Charles with little or no resistance. Ferrantino followed his father in flight to Sicily in mid-March, and on March 28 Charles entered

Naples in triumph. He informed Ferrantino's envoy, who had come to offer Ferrantino's homage as a vassal, that he intended to take the title of king for himself. He and his men settled in to enjoy the fruits of their easy victory.[23]

Louis of Orléans had remained in Asti during Charles's promenade to Naples, while he reportedly seduced the daughter of his host. According to St-Gelais, it was by order of the king that Louis remained behind to protect the route back to France, should a quick retreat to France be necessary. However, Louis may have pushed for the decision to leave him behind in order to seize any opportunity to oust Ludovico. Commynes related that Louis was frightening il Moro with his menacing talk about the Milanese tyrant.[24]

For his part, Sforza had quickly repented of his role in bringing the French into Italy. He had expected a drawn-out war for Naples in which he could serve as mediator. The arrogance of the French offended him, and he was angered that Alexander and Charles had left him completely out of their negotiations. Most of all, he feared the presence of Louis at Asti. He easily imagined the French army returning to the north and ousting him for the king's cousin.[25] All the other powers of Europe were also upset at Charles's audacity and easy victory. As he crossed the Neapolitan border, Ferdinand and Isabella had sent an envoy demanding that he halt. After the expulsion of his relatives from Naples, Ferdinand set to work to draw the emperor, the pope, Venice, and Milan into an anti-French alliance, creating the League of Venice. On March 31, 1495, Commynes, who had gone to Venice as ambassador the previous autumn, was called in by the doge and informed of the league. Its purpose, he was told, was to protect its members from the same fate as Naples. Well aware of the potent threat the League posed to Charles, Commynes wrote to Louis to prepare the defenses of Asti for attack: "if that place were lost, no help could reach the king from France." He also sent word to the duke of Bourbon to send Asti aid from France.[26]

Louis was soon made aware of how dangerous his situation in Asti had become. On April 6 il Moro dispatched a force of 7,000 horsemen and 3,000 footsoldiers against Asti and sent Louis an ultimatum to allow his forces into the city. He also demanded that Louis stop using the title of duke of Milan. Louis responded with action, showing "the energy and courage which Orléans himself rarely failed to exhibit in moments of crisis."[27] He shored up Asti's defenses and sent urgent appeals to Bourbon for help: "I have just received a packet of letters from Venice. They show clearly the situation of the king's affairs in Italy, and by God, cousin, they call for your diligent attention. Especially send me men with whom I can hold the mountain passes to keep open the route for reinforcements and save His Majesty's person. . . . If we do not help him here, the king will be in most serious danger." Louis also ordered d'Amboise to send money from his personal accounts.[28] Since Sforza was slow to attack, the desperate situation at Asti was soon remedied. Several lance companies that were marching to Naples halted in Asti, and Bourbon quickly dispatched enough manpower, so that in less than a month, Louis's forces increased from 2,000 men to over 6,000. Since it was not in Louis's character "to wait until one comes to put him under siege," he took the offensive, despite Charles's orders that he stand ready to bring his forces to meet the king if he called for them. As Francesco Guicciardini, the Florentine historian, stated, "It is difficult to resist what appears beneficial to oneself."[29] Meanwhile, Charles left from Naples on May 20 with about half of his army, leaving the remainder to occupy the realm. He had written to Anne that he hoped to return to France in mid-April, so the retreat was not entirely motivated by the creation of the League of Venice.

Orléans had become aware of the dissatisfaction with Sforza's rule in the city of Novara just across the Milanese border from Asti. When two nobles from the city offered to place it in Louis's hands, he acted. On June 10 a French company was let into the city, and three days later Louis made a triumphal entry before a crowd that shouted *"Orléans! Orléans! Francia! Francia!"* In Guicciardini's opinion, if Louis had then marched to Milan, he would have taken il Moro by surprise and given the signal for general rebellion against the highly unpopular Sforza. Louis, however, moved cautiously, attacking a fortress near Novara and getting bogged down in a siege. Ludovico regained his balance and sent a large force to Novara. When Sforza's men inflicted heavy losses on a French cavalry unit, Louis retreated inside the walls of Novara with his forces.[30] Louis had bungled the situation badly. His principal obligation was to protect the passes across the Alps for the king's safe return and go to his aid if needed, not conquer Milan. The occupation of Novara also made Venice commit fully to the war against France.

Charles soon needed help. As he moved northward from Rome, the allies collected an army about three times the size of his. As the French moved across the Appennines, indecision among his enemies left open the passes until the French forces arrived at Fornovo on the Taro River, a tributary of the Po. On the morning of July 6, 1495, Charles mounted a great black charger and addressed his troops: "Today I shall learn who are my friends, and with them I go forth to live or die."[31]

In the battle that followed, Charles, the special target of a charge led by the marquis of Mantua, "showed great boldness and defended himself nobly."[32] The superior French artillery and their ferocious fighting style, to which the Italians were unaccustomed, were important factors in the outcome of the battle, but as crucial was the presence of the huge French baggage train loaded with the spoils of Naples. Left lightly defended because of the lack of manpower, the baggage lured a large portion of the allied cavalry away from the fighting. Deprived of much of their manpower at the critical moment, the Italians fell back before the French. With most of the French baggage in their hands, the Italians claimed victory, but the French won what they needed—a safe retreat to Asti. They arrived there on July 16, after what Commynes, who claimed that he had been in many campaigns, called the most arduous march of his life.

Most of Charles's men were given the chance to rest at Asti, but some had to be sent to relieve Orléans under siege in Novara. His situation was becoming more and more dangerous, not only because of rapidly dwindling supplies and manpower, but also because the Venetian army that had fought at Fornovo had joined the forces besieging the city. Two attempts to slip in reinforcements failed, and word came out that most of the men, including the duke, were ill. Louis was reported to have quartan fever, a form of malaria in which a high fever reoccurs every four days. Nonetheless, he energetically attended to the defense of the city. He showed his solidarity with his men by eating their food and sending the delicacies from his table to the sick and wounded.[33]

The exhausted French at Asti could not mount a strong relief attempt, and after some bitter arguing in the royal council, it was agreed to negotiate Novara's fate. The Italians were ready to negotiate, as disease was also reducing their forces. Commynes, leading the French negotiating team at Vercelli, asked that Louis be allowed to visit the king. The allies agreed to the request, but when Marshal Gié arrived at Novara to escort him to Charles's camp, Louis's troops refused to allow him to leave until Gié placed his two nephews in the citadel as hostages to Orléans's return. Three days later a truce was agreed upon by which the French forces would leave with military honors and the townspeople pledged not to admit either side until a permanent peace was concluded.

Commynes gave a pitiful picture of the men who came out: Of the original 7,500 men in Louis's force, 2,000 had already died; of the rest, only 600 could have defended themselves. On October 9 the Peace of Vercelli returned Novara to Sforza, who renounced his claim to Asti. The French king agreed to end his support of Louis's claims to Milan. Again there was bitter debate in the royal council over whether to accept the treaty. Louis's friend, the prince of Orange, who had just arrived from France, strongly supported it. According to Guicciardini, Orléans took up the words of the prince "with such sharpness that he and the prince proceeded hot to abuse; and Orléans gave him the lie before all the council."[34] But because the king wanted to return to France, the peace terms were accepted.

On October 22, 1495, Charles broke camp. He reached Grenoble five days later. St-Gelais wrote that Orléans was disheartened for having to leave Italy in such a manner. Nonetheless, he took an active part in the jousts, hunting, and pleasures in which Charles indulged, while the court stayed in Lyon.[35] They ignored the bad news from Naples, where the French army that had remained needed weapons, supplies, and money. Ferdinand of Aragon had sent an army to Sicily before Charles had left Naples. It had then crossed to the mainland and engaged the French in July 1495. Although the French won the battle, the Neapolitans took advantage of the absence of the French troops to open their gates to King Ferrante. Most of the kingdom of Naples returned to Ferrante's control, but the French held on to several key fortresses.

In December 1495 Charles received a much worse piece of news. His three-year-old son had died from measles. Charles Orland had been a strong, healthy child, about whom Commynes commented: "He was bold in his speech and he was not afraid of things that other children usually fear."[36] The queen's grief was very bitter and long, so much so her husband became concerned about her health. He tried to bring her out of her melancholy by throwing a ball for her. Among those attending was Louis of Orléans, whose cheerful demeanor deeply offended Anne. She took his good mood as a display of pleasure at being once more first in the line of succession because of her son's death. As a result she would not speak to him for a long time.[37] Some sources have argued that Louis was only following royal orders to appear merry at the ball, but he probably let his glee at having a renewed chance at ascending the throne show through. Louis was also accused of trying to hasten the fragile king's death by wearing him out with sports, hunting, and womanizing.[38]

Another death soon after the dauphin's also affected Louis's life—that of his cousin and confidant Charles of Angoulême, who left his nineteen-year-old widow Louise of Savoy with two children, Marguerite and Francis. Francis was now next in the line of succession after Louis. In his will, Charles had designated Louis as the guardian of his children, but Louise contested it on the grounds that an old tradition of Angoumois established the age for the right of guardianship at a younger age than elsewhere in France. She took the dispute to the royal council, where it was settled by naming Louis as honorary guardian while Louise had day-to-day authority over her children. This dispute embittered the relationship between Louis and Louise.[39]

Queen Anne became pregnant twice more after the death of her son, but one pregnancy resulted in a son who lived only for five weeks and the other in a stillbirth. After the second, which occurred in early 1498, the king dramatically changed his lifestyle. According to Commynes, he "made up his mind to live properly and according to God's commandments, to put justice and the Church in good order and also to regulate his finances in such a way that he would raise only 1,200,000 francs upon his people by way of taxes."[40] Commynes then enumerated some of the acts that Charles performed to make good his pledge: requiring that bishops reside in their dioceses, giving large amounts of alms, and spending long hours hearing the complaints of the poor and giving justice. Charles even rebuked Louis, who had been his boon companion in much of his womanizing. In February 1498 Charles was reading a manual of confession when he came upon the chapter on sins of the flesh. He said to Louis: "My brother, this book speaks to you!" The duke harshly replied that if he had a different wife, "it would not be so."[41]

Louis's relationship with Jeanne had not changed significantly. It is true that when he was in Asti, he sent her letters in which he used the salutation "Madame m'amye," a phrase that was much more intimate than is suggested by the literal translation.[42] He signed the letters "Vostre amy." They contained information about his military activities and asked her to pray for him. After returning from Italy, Charles frequently would tell Louis: "My brother, go and see my sister." Louis felt he dared not disobey for fear of being thrown back into prison.[43] When Jeanne was at the court, Louis was forced to dine with her or escort her to balls and tournaments. That, apparently, was an important reason why he left the court in late 1497 to attend to his duties as governor of Normandy.

Another factor in Louis's removing himself from the court was a rift that opened between him and the king over Italy. Soon after his return Charles began to plan for a new expedition to Italy. Commynes reported that in early 1496, Charles decided that Orléans would lead an army to Asti with the expectation of help from a number of the smaller Italian states. In July Charles ordered the fleets of Brittany and Normandy to prepare to sail to Naples, and at the same time a Milanese spy reported that Louis was seen in Lyon with 25,000 troops headed for Asti.[44] Louis sent his baggage ahead and was ready to leave when he asked for the matter to be discussed in the royal council. Two meetings of the council resulted in the recommendation that Louis proceed, but, as Commynes put it, he "had avoided leaving because he saw the king in rather poor health and was to be his heir if he should die." Louis said that he would go only if the king gave him a direct command and allowed him to attack Milan. Charles would not, because "he never sent anyone to war by force." Thus, the expedition was halted, displeasing Charles, who was looking forward to his revenge on Sforza.[45]

Perhaps it was Charles's pique at Louis's refusal to lead the new Italian expedition that led him to order an investigation of Louis's government of Normandy. Georges d'Amboise was serving as Orléans's lieutenant in governing the province, and he bore the brunt of the suspicions of malfeasance. The rumors also included talk that Louis and d'Amboise were plotting anew against the king. St-Gelais insisted that d'Amboise acquitted himself completely of all charges. Nonetheless, the atmosphere in March 1498 was so tense that the bishop and the duke, who was then in poor health, closeted themselves at Blois in anticipation of a royal order exiling them, Georges to Rome and Louis to Asti or perhaps Germany.[46]

It was at that tense moment that a royal courier rushed breathlessly into the château at Blois. Several historians have embellished the story of his arrival with a melodramatic gloss of how Louis's men began to dash about preparing for a quick getaway for the duke as they expected to hear that he was under arrest.[47] The true story is dramatic enough. When the courier caught his breath, he blurted: "Sire, the King is dead!"

Charles VIII had died on April 7, 1498, at Amboise. He had been ill for several days but felt well enough that morning to watch some of his courtiers play tennis in the empty moat of the castle. As he walked with the queen through a dark, dirty passageway to the moat, he hit his head hard on the top of a low doorway. He seemed to have shaken off the blow, and he watched the games for about two hours when suddenly he said that he hoped he would never sin again and then collapsed. He lay in the moat on a dirty straw mattress for nine hours, briefly recovering his voice three times to pray. Commynes commented: "And so this great and powerful king died, and in such a miserable place, when he possessed so many magnificent houses."[48]

It has been generally agreed that Charles did not die from a concussion, although the blow may have hastened the onset of whatever killed him. Contemporary sources use the term apoplexy.[49] Charles's unexpected death raised the suspicion of poisoning. Following the adage "See who would profit," the suspicions were directed at Louis of Orléans, il Moro, and the Venetians. Charles had eaten an orange just before going to the tennis game, and since oranges came from Italy and were regarded as especially suitable for poisoning because their strong smell and taste would hide the poison, naturally the Italians came under the strongest suspicion. Both the Venetians and Sforza had much to fear from a new Italian expedition, although il Moro is said to have come to an understanding with Charles just before his death. Clearly he had a great deal more to fear from Louis as king.[50] Certainly the timing of Charles's death was most opportune from Louis's point of view. The dauphin was dead and the queen had just had a stillbirth, assuring that no posthumous son would appear to take the throne. Louis's current estrangement with the king has been seen as providing further motivation. On the other hand, there is no contemporary evidence of Louis's complicity, and in the general view he was deemed incapable of it. In the absence of any evidence that Charles was poisoned in the first place, the accusations can be given little credence.

Louis's right to the throne was not entirely free of possible challenge. It was only the second time that the crown had passed to a cousin of the dead king since the time of Hugh Capet. The first, of course, was the highly controversial succession of Philip VI in 1328. As one who had been imprisoned for lèse-majesté, a case against Louis presumably could have been made. The Venetian ambassador reported that Ludovico Sforza wrote to the duke of Bourbon suggesting that he work to prevent Louis's succession.[51] As Machiavelli wrote:

> There was controversy after King Charles's death as to whether, because of his dereliction and defection from the Crown, he should have lost the right to succeed. He was a wealthy man, however, . . . and able to spend money, and so forth. Besides, the only one who could have been king if he was passed over was a little boy, . . . so for the above reasons and because he had some supporters he was made king.

There was no mention made of Louis's suspect parentage.[52]

As Machiavelli noted, there was no challenger to make such a case. After Louis in the line of succession came three-year-old Francis of Angoulême and then nine-year-old Charles de Bourbon de Vendôme; neither was a viable alternative. The important men of Charles's court appreciated that, and they knew that it would be best for the government and their careers if they saluted Louis as king without hesitation. The prince of Orange went to Blois the same night. Soon Marshal Gié and Sieur du Bouchage, who had been the dauphin's governor, arrived with several more high-ranking courtiers. As Commynes said, "Everyone ran to the duke of Orléans."[53] However, Louis would not be secure on the throne until Anne and Pierre de Bourbon recognized him as king. While they may have lacked the power to deny the crown to him, they could have made it very difficult for him to exercise authority. Fortunately for him, they responded immediately with a letter of congratulations and set out for Blois to salute him as king, where they arrived on April 13. Pierre had become close to Louis in the years since his release from prison. One story has it that his wife had assigned him to keep a close eye on Louis in order to prevent him from gaining too much influence over Charles, but they soon became friends.[54] Thus, what could have been a serious crisis for the monarchy passed without problem, and the accession of Louis XII to the throne took place smoothly and without opposition. Louis was now, as he proclaimed in a letter of April 16, "By the grace of God, King of France, Sicily, and Jerusalem and Duke of Milan."

5

The Reign Begins

Two months shy of his thirty-sixth birthday, Louis of Orléans had become king. He was the third oldest at the moment of succession of the thirty-two kings from Hugh Capet to 1789. Louis VIII and Louis XI were both slightly older. His range of experiences was unique among new French kings: imprisoned for treason, although acts of rebellion by heirs to the throne were by no means unknown; commanding an infantry force in battle and being captured; commanding a fleet at sea; and governing a city under siege. In several respects, however, his early life was similar to Louis XI's. Both men had long periods of estrangement from the king and had been away from the court for several years, but Louis XII's imprisonment was a great deal harsher than Louis XI's exile at the Burgundian court. Both had experience as governors of large provinces and commanders in battle. But while the Spider King allowed his experiences to make him a bitter and suspicious man although a very effective ruler, Louis XII, the "Father of the People," became a far more sympathetic figure after his succession. No other French king was ever quoted as saying: "I greatly prefer that the whole world betray me than that I should betray one single person!" or as regarding peace "as the greatest good that God can give His creatures."[1]

By 1498 Louis was a mature person in physique and personality. A Venetian ambassador described him in 1502 as tall and quite lean but with heavy thighs. He ate mostly boiled beef but liked wine, especially the wines of Beaune, and may have imbibed of it a little too much fairly often. He had a weatherbeaten face, a result as much of hunting nearly every day as of the time spent in the field with the army. His portraits and busts reveal that he had a rather small head with large eyes, a long thin nose, thick lips, and straight reddish hair cut in a page-boy style. None of the contemporary portraits present him as regal in appearance, even when mounted in full armor on a charger. A Venetian ambassador reported that Louis had a "very good countenance, a smiling countenance," and laughed

easily; but he also wrote that he was avaricious and miserly. An earlier
ambassador had also commented on his miserliness, but he attributed it to
Louis's desire to pay his troops on time.[2] Several other contemporary
sources refer to his parsimony. Louis's character and virtues were seen as
rather common, which helps to explain the insult *roi roturier* (commoner
king) that some nobles used for him.

Louis was willing to take advice and listen to opinions contrary to his own,
but he also had a stubborn streak that often make it difficult for his advisers
to persuade him to a different course of action. In 1509 Florimond Robertet,
one of those closest to him, told the Florentine ambassador: "The king's character is not easy to deal with; he is not easily brought around to what is not
his opinion, which is not always correct." Even Cardinal d'Amboise,
Robertet said, did not always succeed in getting him to do as he would like.[3]

Louis's letters have "an air of solicitude, sincerity and candor," according
to their seventeenth-century editor.[4] The king had a free and easy manner
with the people at his court, and certainly with the foreign ambassadors. He
conversed with them at length and was very forthcoming with information
and news. Their dispatches quoted him frequently and reported his opinions on events. A Venetian ambassador provided an example of his intimate
way with ambassadors in a report from August 1513. Louis begged the
ambassador to be careful about keeping secret the news he was giving him,
because when Venice and France were at war several years earlier, Louis
had learned everything that was being sent from Venice. The king said this
"with a great expression of sincerity."[5] When things were going well for him,
there also was a good amount of humor in the conversations. Louis was very
kind-hearted on a personal basis and solicitous toward the French people,
especially the poor, but he was often indifferent toward the sufferings of
other peoples, especially when his forces were inflicting the misery.

Louis's age put him past midlife for men of his era, and he apparently
looked older, since observers remarked that he appeared a little worn out.
Perhaps the reason for this was that he was frequently stricken with high
fevers. They may have been caused by either malaria or Graves' disease
(resulting from the overproduction of hormone by the thyroid gland).
Both diseases can cause recurring episodes of high fever several years
apart. Unlike malaria, which Louis caught in Italy in 1494, Graves' disease seems to be hereditary, and Louis was said to have had the same
symptoms that accompanied the death of his mother. [6] Stress and overex-
ertion can bring about relapses of either disease. While often debilitating
for weeks on end, neither disease is necessarily fatal. Those afflicted by
one or the other can lead fairly active lives for years, although death can

result from a high fever or other complications.[7] Whether Louis had either disease or not, he maintained an active lifestyle even after his almost fatal illness of 1505 and fathered a child at age forty-eight.

Louis's bitter experiences as a young man seem to have taught him patience and a concern for the less fortunate, qualities not obvious in him before 1498. His living conditions for most of his earlier life—in an impoverished household, in prison, in the field with the army, in a besieged town—appear to have made him little concerned for sumptuous surroundings. One of the ubiquitous Venetian ambassadors reported in 1499 that the king had received him in an inn at Etampes, albeit a fine inn, and not the château.[8] As king, Louis earned a reputation not only for plain living but also for plain speaking. In 1501 the archbishop of Besançon, the principal adviser to Philip of Austria, said about him: "No one hates cheating, craftiness and all hypocrites more than he."[9] Louis never put a gloss of diplomatic niceties or court elegance on his words. Perhaps that trait made it difficult for him to believe that others were fooling him. His gullibility was a trait on which several of those who dealt with him remarked, most notoriously by Ferdinand of Aragon, whom a contemporary called "the most dexterous rascal amongst the kings of his day." When Ferdinand's ambassador to France told him that Louis refused to make an alliance with him because Ferdinand had already tricked him twice, he is supposed to have cracked: "By God, he lies, the drunkard! I've tricked him more than ten times!"[10]

The new king's previous life did not turn him into an embittered revenge seeker. He confirmed all of Charles's officers in their positions and continued their pensions.[11] Those who had been the most active in the government of the Beaujeus and most engaged against him were treated warmly when the new king went to Amboise the day after Charles's death to pay his last respects. Upon entering the chamber where Charles was laid out, Louis, "with great tears in his eyes," asked God's pardon for him. When Louis left the bier, he saw a large crowd of royal officials, including Louis de La Trémoille, his vanquisher at St-Aubin, at the far end of the room. The king summoned him forward and asked La Trémoille to be as loyal to him as he had been to his predecessor "and confirmed him in his offices, estates, and pensions."[12]

It is often written that Louis then made his famous statement: "It is not honorable for the king of France to avenge the quarrels of a duke of Orléans!" That comment was in fact made several days later when a delegation from Orléans asked him to forgive the city for its lack of support for him in times past and, specifically, for having closed its gates to him in 1487.[13] The sense of the statement applied equally well to his treatment of

La Trémoille and Charles's officers in general. In respect to Anne of Beaujeu and her husband, Louis granted them something they badly wanted but had not received from Charles—the right to pass on the Bourbon estates to their daughter Suzanne should they die without a son. In their marriage contract Louis XI had insisted on enforcing the law of appanage by which their estates would revert to the monarchy in default of male issue. On May 12, 1498, the new king agreed to allow Suzanne to marry the heir of the Montpensier branch of the Bourbons (the future constable, Charles de Bourbon) and join the vast properties of both families should her parents die without a son, as in fact they did.[14]

Louis XII also won over the late king's family and friends by his handling of the funeral. He stayed in Amboise for a day attending to the details of the transport of Charles's body to Paris and then returned to Blois. Charles's body remained at Amboise for eight days, while Masses were said around the clock. Commynes remarked that everything "was richer than for any other king."[15] A funeral cortege of some 7,000 nobles and royal officials rode with the body while 4,000 poor people carrying torches formed the vanguard. At Notre-Dame de Cléry near Orléans, where an urn holding Charles's heart was entombed, Louis XII and Pierre de Bourbon attended a funeral Mass. It was the only time once the formal obsequies began that the new king was in attendance on the body of his predecessor. Following the ritualistic fiction that "The king never dies!" tradition dictated that the dead king and the living king could never be seen together. Louis returned to Orléans, where he remained until after the funeral.[16]

On May 1 the majestic ritual of the royal burial took place in the crypt of St-Denis in late afternoon. The *grand écuyer,* Pierre d'Urfé, first crying *"Le Roi est mort!"* dipped the point of the royal standard into the tomb and quickly lifted it out, shouting *"Vive le Roi!"*[17] Admiral Graville wrote shortly after: "Never in memory has another king of France had so much richness and so great a company of great men" for his funeral.[18] The cost of the ceremonies was 45,000 francs, according to Commynes, and St-Gelais stated that Louis paid it out of his private funds accumulated before his succession.[19] Louis's final years as Duke of Orléans had not been as impoverished as the early ones, since he had a royal pension and salaries from his offices that totaled at least 44,000 *l* a year.[20] Louis commissioned an Italian sculptor, who had come to France with Charles, to design a mausoleum of black marble and bronze. The statue of Charles on it was destroyed in 1592, and the mausoleum itself was wrecked in 1793.

Louis remained outside of Paris until the rites were completed. He then arrived at the Château of Vincennes on May 2. The magistrates of the

Parlement came out to pledge their service and loyalty, and in his first formal act as king, Louis confirmed them in their offices.[21] The presidents of the Parlement admonished him to administer good justice. All the major officers of the crown were present for a series of meetings as Louis organized his court and government.

The French court provided a living for several thousand persons, either directly or as the sole customer for a vast array of merchants and artisans who followed it. The task of overseeing all of these people belonged to the *grand maître*, who also had the responsibility of introducing foreign ambassadors to the king, choosing the site for the king's lodging when the court was on the road, and directing the security of the royal person. Upon the death of Guy de Laval in 1500, the position went to Charles d'Amboise, the nephew of Georges d'Amboise, who spent as much time at the court as he did in Milan as its governor. After his death in 1511, Jacques de La Palise had the office. Six companies of 100 fighting men apiece safeguarded the king, which included two companies of French *gens d'armes* selected from among the best families. For most of Louis's reign, Huguet d'Amboise and Louis de Dunois commanded them. Claude de la Châtre and Jacques de Crussol served as captains of the two companies of French archers; Béraud Stuart, the company of Scots archers; and Robert de Floranges, the royal Swiss. The tasks of the four companies of the royal archers included guarding the person of the king and patrolling the site where he was. The Scots archers had those responsibilities after dark. These companies provided the king, as well as the king of Scotland for the Scots archers, with a major source of patronage, since an appointment to them was both prestigious and lucrative. The annual salary for a royal guard was 200 *l.*[22]

The major division of the court was the *Hôtel du roi*. Its principal officer was the grand chamberlain, who had supervision of the royal chambers. Because his post gave him free and constant access to the king, usually the chamberlain had broad influence over him. La Trémoille had taken up the post under Charles and kept it through Louis's reign. Other officers of the household included the *grand panetier* (breadcarrier) and the *grand échanson* (cupbearer), who supervised the ushers and servers of the royal table. A member of the prominent Cossé family served as *grand panetier*, with a salary of 3,333.3 *l.* The kitchen staff was divided into the *bouche*, whose members had the honor of preparing the meals for the royal table, and the *commun*, which served the rest of the court. Also part of the *Hôtel du roi* were seven royal physicians, two barbers, six surgeons, and an astrologer, Antoine du Hamelet, who had also served Louis XI and Charles VIII. He received 120 *l* a year. In 1499 there were some 320 persons who had positions in the royal household drawing a total salary of 81,080 *l*, with a median annual salary of 240 *l*.[23]

The court also included the queen's household, the chapel, the *écurie* (royal stables), and the two divisions of huntsmen, the *vénerie*, and the *fauconnerie*. Queen Anne's household, which was substantial, was funded largely if not entirely by the duchy of Brittany, which gave her revenues of nearly 400,000 *l*.[24] The head of the chapel for Louis was René de Prie, bishop of Limoges, made a cardinal in 1507. The twenty royal almoners were the most prominent members of the chapel, with the grand almoner being one of the great officers of the realm. He had the right, unique among the French prelates, to eat at the royal table. He supervised the Hospital of the Quinze-Vingts, founded by St. Louis, and, by extension, oversaw the hospitals of the entire kingdom. In 1499 Laurent Bureau, bishop of Sisteron, held the office. He received an annual salary of 800 *l*, while the other almoners received 200 or 400 *l* a year. Their first duty was the distribution of royal alms. The king had an obligation to give to the poor, but royal generosity was limited. In the fiscal year that extended from October 1, 1506, to September 30, 1507, Geoffroy de Pompadour, now the grand almoner, distributed 6,500 *l* from the royal treasury. Much of that sum went to the clergy for Masses and devotions, but the roll of alms included such items as two *l* for a woman named Loise de Pre for the nourishment of her children and three *l* for Jeanne la belle for her dowry. The sum of 6,500 *l* was the amount of the ordinary alms; at special events such as the king's coronation or first entries, his almoners gave out additional sums.[25]

Prominent clerics who served in the royal chapel for Louis XII included Guillaume Petit Parvey, a noted humanist, who became a royal almoner in 1510. A Greek scholar, he was a close friend of Jacques Lefèvre d'Etaples, the noted humanist. Jean d'Auton, the official chronicler of Louis's reign, and the poet Jean Marot were other clerics of the royal chapel. Louis's confessor for much of his reign, Jean Clérée, a doctor in theology, did not have as brilliant a career, but it was he who was called to the king's sickbed in 1505 "to exhort him to do what was necessary to save his soul." Clérée died in 1507, and Antoine de Forno, the bishop of Marseille, became royal confessor.[26]

The *écurie* provided horses and couriers for the king. The several extant rolls of its members and expenses show clearly Louis's efforts at economizing, but the decline in the size of the *écurie* may also have reflected his preference for going by boat whenever possible. Its personnel dropped from over 200 men in 1496 to 134 in 1500 to 120 in 1510. Louis, like any nobleman of the era, loved horses, especially his great charger Testegaie, but he still reduced the number of horses in his *écurie*.[27] The *vénerie* was the division of royal huntsmen responsible for hunting with dogs, and the *fauconnerie*, hunting with falcons. Louis loved to hunt throughout his life, despite serious health problems, and was said to have "waged war without pity on poachers." He is noted as the first French king to have preferred hunting with hawks. Hawks appear frequently in his accounts throughout his life. He received several famous white hawks of Cyprus though Venice. His favorite, Mugnet, the "terror of herons," is supposed to have expired at the foot of Queen Anne's deathbed in 1514. His *fauconnerie* had 100 huntsmen and 300 falcons and cost 30,000 *l* a year. His *vénerie* was much smaller—six huntsmen and fifty dogs. A poor gentleman gave Louis a white dog named Souillard, who was the ancestor of the famous royal pack of white dogs that lasted through the sixteenth century.[28] Like all kings, Louis had a court jester, called Triboulet, but the word appears to have been a stock name for all royal fools. Louis's Triboulet went on to entertain Francis I and gained lasting fame when Rabelais designed a blazon for him.[29]

Entertainment must have been important to Louis, since he put on numerous tournaments and festivals during his reign. D'Auton described one such festival at Mâcon in September 1503. Among the novelties and pastimes was a German rope walker who performed on a rope strung between the towers of the citadel and a church, 250 steps in length and 150 feet off the ground. In view of the king and 30,000 persons, he danced, did somersaults, and hung by his teeth. A tumbler from Florence astonished the crowd with her somersaults. Louis's accounts for the next year mention thirty-six *l* for a rope walker who entertained him at Blois.[30]

When Louis was at Vincennes in May 1498, however, his major concern was preparing for his coronation at Reims. Although he must have felt secure enough on the throne, since there was no viable alternative to him, Louis still was eager to be crowned to forestall any threat to his succession.[31] As of 1498 the coronation was no longer absolutely necessary for a new king to govern, but it served as the affirmation of his right to the throne. A king who went uncrowned for several months would find his authority diminishing. The case of the Dauphin Charles, who went uncrowned from 1422 to 1429 and who had virtually no authority until Jeanne d'Arc led him to Reims for his *sacre*, was recent enough to have had an impact on the matter.

Louis arrived at Reims on May 26, the day before the ceremony. He made his first "joyful entry" of his reign into Reims, but that event was always overshadowed by the *sacre* the next day.[32] Early on the morning of the coronation, by tradition a Sunday, the tenants of the four most ancient baronies of the realm went to the abbey of St-Remi to order its abbot to carry the ampulla of sacred oil, first used at Clovis's baptism in 496, according to legend, to the cathedral.[33] They brought the abbot a great white horse to ride the short distance to the cathedral, while they stayed at St-Remi to serve as hostages for the safe return of the ampulla. The archbishop-peer of Reims, Guillaume Briçonnet, met the abbot at the cathedral doors. By then the king had arrived in the company of the bishop-peers of Laon and Beauvais, who had summoned him from the archbishop's palace, where he had slept, to the *sacre*. The rest of the nine peers of the realm escorted the king to the main altar. The three other bishop-peers—the bishops of Châlons-sur-Marne, Langres, and Noyon—were at Reims for the coronation. All of the six lay peerages, however, were present by representation; for example, the duke of Bourbon represented the duchy of Guyenne. Five of the peerages—Burgundy, Normandy, Guyenne, Champagne, and Toulouse—had all reverted to the monarchy and were vacant; while Flanders, which still had an incumbent count, Philip of Austria, was represented by his great-uncle.

Each of the twelve peers had a special task in the ceremony; for example, the count-peer of Flanders carried the royal sword and the count-bishop of Noyon, the royal ring. The archbishop-peer of Reims had the major role: He anointed the new king with the sacred oil drawn with a needle out of Clovis's ampulla and placed the crown on his head. During the procession that followed, the twelve peers held the crown on the king's head to symbolize their willingness to help the him rule and his need of their support and service. The archbishop of Reims then officiated at a solemn Mass at which the king took the Eucharist in both bread and wine. Coronations were the only time in late medieval Catholicism that a lay person was ever permitted to take the cup, and it signified the quasi-sacramental nature of the *sacre* in which the king received special divine grace to rule wisely and justly. Earlier in the Middle Ages, the coronation was in fact regarded as a sacrament and had taken most of its ritual from the consecration of a bishop.

After the service, the king was escorted back to the episcopal palace where a grand banquet was served. On the following day he left Reims for the shrine of Saint Marcoul at Corbeny on the road to Paris, where the new king traditionally made his devotions to the saint, a Norman churchman of the sixth century who had a reputation for healing a disease called scrofula. (Scrofula was a form of tuberculosis of the lymph glands, which caused an ugly disfigurement of the skin on the neck but was rarely life-threatening.) The touch of a newly crowned king was thought to be especially effective in healing scrofula, and the disease was called "the king's evil." The touching at Corbeny had become a necessary proof of the new king's right to the throne. Of the twenty persons Louis touched there, fifteen were said to have been healed.[34] Each of those touched was given a new silver coin with the new king's arms, by tradition the first time the new coins were distributed. Probably the improved diet made possible for those who received the money caused the disease to go into remission.

From Corbeny Louis made his way in short jaunts to St-Germain-en-Laye just west of Paris, while preparations for his formal entry into Paris were under way. Although a king would make numerous "first entries" into the cities of the realm in the course of his reign, the entry into Paris was special. It was, along with the king's coronation and his funeral, one of the great spectacles of a reign. Tradition rigidly bound the other two in respect to rubric and decoration, while the Parisian entry allowed for greater freedom to introduce new themes and styles; while the themes and decoration never would be radically innovative, they would reflect developments in French culture.

The first entry into Paris was expected to take place within a month or two of the coronation. It was the major remaining aspect of the "joyous coming" of a new king or a feudal lord of the Middle Ages in which he received the homage of his vassals and cities. A substantial sum of money was granted to the king as a gift from his grateful subjects. Louis refused the money, a sum of 300,000 *l*, and returned it to the people, an act that endeared him to his subjects. The Venetian ambassador wrote at the end of May that he was "greatly loved, even adored" throughout the realm.[35] Although the great vassals of the king still had the obligation of hospitality to receive the king into their châteaux, by the late 1400s the "joyous entry" was restricted to the major cities. Part of its purpose was to provide the king with the opportunity to reconfirm the dozens of royal officials of the cities in their offices, since a new king had the right to replace all of them. Equally important a reason was the opportunity for the bourgeoisie to impress the monarch, the nobility, and the urban lower classes with its wealth and sophistication.

A joyous entry was also an opportunity to reaffirm the traditional relationship between king and city. Early on July 2, an enormous procession of Parisian officials and guild members, royal officials, nobles, and princes, all carefully arranged by rank, conducted the king, who wore golden armor and a blue hat, the royal colors, from St-Denis to Notre-Dame. They reversed the route of Charles VIII's funeral cortege of three months earlier. In between the terminal points there were several stations where the municipal and royal officials and various guilds and corporations were responsible for decoration and pageants. The ornamentation and pageants were largely medieval; there is little sign of any new themes in this entry, but it was clearly less religious in tone than previous ones.[36] At the first station at the Porte St-Denis, the city of Paris sponsored the erection of a giant lily with seven blossoms. Persons dressed to represent Nobility, Humanity, Richness, Liberality, Power, Fidelity, and Charles V, through whom Louis's right to the throne had come, were positioned among the blossoms. At the second station, by the convent of the Filles Dieu, two men dressed in Louis's livery colors of red and yellow carried a huge porcupine wearing a crown, which was Louis's device. His grandfather Louis I of Orléans had taken it from the city of Blois, where its use was highly appropriate, since the porcupine with its quills was symbolic of a stout defense. The symbolism of the porcupine worked well for a king, not only for its defensive prowess, but also for its reputed ability to project its power by throwing its quills at its enemies. Louis's motto *Cominus ac Eminus*, "From near and afar," referred to the alleged ability of the porcupine to defend itself with its quills both at close range and at a distance. As a poet denouncing the English invasion of 1513 put it, "The porcupine is very strong and terrible." Another royal device was a capital L with a crown atop it decorated with the fleur-de-lis. A variant was L and A tied together with a bow. Porcupines appeared on gold coins, and the L on silver coins, while both devices were emblazoned on heavy guns forged for Louis.

The Church of the Holy Trinity was the next stop, where a religious brotherhood, the Confraternity of the Passion, staged Abraham's sacrifice of Isaac juxtaposed with the crucifixion of Christ, in which "blood ran incessantly from the crucifix."[37] It was the only openly religious theme of the stations. Next, at the Porte aux Peintres, there was a stage with figures depicting Good Times, Peace, the French People, and the king as the Good Shepherd. They were set in a garden representing France as the earthly paradise. The procession passed onto the Ile-de-Cité where it stopped at the Châtelet. Within a yellow and violet pavilion were portraits of the new king and his ancestors going back eight generations to Saint Louis. The emphasis on the new king's descent from the king known for his administration of justice reinforced the symbolism of the presence of a figure dressed as the king with Good Counsel and Justice at his side and Injustice under his feet.

The Palais-royal was the last station, where the officials of the financial court, the Chambre des comptes, sponsored a pageant. They erected a large shield supported by two stags. On the shield were the porcupine device of the new king and the coats of arms of the duchy of Milan and the Visconti family. A Latin inscription described the porcupine's fighting prowess: "I pierce the rebels with the puissant darts of my back. And rend with my teeth any I have missed."[38] Clearly the tableau revealed Louis's intention to make good his claim to the Visconti inheritance. His coat of arms included the fleur-de-lis of France and the red serpent of the duchy of Milan.

Then it was on to the doors of the cathedral, where the Parisian clergy, numerous bishops and abbots, and the students and faculty of the university saluted the king and a faculty member gave a speech. The king, in a reaffirmation of his coronation oath, swore to maintain the church in its liberties and rights and pledged to defend it against infidels, pagans, Jews, and Muslims and expel from the realm all heretics. He further promised to give justice to all persons, the small as well as the great. The doors of Notre-Dame were thrown open and a Te Deum sung as the king entered. Then Louis was conducted to a grand banquet in the Palais royal, where all the princes of blood and great nobles of the realm were seated.

The Parisian entry was an event in which the Parisians flattered the king and told him that they expected from him justice, economy, protection, and faithful defense of the church. It was also an opportunity for the Parisians and the court to be entertained. For the next week the festivities continued with banquets and jousts. In order for the crowds to see the jousts, a great deal of scaffolding was erected. One scaffold, jammed with people, collapsed. Some thirty people, including two noblemen, were killed, and 150 injured. The king ordered his Swiss guards to clear away the dead and injured, and in thirty minutes the jousts had resumed, "as if nothing had happened, without pity or concern for the deceased." A popular jester later criticized Louis for his indifference to the suffering people.[39]

As was traditional, the shields of the knights who were jousting were hung on an artificial tree. Louis's shield was noted as bearing an "ornate crown of imperial form"—it had two intersecting arches over the top instead of the traditional French open crown with fleur-de-lis. This was one of the first French uses of the imperial crown, which a century later had become standard across Europe. Its use may represent the Valois rivalry with the Habsburgs, or it may reflect French pretensions in Italy from where the imperial title came.[40]

Perhaps the crown that Louis XII now wore was less prestigious than that of the Holy Roman Empire, but no prince would not have preferred to wear it. The realm it represented was the largest, wealthiest, and most populous in western Europe. In the previous 150 years, France had expanded beyond its longtime borders set by the Treaty of Verdun (843), having annexed Dauphiné and Provence. Nonetheless, it was still about 20 percent smaller than present-day France.

Only in the central Pyrenees did the borders of 1498 coincide with today's. In the western Pyrenees, Navarre was a sovereign kingdom, although the French king regarded it as his fief. In the eastern Pyrenees, the provinces of Cerdagne and Roussillon, which had passed back and forth between France and Aragon, were again under Aragonese rule. On the frontier with Italy, the duchy of Savoy was an independent principality controlling the region from Geneva to Nice. West of Geneva lay the Franche-Comté and the county of Dombes, properties of the House of Burgundy that had passed to the Habsburgs. To the north, Alsace and Lorraine were units of the Holy Roman Empire governed by a myriad of nobles. Along the northern border, Flanders and much of Artois were also under Maximilian of Habsburg, although they were legally fiefs of the French crown. West of Flanders along the English Channel was English-held Calais, a reminder of the Hundred Years War. Beyond the borders were several small enclaves under French sovereignty; the most important was the city of Tournai in Hainault. Within the realm were two important independent enclaves, papal-ruled Avignon and the principality of Orange. Louis XI had purchased Orange from the House of Chalon in 1475 for 40,000 *écus,* but in 1500 Louis XII returned it to Jean de Chalon for his services to him since 1485.[41] Except for Avignon and Orange, all of the above-mentioned lands were sources of a great deal of diplomatic activity, controversy, and, foremost, war.

In 1514 Louis XII commissioned Louis Boulenger from Albi, an "expert geometrician and astronomer," to measure his realm. He concluded that the circumference of France came to 800 leagues (roughly 2,400 miles), and the area, 40,000 square leagues, close to the true figures. Boulenger indicated that there were twelve archdioceses and ninety-two dioceses, eighteen duchies and eighty-six counties, and 600,000 towns and villages, from which he interpolated that the population of France was 100 million people, a wildly exaggerated number.[42] The real population of France of Louis's time cannot be determined, largely because there was nothing like a census taken and tax rolls provide a poor substitute. Given the inexactness of historical demography, an estimate of 14 million people is plausible for 1498.

Whatever number is used for the population, there is no question that it was rapidly increasing from its nadir of about 1450. The century after the Black Death had seen a continued decline in population caused by recurring plague, disastrous harvests, and the violence and destruction of the Hundred Years War. With the end of the war in 1453 and an improving climate, the population began to rebound. Louis XII's reign was a time of vigorous population growth and the attendant economic growth.[43] The return to cultivation of land abandoned in the early 1400s provided a boost in the grain supply that naturally led to a population increase. The weather largely cooperated throughout Louis's reign. There was one year of famine at Tours (1501) caused by an extremely cold winter, which also caused a destructive ice jam on the Loire. The winter of 1505-6 was probably colder, since there are reports of extreme cold and snow from all across France. But heavy snow, which on January 6 covered the ground at Marseille to the depth of four hands, saved the winter wheat from being killed.[44] With the grain supply increasing at least as fast as the population during Louis's era, the price of grain remained quite stable. To ensure that it would, he banned the export of grain from the realm in 1507—which was, however, something virtually every king did. The price of a *setier* of wheat (156 liters in the Parisian system of measurement) at Paris on November 12 was a good indicator of how good the harvest had been that summer. During Louis's reign the median price was 1.56 *l* (1508), with a high of 2.11 *l* (1501) and a low of 0.83 *l* (1509). Most other commodities also were generally stable in supply and price.[45] Rents remained steady, which meant that the peasant tenant holders—the vast majority of the peasantry—were able to maintain their standards of living. Wages for rural laborers rose considerably, so the portion of rural society that depended on wage income saw its conditions improved. That in turn meant a reduction in the number of vagabonds and brigands on the roads of the realm,[46] since the rural laborers were the most marginalized group in society. Any downturn in their fortunes sent large numbers out of their villages and into a life of crime. Louis's reduction of taxes in the first years of his reign also benefitted the peasants and made him very popular among them.

The nobles, who constituted a significant part of the rural population, also prospered. Increased production with the return of fallow fields to cultivation profited them, while prices remained largely stable.[47] The wars of Louis's reign afforded them the opportunity to ply their profession and gain wealth from ransoms, plunder, and royal wages, while the wars were fought mostly outside of the realm and caused little harm to their properties. In short, the 90 percent of the French population living in the countryside enjoyed "exceptional affluence . . . when the wounds of the Hundred Years' War had been healed."[48]

When the rural world flourished in the early modern period, the urban one did also. The urban population took off in the late 1400s at a pace faster than the rural, largely a consequence of immigration from the villages. After 1450 higher wages in the cities attracted labor from the countryside, although by 1500 urban wages had flattened out and remained largely stagnant for the next several decades. The growth of cities continued but at a slower pace. Still, at the end of Louis's reign, Claude de Seyssel, the noted political theorist, could comment: "For one merchant in the time of King Louis XI you can find over fifty in the present reign and there now are in the small towns more merchants than once were found in the great cities."[49]

Paris was, of course, the largest city. A Venetian ambassador suggested in 1502 that its population was more than 300,000 people[50]; but that number is probably much too high, since a well-founded estimate for 1547 is 220,000. Foreign immigration, largely from Italy and Spain, was a factor in the growth of several of Paris's rivals. Lyon, which at some 40,000 people vied with Rouen as the second city of the realm, had a very substantial Italian community that helped make the city the French leader in banking and commerce. Bordeaux, with an estimated population of 20,000 in 1500, became the home of several thousand Iberian Jews after the expulsions of the 1490s.[51] The major French exports were grain, wine, woad for dye, coarse cloth, and salt. Fine cloth, spices, precious metals, and furs were the major imports. In Louis's reign spices carried by the Portuguese from the Indies began to appear in France. Merchants from Languedoc who dealt in spices brought through Italy asked Louis in 1513 to prohibit the import of Portuguese spices, but he refused because of the need for good relations with Portugal against Spain.[52] Cities such as Bordeaux, Nantes, St-Malo, and Rouen prospered from foreign trade, but the biggest winner in that respect was Marseille. Once Provence was annexed in 1481, Mediterranean trade was largely diverted there at the expense of Languedocian ports such as Narbonne and Arles, which were also hampered by the silting up of their harbors. Despite constant complaints about the flow of bullion out of France, exports and imports were nearly in balance, with the greater quantity of exports largely balancing the more costly imports.

Internal transportation across France was still extremely difficult. Except in those few places where Roman roads were kept in good repair, roads were muddy or dusty ruts for travel on foot or horseback. Carriages were still almost unknown. Only a small amount of trade traveled across land; for both commerce and persons river boat was the vastly preferred mode of transportation. The royal court frequently traveled up and down the Seine and the Loire. Blois was favored as a royal residence in part because it was within an easy boat ride on the Loire of several other royal residences. France was blessed with rivers, so that it was possible to go by boat, for example, from Harfleur to Marseille with only one short portage. But the rivers, especially the Loire, were inconsistent, frequently too high or too low, and blocked by sandbars and fallen trees. Regardless of the mode of travel, highwaymen and pirates were a constant fear.

Nonetheless, the French traveled a great deal on business or pilgrimages. The royal court was highly peripatetic, despite the great number of persons and items that traveled with it; but Louis XII moved about less than most kings of the Renaissance, spending much of his time at Blois. Rudimentary postal services run by the monarchy and the University of Paris existed in 1500. They were expensive but relatively quick. It took a letter sent in the summer from Brussels forty-four hours to reach Paris, sixty hours to Blois, and ninety-six to Lyon. Winter added at least another day. The announcement of the election of a pope in 1503 reached Blois from Rome in less than four days, but it took nearly seven days for news of Charles VIII's death to reach Rome. In 1505 a royal courier on an urgent mission made the journey from Blois to Hennebont in southwestern Brittany, stopping to deliver a message in Nantes, in two and a half days. Along the way he requisitioned twenty horses for which he paid an average of fifteen *sous*, and he paid four *sous*, nine *deniers* in tolls.[53]

The difficulty of communication meant that the spread of the king's French from the north was a slow process. In the provinces of the west and south, the ordinary peasant probably knew only a few words of the king's French, which replaced the local dialect of the ordinary people of Bordeaux only by 1500.[54] Breton was an entirely different language, being Celtic, not Latin, and its clear distinction from French surely was a major factor in Breton autonomy. Since Latin was still used in the law courts, there was no strong incentive for the speakers of Breton and the dialects of the Midi to learn French. In 1498 most people in the realm regarded themselves as residents of their towns or cities first, then of their provinces. The idea of being a *bon françois*, which is found a century later, would have been highly unusual then.[55] The king was a far-off figure whom most never saw, who demanded taxes, and whose justice was fitfully applied. At mid-reign Louis XII may well have been the best loved king in French history, but whether his popularity translated into making the monarchy more visible or more powerful in the distant corners of the realm is impossible to assess.

6

Matters Matrimonial

There was little that was unusual or innovative about Louis XII's coronation and Parisian entry, but what was highly peculiar was the absence of a queen at his side during these festivals. Becoming king had not changed his attitude toward Jeanne of France. If anything he felt all the more strongly his lack of a son. The greater the inheritance, the greater the need for an heir! While it will never be known whether Jeanne actually could have had children (she seems to have been sure she could), Louis's revulsion at the sight of her made it impossible. When she heard that he had become king, she sent him letters of congratulations, but he apparently ignored them. His refusal to invite her to the coronation not only was an obvious demonstration that he did not regard her as his wife, it was also an insult to a daughter of a king.

That Louis would seek an annulment was a foregone conclusion the moment he became king, for there was a great deal more at stake than even the question of the royal heir. Anne, Charles's widow, had reverted to her status as duchess of an autonomous Brittany. Her marriage contract with Charles had specified that should he die before her, the duchy would regain its status prior to their marriage. However, it also included a clause requiring her to marry the successor to the throne should Charles die without a son. Three days after she became a widow, Anne reestablished the Breton chancellery and appointed the prince of Orange to govern for her until she returned to the duchy.[1]

Louis and Anne knew each other very well, regardless of whether he had been in love with her since his first sight of her in 1485. Although they had been estranged for a time after her son's death, their relationship warmed up again when they cooperated in opposing Charles's plans for renewed war in Italy. Anne had been strongly opposed to the Italian expedition from the first; when Charles had written to her in 1495 for more troops, she replied that she would send him widows instead.[2] She was now twenty-two years old. She was regarded as pretty with her small, neat features, although she walked with a limp because one leg was shorter than the other. It was a minor flaw in an era when much of the population had obvious physical defects. She was described as being knowledgeable in government and culture, generous with her money, and very strong willed. Clearly, she was capable of child bearing, which was more important than her appearance and virtues, but her greatest asset was the fact that she controlled the fate of Brittany.

Anne had grieved deeply for Charles. For two days she neither ate nor slept but wept incessantly. She refused to wear the white dress of a newly widowed queen without a child (from which came the term "*la reine blanche*") for forty days until it could be determined whether she was pregnant. Instead, she wore black as a measure of her grief. The same afternoon that Louis arrived at Amboise after Charles's death, he went to Anne's side to offer condolences: "The good Prince comforted her the best he could."[3] Formally there could be no contacts between them, but Anne wrote Louis a brief letter on a scrap of paper thanking him for his condolences and signed it "She who is and always will be your good sister, cousin and ally." But when the subject of remarriage was raised, Anne objected that Charles had been married twice (first to Margaret of Austria) and God had punished him by denying him an heir. When the period of mourning had passed, she busied herself reestablishing the autonomous ducal government in Brittany and began to mint coins with her arms.[4]

In regard to Jeanne, Louis could not bring himself to confront her directly. According to La Trémoille's biographer, Louis, soon after his coronation, sent the great captain to ask her to agree to an annulment.[5] La Trémoille was surely chosen for the delicate task because, as Louis XI's devoted servant, he would lessen the insult to her father. There is no indication of where he met her, but it probably was at Tours, where she had remained since her brother's death. His words to her could hardly have been more gracious:

> Madame, the king strongly recommends himself to you and has told me to tell you that there is no woman he loves more than you for the graces and virtues that shine in you. It is deeply displeasing to him that you cannot have issue, for he would like to end his days in so saintly company as yours. But you know that the royal blood of France is beginning to be diminished and your late brother Charles has died without children. If the same happens to the present king, the kingdom will change dynasties and could fall into foreign hands. For that reason he has been counseled to take another spouse if you will give your consent. By right there has been no true marriage between you two, because he did not give his con-

sent but it was done by force and the fear that monseigneur your late
father in his wrath aroused in his person. Nonetheless he has so much
love for you that he would prefer to die without issue than displease you.

Jeanne's reply to so courteous but difficult a request was equally courteous but firm: "Had I thought that there was no real marriage between the
king and me, I would beg him to leave me to live in perpetual chastity
because that is what I desire the most . . . to live spiritually with the
Eternal King and be His spouse."

When La Trémoille reported Jeanne's words to Louis, he gave a great
sigh and said:

> I am in great pain over this affair. . . . I know the goodness, sweetness and
> benevolence of this woman, her royal blood, her incomparable virtues and
> her righteousness but on the other side I know she cannot have issue and
> by default the kingdom of France will fall into ruin. Although I have not
> had a true marriage with her nor have had marital relations, nonetheless
> because for a long time she has been regarded as my spouse and my mis-
> fortunes have been sweetened by her, it vexes me to leave her.

For these reasons, the story goes, the king deferred for a time seeking an
annulment, but pressed by the princes of France, he decided to seek a
judgment on whether it was a true marriage.

What is one to make of all this? The account was written several
decades later, so we need not accept it as verbatim. Historians have taken
Jeanne's statement as accurately revealing her motivation, and her life
after the annulment bears out such a view. She was also determined to
prevent any insult to the memory of her father. While granting them as
powerful reasons for her decision, one has to wonder if Jeanne also hoped
that should Louis fail to gain an annulment, his powerful need for a son
would force him to treat her as a real wife.

If the statement that Louis put off seeking an annulment for a time is true,
it was a very short time, hardly more than a month. What persuaded him to
go forward was certainly not pressure from the princes, but Anne of
Brittany's sudden decision to marry him within a year should he gain his
freedom. Negotiations between them, with Georges d'Amboise and La
Trémoille as the intermediaries, began in late July. On August 18 Anne
signed a promise of marriage, and the next day Louis pledged to evacuate his
troops from the five Breton strongholds the French held in a year's time if
the marriage did not take place. However, the king sent secret messages to
his captains in the strongholds to hold them at all costs until further notice.[6]

Anne's change of heart probably depended on evidence that the papacy would look favorably on Louis's request for an annulment. Immediately after his accession, Louis had sent a friendly message to Alexander VI announcing his succession. In early June the pope dispatched a high-ranking envoy to France to congratulate the new king. The envoy was instructed to extract from Louis a promise to lead a crusade against the Turks, a pro-forma request made of every new Catholic king, and a pledge not to seize Milan. There was no specific mention of Louis's marriage.[7]

Encouraged by the pope's profession of friendship and Anne's change of heart, Louis sent a request to Rome that his marriage to Jeanne be dissolved on the grounds of nonconsummation. On July 29 Alexander agreed to appoint a commission to examine the case. At the same time, he forwarded a suggestion that Louis might find it fitting to be generous to his son Cesare Borgia. Alexander openly acknowledged his three children from his younger days, and with the assassination in 1497 of one son, his ambitions for his family had settled on Cesare, who had been made a cardinal at age seventeen but was still in minor orders. In June 1498 the pope released his son from the clerical state on the grounds that he had coerced his son into the Church in the first place. Cesare was now free to marry and create a Borgia dynasty. Alexander wanted him to marry a daughter of King Federigo of Naples, but both father and daughter flatly refused. The pope looked to Louis for help in forcing their consent, and he also sought French properties and pensions for Cesare in order to establish him as one of the great men of Christendom.[8]

In late July 1498 a Portuguese diplomat, Fernando d'Almeida, the bishop of Ceuta in North Africa, arrived in France to negotiate with Louis. The king agreed to promote Cesare's marriage to the Neapolitan princess and give him the counties of Valence and Die in Dauphiné near Avignon. The Valentinois would be raised to a duchy, and Louis granted several additional sources of income so that Cesare would receive 20,000 l a year. Cesare would also receive command of a company of 100 lances and the rule of Asti after the French won Milan. When Alexander approved of the terms, Louis sent six galleys to Italy to escort Cesare to France.[9]

While it was not stated in the agreement, the pope agreed to form a tribunal to hear Louis's request for an annulment. He named to it the bishop of Ceuta and the bishop of Albi, Louis d'Amboise.[10] The bishop of Albi was the brother of Louis's closest confidant (Georges cosigned the royal order establishing the commission) and an active member of the government. Since he had been a key adviser to Louis XI and had officiated at the marriage of Charles VIII and Anne of Brittany, he was not necessarily prejudiced against Jeanne, being her friend as well as Louis XII's. In 1488 Jeanne had written a letter to him that indicated a close relationship between the two.[11]

On August 10 the papal tribunal acknowledged receiving its commission and called on Jeanne to prepare her defense. Louis named four canon lawyers, led by Antoine de L'Estang of the prominent Norman family, to represent him, and ordered three canon lawyers from Tours to serve as her counsels. His lawyers laid out the grounds for granting an annulment: consanguinity in the fourth degree between Louis and Jeanne; the spiritual consanguinity between them since Louis XI had been Louis's godfather, which was in canon law as powerful an impediment to marriage as were blood ties; the coercion used by Jeanne's father; and nonconsummation. Prior to his succession, Louis's treasurer had compiled a dossier of materials for the case were it ever heard.[12] The two judges quickly accepted as valid the papal dispensation of 1476 for the first two points, thereby removing them as grounds for dissolving the marriage.

In order to avoid raising the difficult issue of whether the marriage had been consummated, the royal lawyers concentrated on the question of coercion.[13] They presented a list of twenty-nine witnesses who could testify to the threats Louis XI had made to force the duke of Orléans into the marriage. However, Jeanne's counsels raised the point in canon law that "cohabitation purges coercion."[14] As it became clear that Jeanne, contrary to Louis's hopes, was not going to accept passively the dissolution of her marriage, and that the judges were taking "cohabitation purges coercion" seriously, the pope involved himself by appointing a third judge, the bishop of LeMans, Philippe of Luxembourg. He was an old friend of the king and was regarded as less likely than Louis d'Amboise to be impartial.[15] Whether Alexander VI had an inkling of the difficulties in Louis's case is not clear, but it is possible that a fast courier could have gotten word of the problems in the hearing to Rome by August 31, the date of Luxembourg's appointment, if the pope had acted immediately upon receiving it. The justification for adding a third judge was that the bishop of Ceuta was needed elsewhere, although he served to the end.

Luxembourg had not yet received his commission and the notice of his appointment as a cardinal when Jeanne of France addressed the tribunal at Tours. She admitted her ignorance of law and expressed her great displeasure at what she was being forced to do. She added that she hoped the judges would not be offended if she did not address herself simply to their questions but expounded on them, and she asked that her statement be added to the record of the procedure.[16] She stated that she did not believe her marriage had been coerced and said that while she knew she was not as attractive as other women, she believed she was capable of having children. The royal counsel asked if she would submit to a physical examination by wise and prudent women, but she flatly refused by right of her royal blood.

After a week's recess, the tribunal reassembled at Amboise with the cardinal of Luxembourg present and Jean de Vasse of Bourges now serving as Jeanne's new chief counsel. Her previous one had resigned, citing his fear of the king, which prevented him from properly representing his client. De Vasse appears to have done an excellent job. There followed the testimony—oral or written—of the twenty-nine witnesses who knew something either of the circumstances of the marriage or of Jeanne and Louis's life together. They were mostly members of their household, friends, and advisers, and included the old bishop of Orléans, who had performed the marriage ceremony but was too feeble to testify in person. Only three witnesses were presented for Jeanne, and they did little to strengthen her case. In his rebuttal, de Vasse made a powerful argument on the point of "cohabitation purges coercion." He argued that Louis had had several good opportunities to denounce his marriage earlier: when he appeared before the Estates-general in 1485, for example, or when he was in Brittany in 1488 and had denied seeking Anne's hand because he was already married, but especially when he was in Asti in 1494, where he was sovereign lord. Not only had he not denounced his marriage there, he also addressed letters from Asti to Jeanne in terms of marital intimacy. Louis's lawyers replied that he had been forced to pretend that Jeanne was his wife in fear of her father and brother, his predecessors. The king made the same case when he allowed himself to be interrogated by a representative of the tribunal at Mantes on October 29.[17]

With the king's position in some trouble, his counsels played their trump card—the letter of Louis XI to Antoine de Chabannes. The letter has been quoted earlier, but it is worthwhile to cite the key sentence again: "I warn you that I hope to make this marriage and those who oppose it will not be sure of their lives in my realm." In 1488, when Louis was in Brittany and was thought to be preparing a case for an annulment, Charles VIII had ordered Chabannes to hand over the letter, but he had failed to deliver it. After Chabannes died, the letter passed to his son Jean, the son-in-law of an illegitimate daughter of Louis XI's. This half sister of Jeanne's was fond of her; and when at the beginning of the proceedings, Louis asked Jean de Chabannes to give up the letter, she strongly objected. It was only three months later that royal pressure convinced Chabannes to turn it over.[18] The royal lawyers had several prominent members of Louis XI's court attest to the authenticity of the signatures of Louis XI and his secretary. Jeanne's counsel also examined it and could not impeach it.

As powerful a piece of evidence for coercion as the letter was, it still did not refute Jeanne's argument that "cohabitation purges coercion." If she could convince the judges that the marriage had been consummated, they might yet be persuaded to deny the annulment. Louis had denied ever having marital relations with her and produced several witnesses, including Gié, who said that Louis had told them he had not consummated the marriage because of the physical defects of his wife. With Jeanne refusing by privilege of her royal blood to submit to a physical examination, the case came down to the solemn word of the two principals. On December 4 Louis faced the tribunal in a church at Legeuil on the road between Tours and Paris and swore on the Gospels that the marriage had not been consummated. It was tradition that the word of a consecrated king was the strongest possible evidence; with Louis's oath, the tribunal had no real choice but to decide in his favor. On December 17 the tribunal sitting at Amboise returned its verdict in favor of an annulment.[19]

Louis immediately granted Jeanne the title of duchess of Berry and a pension of 30,000 *l* a year.[20] He returned her dowry of 100,000 *écus* to her, which he had never touched. She withdrew to a château near Bourges, the capital of the duchy of Berry, and took an active role in its government. There, "having been made a virgin again by the oath of my husband,"[21] she turned to religion and began to organize a religious order of women called the Order of the Annonciade in honor of the Virgin Mary. She succeeded in gaining papal approval for the rule of her order in 1501, but regarding herself as still a married woman, she did not take her vows until 1504. She was reported as saying several times after 1498 that the annulment freed her of "a heavy burden."[22]

Jeanne had no known contact with Louis after the decision against her, but he was said to have observed her at prayer from behind a pillar in the chapel of her convent and remarked that she was a saint. When she died in 1505, he ordered that she be buried "with every possible honor." Later he went to Bourges to pray at her tomb. Her reputation for saintliness, based in large part on the dignified humility in which she accepted the verdict on her marriage, was widespread by the time of her death. Soon numerous miracles were attributed to her. In 1742 the church beatified her and in 1950, canonized her a saint.[23]

Jeanne has had vast sympathy over the centuries, not least of all from the church itself, and numerous authors have concluded the annulment was unjustified.[24] In the lifetime of Louis XII, the noted theologians

Olivier Maillard and Jean Standonck always insisted that Jeanne was the true queen. There was a great outpouring of popular support for Jeanne in late 1498. The word that the king wanted to divorce his wife had spread like wildfire across the realm. It was a time when very few marriages were broken for any reason, and the common people had little understanding of the legal grounds for the king's case. It was assumed that Jeanne's infertility was the only issue, and it was felt that Louis ought to have accepted God's will in the matter. The papal tribunal was denounced as a sham, and when its verdict was announced at Amboise, a large crowd denounced its three members as Herod, Ciaphas, and Pilate, who had also condemned an innocent person. The analogy gained credibility when a violent storm struck Amboise at the moment the judges announced their decision.

At Paris the reaction was much the same. Standonck, the rector of the Collège de Montaigu, proclaimed that a wife could not be put aside except for adultery; Maillard, a fellow member of the faculty of theology, greatly angered Louis's confidants by his intemperate language on the subject; and Thomas Warnet, a master of the Collège de Montaigu, preached against the annulment. When Maillard was threatened with being tied in a sack and thrown into the Seine, he replied it made no difference to him whether he went to heaven by land or water.[25] The popular satirists of the time, the Basoche, lampooned the king in their verses.

The popular reaction was made stronger by the long-expected arrival of Cesare Borgia at the court on December 18, 1498. He carried with him a papal dispensation for the impediment of consanguinity between Louis and Anne, necessary because Anne's grandmother was Louis's aunt. Alexander had issued it in anticipation of a verdict annulling the marriage.[26] Cesare had left Rome in early October with 200,000 ducats and a cardinal's red hat for Georges d'Amboise. The pope had spared no expense in making his son's appearance and entourage as brilliant as possible. His horses, for example, came from the famous stables at Mantua, and their bits and stirrups, reportedly even their shoes, were made of silver.

The Borgia entourage crossed the Mediterranean in French galleys and disembarked at Marseille, where by royal order 400 horsemen and the archbishop of Aix escorted Cesare to Avignon.[27] There Cardinal della Rovere, the governor of the papal enclave, entertained him. This enemy of the Borgias was full of praise for Cesare in his report to the pope and noted how high in the king's favor he stood. Borgia was slow to reach the royal court, either because he had been told not to appear with the bull of dispensation for consanguinity before the annulment was a fact or, as Louis put it, "he was in a land of beautiful women and good wine." Cesare arrived at the Château of Chinon, where Louis was on the day after the verdict was announced. For those who were angry with Louis for putting aside his saintly wife, Cesare's arrival was an event as unwelcome as the thunderstorm of the previous day that had blasted Amboise. His presence seemed to be proof of an unholy alliance between king and pope.[28]

Cesare's arrival created a delicate problem of etiquette: How did the king greet an illegitimate son of a pope? An amusing solution was found. Cesare stopped just short of the château, and Louis, supposedly out hunting, happened to meet him by accident. By granting him his fiefs there, the king could host him as a great nobleman without further worry about protocol. Cesare handed over the bull of dispensation and d'Amboise's red hat. Louis was then obliged to find a wife of proper rank for him. Princess Carlotta of Naples, who had been born in France, was in residence at the court as a maid-of-honor for Anne of Brittany, but she made it very clear that she would not marry Cesare. Louis could not force her because it would have created an uproar among the French people and, given his own experience, been very hypocritical. He offered his niece, the daughter of Mary of Orléans and Jean de Foix, but she also refused. Finally Alain d'Albret put forward his daughter Charlotte, a young woman said to be of great beauty and intelligence. Albret had high rank, since his eldest son was king of Navarre, and the wealth to offer a dowry of 30,000 *l.*[29]

After lengthy negotiations the two parties signed a marriage contract on May 19, 1499, which contained clauses obliging Alexander to aid Louis in occupying Milan and Naples and giving a red hat to Charlotte's brother.[30] The wedding took place immediately, and the morning after, Cesare boasted of his prowess as a husband, which Louis repeated in a letter in his own hand to Alexander. Cesare was said to have bragged that he made "eight trips" on his wedding night. Court gossip said he actually made eight trips to the privy, because an apothecary hired to concoct him an aphrodisiac gave him a laxative instead. Shortly after the wedding Charlotte became pregnant, but Cesare never saw the child, a daughter named Louise, because he left France before her birth, never to return. His abandoned bride made her way to Bourges where she joined Jeanne of France in a life of religious devotion.[31]

By the time of Cesare's wedding, Louis had celebrated his marriage to Anne of Brittany. On January 7, in the castle of Nantes, Louis and Anne signed their marriage contract in front of forty witnesses, mostly the great nobles and prelates of Brittany and France.[32] It dictated that the duchy, which would keep a separate government, would pass to the second son should the marriage produce more than one, or to the second daughter in default of any sons.

If there were no children at all, Brittany would go to Anne's closest relative. Should Anne die before Louis, he would have the usufruct of the duchy until his death. Clearly she intended to maintain the autonomy of her homeland and prevent its absorption into the kingdom of France.

The next day the wedding was celebrated in the cathedral of Nantes, but no contemporary account is extant. However, the Venetian ambassador did report that Louis had bragged on the morrow of his wedding night about how virile he had been with his bride. His ardor "was in no way displeasing to the Queen."[33] Throughout their fifteen years of marriage, there was not the slightest hint of scandal involving their relationship. Louis's dissolute lifestyle of prior years was completely changed. He quickly proved wrong the papal nuncio's remark of November 1498 that he "devotes himself entirely to lascivious pleasures to the utmost."[34] Their public life at court also was highly regular. Their evening meal was taken quite early, and after a short, subdued entertainment of music, poetry, or perhaps a brief play, they retired. When they were apart, a Florentine ambassador reported, Louis wrote to her in his own hand every day.[35]

Clearly the royal couple were happy together, even if they had their disappointments, especially over their lack of a son, and spats, largely over Anne's undying devotion to her duchy, although she could not speak Breton.[36] As duchess, she was fully committed to maintaining Brittany's autonomy, and she used her influence over Louis to that purpose. She insisted on having her own bodyguard of 100 Bretons, who accompanied her everywhere in public. Since they frequently could be seen waiting for her on a small terrace at Blois, where the court usually was in residence, it became known as the "Porch of the Bretons." Anne ran the Breton government without interference from Louis; she even received and sent ambassadors and submitted nominations for Breton sees and abbacies to Rome.[37] Although Louis's authority in Brittany was no greater than that of his predecessors, his marriage with Anne assured that the duchy, so often a source of major problems for the French monarch, would be quiescent during his reign.

Bretons and French alike generally had affection for Queen Anne. She was far more generous with her extensive wealth than was Louis, who from the beginning of his reign hoarded his money for his campaigns in Italy. In 1508, for example, she gave 10,000 *l* to Jacqueline d'Astarac, Commynes's niece, for her marriage to a member of the prominent Mailly family of Picardy.[38] In contrast, the courtiers and hangers-on at the court thought Louis miserly. The common people were less inclined to think so, since he granted a 10 percent reduction in the *taille* as a wedding gift to his realm.

The king clearly felt a need to justify himself to his people for his remarriage, as two days afterward he sent a letter to the Chambre des comptes explaining and defending his actions. Because it was hardly probable that the *"gens de mes comptes"* were the only ones to receive it, it is likely that he intended it as a public statement at least to the higher levels of French society. He declared that he had gained the throne by "true succession" and briefly described the acts by which the marriage to Jeanne had been forced on him. Upon his succession, he had asked the pope to appoint a tribunal of great prelates to judge the truth of the case, aided by a vast number of those knowledgeable in church and civil law. Louis asserted that Dame Jeanne had a full and fair hearing, as had he. For every good reason, the judges decided in his favor and freed him to marry the duchess of Brittany. The marriage, Louis declared, was fully sanctioned by the church, and the reason for it was to provide an heir for the peaceful succession to the throne, which would assure the peace and repose of the realm and his subjects.[39] The letter reveals that Louis had a concern for public opinion that was largely absent in the kings of the next centuries.

The annulment and remarriage had eroded much of the popularity and goodwill always given to a new king, which Louis had fostered by his first acts of government. Before he could hope to lead an expedition to Milan or Naples, he had to rebuild popular support. On the positive side, however, he was now free of the immense psychological burden of the marriage to Jeanne of France. He could marry a spouse with whom he could have children and lead a normal life in so far as it was possible for a king. The annulment also seems to have allowed him to become more caring, as he revealed in a program of concern for the welfare of his people. It enabled him to regain his popularity and raise it well above that of any other king of the era.

7

Monarchy, Ministers, and Money

L ouis XII's great popularity, rebuilt within a year of his annulment, may have enhanced his ability to rule France and surely helped him through the difficult last years of his reign, but it was hardly a necessary attribute of effective kingship, as Louis XI amply demonstrated. Kingship in Louis's era drew from three different sources—Christianity, Roman law, and feudalism—for its theoretical underpinnings and practice. This resulted in considerable confusion and contradiction in the concept of kingship as expressed by writers of the period and, it might be argued, in its practice as well.

No French author from that era could ignore the strong religious overtones of contemporary kingship. It came from God, to whom alone the king was responsible. On Judgment Day a king would account not only for his own sins but also for his stewardship of the realm and its people. The French king, chosen to rule by the Eternal Lawgiver, had the law of the realm "in his breast." Advocates of true royal absolutism or, as those of the era would have said, royal despotism, who drew heavily on Roman law, were rare in the late fifteenth century; but even those who were not absolutists in that sense approved of the maxim: "What pleases the king has the force of law!" They did not interpret it as creating a foundation for despotism. The king indeed had the power to make law, but that law had to be for the good of the realm to be legitimate. It could not please the king to ordain bad law. According to Claude de Seyssel, who was the major French political writer before Jean Bodin and a member of Louis's government, a good king allowed himself to be bridled by religion, justice, and polity. By the last term Seyssel meant the laws and edicts that past kings had mandated for the good governance of the realm and the maintenance of royal authority. A king who allowed himself to be subject to law and tradition was far more praiseworthy than one who tried to rule arbitrarily.[1]

It may well be that Seyssel thought so highly of Louis XII, clearly his ideal king, because Louis rarely used the phrase "For such is Our pleasure!" by which kings usually signaled that they were making a decision that was unpopular or arbitrary.[2] Seyssel also commented that the French monarchy "has some of the traits of aristocracy." That term implied the need to consult "the better and saner part" of the people, and although Louis only once convoked a meeting that may have warranted the title Estates-general, he held many meetings of provincial and local assemblies. The consultative aspect of the French monarchy reached its peak in the Renaissance era under Louis.

Aristocracy also connotes the presence in the state of a group of elites with special privileges and influence. Seyssel fully acknowledged there was such a group in France with a broad range of advantages and powers. Those privileges originally arose from the fact that the nobles' ancestors had put life and limb at risk defending king and realm, as would the present generation when the king called on them, or so the theory went. As the lord of a hierarchy of feudal vassals, the monarch was the "first aristocrat." In 1468 the number of men who were expected to answer a royal summons to service as cavalrymen, the essence of noble status in the feudal system, was estimated at about 20,000.[3] Using the most common multiplier in demography of three other family members for every warrior, the total of 80,000 noble persons, plus several thousand nobles in religious life, seems plausible.

The close identification between noble status and access to land remained largely intact in Louis's era, although the monarchy recognized the possibility of a nonnoble acquiring a *seigneurie,* land that a nobleman properly held, by requiring the payment of a fee called the *franc-fief.* The fee acknowledged that the king needed compensation for the loss of military service for a fief now in the hands of one who could not provide it, although many of the sons of these *anoblis,* new nobles, would appear in the military. In the late fifteenth century, what had been a quiet practice of providing limited social mobility for wealthy commoners largely for the purpose of replenishing the nobility, which constantly saw its families die out, was supplemented by royal revenue devices providing noble status for payments to the monarchy. One such device was the *lettre d'anoblissement,* the patent of nobility. It was usually granted for a hefty sum, although occasionally the king gave one for great service in war. There is no doubt that the old nobility, the *noblesse de race,* also called the nobles of the sword, resented those new nobles. However, the sword nobles, reluctant as they were to acknowledge the newcomers as noble, were willing to admit that the king had the power to ennoble men who had the right credentials, in particular great wealth, through the *franc-fief* and patents of nobility. They were far more resentful of a new practice now beginning to appear: the ennobling of royal officeholders in the judicial and the fiscal systems. Most officeholders had come from the nobility until the late fifteenth century, so the concept that serving the king as an officer conferred noble status had not been very controversial until then. With the dramatic change in the social origins of the officers and the surge after 1500 in venality, the practice of selling royal offices, the old nobility saw its interests under attack. What in the past had been an eventual full acceptance of the *anoblis* took much longer in respect to these nobles of the long robe, the *noblesse de robe*. Their claims to noble status became a focus of complaint from the nobles of the sword. The practice of law was not regarded as a noble enterprise, and perhaps it was the entrance of bourgeois lawyers and their sons into the nobility through officeholding that so raised the ire of the nobility of the sword toward the nobles of the robe during the sixteenth century.

In Louis's reign a number of wealthy haute-bourgeoisie entered the nobility, buying up offices and seigneuries, but they were hard-pressed to match the income of the wealthiest of the old nobility. The duke of La Trémoille, whose numerous estates were concentrated in west-central France, received an average annual income of 27,600 *l* from them between 1486 and 1509.[4] The expenses of nobles were every bit as high as their incomes, if not higher. Every noble who could afford it had a retinue of lesser nobles, a court, and a bureaucracy of officers to collect their revenues from their estates. A man was not a *gentilhomme* unless he hunted and fought; hunting dogs and hawks, horses, groomsmen, arms, and armor were costly needs. Louis XII was quoted as saying that most of the nobles of his realm were bankrupted by their dogs and horses.[5] Luxuries, dowries for their daughters, and funerals appropriately expensive for the family's rank strained noble resources. The wills of nobles contained large sums for Masses for their souls and alms for the poor as a way of atoning for a sinful life and often pushed many families into debt. Key to the concept of nobility, however, was a public display of largesse: to the poor certainly but not in large amounts, to the church, to relatives, but especially to the nobles of one's retinue. Miserliness was the characteristic of a commoner, which was the meaning of the great insult thrown at Louis XII when the nobles called him *roi roturier* for what they regarded as his lack of generosity toward them. Not only the king, who obviously was the richest source of gifts and pensions, but every wealthy nobleman was expected to provide largesse to those lower in the feudal hierarchy. The king and greater nobles also had offices that provided the lesser nobles a salary and the opportunity for graft, although the number of bourgeoisie in such offices was far higher in 1500 than a century earlier.

The most prized form of largesse was the royal pension, which often was very substantial. For example, Louis XII provided a pension of 10,000 *l* to Louis de La Trémoille, and the princes of blood and members of the royal family drew more than that from the royal fisc. The pension rolls also included nobles who received as little as 100 *l.* The annual total of royal pensions reached 500,000 *l* and more, except for several years under Louis, when it dropped to below half of that. A large pension almost always went with high office in the royal administration and a hefty salary. For example, La Trémoille received 4,000 *l* as governor of Burgundy, while the governor of Languedoc received 12,000 *l.* The king also frequently dispensed gifts in gold or in the form of the revenues from a specific toll or tax. In 1501, for example, Louis granted the annual income from a confiscated estate to Ferry de Mailly, a prominent Picard nobleman.[6] In general, Louis was less generous than most other kings of the era.

The nobles who received such sums from the king would in turn distribute much of the money to their retainers. For this system of patronage, which historians of England often call "bastard feudalism," historians of France prefer the term "clientage." As of 1498, traditional feudalism, with its lord-vassal relationship, largely remained in place in France, even if the bonds of feudalism were weaker than in the past, while clientage, by no means new to the realm, was rapidly becoming more widespread. A modern historian, J. Russell Major, has argued that as the bonds created by fealty weakened, no longer binding lord and vassal together, clientage emerged as a means of reestablishing the ties between the greater and lesser nobles.[7] Nor had family ties and kinship disappeared as a means of bonding nobles together with common goals and interests. The result was a confusing network of relationships among the nobles, most difficult to untangle, in which a nobleman might have been serving as the vassal of one aristocrat, acting as the client of another, and having family ties to a third.

A patron-client relationship was created when someone lower in the aristocratic hierarchy agreed, often by an oath, to serve someone higher placed. The client could expect both military and legal protection, even against the royal courts if the patron was well enough placed. The client gained from his patron gifts, pensions, and frequently offices, which may have come either from the patron's own resources or the king's. Access to royal largesse for the benefit of clients was a key measure of influence for the great nobles. A very clear example of this practice comes from Charles VIII's reign. In 1484 the king gave the captaincy of the Château of Chinon to Pierre de Beaujeu, who in turn gave it to his chamberlain with all the rights, privileges, revenues, and wages that pertained to the office.[8] In return for such favors, he expected the latter's loyalty and service. The client whom a patron placed in a royal office was expected to look after the patron's interests in the discharge of that office. For most clients the principal form of service was military. Every prominent nobleman had his retinue, dressed in his colors, which accompanied him wherever he went. When the patron went to war in royal service, he brought his clients as well as his vassals with him. A large portion of the *gens d'armes* in the royal service were first of all clients of the great aristocrats. When one of the grand nobles revolted, as Louis himself had done, his clients and vassals were expected to go with him into rebellion, denying the king the use of that manpower.

Frequently, the rebellious grandees were royal governors of major provinces. With very few exceptions, Louis's governors were from the princes of blood and the highest levels of the nobility; he was fortunate that none made any attempt at rebellion. Since the governorships for the most part were created originally for the command of frontier forces, in 1498 they were in place in nine frontier provinces and the Ile-de-France, the only interior province with a governor, perhaps because of the importance of Paris. The interior provinces had been mostly appanages of the princes of blood when the governorships had appeared and had not been assigned governors. After the duchy of Orléans had reverted to the crown upon Louis's succession, only the Bourbonnais remained in appanage. Upon their reversion, the monarchy made no move to place governors in those provinces. Prior to Louis's reign, governorships often had remained vacant for long periods of time. Starting in 1504, they were filled almost continuously until 1789.[9] The governors received salaries as high as 12,000 *l* a year in addition to a royal pension. They frequently collected additional salaries for their major responsibilities at court or, more likely, with the army. Typically the governors were captains of companies of *gens d'armes*. As such, rarely were they in their provinces. Their lieutenants, also appointed by the king, generally made the routine decisions of the provincial *gouvernements* in place of the governors. Those decisions largely involved recruiting for the army, maintaining fortifications, and responding quickly to any invasion. In the Midi in particular, the governors had broad powers of patronage over the royal offices of their provinces except for the Parlements.

Administration of royal justice in the provinces was in the hands of officers called *baillis* in the north and *sénéschaux* in the south. These offices had been created when feudalism was in full sway to provide something of a royal presence among the local fiefholders. They were filled by the local nobles, who often served as military captains as well. In the past their responsibilities had been very broad, involving virtually every aspect of government from tax collection to justice. There were some 100 *bailliages* and *sénéchaussées* in the realm as of 1515; the number continued to increase thereafter. They in turn were subdivided into smaller units, whose officers were responsible for government at the local level, especially justice. In Louis's time there may have been as many as 1,455 such royal officers, not counting their subalterns. However, control of the fiscal system had slipped away from them and their superiors, and a parallel financial structure had been created, which will be discussed later. In an ordinance of 1499 Louis addressed himself to the problem of absenteeism among the royal officials in the provinces, but the increasing number of other offices they held made it inevitable.[10]

Governors were ex officio members of the royal council, but since few attended on a regular basis, they usually had little influence on royal decisions, unless they were active in the council for reasons other than their governorships. The council's presiding officer when the king was absent was the chancellor, the chief officer for justice and administration in the realm. He had custody of the three royal seals, including the Great Seal, which was used to seal all royal decrees giving them legal authority. The seals did not change from reign to reign except for the name of the king. During the major royal processions, the chancellor walked or rode immediately before the king while the Great Seal was carried in a special casket in front of him. As the chief of justice he had the right to wear the robes of the presidents of the Parlement, over which he presided when he attended it. He had the power to condemn and pardon without consulting the king except in cases involving treason and the king's person. He had the right to refuse to seal a decree that he felt was inappropriate, but the king, having heard his objections, could order him to seal it. As head of the royal chancellery, the chancellor had a hand, often the main one, in drawing up every royal decree and edict. His influence was paramount in the appointment of numerous royal officials. He officially spoke for the king before the Estates-general, in the Parlement, and at church synods. The chancellor often received the homage of the great vassals of the king in his place.

The chancellor almost always came from among the presidents of Parlement because of his role as chief of justice. His appointment was for life, although Louis's acceptance of Charles VIII's chancellor seems to have been the final step in establishing that principle. He received 10,000 *l* a year with 2,000 *l* more for entertaining.[11] His life tenure gave him a great deal of independence from the monarch and allowed him to object to royal decrees. Should his criticism offend the king too much or should he become incapacitated, the king could pass most of his duties to the *garde des sceaux*. It appears that Louis XII largely created that office, when the chancellor of the middle years of his reign, Jean Ganay, became too ill to carry out his duties. Louis named Etienne de Poncher *garde des sceaux*, and that ambitious and capable man essentially defined the office for the future, establishing its tasks, besides having physical custody of the royal seals, as overseeing the royal chancellery and appointing its personnel.[12]

Louis XII inherited Chancellor Guy de Rochefort from Charles VIII, succeeding his brother Guillaume who had died in 1497. The brothers had been part of the large pool of bureaucratic talent at the Burgundian court and rose rapidly in the French government after joining it in 1477. Louis reconfirmed Guy in office in June 1498.[13] While he possessed broad authority as chancellor, Guy de Rochefort apparently did not carry much personal influence with Louis. Two men who did influence the king were the royal secretaries, Florimond Robertet and Etienne de Poncher. Robertet's knowledge of Italian, German, Spanish, and perhaps English allowed him to rise in the service of Pierre de Bourbon. He served as a secretary to Charles VIII, and, when Louis became king, he became his personal secretary, countersigning most of the letters and decrees signed by the king. In 1501 he became treasurer of Normandy, a position high in the fiscal system of the government that did not require him to be absent from the court. He spent more time with the king than perhaps any other officer, but it is difficult to point to any specific examples of his influence until after Georges d'Amboise's death in 1510. Poncher was the one relative newcomer to power during the first years of Louis's reign. Born at Tours, he studied law and received a seat in the Parlement of Paris in 1484 through Louis's influence. In 1498 he became a royal secretary and, in 1503, bishop of Paris, an office that did not keep him away from the court.

By far the dominant member of Louis's court was Cardinal Georges d'Amboise, although he held no formal office. At the end of August 1498, a Milanese spy reported that he "ruled supreme," and in 1502 the Venetian ambassador reported that he did all the business for the king. Five years later a report from papal nuncio in France stated flatly about d'Amboise: "He is the true king of the French."[14] Born in 1460 to a midlevel Norman noble family, he was two years older than Louis. They had known each other from their early years, and Georges entered Orléanist service at the very beginning of his public career. He won Louis's enduring confidence and affection. The credit his father had with Louis XI gained Georges the bishopric of Montauban at age nineteen, having already been an abbot for four years. He became archbishop of Narbonne in 1482. Louis's influence as governor of Normandy was an important factor in d'Amboise's becoming archbishop of

Rouen in 1493. Rouen was probably the most prestigious and wealthiest diocese in France, providing its bishop with some 17,000 *l* in income. In 1503 he gave 20,000 *l* to Louis for the Italian war.[15] His elevation to cardinal was one of the favors Alexander VI gave Louis shortly after his succession.

Although d'Amboise profited from the common practice of that era of combining a major church office with vast political influence, he set a good example, not much imitated, of refusing to be a pluralist. His use of the revenues of the see of Rouen was also exemplary, but a Venetian ambassador surely exaggerated when he wrote that the cardinal gave all of his episcopal income to the poor.[16] He did contribute heavily to the reconstruction of the cathedral of Rouen, but much of the vast wealth he accumulated in royal service was invested in his Château of Gaillon.

D'Amboise's authority in the church, already great, was vastly increased in 1502 when Alexander VI made him legate *a latere*. The result was the creation of essentially a tripod system of authority in the French church among king, pope, and cardinal. However, d'Amboise was dedicated to the king's interests, and there was no conflict between them over church policy. The cardinal's authority as legate included the right to approve the *décime*, the clergy's "gift" of 10 percent of its income to the king; he seems to have used his influence to discourage Louis from requesting it. D'Amboise's ambitions went beyond having a major role in governing the French church. Numerous observers commented on his burning ambition to become pope. Several of Louis's decisions involving Italian affairs were said to have been made largely in consideration of how they might enhance his friend's chances of being elected to that office.[17] In the election of 1503, d'Amboise came close, but he never had another chance at St. Peter's throne.

D'Amboise's role in Louis's government extended beyond domestic policy and the church; he was also deeply involved in foreign affairs as a diplomat and Louis's governor of Milan for four years. Little wonder that the expression "Let George do it!" (*Laissez faire à Georges!*) is supposed to have originated in Louis's time.[18] In the first months of his reign, the Parisian satirists, the Basoche, severely criticized Louis for giving so much power to d'Amboise and his brother Louis, the bishop of Albi.[19]

When d'Amboise was away from the court, his role in influencing policy passed largely to Pierre de Rohan, Sieur de Gié, until Gié's disgrace in 1504.[20] He came from a cadet branch of a very prominent Breton family. As a great grandson of Bonna Visconti, he was related to Louis. His father died soon after Pierre's birth in 1451, and he was raised at the court of Louis XI, who gave him high offices at a very young age, including a marshal's baton in 1476 at age twenty-five. He cast his lot with the French monarchy against his Breton relatives and Louis of Orléans, but he quickly moved into Louis's inner circle after the latter's succession. Despite his military office, he was constantly at court and was one of the most frequent participants in the royal council until his disgrace removed him from the court.

Gié, d'Amboise, Rochefort, Poncher, and Robertet were the usual members of the *Conseil Secret*, also known as the *Conseil des Affaires*, because its members were referred to as *les gens des affaires de Sa Majesté*.[21] All matters of importance about war, finances, justice, patronage, and religion were first discussed in the Conseil Secret. It met in the king's chambers, usually in the early morning. Only after it had reached a decision, or if it could not reach one, was an issue brought to the *Conseil des Parties*, a much larger royal council. In July 1498 Louis published a list of those who were eligible to attend the Conseil des Parties, which met in the afternoons and often without the king. It included the princes of blood, the bishops, the major royal officials, and the presidents of the Parlement. Rarely would a majority of them be at court at one time, but when truly critical matters were going to be discussed, such as war, the king would expect most to assemble for consultation.

Louis XII's reign was a period of transition in which the distinction between the two royal councils had not yet been clearly defined, and on occasion, important matters were taken directly to the Conseil des Parties. For the most part, however, a small group of the king's closest confidants made decisions in the Conseil Secret, where there was little chance of a bitter division in the royal council of the kind that had occurred in 1484. The emergence of the Conseil Secret was another step in stripping the feudal nobility of its traditional influence over the king and in enhancing royal authority. Nonetheless, Seyssel probably identified the principal motivation for the development of the Conseil Secret: the vastly increased confidentiality that involving only a small number of men in state secrets made possible.[22]

While attendance at the Conseil Secret was fairly consistent, the personnel of the Conseil des Parties varied greatly. Prominent nobles, prelates, and royal officials from the outer provinces were invited to attend when they came to the court. In the first sixteen months of Louis's reign, sixty-six persons signed edicts accepted by the Conseil des Parties, indicating their presence at one or more meetings, although many meetings did not result in an edict. Exactly half of that group signed only one decree out of the forty known for that time. They included such figures as the first president of the Parlement of Toulouse and a Breton bishop.

Georges and Louis d'Amboise, Rochefort, and Gié were the most frequent
signatories. Three other d'Amboises signed at least one edict. Most who
attended the Conseil des Parties in the first years under Louis had been
active in the reign of Charles VIII as well.[23]

By 1498 many of the judicial functions of the medieval royal council had
devolved to a distinct institution, the *Grand Conseil.* Despite the evolution by
1300 of a separate judiciary body, the Parlement, the royal council had continued to take an active role in deciding cases involving important persons
or issues. Since the council traveled with the king, it had been difficult to get
cases heard and decided. The *cahiers* of the Estates of 1484 contained a bitter complaint about the situation. In 1497 Charles VIII had taken a major
step toward establishing a separate body by defining the types of cases it
would hear and placing it in Paris, despite the vigorous protests of the
Parlement. At the beginning of his reign, Louis XII issued an edict establishing its membership as being the chancellor and eighteen magistrates. He
mandated that cases involving persons of high dignity and disputed elections of bishops and abbots be brought to it.[24] As had happened before with
the Parlement, the absence of the king from the Grand Conseil meant that
cases of great significance because of the persons or issues involved were
still appealed to the royal council. However, the creation of the Grand
Conseil did reduce the judicial business of the royal council. Since it did not
have the tradition of independence that the Parlement had developed over
two centuries, it was far less likely to challenge the royal will.[25]

Despite being a royal institution, the Parlement had an amazingly strong
sense of independence from royal control. The term "Parlement" could refer
in a broad sense to the set of judicial institutions placed around France or,
more specifically, to the Parlement of Paris, the original institution. The
Parlement grew out of the king's feudal obligation to dispense justice with the
aid of his nobles. By the mid-thirteenth century the caseload had become too
heavy and specialized for the king and his council to handle. A separate body
of judges, the Parlement, was given a fixed abode in the Palais Royal at Paris.
It soon began to function as a court of first instance for cases involving
offenses against the royal person and his rights and properties. It also served
as an appeals court for cases from the courts of the *baillis* and *sénéchaux*,
although the king often took appeals from it to the royal council. In 1499
there was a total of eighty-three magistrates in the Parlement of Paris.

The most important power that had devolved on to the Parlement was
the task of registering royal edicts in an official record. The Parlement
soon had gained the right to refuse to register edicts that it regarded as
violating the fundamental laws of the realm, the best interests of the

monarchy, or the privileges of the various orders of the realm. The king could then order Parlement to register a disputed edict by a *lettre de jussion.* If it still refused, he could appear in person, resume the authority he had delegated to court, and order the registration of the edict.

The Parlement of Paris always regarded itself as the sovereign court of the entire realm with no appeal except to the king, and it looked down on the provincial parlements that began to appear in the fifteenth century as mere branches of itself. The difficulties of travel to Paris and the need to satisfy local particularism in remote provinces led to the creation of Parlements at Toulouse, Bordeaux, and Grenoble. Charles VII erected them as sovereign courts for their provinces, which meant that appeals from them went to the royal council, not the Parlement of Paris. The dukes of Burgundy had their equivalent of the Parlement for their duchy. After 1477 the court existed in a legal limbo until Charles VIII gave it official status and residence at Dijon in early 1498.

In Normandy, the English administration had left behind an institution called the Exchequer, which had become more a judicial court than a financial body. Lacking supervision from London in the last decades of English rule, the Exchequer had fallen into some bad habits that were allowed to continue after 1453. There was no consistency in its membership, since the grands who had the right to sit on it attended erratically—not that regular attendance would have been a great burden, since it met only once a year but never in the same place. Bribe-taking and favoritism were rampant, and decisions were excruciatingly slow. Louis had become aware of the problem when he served as governor of Normandy. After becoming king, he summoned a group of prominent Normans to Paris to tell them he planned to create a parlement for the province. They asked that the provincial estates be convoked for consultation. When the Norman estates met at Rouen in early 1499, Chancellor Guy de Rochefort, speaking for the king, declared: "The King is the debtor and owes justice to his people. . . . He wishes to put order in all the courts and jurisdictions."[26] Louis then established a "Perpetual Exchequer" permanently placed at Rouen; the estates requested continuing the old name. The grand sénéschal of Normandy was completely relieved of the power of overseeing justice in the province. The personnel of the new institution, which Francis I renamed a Parlement in 1516, was set at four presidents and twenty-eight magistrates.

In Provence, a quite similar state of affairs existed, although the failures of the grand sénéschal of Provence and the old *Conseil Eminent* were not quite as notorious as in Normandy. Louis established a parlement at Aix in 1501 with one president and twelve magistrates. At the end of his reign, there were seven parlements. The disputes over jurisdiction between Paris and the provincial courts were often fierce. Kings sometimes sent cases of special significance to the provincial parlements rather than have them heard in Paris, as the provincial courts tended to be more amenable to the royal will.

The Paris Parlement's apologists often called it the Senate, a reference to the Roman Senate, as the first president did in his address to Louis XII in July 1498.[27] That grandiose view of the court's power and independence often led to clashes with the monarch. While Louis had several disputes with the institution, mostly over the affairs of the church, it rendered him good service in the first political crisis of his reign. In the summer of 1498, he issued an edict that mandated a broad reform of the University of Paris, one of the most powerful and independent bodies in the realm. The principal problem with which the edict dealt was the presence in Paris of a great number of former students, perhaps as many as 20,000, who hung on for years in the city with few responsibilities and little money.[28] They continued to claim the privileges and protection of the university, especially the exemption from the tax on wine and goods consumed by university members. Their behavior was frequently outrageous, and they often caused the numerous riots between students and townspeople that plagued the city. They claimed the right, in which they were supported by the university, to be tried in its special courts, which were notoriously lenient on students.

Louis's edict mandated that the privileges of students be restricted to those who had been enrolled in a university for the previous six months. It limited the length of time that such privileges could be claimed—from four years for those enrolled in the faculty of arts up to fourteen years for those pursuing a master's degree in theology. Large fines and harsh punishments were set for those found violating the edict.[29] The uproar in the University of Paris was enormous, not only from those directly affected but also from the entire faculty and student body, which were always fiercely protective of the institution's privileges. They first denounced Cardinal d'Amboise, whose purview over ecclesiastical matters probably did make him the instigator of the reforms. The black mood of the students was revealed by the sketch of a heart pierced by a dagger that was nailed to the door of Chancellor Rochefort's house in Paris. He was "liberally defamed" by the university members. Placards were posted threatening his death if he were not sent into exile.[30]

In appealing to Louis, the university used the fiction of the evil adviser to avoid attacking the king directly. He refused its petition, as did the Parlement, which at another time might have been sympathetic to the university. The university responded by calling for a "cessation of sermons and lectures": Not only would the university shut down, but all the clergymen in Paris who had been students there and had sworn the oath of loyalty to it were to cease giving sermons. The cessation was the device by which the university had won its privileges in 1200 and protected them since. Letters signed by the rector were sent across France announcing the end of classes until its privileges were restored. The students responded to the king's edict by rioting in the streets. The Parlement, whose duties included the police of the city, asked Louis to come in force to restore order. The king, who was in Blois, gathered a small army and marched to Paris, arriving there in early June 1499. His presence with an armed force quieted the turbulence. While he refused to soften his edict, he was conciliatory toward the university. Its leaders had met him outside of the city and begged his forgiveness. He granted a blanket amnesty, except for Jean Standonck, whose very vocal denunciation of Louis's annulment had already brought him to the king's attention, and three accomplices. They were sent into exile, and some others thought it prudent to leave France before receiving a formal punishment. Louis eventually pardoned them in April 1500, and they returned to Paris. Louis's forceful action ended the practice of the cessation for the University of Paris. Royal power had at last effectively curbed what had been certainly the most independent of the medieval corporations. Kingly authority had made an important stride forward.

Louis's edict policing the university was part of a much larger plan for reform of justice and administration that he probably had in mind when he came to the throne. He was an experienced governor by then with a good understanding of the system of government and its deficiencies, and he had heard the Estates of 1484 on how to improve it. The result was the Ordinances of Blois of March 1499, one of the major pieces of legislation in the history of the French monarchy. It consisted of a lengthy preamble and 162 articles. The preamble described the king's obligation to give justice to his people, which is the "principal and most necessary part of all monarchies and realms." Because France is first among the world's realms, it also must be superior in justice. The preamble went on to provide the rationale for the reforms. Because of war and the confusion of the times, the work of past kings in creating a system for administering justice had been disrupted. Therefore, the king had assembled at Blois a number of prelates, princes of blood, presidents of the parlements, *sénéchaux*, and *baillis* to advise him on reforming justice. The preamble was careful to assert that the 162 articles contained no new law but only a return to the good law of the past.[31]

The first several articles pertained to the church. The king ordered that the "holy rules" of the Council of Basel and the Pragmatic Sanction of Bourges be observed.[32] He revised the rules for giving church benefices (a church position with an income) to university graduates. The Pragmatic Sanction had ordered bishops to fill one-third of the various benefices that became vacant in a year with university graduates. The rule had been intended not only to provide a living for those who had earned an academic degree, but also to ensure that a significant portion of the clergy was educated. Since many benefices were lucrative sinecures, they were often the causes of bitter disputes. Louis hoped to solve the problem by ordering the bishops to stop hiding the benefices that became vacant in order to fill them with their own clients and to make the vacancies known to university authorities. The universities for their part were to provide a list of new degree holders to the bishops to use in filling benefices.[33] The edict helped Louis regain his popularity in the University of Paris.

The majority of the 162 articles dealt with the system of justice. Louis was well regarded for his attitude toward justice. Giovanni Botero, writing a century later, said that the king "raised his hat to the gallows, saying he was king by means of justice."[34] The *cahiers* of the Estates of 1484 had been very harsh in their criticism of the judicial system, and Louis obviously remembered their complaints. Several articles of his edict were designed to protect persons accused of crime. Formal indictments were required before a trial could be held. Judges were told that they had to interrogate the accused and witnesses themselves instead of having their clerks do it. The local language was to be used in the court procedures, not Latin, and the interrogations were to take place as quickly as possible after an arrest. Torture was to be used only once on an accused person who refused to confess, and admissions made under torture had to be repeated the next day for them to serve as proof of guilt. Other articles were designed to speed up the rendering of justice, such as requiring judges to pass sentence within six months of the interrogation. In criminal cases, an even split among the judges rendered a verdict of acquittal.[35] Louis also sought to deal with the cost of justice. He mandated a reduction in the fees paid to the courts and lawyers and forbade the paying of bribes except for small gifts. On several other occasions, Louis revealed his suspicion of the readiness of government officials to take bribes. Perhaps the best example occurred in 1505 when he required his envoy to Rome to sign a pledge not to accept any gifts while he was there.[36] Ironically, Louis himself had a notorious reputation for bribing the officials of other governments.

In regard to the judges, the Ordinances of Blois made sorely needed reforms. Article 40 prohibited the sale of judicial offices in the strongest terms and mandated that if the chancellor by mistake had sealed letters patent for offices that had been sold, they were null and void. However, Louis had to repeat his decree in 1508, and under Francis I, the sale of judicial offices became as common as the sale of financial offices, which Louis did allow.[37] Other articles concerning the judges included one forbidding father and son or two brothers from serving together in the same Parlement. Absenteeism from the courts except for other royal service was interdicted. He even set out the number of days and hours per day that the *parlementaires* were to be present and required them to possess a book of all royal edicts. Yet another article obliged the members of the Parlement to assemble one Wednesday a month for self-examination of their procedures and behavior. The *mercuriale,* from *mercredi* (Wednesday), became a standard part of the procedures of the Parlement, but it never met as often as intended. In 1500 Louis attended a *mercuriale,* the only king to do so until the infamous *mercuriale* of 1559 attended by Henry II. Article 48 established the prerequisite of a degree in law for appointment as the lieutenant of a *bailli* or *sénéchal.* Since the lieutenants did most of the judicial work of those offices, this resulted in a significant improvement in the local courts by taking justice out of the hands of the local nobles and giving it to professionals.

The reforms of 1499-1500 did not eliminate the nobility from the administration of justice completely. They continued to sit in the Grand Conseil and the parlements, but, so Voltaire later argued, Louis's judicial reforms were the beginning of the separation of the nobles of the sword from the nobles of the long robe. With justice largely removed from the hands of the nobles, who were at best amateurs in law, it passed to professionals with their law degrees. Service to the king, whether in war or at court, had always been regarded as ennobling those who did it. Such status was not hereditary, but the officeholder would be eager to pass his office and noble status to his heir. Since the purchase of judicial offices was forbidden, the solution was resignation *in favorem,* a practice that allowed an officeholder to resign his office to whomever he pleased, usually a son or a nephew. An office, whether royal or ecclesiastical, was regarded as a property right, much like a piece of land. A resigning magistrate usually included the right of regression in the document of resignation, which allowed him to return to the office should his designated successor die before him. In this way "dynasties" in Parlement began to appear with generation after generation of a family becoming ennobled by their service in the courts. Since it was a tradition that three generations of living nobly made noble status permanent, such families eventually became ensconced in the nobility of the long robe, albeit at a somewhat lower level of prestige than for the nobility of the sword.

When Louis became king, he gave numerous royal offices to his friends, creating some to accommodate all of them. He also created new financial offices to defray the costs of his Italian war, allowing venality in the financial offices, although he was opposed in principle to selling offices. Botero quoted him as saying: "Those who bought offices sold afterwards at retail very dearly what they had bought wholesale at a good price."[38] It was, however, not entirely due to venality that the fiscal dynasties of several families from Tours developed, since members of those families were already in office when the practice began. The Tourangeaux families made up a "who's who" of Louis's administration — Berthelot, Briçonnet, Ruzé, Poncher, Beaune, and Gaillard. They intermarried constantly, and marriage tied other prominent officials to them, such as Florimond Robertet, who married a Gaillard.

The fiscal offices in question included the *Chambre des comptes*, the *Cour des trésors*, and the *Cour des aides*.[39] Their incumbents collectively were called *gens des finances*. The first was the fiscal policy-setting offspring of the medieval royal council. Its purview over royal finances was very broad, although the royal council occasionally intervened, and it supervised the revenue-gathering officials. Its duties also included collecting records on new fiefholders and the performing of homage for the feudal system. The Chambre des comptes collected its records in Paris, and the fire of 1737 that destroyed most of the collection was a serious blow to historians. Its judicial function was largely the settling of disputes between tax collectors and the government. It was a sovereign court in that it had the power of registering royal edicts on finance and the right to refuse to accept those it regarded as improper. However, the king could order it to register his decrees with a *lettre de jussion*. Upon Guillaume Ruzé's death in 1506, the office of first president of the Chambre went to Jean Nicolay, a protégé of Cardinal d'Amboise; his descendants held it until 1789. There were provincial Chambres des comptes at Aix, Dijon, and Grenoble. The last two were clearly subject to the authority of the Parisian chamber, but the first appears to have been independent.

By 1498 the Chambre des comptes had lost much of its earlier authority to the other two fiscal courts and had become essentially the accountant of royal finances. Perhaps as a consequence, Louis reduced its bureaucracy by 40 percent by 1511. The Cour des trésors' competence pertained to what were called the king's ordinary revenues, those from the royal demense. They were the products of the king's role as feudal lord, both of the entire realm and of smaller properties where he was the feudal seigneur. They included rents and profits from agricultural land, vineyards, forests, and fisheries; tolls from roads and bridges; and dues, fees, and fines that came to the king as the lord of his vassals. The medieval king had been expected "to live off his own": drawing enough from these types of revenue to carry on government without taxes. In fact, the ordinary revenue was quite small, although the nature of the sources makes it impossible to establish an exact figure. One estimate for early in Louis's reign put it at 231,000 *l.* Improved collection and the prosperity of his reign increased that figure to about 500,000 by 1515. Nonetheless, it was flatly impossible that Louis could have lived "off his own," as an author of the next century claimed.[40]

The four royal treasurers supervised the collection of the ordinary revenues in the four great divisions of the kingdom—Languedoc, Languedoil (the Ile-de-France and the north), Normandy, and Oultre-Seine-et-Yvonne (the center). Several frontier provinces such as Picardy were outside of the four divisions, and Louis established a special treasury for his family revenues from Blois. At the local level, the *baillis* and *sénéchaux* supervised the collection. About 420 officers were required to collect the king's ordinary revenues. Most of these revenues were farmed: Wealthy merchants and bankers would bid at a public auction for the right to collect a specific revenue for a given region. A short candle was lit, and the high bid when it burned out was the winning one. The high bidder paid the bidded amount immediately to the royal officials and then collected that amount and more, often much more, for his own profit. But he also had to swallow any shortfall. The system provided the king with a sure source of revenue while permitting the revenue *fermiers* to make a profit. There were frequent complaints that the revenue farmers of an area were in collusion, allowing each member of their group to be high bidder for a tax well below its real worth.

Most of the royal revenues came from the extraordinary revenues, the term for taxes. It was a commonplace of this era that the king ought to have been able to draw 20 million *l* in taxes annually from his realm, an average of 20 *l* from each of the one million towns and villages that supposedly existed in France.[41] The reality, of course, was a great deal less than that. The Cour des aides supervised the collection of the extraordinary revenues. Its title referred to the oldest of the taxes, the *aides*, which were based on the feudal lord's right to financial aid from his vassals for war and other obligations. It was supposed to have been first collected for John II's ransom in 1357. By Louis's time the *aides* had become a permanent sales tax placed on nearly every commodity sold in the realm. Certain luxury items, such as spices used by the nobility and clergy, were exempt, as were small sales of under five *sous* of the sort found in a small village. The *aides* were imposed at either wholesale or retail but not both, except for wine, which was taxed at one-twentieth of its price at wholesale and one-eighth at retail, the *vingtième et huitième* of so many tax documents of the time. The importance of wine in French life even then is obvious from its major place in the fiscal system. Louis frequently gave gifts of wine to foreign dignitaries and rulers.

The *aides* were almost entirely farmed out. There was a strong prejudice against *grosses fermes* for the *aides*, so a farmer collected the tax on a specific commodity in a small region. The government preferred to have as the farmers of the *aides* merchants who knew both the market for a particular commodity and its merchants. It was felt this would not be true for grand farmers, who, it was suspected, would conspire among themselves to keep their profit high. The portion of royal taxes that the *aides* comprised had fallen greatly in the fifteenth century; the trend continued in Louis's reign. In 1497 the treasury collected 531,000 *l* from the *aides*, which rose to 654,000 by 1514, but the proportion of ordinary and extraordinary revenues that they represented declined from 14 percent in 1497 to 11 percent in 1514.[42] Louis agreed with the common view that the *aides* were a fair tax because everybody paid them, even if the nobles and the clerics had exemptions for some items. Part of Louis's popularity rested on the fact that he made everybody pay the taxes on wine.[43]

The tax on salt was called the *gabelles*. As a necessity of life whose sources were severely limited, salt lent itself well to large-scale royal taxation. However, few aspects of the royal fiscal system were more complicated than the *gabelles*. They were imposed at wholesale at a specific amount per unit weight of salt and did not depend on its price, which the government did try to control. The provinces of north and central France did not produce any salt and so were the most vulnerable to the tax. These *pays de grands gabelles* paid the highest salt tax by far. The salt was brought to royal salt warehouses, *greniers à sel*, in districts and towns and then sold to the populace with a hefty tax imposed, generally around 75 percent of its value. Families were required to buy a specific amount a year regardless of whether they used that much. In the lands of the *petits gabelles*—the Midi and Burgundy—the *gabelle* was levied at 20 to 25 percent of the retail value. There salt merchants were less controlled than in the north. The immediate areas of salt production, the coastal margins of the Atlantic from Normandy southward and the Mediterranean, were free of the tax. The large difference in the price of salt within the realm encouraged large-scale smuggling, although the increased rate of taxation of later centuries made smuggling worse than in Louis's time. In the years from 1489 to 1514, the take from the *gabelles* increased from 150,000 *l* per annum to 284,000. Louis was quoted as saying that it was the easiest and lightest subsidy that had ever been levied, "because folk from all estates pay it." Exemptions from it were very few, limited to those of the highest status. The Chambre des comptes had to verify any exemption claimed.[44]

The newest tax, the *tailles*, was also the heaviest. Once the *tailles* had become permanent in 1439, the tax provided 1,200,000 *l* for Charles VII's treasury. That sum rose rapidly under Louis XI, reaching 4,700,000 *l* in 1483, but Anne of Beaujeu and Charles VIII reduced the *tailles* considerably, probably in response to the Estates of 1484, which had requested that they be maintained at 1,500,000 *l*. By 1498 they had declined to 2,114,157 *l*, although there was a large deficit that year.[45] There were two types of *tailles*. In Languedoc, it was a tax on *terre roturière*, property that did not confer a title of nobility on its holder. When such a piece of land was purchased by a nobleman, it continued to be liable to the *taille*. In the rest of the realm, the taille was *personnelle*, a tax on the land and wealth of nonnobles. When a noble purchased a piece of property or a commoner property owner gained a patent of nobility, those properties escaped the *taille*. When that happened, the tax on the rest of the taxpayers of the parish was increased, since a parish was assessed a specific sum. Disputes over whether a piece of land had escaped the *taille* were frequently carried to the Cour des aides and sometimes to the royal council. The reason for the exemption for the nobility was that the tax had been created explicitly for the support of the army imposed on those who did not serve in the military. It was expressed in terms of supporting 2,500 lances. The clergy was also exempt.[46]

When the king and his council had fixed the total amount of *tailles* for the forthcoming year, the sum was divided among the four *généralités des finances*, which made up most of the realm. They corresponded closely to the four treasuries of the demense and were headed by the *généraux des finances*. These units were subdivided into some 90 *élections*, so-called because in the past, the taxpayers had elected the *élu*, the officer who supervised the collection of the *taille* in each district. The *élus* informed the parishes of their assessments, and parish assessors informed the taxpayers of their tax based on the assessors' estimate of their wealth. By Louis's time the *élus* were no longer elected but were appointed royal officials who also supervised the collection of the *aides* and the *gabelles* in their *élections*. The money was actually collected by officers with varying titles, the most common being *réceiveur des tailles*. It has been estimated that there were 1,139 tax officers in place in 1515. At those times when the annual total of the *tailles* had already been set and the king needed more money, usually for war, he resorted to a surtax called the *crue* (fresh), because it was freshly imposed on top of the *taille*. The large cities were exempted from the *tailles* on the grounds that it would be difficult to assess the wealth of the great number of persons who did not own property. Instead those cities would agree to an *octroi* (grant) of money to the king, which was collected largely from tolls and tariffs.

The *tailles* and the system of *élus* predated 1453, and the provinces that had reverted to the crown after that — Guyenne, Gascony, Brittany, Burgundy, and Provence — along with Languedoc and Dauphiné had a somewhat different system of levying direct taxes from the rest of the realm. The tax had a different name in several of these provinces; in Brittany and Provence, for example, the term *"fouage"* was still in use, from the hearth tax of earlier centuries. The Estates of those provinces met annually to agree to levy the sum requested by the king and also met to agree to any *crue* requested. They were called the *pays d'état*, while the rest of the realm made up the *pays d'élection*. The distinction remained in effect for several centuries, and consequently, in the *pays d'état* the provincial estates continued to meet. There were also several provinces, such as Normandy and Burgundy, where the provincial estates and the system of *élections* existed together during Louis's reign.[47]

When Louis XII reached the throne, he found a deficit of 1,400,000 *l*. Nonetheless, he moved quickly to reduce the *tailles* by 200,000 *l* to 1,932,704,[48] and he refused the 300,000 *l* for his "joyous coming." The Italian wars forced the *tailles* back over 2,000,000 *l* for three years, but then Louis was able to reduce them substantially, to 1,650,000 *l* in 1503 and after a small increase in 1504, down to 1,500,000 in 1506.[49] But having reduced the base rate of the *tailles*, Louis several times had to ask for *crues* of 300,000 or 500,000 *l*.

In order to meet his budget, Louis had to reduce expenses.[50] One place for reduction was the pensions for the nobility and foreign princes, which in 1497 came to 498,000 *l*. He is said to have reduced them by half, but if that was true, they shot up again with the onset of the Italian War. In 1500 the pensions for 260 persons totaled 416,544 *l*, but they dropped again to 247,000 *l* in 1503, and declined again to 202,000 *l* in 1505. It appears that Louis reduced the number of persons on the pensions rolls rather than decreasing the pensions for those still receiving them. Pierre de Bourbon, for example, received 10,000 *l* for the duration of Louis's reign.[51]

Louis, like every king, resorted to other sources of income to meet his needs for money. The church's great wealth was always tempting; but as long as Cardinal d'Amboise was his principal adviser, Louis made little effort to avail himself of it. The chief means of tapping into the clergy's wealth was the *décime*. Prior to d'Amboise's death in 1510, Louis used the device three times: for 235,466 *l* in 1501 and 1503 for proposed crusades against the Turks, and 271,386 *l* in 1509 for war in Italy.[52]

Borrowing was another way of making royal ends meet, especially when Louis's goal of reducing the tax burden on his people clashed with his desire to make good his dynastic claims to places in Italy. He drew rather little on the Italian bankers of Lyon for loans. Instead he depended heavily on forced loans from the bigger cities or wealthy individuals, often members of the government. The king did not pay interest on such loans, and under some monarchs the lenders were fortunate if the principal was repaid, but usually those who had been pressed into lending to the king received some sort of benefit. One form of royal borrowing that was becoming more common was known as the *rentes*. It referred literally to the renting of a revenue: Someone who had a dependable source of income would turn it over to another for an agreed-upon number of years in exchange for a loan. The revenue served as interest for the loan, generally at *denier* 12 (8 1/3 percent), which was seen as not violating the church's ban on interest-taking as usury. The principal would be repaid in a lump sum at the end of the contract. The monarchy often extended its contracts indefinitely. The tolls collected in the cities were frequently used as security for *rentes*, but it was only under Francis I that *rentes* collected by the city of Paris emerged as a major source of borrowed funds.

Very little of the money raised by the monarchy actually was collected in the king's treasure chests, which were kept with his person until 1532, when they were placed permanently in the Louvre. Most royal expenses were paid via letters called *quittances*, which authorized the bearers to collect the specified sums from the treasurers of the fiscal divisions of the realm. The *quittances* usually designated the specific revenue sources that were to be drawn on in order to pay them. For example, in 1508 Thomas Bohier, *Conseilleur des finances* in Normandy, was sent a *quittance* directing him to pay the expenses of the royal Ecurie from money collected from the *huitième* of wine in Beaumont, the *aides* of Laval, and the *tailles* of Loudon.[53]

Louis XII spent a very busy first year of his reign implementing his ideas, presumably thought out in advance, of what good government was. They have been attributed both to his reading of Seneca during his imprisonment and the Estates of 1484. Either was a plausible source of his reform program, but he was also surrounded by a coterie of experienced royal officers. Louis seems to have had a sense of urgency to reform the government before he embarked on his grand expedition to Italy. For the rest of his reign, he fine-tuned the reforms of 1498-99, but he never again attempted anything of their magnitude.

8

Vive le Duc de Milan!

Having largely implemented his reform of the government, secured internal peace and stability, and earned his people's affection by his fiscal policy, Louis XII turned his attention to fulfilling the consuming passion of his life—the conquest of Milan. He hated Ludovico Sforza, not only because il Moro had usurped his rightful title, but also because he had humiliated Louis at Novara in 1495. The Venetian ambassador reported that Louis thought of nothing but the ruin of Sforza and would give ten years of his life to see to his destruction. He refused to refer to Ludovico as the duke of Milan, simply calling him Signor Ludovico.[1]

The king moved to quiet any opposition in France to the new Italian expedition by promising that the revenues of Milan would pay for the war and by seeking loans and grants from other Italian states, especially Venice. He also acted to keep the other European states from aiding il Moro or attacking France while the Italian expedition was going on by settling disputes with his neighbors and forging alliances. Among France's neighboring sovereigns, no one hated the French as much as Maximilian I, the Holy Roman Emperor,[2] who would be the quickest to take advantage of an opportunity such as the movement of French troops to Milan. The emperor was hunting when the Milanese ambassador brought him the news that Charles VIII had died. "Now is the time to put away the deer," the ambassador told him, "and perform deeds worthy of your name and title."[3] Maximilian expected that the Bourbons and the other lords with whom Louis had been at odds would dispute his succession, and he was eager to fish in such troubled waters. Calling the German nobles together, he harangued them with the long list of injuries the French had done to him and his family, and to the empire. He concluded: "Now you know well the treason, betrayals, and injuries I have suffered, and the good reasons you and I have . . . to dip our swords in French blood."[4]

The emperor assembled a small army and, in July 1498, crossed into Burgundy, which he always intended to recover for his dynasty. The local

French units quickly routed his ill-prepared forces. Louis responded to Maximilian's aggression by acting to detach his son and heir, Archduke Philip, from him. Philip, now twenty years old, was the ruler of the Low Countries and claimed Burgundy as the heir of his mother, Mary of Burgundy. Guicciardini called him pacific by nature and noted that he ruled a people (the Flemings) who were utterly opposed to a war with France since it would disrupt their commerce.[5] Far less hostile to France than was his father, Philip responded to Louis's overtures, and a treaty was signed between them in August 1498. It settled the dispute over the nature of the archduke's rule over Flanders and several towns in Artois. Philip agreed to do feudal homage for them, while Louis pledged to return the disputed towns to him. They also agreed that Philip would not challenge French rule over Burgundy during their lifetimes. In the following July, Chancellor Rochefort went to Arras to accept the archduke's homage in one of the more splendid ceremonies of Louis's reign.[6]

In August 1498, with his forces defeated and his son negotiating with the enemy, Maximilian agreed to a truce.[7] With Maximilian temporarily neutralized, Louis turned his attention to Henry VII. The king of England regarded the new king of France more highly than his predecessor, for they had worked together in defending Brittany a decade earlier.[8] Louis was eager to avoid a conflict with England, because the English easily could cause trouble for France from their stronghold at Calais. Louis was quick to be accommodating to Henry. In July 1498 Louis offered to renew the Treaty of Etaples, which Henry and Charles VIII had negotiated in 1492. Since it included an annual pension of 50,000 *écus*, Henry had good reason to agree. In the negotiations, the French even hinted that they were prepared to abandon the "auld alliance" with Scotland. Perhaps that is why Louis had been slow to make contact with the Scots; as of August 1498 he had not yet officially informed them of his accession.[9] There was, however, little possibility that an alliance as useful for France as the one with Scotland was would be allowed to lapse. By early 1499 the "auld alliance" was as firm as ever.

Although Henry VII continued to pursue the marriage of his son Arthur to the Spanish Infanta Catherine, for the next ten years England was effectively neutralized as far as any alliance against France was concerned. When Louis turned his attention to the Spanish monarchs, he found a tougher case. Ferdinand of Aragon, who largely directed policy toward France for his wife, Isabella of Castile, had long demonstrated both his hostility toward the French and his ability to shift positions without notice. Technically, he was still a member of the League of Venice and at war with France, although there had been very little action recently and the League was rapidly decaying. In June 1498 he sent an embassy to France on behalf of his Italian allies to discuss a formal truce. At first the negotiations went poorly, and the Spanish ambassadors had already left the court. Louis, under the pretext that he was going hunting, rode after them and persuaded them to reopen the negotiations. His effort resulted in an agreement of early August. It did not resolve any of the territorial disputes between the French and the Spanish monarchs, which were passed over without mention. The treaty was simply a pledge of mutual friendship and nonaggression, but it was enough to persuade Louis that he had nothing to fear from Spain.[10]

With the three major states pledged to peace with France, Louis still had to attend to two more neighbors, the Swiss Confederation and the duchy of Savoy, which could create difficulties in his forthcoming expedition to Milan. The Swiss cantons were still legally part of the Holy Roman Empire, and they had a vaguely defined obligation to obey the emperor in war and foreign policy. The cantons around the major passes across the Alps from Italy were attracted to Italian affairs, and Ludovico Sforza had been diligently courting them. For other Swiss, the long tradition of service with France caused them to maintain a pro-French attitude. The Confederation had agreed in 1495 to provide Charles VIII with mercenary troops, but the agreement ended at his demise, and some 12,000 *l* had been left unpaid. Although Louis immediately upon his accession sent an agent, Antoine de Baissy, the *bailli* of Dijon, to the Swiss pledging payment of the money and asking for a renewal of the contract, they were unwilling to commit themselves. By the end of 1498, however, Maximilian's aggressive posture toward the Swiss made them far more amenable to Louis's proposals. In March 1499 the Confederation accepted a new contract for ten years, which called for an annual subsidy of 20,000 *l* from Louis for allowing him to recruit an unspecified number of troops in the Confederation. Louis pledged to protect the Swiss homeland and educate two Swiss students at Paris at his expense.[11]

Savoy ought to have been a close ally of France, since the ducal family had intermarried widely with the French royal family, having furnished wives for Louis XI and Charles of Angoulême. As frequently has happened, however, the small state was eager to blunt the power and influence of its larger dominating neighbor. Under Duchess-dowager Bianca, who was governing for her son Philibert, Savoy was a firm ally of Milan. Since Milanese diplomats were unwelcome in France, the Savoyard representatives there kept Sforza informed of events in France, such as

Charles VIII's death and Louis's succession.[12] Louis XII set to work to detach Savoy from Milan. He provided liberal sums of money to the duke and his entourage, and in February 1499 Philibert agreed to meet a French agent. By May an alliance had been hammered out by which Philibert was committed to allow French forces to cross his borders and purchase supplies and recruit troops in Savoy. Philibert would receive a pension of 22,000 *l* for himself and 10,000 *l* for his half brother in addition to the command of a French company of 100 lances.[13]

In Italy itself Ludovico had been busy estranging himself from his fellow Italians in the League of Venice, while Louis had been cultivating Venice, the major Italian power, from the moment of his accession. He sent a warm letter to the doge announcing his succession and urging an alliance. Venice immediately sent an agent to the French court, who reported on the friendly welcome he had received. Louis told the Venetian that he thought more highly of Venice than of any other Italian state. However, when the Turks took the Venetian-held fortress of Lepanto in late 1499, Louis told Venice's ambassador: "You Venetians are wise in your deliberations and have great riches, but you lack spirit and courage in war. You have too much fear of death. We undertake war with the spirit of win or die."[14]

Based on the agent's report, the Venetian Senate sent a full embassy of three diplomats to France. They were welcomed effusively and even granted a daily allowance of 50 *l*, something previously unheard of. Louis treated the ambassadors with utmost courtesy; after several days of ceremony, he met with them and proposed an alliance to them. When the ambassadors' report arrived, Venice made a quick decision in favor of a limited alliance. When Louis and his advisers were informed of the Venetian Senate's terms in mid-September, they found them to be too limited. Prolonged haggling, especially over the French request for a subsidy of 100,000 ducats from Venice, dragged the negotiations into 1499. Finally, in February, Louis accepted terms largely as offered by Venice, despite the objections of all but one member of his council. Venice would provide 1,500 men-at-arms and 4,000 infantrymen at its own expense for the war on Sforza, but no subsidy. The city was to get several cities in the eastern part of the duchy of Milan, and it had the right to withdraw from the fighting if the Turks mounted a serious threat against it. On April 15 Louis swore the terms of the alliance.[15]

Cesare Borgia had already committed the pope to supporting the war on Milan, and Florence had proclaimed its neutrality. Sforza was virtually isolated, except for a tacit alliance of dubious value with the Ottoman Empire. He had some reason to hope that the mercurial Maximilian, whose second wife was his niece, would come to his aid, but in early 1499 there was no evidence that the emperor would break his truce with France. The one cause for optimism Ludovico had was the often-repeated report that the French disliked the idea of war in Italy, fearing that it would be a pretext for raising taxes, and the nobles especially were hostile to it, as implausible as that was.[16] Sforza's ambassador to the papacy assured Alexander VI that his master did not fear the French because he had both the manpower and the gold to withstand them.[17]

Louis also worked to foment dissension within Sforza's possessions. Gian Giacomo Trivulzio, a leader of Milanese opposition to il Moro who had been in exile in France, was made governor of Asti to encourage his friends in Milan. Louis also began an economic campaign against Genoa, which had been absorbed into Sforza's state. The importing of a number of items from Genoa was banned; Genoese merchants were ordered to depart from France within six months; and Genoese bankers were barred from participating in the money exchange at Lyon. These measures quickly built up pressure for an accommodation with France within the city.[18]

From the moment of his accession to the throne, Louis XII had been building up the French army to use in Italy. Charles VIII had assembled a potent force for his expedition in 1494, but after his return he had allowed it to atrophy. Had all the diplomatic and domestic arrangements been in place in the spring of 1498, Louis could not have attacked Milan until his army was ready. Louis and his people still regarded the knights, the *gens d'armes* as they were called in that era, as the flower of French men of war. Over the previous two centuries, faced first with ever more powerful crossbows and then with firearms, the *gens d'armes* had taken on more and more armor, encasing themselves and their horses with plate armor. The expense of equipping oneself as a knight and procuring the great horses now needed had made it impossible for all but the wealthiest nobles to serve as heavy lancers. Charles VII had recognized the problem in 1439 when he reorganized the French cavalry. Faced with a rowdy mass of ill-disciplined nobles more loyal to local magnates than to the crown, he acted to gain greater control over the fighting men. In his edict of 1439, he established the *compagnies d'ordonnance*, which were intended to remain intact for the duration of the war with England, and mandated royal pay for them. The twenty companies he established were each to have 100 lances, consisting of a heavy lancer, three support troops, and two valets. The support troops were all mounted but often dismounted to fight. It is not clear from what social class Charles intended to recruit the support troops, but soon after 1445 they were petty nobles, who could not afford the equipment of the lancer.

The *taille* had been established to pay the lance companies. Contrary to royal promises, neither *taille* nor lance companies disappeared after the French victory in 1453. However, the strength of most companies declined to fifty lances, although several companies commanded by members of the royal family or great nobles still had 100. The number of men in a lance dropped to four. A further source of heavy cavalry was the king's mounted bodyguard, the 200 *gens d'armes de l'hôtel*, recruited from the higher nobility, and his 200 Scots archers, who actually were heavy lancers. Both units fought with the lance companies when the king was in the field with the army. Charles VIII had assembled some 3,000 lances in 1494, but that number dropped drastically in the next years. Louis is said to have found only thirteen companies with a total of 750 lances in 1498. Setting to work immediately upon his succession, he increased the number to 3,000 lances in a year's time,[19] but whether they were all good fighting men is unknown. A lancer received 180 *l* a year as a salary, but many drew larger pensions from the king because of their high standing in the realm.[20]

A lancer's heavy armor made it difficult for him and his horse to move or turn quickly, but it did make him close to being invulnerable to most weapons and missiles encountered on a battlefield of the day. Only artillery was likely to do serious injury to an armored lancer, but it was highly inaccurate. Yet the relatively small number of lancers and their lack of speed greatly reduced their capability to dominate the battlefield of the era. Few if any persons recognized the deficiencies of the heavy lancer, and most agreed with Machiavelli's statement that "today the French men at arms are the best in the world."[21]

In addition to the *gens d'armes* of the lance companies, the French king could also call out the *ban et arrière-ban* if he needed more horsemen. That was the term for the feudal levy, obliging the fiefholders to military service, although there were some exceptions, such as for the noble members of the sovereign courts. Those commoners who held fiefs had to pay a fee in substitution for service. It was commonly acknowledged that a large portion, perhaps as high as 75 percent, of those obliged to serve when the ban was summoned, did not appear. Pierre de Gié, who was one of the two marshals in the French army, began a census in 1503 to determine exactly how many men were liable to service from the ban. He was able to procure counts for only two *bailliages* before he fell into disgrace.[22] The manpower assembled by the *ban* was poorly equipped and trained and generally ill-disciplined. It was usually called only if the realm was threatened with invasion. The French army of 1498 had no light cavalry—that is, horsemen equipped with missile weapons—although it had a few mounted hand-gunners and crossbowmen, who dismounted to fire their weapons. The usefulness of light cavalry as skirmishers had been made obvious in Italy in 1494, and Louis began to recruit Albanian light horse, which the Venetians had used effectively.

In respect to the infantry, the deeply ingrained fear among the French nobles of putting weapons in the hands of their peasants, a product largely of the Peasants' Revolt of 1358, meant there were very few native footsoldiers in the French army. The efforts of Charles VII and Louis XI to create a native archer corps of 10,000 men, who were to be free of the burden of paying the *tailles*, failed badly. Only in Gascony, where the English had made use of local infantrymen, was there something of a military tradition among French commoners; Gascons appeared in some numbers in the French army under Louis XII. Further retarding the development of a native infantry was the French tardiness in adopting firearms. One reason was the poor quality of French-made arquebuses (muskets), which forced the French to buy Italian models whenever possible. Another was the attitude of the French nobility, expressed as late as 1570 by the noted French captain, Blaise de Monluc: "Would to God that this unhappy weapon had never been devised, and that so many brave and valiant men had never died by the hands of those who are often cowards and shirkers, who would never dare to look in the face those whom they lay low with their wretched bullets."[23] The few companies of non-Gascon French infantrymen that did exist used the pike or the crossbow. Their pay was haphazard, and their discipline worse. Botero in the late sixteenth century stated that Louis dismissed them because they committed so many murders and assassinations; therefore, he had to hire vast numbers of Swiss mercenaries, which placed a heavy tax burden on his people.[24]

In hope of reducing the heavy expense of mercenaries, Louis would agree in 1503 to Gié's plan to create a French infantry force of 20,000 crossbowmen, archers, and pikemen. According to Gié, the cost of that size a force would be about the same as for 200 *gens d'armes*, or about 36,000 *l.* His plan became caught up in the court politics during the period of Louis's serious illness of 1504. Gié's alleged intention to use the new infantry force to seize power was one of the accusations against him when he was charged with treason in 1504. With his disgrace, the plan for a potent native infantry was scrapped for a time.[25]

The French artillery train was of vastly better quality. Already for three decades France had a reputation for having good artillery. It was under the jurisdiction of a *grand maître de l'artillerie*, who in 1498 was Jacques de Genouillac. The 130 great pieces cast from bronze, known as culverins, fired iron balls, not the stone balls used in the wrought-iron bombards found elsewhere in Europe, which made culverins much more effective against fortifications. A culverin used considerably more powder than did a bombard, but France had plenty of saltpeter, the key ingredient of gunpowder. Despite the recently developed gun carriage, which greatly reduced the difficulty of moving guns, the artillery still required a huge number of horses. In 1499 Louis bought 1,800 horses at Lyon for it. For the most part, culverins were still too unwieldy to use effectively in the field; they were primarily siege weapons. The French had demonstrated in 1494 how effective their artillery was in reducing Italian castles.[26]

French troops had a notorious reputation both at home and in Italy for bad discipline and rowdy behavior. In part, it was the result of irregular pay, which forced them to take what they needed from the local people. A major goal behind Louis XII's reform of the royal fiscal system was the provision of regular pay for the army. He issued an edict establishing severe punishments for those who looted civilians. While the edict certainly did not eliminate bad behavior by the troops—an impossible task— it did reduce it considerably and earned for the king the gratitude of the people. In 1499 a comment was made that the king "is obeyed as if he has been reigning for the past 100 years."[27]

Louis also needed to raise a great deal of money for a campaign in Italy, but he did not want it to be a heavy burden on his people. To fill his war chest, he used such expedients as imposing a strict discipline on the tax system and insisting on a rigorous honesty on the part of the fiscal officers. When a treasurer-general told him that there was no gold to be had from his accounts, he told the officer: "I know that you will find it for me, and I will show you that I will be obeyed, not like the late King Charles, but like old King Louis."[28] Pensions were drastically cut, and Louis rescinded the grants of financial offices that Charles VIII had made and obliged their incumbents to buy them back. Provincial estates were summoned to provide subsidies for the military campaign. The Venetian ambassador reported to his government: "To hold the estates consists of one thing: the king opens up his revenues and expenses and asks for a subsidy." In April 1499 the king told the Venetian that he had enough money for two years of war.[29]

At the beginning of 1499, the Venetian ambassador reported that the king was sending 12,000 infantrymen, 1,500 lances, and the 200 gentlemen of his household to Asti.[30] Louis made one last attempt to get Sforza to recognize his sovereignty by offering to let him remain in power in return for an annual tribute. When in July Sforza refused, the remainder of the French army at Lyon was sent on to Asti. According to the best estimate,

27,000 men, of whom 10,000 were mounted and 5,000 were Swiss, gathered there in August.[31] The command of the army should have gone to the constable, who led the French army in the absence of the king. Charles, however, had left the post vacant since 1488, and Louis never filled it. Both kings probably felt threatened by the vast authority that tradition gave the constable. Thus, one of the two marshals, Gian Giacomo Trivulzio, was named the commander. He was a native of Milan and an experienced condottiere, who had gone to France during the reign of Louis XI. While he did not have as much experience in battle as did several of the French captains, he knew the region around Milan; and it was regarded as appropriate that a local nobleman lead the French into Milan.[32]

Louis and his captains had worked hard to assure the logistics of the campaign. The export of wheat from Provence was prohibited, and commissioners were dispatched across Provence and Dauphiné to purchase victuals. The treasurer-general of Languedoc was brought to Lyon to serve as the paymaster for the army. Louis also established a "provost of justice" in each military company to prevent pillage and rape in the regions through which the army passed.[33] As the French army moved through Savoy, Louis left Queen Anne, who was pregnant, at Romorantin in central France, where the court had moved because of plague at Blois, and went to Lyon. Arriving at Lyon on July 10, he made his formal entry into the city. He remained there during the forthcoming campaign because, as d'Amboise told the Venetian ambassador, he felt that Sforza was not worthy of the honor of facing the king of France in battle.[34] It took fifteen days for the main body of troops to reach Asti. Sforza had done little to prepare for the attack; apparently he had believed the reports that the French would not strike that year. He was dependent largely on mercenaries—mostly Italian for his cavalry and mostly Swiss for his infantry, totaling 23,000 men.[35] Maximilian had promised a large force to aid him, but as was usual for him, he failed to follow through.

On August 10 Trivulzio led his army out of Asti into Milanese territory. He quickly came to the fortified town of Rocca di Arazzo, the first of a series of strongholds that guarded the western part of the duchy of Milan. Once the batteries were in place, it took only five hours to open a breach in the wall. After rushing the breach, the French seized the town and massacred the garrison as well as numerous civilians. Louis XII had ordered a slaughter in the first fort taken by storm to encourage the quick surrender of other strongholds. The legal rationale was that the defenders had committed treason against their rightful lord by resisting his army.[36] In general, with a few exceptions such as the one just noted, Louis kept a tight rein on his troops, especially when he was with them. The Florentine Luca Landucci, after lamenting the atrocities of Cesare Borgia's troops in 1501, commented: "When the King of France was here, we did not hear of the smallest case to do with women; and the French were in our houses together with gentlewomen, but there was never an idea of their behaving badly."[37]

The French repeated the episode at Annone several days later, and it had the desired effect of persuading three more strongholds to surrender without resisting. This brought the French army to Alessandro, the second city of the duchy. On August 25 Trivulzio began to batter its walls. The vigorous defense of its walls suddenly ended when the governor and most of the *gens d'armes* slipped out of the city before dawn on August 29.[38] With the Venetians entering the duchy from the east and the French setting up their batteries before Pavia, the last stronghold protecting Milan itself, Sforza realized that there was little purpose in continuing to resist. On September 2 he and a band of cavalrymen fled from Milan and headed northward toward the empire. Three days later a meeting between Trivulzio and the civic leaders of Milan established the terms for the city's submission to Louis XII. The civic leaders took on the task of persuading the garrison of the citadel to surrender in exchange for a pledge barring French soldiers from Milan. Meanwhile, the city of Genoa agreed to accept a French governor. Louis named his cousin Philip of Cleves to the post.[39]

When Louis learned of the surrender of the citadel of Milan on September 17, he immediately left Lyon. When he later saw how well built the citadel of Milan was, he called its commander the new Judas for his quick surrender. On October 6 Louis made his triumphant entry into the city, which was done "according to the ancient custom of the Romans." Its centerpiece was a arch of triumph decorated with paintings of Louis and topped by an equestrian statue of him. Numerous Italian princes, prelates, and ambassadors, including one from the pope, came to congratulate him. When Louis, who presented himself as duke and not king, reached the main gate, Trivulzio presented him with the key to the city. Coins with the legend "Louis, king of France and duke of Milan" were distributed. According to Jean d'Auton, Louis's official historian, the Milanese people, wild with enthusiasm, shouted *"Francia! Francia!"* as the king, dressed in the ducal robes, rode through the streets. But the Venetian ambassador, whose official report presented the same picture, wrote to his brother that the people were very sullen.[40]

Louis spent six weeks in Milan establishing his government, making a quick trip to Genoa as well. He named Trivulzio as governor in Milan and established a ruling council he called the Senate but to which the French often referred as a parlement. It had eight Italian members and seven French, and had the same power as the Parlement of registering royal edicts for the duchy, which would not go into effect until they had been registered. Louis greatly reduced the taxes that Sforza had been collecting, perhaps by as much as one-third, but not by as much as the Milanese had been led to believe by French agents before Sforza's ouster. The French troops availed themselves of considerable booty outside of the city, and Louis did intend to pay for the cost of the expedition by efficient collection of taxes; but there is little question that the tax burden was lower than under Sforza.[41]

Louis clearly wished to treat the duchy as part of his rightful domains and not as a conquered territory; he showed the same spirit of reconciliation there as he had in France at his succession. He also offered easy terms to those who had fled with Sforza to the Tyrol. Nonetheless, things soon began to sour for the French. A week before Louis departed for France, an attempt to arrest a Sforza partisan created a disturbance, to which Louis had to go in person to quell. He told the mob that he had not come to their city to impose tyranny but to rule justly. He now had to return to France because of the coming winter but would return to visit once a year. In the meantime, the people had to obey Trivulzio, his lieutenant.[42]

Louis's return to his realm was a triumphal procession through city after city until he reached Romorantin. There he saw his daughter Claude for the first time. She had been born on the day that Louis left Milan but was baptized only after he arrived back at Romorantin.[43] Shortly after that, the court went to Blois, where the plague had subsided.

In Milan, the French position deteriorated rapidly. Trivulzio's power rankled his former Milanese peers; the Venetian occupation of land in the eastern part of the duchy angered the Milanese; and the French soldiers returned to their usual mode of behavior after the king left. Trivulzio proved incapable of restraining the soldiers, and the Milanese quickly repented of whatever enthusiasm they might have had for French rule. Sforza's partisans alerted him to the situation, and he set about to recover his duchy. The emperor gave him permission to recruit soldiers in the empire, and the Swiss were quick to sign on because Louis had not paid the pikemen who had been serving him all they claimed he owed them. A good number of Italian *gens d'armes* also signed on.[44]

In mid-January 1500 Sforza's army crossed into the duchy of Milan. Trivulzio recalled the French troops that Cesare Borgia had taken with him to recover papal lands in the Romagna, which was part of Alexander's price for supporting Louis, but even their quick return did not give

Trivulzio the numbers to match Sforza's. The news of Sforza's occupation of the major fortress of Como to the north of Milan emboldened his partisans in Milan to take arms. On February 1 Trivulzio decided he could not hold the city, and he and his troops retreated to fortresses west of it. Il Moro was welcomed back into Milan on February 5 by a joyous crowd much larger and louder than the one that had greeted Louis XII.[45]

The king was at Loches when the news of the rebellion in Milan reached him three days later. He responded in fury, putting a hefty price on Sforza's head and vowing to wipe Milan off the face of the earth. As always was the case with him, however, his anger quickly abated, and he set to work to recover his loss. He found 400,000 *écus* to fund a new campaign and moved back to Lyon so that he could communicate more quickly with his captains in Italy.[46] Louis dispatched La Trémoille with 700 *gens d'armes* to Asti, and Antoine de Baissy, the usual French agent in the Swiss cantons, went back into the Alps to recruit pikemen. Despite the official position of the Confederation in support of il Moro, Baissy had no trouble assembling 10,000 mercenaries.

By the time La Trémoille reached the French-controlled forts in the western Milanese, some 30,000 troops had gathered under the fleur-de-lis.[47] He took command of them as the king's lieutenant-general. A far more able commander than Trivulzio, he quickly restored order and discipline to the army. The good order of the French army now contrasted sharply with Sforza's; for as good a politician as il Moro was, he never translated his political skills into effective military command. In the city of Milan itself, the people's support for their old ruler dropped as fast as it had for the French.

Sensing his precarious position in Milan, Ludovico left for Novara, where he hoped to stop the French army before it reached Milan. On April 8, 1500, the French army began to set up siege lines around Novara. Sforza's cause received a major setback when the Swiss Confederation ordered that the Swiss in both camps not fight each other. He had a much larger proportion of Swiss than La Trémoille did. With much of the rest of his manpower also deserting, Sforza decided to try to slip away as well. Dressed like a pikeman (or like a Franciscan, according to some sources), he hid among the Swiss as they filed out of Novara. La Trémoille, suspecting it was the case, drew up battle lines around the Swiss and threatened to wipe them out if they did not hand over Ludovico. When a Swiss pikeman pointed him out, Sforza begged that he not be forced to surrender to Trivulzio, the cause of all his troubles, so he was led to La Trémoille to submit. The French commander put him under extremely heavy guard and wrote to the king announcing his capture.[48]

As can be imagined, Louis's reply was ecstatic, but he declared that he could never be happy until he got Sforza across the Alps. He sent his company of royal archers to escort Ludovico to France. On April 17 il Moro was taken from Novara, but he was in such poor health that the journey to Lyon had to be made very slowly. On May 2 his party reached Lyon. A huge crowd gathered to watch as he was escorted to the citadel. The king and the Venetian ambassador were among the onlookers; the latter's report described Sforza as having the appearance of a very sick man, trembling in every limb. The ambassador reported that he was placed in an iron cage and added that Louis had changed his mind about imprisoning him in the tower of Loches because he liked to hunt in that area and did not wish ever to see his prisoner.[49] Sforza was instead taken to the fortress of Lys-St-Georges near Bourges, where he was kept in honorable captivity. After an escape attempt in 1505, he was taken to Loches and put under much more rigorous confinement. He died there in 1508 without ever meeting Louis. The king always refused his requests for interviews because he feared that il Moro would successfully use his great powers of persuasion on him. Sforza's burial place remains unknown.[50]

Louis had not spent all of the early months of 1500 worrying about the Italian campaign. He had passed much of his time in Lyon hunting in the mountains to the east of the city, one of his favorite hunting areas. In late May, after Sforza had been sent on to Lys-St-Georges, the king held a great tournament at Lyon. Fourteen famed knights dressed in white formed the king's party; and fourteen dressed in black made up the queen's, who had just arrived. Her team won the tournament. Jousting and other festivities continued for another fifteen days.[51]

Meanwhile, the French government for Milan was being reconstructed under the direction of Georges d'Amboise. Well before Sforza's capture, Louis had decided to put him in charge of Milan. He had full royal authority; in other words he became the viceroy of the duchy. With him went Jacques Hurault, one of the royal treasurers, and numerous other royal officers. They had left Lyon in February, so they were with the French army when it reentered Milan. On April 6 d'Amboise received the request for royal pardon from the city of Milan. All of the significant people and 4,000 children took part in a penitential procession to the cardinal's residence. After they had all assembled, a prominent Milanese lawyer pledged that the city would never again rebel against its rightful sovereign, the king of France. He added that he hoped the king, like Jesus Christ forgiving St. Peter for betraying him, would be merciful to his people. D'Amboise responded that he hoped Milan would not imitate Peter, who had betrayed his Master three times. The city agreed to provide 300,000 *écus*, down from the 800,000 first demanded, above its regular taxes to defray the cost of the reconquest. The cardinal then pardoned the city in the name of the king for its damnable treason, except for the principal leaders of the rebellion. The event ended with the 4,000 children crying *"Francia! Francia!* Mercy!"[52]

The cardinal was able to impose reasonably good behavior on the French troops, although they did loot Sforza's partisans. Trivulzio proved to be a major problem for d'Amboise, since he encouraged the French troops in their bad behavior toward his personal enemies, and most of the Milanese hated him. D'Amboise was also eager to get rid of a threat to his power in Milan. He sent letters to Louis asking for Trivulzio's recall. Louis agreed to appoint the cardinal's nephew, Charles de Chaumont d'Amboise, as commander of the French army in Milan. With virtually unlimited authority from the king and his nephew now commanding the military there, Cardinal d'Amboise would be the de facto ruler of the duchy of Milan for the next three years, although he frequently returned to the French court. In 1503 his nephew replaced him as governor.[53]

Louis XII had already established the basic system of French rule in Milan with his edict of November 1499. It had created the Milanese Senate or Parlement and a generality for fiscal matters.[54] The tax revenues of the duchy were vast, totaling under Sforza 1,686,000 *l*, according to a French source. Louis was content to take only 622,050 *l*, but local expenses ate up nearly all of that sum, for the pay of the French army in the duchy and the pensions given to the French nobles serving in high positions in the army and the ducal government. In 1510 a surplus of only 5,956 *l* was sent on to the French treasury, but by paying the cost of the large French army in Italy, the Milanese tax revenues reduced considerably the burden of the Italian wars on the French people.[55]

Despite what Louis regarded as open treason against him as sovereign lord of Milan, he was again very generous to the city in victory. It helped to secure his reputation as a generous and merciful king. It made French rule acceptable in Milan for the next decade, as there was little agitation there. The city's prosperity returned, and the export of grain, which Sforza had forbidden in 1499, was resumed in 1508.[56] However, the goodwill of the Milanese did little to help Louis make good his other ambition in Italy, the rule of Naples.

9

A Kingdom Won, a Kingdom Lost

irmly established in Milan, Louis XII now turned his attention to the other Italian domain he regarded as rightfully his—the kingdom of Naples. His claim to that realm was less immediate than the one to Milan, since it came through his status as the successor to Charles VIII, but that did not make him any less determined to make good his rights. The fact that King Federigo of Naples was openly aiding Ludovico Sforza only strengthened Louis's resolve.

The presence in southern Italy of several French garrisons, remnants of Charles VIII's expedition of 1494, gave Louis a toehold in the realm from which his army could operate. Before he could dispatch new forces southward, however, several problems in north Italy required solutions. One involved Florence's dispute with Pisa. The Florentines had conquered Pisa in 1406, but in 1494 the Pisans had ousted them. Since then Florence had Pisa under nearly constant siege, and the Florentine government urgently needed French aid for retaking it.[1] Louis and his advisers were rather miffed at Florence, because it had tried to maintain a strict neutrality between France and Milan, despite a long record of pro-French diplomacy. Their annoyance was tempered, however, by the awareness that any expedition to Naples would pass right by Florence. After the reconquest of Milan, the Florentine government pressed for the implementation of an agreement from 1499, which had pledged French aid for taking Pisa in exchange for 50,000 *écus* to pay the Swiss. The Florentines distributed 20,000 ducats among the king's ministers to encourage them in supporting the scheme against Pisa.[2]

Louis agreed to provide 600 French *gens d'armes* and 6,000 Swiss infantrymen under the command of Sire de Beaumont. The Florentines had insisted on him because he had handed a fortress over to them in 1494, as Charles VIII had ordered, unlike several other captains who had refused. Beaumont, however, was neither as experienced nor as well-regarded a commander as Louis's first choice, Yves d'Alègre. Beaumont found it impossible to maintain discipline among his men as they trudged toward

Pisa. Their behavior was atrocious, and, as was usual in an ill-disciplined army, many deserted.[3]

On June 29, 1500, a combined Florentine-French force set up siege lines and batteries around Pisa. Within a day the French guns had knocked down 100 feet of the city's medieval walls. When the assault troops reached the breach, they were astounded to find that the Pisans had thrown up an earthen wall behind the breach, bristling with guns. The sight of this "double Pisan rampart" so discouraged the besiegers that they refused to go forward.[4] Beaumont began to lose faith in the enterprise, as did his men, who deserted en masse. He wrote to Louis that the goal of the expedition was unattainable. On July 11 the remaining French forces broke camp and retreated to the north.[5]

The king was furious at the terrible showing of his forces and blamed Florence both for insisting on Beaumont and not paying the troops promptly. Niccolo Machiavelli was part of a delegation sent to France to appease Louis and persuade him that Florence was not responsible for the fiasco. Thus, that shrewd assessor of politics and men made his first contact with France and the French king. Among the things we learn from Machiavelli's reports is that the French court traveled incessantly, which made being accredited to the court very expensive for the ambassadors. Machiavelli constantly asked for more money for his expenses from the Florentine government. Louis's image as a parsimonious pincher of *deniers* was obvious to the Florentine delegation, as he demanded that Florence pay extra sums to his troops in Italy and provide a large enough amount to make a second attempt on Pisa. Machiavelli made an interesting comment on what he perceived to be the attitude of the king and his advisers toward the smaller powers like Florence: "The French are blinded by their own power, and only think those who are armed or ready to give money worthy of their esteem. They see that these two qualities are wanting in you [Florence], so they look upon you as Sir Nothing." He recommended that his government should use bribery to win friends at the French court, "who would be stirred by more than natural affection since that is what has to be done by all who have affairs at this court. And he who refuses to do it is like one who would win a suit without paying his attorney."[6]

Machiavelli made it clear in his dispatches that neither Louis nor Cardinal d'Amboise, who had returned from Milan by the time of his embassy, could speak Italian, although Louis seems to have learned some later.[7] Machiavelli not only had to deal with the anger of the king and his minister toward Florence for the failure of the Pisa campaign, but also the diplomacy of Alexander VI, who hoped to add Florence and Tuscany to the realm that Cesare Borgia was carving out of north-central Italy. When his fellow ambassador took ill in early September 1500, Machiavelli served alone at the court and came into close contact with Louis and d'Amboise for two months until a new ambassador arrived. He discerned that they had no real interest in seeing the Borgias successful in their designs for Italy, despite aiding them, but they did not know how to stop the Borgias. Machiavelli suggested that the cardinal had pushed the king into acquiescing in the Borgia program because he wanted to be elected pope and needed the support of the Borgia party. The Florentine also noted Louis's fear of the Germans, by whom he probably meant the Swiss, who were frequently referred to in this era as the "High Germans."

Machiavelli, who became quite close to Cardinal d'Amboise, warned him about the Borgias and the Venetians, who, he argued, were determined to thwart French designs for Italy. The cardinal responded that his master "had long ears and short belief, that he listened to all, but believed in nothing but that which he could touch with his own hands."[8] It was probably at this interview that d'Amboise told Machiavelli that the Italians did not understand war; the Italian replied that the French did not understand politics, for otherwise they would not have allowed the papacy to become so great.[9]

Machiavelli returned to Florence in late November 1500, having largely achieved his goal of placating the French by persuading his government to provide Louis with an additional 20,000 ducats. All of the money, however, had to go to the Swiss in the French army, who, as was their habit, had demanded a large sum to leave the service of the army that had hired them. In this case, they wanted two months' additional pay and a third month's pay for having handed over Ludovico Sforza. When they had first demanded the money, Louis had indignantly refused. They then, in September 1501, proceeded to occupy the fortified town of Bellinzona on the northern frontier of the duchy. Even after Louis gave them the 20,000 ducats he had acquired from Florence, they refused to leave the town on the grounds that Louis had granted them the place in the treaty by which he had recruited them. On several occasions small-scale hostilities broke out between them and French troops from Milan. Eighteen months of negotiations led by d'Amboise failed to get the Swiss to withdraw, and with the new expedition to Naples now under way, which required more Swiss mercenaries, Louis gave in. In April 1503 he conceded Bellinzona to the Swiss in perpetuity.[10] The relative ease with which the Swiss had gained their victory was an ominous portent for the future.

For Louis XII, however, the Bellinzona affair was a minor irritant in the midst of the new expedition to reclaim Naples. The king realized that winning back southern Italy required much more preparation and involved greater risk than had the conquest of Milan. He set about to neutralize or make allies of those states that were in a position to hinder his project. The governments of Europe had much the same reasons for objecting to the French occupation of Naples as they had had for Milan, and several had stronger ones. The papacy, certainly after Alexander VI was gone, would not have wanted to see the French in control of lands on both sides of Rome. The Ottoman Turks had their own ambitions in south Italy, having failed twenty years earlier in an invasion attempt across the Adriatic; they also were aware of the talk about using Naples as a base for a crusade against them. They increased their pressure on Venice to prevent it from aiding Louis.

It was Ferdinand of Aragon, however, who had the strongest reason to object. King Federigo of Naples was his relative; Ferdinand himself had a claim to the realm; and his troops occupied much of it. Either he would have to accept the humiliation of withdrawing them without a fight or risk a war with France. With the pope and Venice allied with France, although the Venetian government did advise Louis against the Neapolitan campaign, Ferdinand decided he was in no position to prevent a French victory in Naples. He looked rather to see what profit he could squeeze out of an unpromising situation. The outfitting of a large Spanish fleet, ostensibly for an attack on the Turks, convinced Louis that Ferdinand could be a real threat to his plans. Accordingly, he sent a secret embassy to Spain to negotiate a treaty with Isabella and Ferdinand. It was signed at Granada on November 11, 1500, and called for the division of the kingdom of Naples between Louis and Ferdinand, with the former getting the title of king of Naples and the northern half of the realm, and the latter the duchies of Apulia and Calabria. The revenues of the kingdom were to be split equally, and if one monarch were to get more out of his part, he was to make it up to the other.[11] The treaty was to be kept secret until both kings were ready to move into Naples.[12]

Louis's contemporaries and modern historians have severely criticized him for the Treaty of Granada. Guicciardini saw it as "greatly wanting in prudence." Machiavelli devoted several pages in *The Prince* to Louis's mistakes in Italy, including the grave one of bringing into the land "a very powerful foreigner . . . who was capable of driving him out." William Prescott, the nineteenth-century historian, convicts both Louis and Ferdinand of "political robbery . . . veiled under a detestable mask of hypocrisy," but he was convinced that Louis bore the greater blame.[13] Louis's policy in respect to Naples deserves censure in several respects, but the worst part was inviting Ferdinand to participate in the spoils. If

Ferdinand was so willing to betray his own kin, how much more quickly would he turn on the French king?

Oblivious to the danger and passing up an offer from Federigo of tribute of 100,000 ducats immediately and 50,000 annually for twenty-four years, Louis set 1,000 lances and 10,000 foot soldiers, including 5,000 Swiss, on the road to Naples in early June 1501. In May he had asked Bologna for the free passage of his army across its territory.[14] He gave the command to Béraud Stuart, who had served there before. Meanwhile, a powerful galley fleet under Philip of Cleves, Louis's cousin, embarked from Marseille with several thousand troops aboard. As the army neared Rome, the French and the Spanish ambassadors at the papal court revealed the secret agreement to Alexander VI. He received the news with enthusiasm and issued a bull naming the two kings as his vassals in Naples, which was still regarded as a papal fief. He deposed King Federigo for negotiating with the Turks, in 1499. The pope entertained the French captains in grand style and ordered Cesare to join them with his forces.[15]

Federigo was ignorant of his relative's treachery until the publication of the papal bull against him. Thus, he had allowed a Spanish fleet to land in Calabria and sent his son to the Spaniards for safekeeping. With several of his key forts already compromised, he gathered his remaining troops in Capua. The city had good defenses, but once the French siege train arrived, the defenders were reluctant to test the French guns. After a few shots they agreed to negotiate a surrender. Apparently the garrison was lax in defending the walls while the negotiations were going on, for French troops rushed the wall and broke in. Although the French had behaved with unusual decorum in the campaign to this point (Stuart was a stern disciplinarian), they abandoned all restraint inside Capua and plundered and raped mercilessly. According to several sources, Cesare Borgia selected thirty or forty of the city's most beautiful women and had them sent to Rome.[16]

When the news of the sack of Capua spread across southern Italy, no one wanted to resist further. Federigo fled to an island, and on August 4 Stuart entered Naples unopposed. He was able to keep his men under control there, so there was no repeat of the treatment of Capua. With all of his realm in French or Spanish hands, Federigo agreed to surrender to the French, since he felt nothing but hatred for his Spanish kin. He was taken to France, where he was granted an annual income of 20,000 *l* on the duchy of Anjou and a pension of 30,000 *l*. He agreed to the terms in order "to avoid shedding of blood."[17] He died at Tours in 1504. His son was sent to Spain, despite the pledge of both allied commanders that he could accompany his father to France.

For the moment the cooperation between the French and Spanish continued, as they turned their attention to the second part of the agreement—a crusade against the Turks. Once Louis had taken control of part of Italy, he was placed under great pressure to lead a crusade. Since the Turks were on the offensive against Hungary and the Venetian outposts in the eastern Mediterranean, Venice and the pope expected him to lead the effort to blunt the Muslim advance. Louis was amenable to the idea, as every Christian king of the era, even James IV of Scotland, thought of himself as the crusader king who would save Christendom. For the Venetians, Turkish advances in Hungary were as frightening as the loss of their eastern outposts; if Hungary was conquered, the Turks would be at the eastern frontier of the republic. Thus, they and the pope directed Louis's attention especially to helping King Ladislaus of Hungary. Alexander did his part by annulling Ladislaus's earlier marriage, allowing him to take a French bride, Anne de Foix-Candale, the daughter of Gaston of Foix-Candale. She had been raised at the French court. A marriage contract was signed in March 1501, and in July 1502 she left Blois for Buda, going via Venice. She died in childbirth in 1506, leaving an infant son who became King Louis II of Hungary.[18]

Louis was more directly involved in battling the Turks in the Mediterranean. Since 1494 the French galley fleet in the Mediterranean had been augmented considerably by using money drawn from the clergy for a crusade. In 1499 Louis sent twenty-two galleys to help Venice defend Lepanto against the Turks, but they could not prevent its fall. Louis wrote to the sultan demanding that he cease his attacks on his ally, but to no avail.[19] Now, in 1501, Philip of Cleves's fleet of some twenty galleys, arriving at Naples, found nothing further to do there and left for the Adriatic. There it joined with the fleets of Venice and the Knights of Rhodes, whose grand-master was one of the d'Amboises. They agreed to attack the Ottoman-held fortress of Mytelene on the southwest coast of Greece.

In mid-October, already late for a campaign in the Mediterranean, which can be treacherous in the winter, the allied galleys unloaded their fighting men and heavy guns to conduct a siege of Mytelene. It was the sort of amphibious operation at which galleys excelled. But when the allied force failed to take the fortress in several days, another feature of galley warfare came into play—the inability of a galley fleet to maintain itself for any length of time off a hostile coast because of the limited amount of water and rations that could be carried. A Venetian report also noted the lack of gunpowder. Six days later the allies reloaded their men and withdrew. They were caught in a terrible storm, which sunk two

French galleys with the loss of over 1,000 men.[20] This ill-fated expedition was the last time the French battled the Muslims in what may be termed a crusade. Two decades of French inactivity in the Christian war with Islam followed, and then France under Francis I began to develop a tacit alliance with the Ottoman Empire directed against Charles V.

The news of the defeat at Mytelene hardly distracted Louis and d'Amboise from the task of establishing an administration for the French part of Naples. Louis first granted a general amnesty to those who had fought against him, since the French regarded them as traitors against their rightful sovereign.[21] Jean Nicolay, a magistrate from the Parlement of Toulouse, was named chancellor of the kingdom with a salary of 1,500 *l.* While Nicolay, as his correspondence shows, seems to have been an honest and capable man, many of the other Frenchmen placed in offices in Naples were not. Louis was largely interested in using the opportunity to satisfy his entourage with church benefices, offices, and estates.[22] The greed of those he placed in power there was a major cause of both the disaffection of the Neapolitan people from French rule and the eventual failure of the French forces. For example, Yves d'Alègre, a well-respected captain, sold a large quantity of wheat intended for the French army to the Venetians. The Spanish captured the Venetian ship carrying the wheat and sent it on to their forces. Perhaps the worst example of Louis's personnel decisions was the appointment in late 1501 of Louis de Nemours as his commander in southern Italy to replace Stuart. Although Nemours was from the great House of Armagnac, he was young and rash and not the man to replace the respected veteran. It created resentment, and more seriously, Nemours was eager to fight the Spanish in order to prove himself.[23]

Louis was keenly interested in the Neapolitan revenues, which he expected to use to make his Italian campaigns self-supporting. The gross revenues assigned to the French king came to 571,000 *l* in 1502, while the expenses of the French administration came to 560,000 *l.* Louis had great trouble getting the surplus money from Naples and may never have received any of it. One of his first acts was to order the minting of a new ducat for Naples with his name, title of king of France and Naples, and bust on one side, and the phrase *Perdem Babilonis Nomen,* "I shall destroy the name of Babylon!" on the other. It is generally assumed that Babylon referred to the Turks, although there is also speculation that the papacy was the target.[24]

The problem of sharing the revenues between France and Spain precipitated war. By the beginning of 1502, relations between the French and the Spanish in Naples had become very edgy. The two sovereigns began to negotiate their differences, but, without waiting for any conclusion, in

April 1502 Nemours attacked the Spanish in Apulia. Inferior to the French in numbers, Gonsalvo de Cordoba retreated into the fortress of Barletta on the Adriatic, which Nemours placed under siege in July.[25]

Louis was deeply angered to hear of the renewed fighting. He immediately returned to Lyon, which he had left only the previous October, and remained there for most of the next two years, to be closer to the action in Italy. He had a postal service established between Lyon and Milan, where news of Italy was collected. The post was regarded as so reliable that foreign ambassadors used it for their dispatches.[26] The king dispatched money and reinforcements to Naples. His attention to events in southern Italy was distracted, however, by Cesare Borgia's activity in Tuscany, which was threatening Florence, France's close ally. Having seized control of nearly all of the Romagna, Borgia was eager to extend his domains. Pisa, Florence's bitter rival, had offered the keys of the city to him and flew his standard on its walls. Florence demanded that Louis rein in Borgia. The king decided to go to Milan in order to deal with Cesare directly. On July 8 he reached Asti and sent a message to Borgia warning him not to make any move against Florence. Cesare, convinced that in person he could overcome any problems with the French king, went to Milan to meet with Louis.

Upon Borgia's arrival in Milan on August 5, 1502, Louis greeted him effusively but did press him into dropping any designs against Florentine territory. He agreed to provide Cesare with 300 lances for his other projects. The two men then rode to Genoa, where Louis made his formal entry into the city on August 26. St-Gelais and d'Auton both made special mention of the 3,000 Genoese women dressed in white silk, damask, or taffeta who participated in the entry procession.[27] The entry ceremonies of French cities did not include many women, certainly not as many as at Genoa, which had a reputation for its beautiful ladies.

It was in the context of the beauty of Genoese women that d'Auton introduced Tommasina Spinola, "one of the most beautiful of Italian ladies." According to the French author, she fell deeply in love with Louis, "a marvelously handsome man." He reciprocated with a platonic love that was completely honorable, the love of a knight errant for his lady. Because of her feeling for him, said d'Auton, she refused to sleep any more with her husband. And Louis responded to her love by being far more generous to the Genoese in regard to taxes and privileges than he had intended to be. This story has held the attention of historians ever since, and they have devoted a great deal of effort to identifying Tommasina Spinola. Although there were seven women with that name in Genoa in 1502, none fits d'Auton's heroine in age. More significantly, none died in 1505, as d'Auton stated that Louis's Tommasina did when she heard the rumor that he had died during his serious illness of that year.[28] There are other versions of the story. One from 1562 proposes that Louis, hearing of the lady's renowned beauty and wondering if it was natural or from makeup, visited her home early one morning while she was still in bed. When she appeared before the king in her negligee without any makeup, Louis found that she was even more beautiful than he had been told.[29] The other version, in Bernard Quilliet's recent biography, finds a far less honorable explanation for the story. Drawing on the fact that in 1502 one of the Tommasinas was twenty-three years old and married to an old man, Quilliet proposes that the city leaders had her try to seduce the king in order to persuade him to be generous to their city. He does not reach a conclusion on whether she was successful beyond noting that Louis was indeed generous to Genoa.[30]

Entertaining Borgia was not the only thing that Louis did in Italy that summer. He thoroughly examined the administration of Milan and found that all but one of his officers were doing their duty loyally and justly. The one who was not was the chancellor, Pierre Sacierges, bishop of Luçon, about whom he had heard loud complaints. Sacierges was promptly replaced, for "the king is not in the habit of reappointing anyone whose abuse of office is obvious." After the ceremonies in Genoa, Louis and Cesare returned to Asti, where Cesare took leave of the king. The king then crossed back into France, arriving at Grenoble on September 15.[31]

Unfortunately for his prospects in Naples, Louis was not paying the same attention to his officers there, since his commander, Louis de Nemours, was flitting away an excellent opportunity to drive the Spanish out. The expected quick victory never came, because Nemours refused to push an assault on Barletta, expecting that it would fall into his hands without one. Meanwhile, Spanish reinforcements were pouring into the region, whereas a large part of the intended French reinforcements had been sidetracked for Cesare Borgia's benefit. In January 1503 a local noble, noting the dramatic buildup of Consalvo's forces, predicted a Spanish victory.[32]

In February the French suffered a blow when a small galley fleet under Prégent de Bidoux, operating in the Adriatic, was caught in the harbor of Otranto and captured. Otranto was a Venetian possession, and Prégent had been misled by its governor's promise not to allow the Spanish to attack him there. Louis was furious with his erstwhile ally when he heard the news. He spotted the Venetian ambassador at Mass soon after and lambasted him throughout the service. The ambassador reported that he could not hear a word of the Mass because of Louis's tirade. The king demanded that Venice compensate him for the loss of his galleys, but the city refused.[33]

The boredom of the sporadic fighting in southern Italy gave rise to three events that have fascinated contemporary authors and modern historians alike. All involved formal individual combat, and the first two included as a participant Pierre de Bayard, *le chevalier sans peur et sans reproche*, as he soon became known. He was from Dauphiné and had been fighting in Italy since 1494, earning a reputation as a bold and powerful man-at-arms. The first episode of the three was called "The Combat of the Eleven," as eleven *gens d'armes* from both sides engaged in armed combat in a tournament setting. The event came about because of French taunts that the Spanish horsemen were cowards for refusing to meet the French heavy cavalry in hand-to-hand combat and their reputation as horse killers. Enraged by the taunts, the Spaniards offered to prove the French wrong. Eleven champions from each side were chosen, and the combat took place under Venetian supervision at Trani. After a time, only two Frenchmen remained mounted, but those two, Bayard and François d'Urfé, fought the nine remaining Spaniards to a draw.[34]

Soon after this Bayard, leading a small troop of French horse, defeated a larger body of Spanish cavalry and captured the captain, one Alonso de Sotomayor. After he had been ransomed, Sotomayor accused Bayard of not treating him as a gentleman. When Bayard heard of this insult to his honor, he demanded that Sotomayor retract his charge or meet him in single combat. Sotomayor, of course, refused to retract it, and on February 1, 1503, the two met, again at Trani, to fight to the death. Since Bayard was the challenger, Sotomayor had the choice of fighting style; aware of Bayard's reputation as a horseman, he chose to fight on foot, as he was the larger and stronger man. Nonetheless, Bayard struck a well-placed thrust with his dagger at his foe's neck and killed him.[35]

The third event took place without Bayard. After a brief fight in which several French *gens d'armes* were captured, the Spanish captain gave the honors of battle to a body of Italian horsemen who had fought with him. The French were deeply insulted that Italians, whom they had constantly defeated, should be so honored. After an exchange of insults, it was agreed that thirteen French men-at-arms would fight thirteen Italians in the same lists at Trani. In the formal combat that followed, victory went to the Italians, to the enormous pleasure of all Italy.[36] Besides demonstrating the level of boredom that must have permeated all the forces in southern Italy, the episodes show that a spirit of chivalry, albeit a decadent chivalry, still flourished at the turn of the sixteenth century.

Real battle came quickly enough after these episodes. It was set up by a whirlwind round of diplomacy that Louis undertook to buttress the tenuous hold his forces had over Naples. He had been able to establish a close relationship with Archduke Philip of Austria, who was Emperor Maximilian's son, Ferdinand and Isabella's son-in-law, and the ruler of the Low Countries. In early 1503 Louis invited him to return to France, through which he had passed on his way to Spain the year before. The two princes met at Lyon and, on April 5, 1503, signed a treaty that was intended to apply to Maximilian and the Spanish monarchs as well as to the signatories. It confirmed the marriage contract from the year previous, betrothing Louis's infant daughter Claude to Philip's son of nearly the same age, Charles. The new treaty provided that once they were wed, the two children would gain the titles of southern Italy. Until that time, a French and a Spanish administrator would govern the two divisions of the kingdom of Naples, and there would be an immediate halt to the fighting.[37]

Festivals were held in Lyon and Paris to celebrate the new peace,[38] while both Louis and Philip sent dispatches to the two commanders to stop fighting and restore recently seized areas. Louis also halted the planned embarkation of more troops for Naples. Ferdinand and Isabella, however, hardly felt obligated by a treaty their son-in-law had signed. Two months earlier they had written to Gonsalvo that they had no intention of ending the war and Philip's trip was intended to deceive Louis. It seems very unlikely that Philip was aware of this.[39] When Ferdinand and Isabella heard of Philip's agreement, they declared that he had exceeded his authority and had been duped by the French king.[40] Gonsalvo was told to ignore Philip's orders and pursue the war. Reinforced by troops from Spanish-held Sicily, the Great Captain took his men out of Barletta. Nemours gathered his forces and moved to confront him in April 1503. Aware of the approach of the French army, Gonsalvo halted his troops below the hilltop town of Cerignola. A ditch already in place around the base of the hill was deepened and widened, and the dirt was thrown up behind it to form a rampart. Sharpened stakes were driven into the floor of the ditch. Most of Gonsalvo's 7,000 men were infantrymen, the bulk of whom were Spanish arquebusmen, flanking a corps of German pikemen.

Nemours's forces were, as was typical for a French army, much stronger in cavalry. He formed his army into the standard three divisions, but their arrangement was highly unusual. His right wing consisted of his cavalry; his center, Swiss pikemen; and his left, German and French crossbowmen; and they formed in echelon—in a diagonal line with his right division forward and his left well back. Several of the most experienced

French captains were reluctant to attack the well-entrenched Spanish line. Nemours was determined to prove his mettle, and the captains of the Swiss declared that they would not stay with the French if he did not order an assault. Nemours led his *gens d'armes* toward the enemy, but they were brought up short by the ditch. As Nemours rode along the ditch looking for a place to cross, he was hit by an arquebus ball and killed. Meanwhile, the center division of Swiss pikemen reached the ditch. Taking heavy fire, they scrambled across the ditch, but they had lost their momentum and were not able to push the enemy's pikemen back from the rampart on the opposite side. With casualties rapidly mounting from the arquebus fire, the French army broke ranks and ran. A hard pursuit by the Spanish inflicted a great many more casualties.[41]

This Battle of Cerignola marked the first time that firearms were the major determining element in a battle. It also was the first time that the Spanish had defeated the French in a major confrontation; thus, it was a major turning point marking the rise of Spain as a military power and its general superiority over France for the next 140 years. More immediately, the defeat at Cerignola proved disastrous for French interests in southern Italy. Most of the French-held strongholds, largely stripped of their garrisons for the battle, quickly surrendered, as the Spanish army passed by them on its way to Naples, which enthusiastically welcomed Gonsalvo. The remaining French forces, 2,000 foot soldiers and 300 *gens d'armes*, withdrew into the powerful fortress of Gaeta on the coast north of Naples.

Still, Gaeta gave the French a toehold for retaking the lost territory, and Louis XII tirelessly set about gathering a new army to send to Naples. In a letter to his officers at Gaeta, Louis indicated that he still hoped that the Spanish monarchs would repudiate Gonsalvo's acts and adhere to the treaty he had signed with Archduke Philip. But in the meantime, he was working day and night to make provisions for their aid by land and sea.[42] In a letter to the city of Paris, he asked for subsidy of 40,000 *l* to help him make good the losses caused by "the evil and disloyal turn" that the Spanish monarchs had made against him "after their son [-in-law] had with their consent sworn the peace treaty." The city offered only 20,000 *l*; Louis came back with a request for 30,000 *l*, to which the city agreed.[43] The other cities of the realm were expected to contribute at the same rate as Paris; but the nobles, generally very niggardly in giving money to the monarchy, contributed more generously. Pierre de Gié gave 25,000 *l* and financiers Jacques de Beaune and Thomas Bohier each contributed 20,000 *l*. The members of the parlements and the fiscal courts were also dunned for money.[44] The *bailli* of Dijon was sent back into the Alps to recruit Swiss mercenaries, and the most respected French captain, Louis de La Trémoille, was called out of retirement to command the new army.

In early June 1503 ambassadors arrived at Lyon from Spain to justify Gonsalvo's acts. Archduke Philip was still present, and he, Louis, and the ambassadors had a very heated exchange. The Spaniards claimed that Philip did not have the authority to bind their rulers. Philip retorted that he had a letter with their seals empowering him to negotiate with Louis. The ambassadors replied that if the French king wanted a treaty with Spain, he needed to deal with them and not depend on something that Philip "pulled out of his sleeve." Philip became so agitated that he had to retire to his chamber, but he soon returned to tell Louis that he had done nothing for which he could be reproached. Louis replied that he knew the goodwill of the archduke and ordered the ambassadors to leave his kingdom in three days or suffer the consequences.[45]

After this episode, Louis decided to force the Spanish monarchs to repudiate Gonsalvo's work by sending a fleet against the Spanish coast and two armies across the Pyrenees in two different places, calling out the feudal levy to augment his forces. None of these forces accomplished anything of substance. In late October 1503 Louis was forced to negotiate a truce for the Spanish theater, which allowed Ferdinand to concentrate on Italy.[46]

In the summer of 1503 Louis was also busy reinforcing and resupplying what was left of his army in southern Italy. In early June, for example, four carracks (large cargo ships) with 500 crossbowmen from Genoa and 7,000 *castres* of wheat sailed for Naples. A month later La Trémoille's army of 1,200 *gens d'armes* and 10,000 infantrymen began to march southward.[47] As his forces approached Rome, word came of the death of Alexander VI. The suddenness of his death and the speed with which his body bloated and blackened were regarded as powerful reasons in that era for suspecting poisoning, but the charge was never substantiated. The Borgias had been helpful to Louis, even if their help was always self-serving. For example, Alexander, shortly before his death, had proposed that the papacy would bear two-thirds of the expense of the war if Cesare would be given the title of king of Sicily.[48] But Louis could hardly have regretted the opportunity to put a true friend on the throne of St. Peter—Cardinal d'Amboise, whose ambition to become pope had long been obvious.

When word of Alexander's death reached Lyon, Louis immediately ordered La Trémoille to halt his forces in the vicinity of Rome in order to influence the conclave electing the new pope. He also expected that Cesare would support d'Amboise's candidacy by directing the cardinals he controlled to vote for him. Cesare, however, was also seriously ill when his

father died and was in no position to exercise the control Louis expected
of him, not that he was as committed to electing d'Amboise as Louis
thought. Thus, a compromise candidate emerged as pope — a sickly man of
sixty-three years who took the name of Pius III and reigned for under two
months.[49] The delay that the election caused for the French army on its
way to Naples proved to be most costly to French plans. The halt in the
heat of the Italian summer resulted in the inevitable desertions and deaths
from disease, especially malaria, so prevalent in the area about Rome.
More seriously La Trémoille himself became ill and returned to France.
Louis replaced him with an Italian condottiere, Francesco Gonzaga, the
marquis of Mantua. The marquis was a respected and experienced captain, but he could not hold the loyalty of the men of the French army the
way La Trémoille had.[50]

Gonsalvo took advantage of the extra six weeks the French gave him to
establish a strong defensive position along the south bank of the
Garigliano River, which entered the sea a few miles south of Gaeta.[51] It
was too swift to ford until well upstream from his position. When the
French army arrived in the vicinity in early October, the marquis, after
some hesitation over how to proceed, decided to bring the French fleet up
the river to build a bridge out of boats and allow the French to cross.
Prégent de Bidoux, who was equal to most tasks asked of him, succeeded
in building the floating bridge, and did it well enough that it lasted for two
months in the river's swift current. Before the Spanish realized what had
happened, a small force of French *gens d'armes* crossed in order to secure
the bridge head. The enemy, rushing to the scene, fell on the French, and
in the ferocious battle that followed, Bayard added to his already stellar
reputation by holding off 200 Spaniards nearly single-handed, if his biographer can be believed. Regardless of the real extent of Bayard's prowess,
the French kept control of the bridge, since a small force could defend it,
but the marquis of Mantua decided not to risk his army against the large
force Gonsalvo had posted just beyond the bridge.

Both armies settled in close to the bridge to wait for their opportunity.
By this time, it was November, and the weather had become atrocious.
The locals regarded the rains as the worst in memory. The armies quickly
stripped the region bare of food and fodder. In that respect, the French
should have been in the better situation, since they were closer to Rome
than the Spanish were to Naples and ought to have been able to draw supplies from there more easily. However, the French agents in Rome had
been busy pocketing much of the gold sent to support the army in the
south.[52] Thus, the French forces were as miserable as the Spanish, and

neither the French *gens d'armes* nor the Swiss mercenaries accepted their situation as stoically as did the Spanish peasants who made up most of Gonsalvo's army. Perhaps even worse for the French, the lack of fodder was decimating their horses, and the strengths of their army—the gendarmerie and the artillery—both depended on horses.

In late December 1503 Gonsalvo, eager to relieve his men of their misery, decided to make his move.[53] The materials to make a bridge of boats were quietly gathered, and it was then thrown across the Garigliano under the cover of darkness. Distracted by a dawn attack on the bridge they controlled, the French did not realize the Spanish had crossed the river until Spanish units attacked them on their side of the river. The French captains hastily decided on a fighting retreat to Gaeta, calling on Prégent to bring his galleys upriver and load the heavy artillery. The hopes of some Frenchmen for a quick return to France were dashed when several of Prégent's galleys, loaded with heavy guns and men, sank at the mouth of the Garigliano. A squad of *gens d'armes* formed the rearguard of the French army. Bayard, who according to his biographer had three horses killed under him, and the other heavy troopers managed to delay the Spanish until the majority of the French had reached the fortress of Gaeta.

The security of Gaeta was only temporary, as Gonsalvo quickly arrived to lay siege to it. The French were not prepared, mentally or physically, to wage a strong defense of the fortress. Gonsalvo had just arrived when a herald approached him with a request for a truce. Knowing that his forces were hardly better prepared for a long siege, Gonsalvo granted terms. The French would evacuate Gaeta, leaving all of their guns and supplies behind, and be free to return to France either by sea or through Italy. On January 1, 1504, the Spanish entered the last major French stronghold in the kingdom of Naples. A few French units remained scattered across the region. In particular, the noted captain Louis d'Ars held the fortress of Venosa in Apulia. The Spanish set about to clear them out, but Venosa held out until Louis, despairing of the situation, ordered d'Ars to abandon his post and return to France. D'Ars and his small band of men proudly and in good order made their way across Italy, unlike the several thousand survivors from Gaeta, many of whom never made it home. When d'Ars reached the court at Blois, Louis, trying to salvage some pride and honor from the debacle in Naples, treated him like a conquering hero.[54]

When Louis received word of Gaeta's surrender, he waxed philosophical: "If this time the scourge of fortune has struck to the quick, at another time good luck will let me recover my loss, . . . for my misfortune is not without remedy."[55] In fact, he was not at all willing to leave his claim to the kingdom of Naples to the whims of fate, even if in the foreseeable future there was little chance of assembling another army to win it back by force. Louis turned for the time being to complicated diplomatic maneuvers to secure his rights in southern Italy.

Nor was the king philosophical in his response to those he considered responsible for the disaster in Naples. He refused to send the surviving officers and soldiers of the defeated army money or transportation to return them to France. It is true, however, that with the loss of most of Prégent's galleys at the mouth of the Garigliano River, there were only five galleys left in the French fleet in the Mediterranean, and Louis dared not risk them at sea in the winter storms.[56] The French troops, completely destitute, straggled northward through Italy; the Italians ill-treated them in retaliation for the insults and arrogance of the previous summer. Even hardened observers were moved to compassion by the sight of these men "robbed and plundered by the peasants . . . and coming naked into Rome." A Florentine wrote: "The King of France did not send them any succor but seemed to have forgotten them."[57] There is no count of how many soldiers did reach their homes, but based on the Italian reports, the number was small. Even the highest-ranking officers such as Yves d'Alègre were not able to return to France—in their case because Louis refused them permission to reenter his realm. Louis's governor at Milan was told to hold all those captains and men-at-arms who had ill-served the king in Naples.[58]

If Louis's treatment of the defeated army was harsh, he was even more bitter toward his financial officers for Naples. They were accused of having defrauded the king of 1,200,000 *l* intended for the army. Louis de Sandricourt, the *bailli* of Blois and a companion of Louis's from his youth, told him that by their malfeasance his treasurers had caused the deaths of 30,000 French troops and 2,000 *gens d'armes*. Some twenty fiscal officers, serving in both France and Italy during the campaign, were accused, but the number convicted was much smaller. Five were condemned to having their properties confiscated, three of whom were given the additional penalty of being pilloried. Two officials, condemned to death, were pardoned but imprisoned. One of them, the *bailli* of Dijon, the most prominent of the officials charged, was soon returned to his offices. Apparently no one was executed. The trials were held in a number of towns across France, giving rise to the speculation that Louis was trying to restore popular confidence in the royal administration and convince the people that the debacle in Naples was the fault of wrongdoers.[59] Nonetheless, all of Louis's efforts to punish his fiscal officers, his callous neglect of the sufferings of his troops, and fervent wishes failed to change one very salient point: The kingdom of Naples, so easily won ten years earlier, had been irretrievably lost.

10

Father of Claude, Father of the People

Before the investigation of the fiscal officers was completed, Louis, now forty, fell seriously ill while at Lyon in January 1504.[1] His contemporaries attributed his illness to being heart-sick over the loss of Naples, and stress does exacerbate both chronic illnesses, malaria and Graves' disease, which Louis may have had. The contemporary sources confuse this illness with the more serious episode of 1505, so it is difficult to determine exactly what happened when; for example, whether it was in 1504 or 1505 that Francis of Angoulême was told to come to the court to prepare for his succession. It is clear that in both episodes, Louis's physicians and those close to him thought he was dying, but in both, he rallied after several months to resume his normal life. In 1504, after a month of being prostrate in bed, Louis was well enough to be taken to Blois. His physicians felt his native air would be good for him. By May he had recovered sufficiently to resume nearly his usual routine.[2] However, his habits became more sedate, and for the next ten years his private life became very regular.

In 1504 the danger that the king would die and nine-year-old Francis would have to take the crown led to discussions about the need for a possible regent. Louis wanted Anne to serve, but there was a problem with that scenario: She had not yet been crowned as Louis's queen. Neither the queen's coronation nor her formal entry into Paris had taken place when tradition dictated—two years after her husband's succession. They had been planned for January 1501, two years after Louis married her. He had sent a letter to Paris ordering the city to prepare for her entry. However, this was the first time the realm had faced the question of how to treat a queen who was married to two kings, since she had already been crowned and made an entry in 1492 for Charles VIII. Some courtiers felt Anne did not need to go through the ceremonies again. That view, along with the earlier criticism of her in Paris, especially from the university, led Louis abruptly to cancel the plans.[3] Anne resisted any suggestion that she undertake the two ceremonies until Louis's ill health made it very possible that she would serve as regent for Francis of Angoulême. In October 1504 Louis sent a letter to the Parisian municipality informing it that his "very beloved and dear companion the Queen has decided to make her entry into our good city of Paris." He requested that the city prepare to greet her the same as it would for "our own person." The city agreed to give her a gift of 10,000 *l* this time, instead of the 5,000 *l* it had offered in 1501.[4]

On December 18, 1504, Cardinal d'Amboise crowned Anne at St-Denis. There was one innovation in the ceremony. Before it began, Anne took off her wedding ring and sent it to the cardinal; in the course of the coronation, he gave it back to her as a sign that the queen was wedded to the realm. It seems to have been the first time this symbolism was used in the queen's coronation. The queen was hailed as the second person in the realm after her husband, worthy of receiving all his rights, honors, and powers. This suggests that the groundwork for the appointment of Anne as regent, should Louis soon die, was being prepared.[5]

Two days later Anne arrived at the St-Denis gate of Paris. From there she was escorted into the city by her husband, who by tradition was absent from her coronation, and the city's leaders and principal churchmen. An actor recited a poem that described the fealty the city owed to its "principal princess." At the five stops between the gate and Notre Dame, Anne and her entourage were entertained and edified by mystery plays and poetry. After a stop for a prayer at the cathedral, the party went on to a banquet put on by the city. Both in motif and decoration, Anne's entry was still largely medieval.[6]

The royal couple stayed on in Paris for several weeks for the tournaments and other games staged for their entertainment. Putting a pall over the festivities, however, was Pierre de Gié's trial for lèse-majesté. While the king was incapacitated in 1504, Gié had run the government, since Cardinal d'Amboise was in Germany negotiating with Maximilian. While the cardinal was hardly well loved at the court, his power and influence were not as greatly resented as Gié's. As a Breton noble, he was an outsider, and his second marriage to Marguerite d'Armagnac, sister to the duke of Nemours killed in the Battle of Cerignola, was also a cause of resentment, since she passed him the title of duke of Nemours and its vast estates. Conveniently, Gié's oldest son married the younger sister, Charlotte, to ensure that the Armagnac inheritance stayed in his family. When d'Amboise returned to the French court in March, he set about to reduce his rival's power.[7] There is no evidence the cardinal intended the complete destruction of the marshal's authority, but that was the consequence of what he began.

On March 22, 1504, a young member of Louise of Savoy's household, Pierre de Pontbriand, whom Gié had placed there, approached the king as he was being carried on a litter through the gardens of Blois.[8] Pontbriand tried to make an accusation against Gié, but Louis brushed him off. The young man returned two days later, blocking the king's path until he heard him out. Louis then told Pontbriand to relate the charges to d'Amboise. The cardinal was quick to see how the accusations could be used to undo Gié's power. He had a deposition drawn up and taken to the marshal. According to the royal *procureur général*, Pierre Bonnin, who zealously prosecuted the case, Gié "wept and lamented when he read it, saying that he was lost and confessing that it was true." Bonnin also deduced his guilt from the fact that he then fled the court "like a fugitive, without saying *adieu.*"[9] It is certainly true that by leaving the court the irate marshal gave the appearance of guilt and, more important, removed himself from the scene, giving his enemies the king's ear. Among those enemies, Queen Anne figured very prominently. She hated Gié for his role in defeating her father during the Breton War early in the reign of Charles VIII. The records of the case made it clear that Gié also disliked the queen and was well aware of her attitude toward him.

The charges against Gié made up twenty-three articles in the indictment. Nearly all of them in some fashion centered around his office as guardian for young Francis of Angoulême. When Louis became king, he had given the guardianship over his young relative, established in the agreement of 1496, to Gié. Recognizing the potential for power and influence the office offered him, Gié was far more active than Louis had been. Louise of Savoy was very jealous of her place as mother to the successor to the throne, her "Caesar" as she called him in her diary, and she chafed under Gié's supervision. Several incidents, such as when one of his men, told to escort the prince to Mass, found the door bolted to Louise's chamber, where Francis slept, and broke it down, created bad blood between them.[10]

The charges against Gié ranged from the petty to the truly serious. Among the former was the accusation that he had told Louise that Queen Anne hated her. The heart of the indictment was the charge that the marshal was planning a coup d'état in connection with the king's illness of 1504, which Gié was said to have been convinced was terminal. The indictment accused him, anticipating the king's death, of ordering his men at Amboise, Angers, Loches, and Tours to take control of the roads and bridges and not let anyone pass. His alleged purposes: first, to prevent Queen Anne from returning to Brittany as she had after Charles VIII's death; second, to take control of the person of Francis of Angoulême so he could dominate the new government; and third, to usurp Anne's position as head of the regency council for the new king. The often-repeated story that Gié's men actually stopped the queen in her barge, loaded with her jewels and household goods, as she was about to leave for Brittany seems to be apocryphal. There is no mention of it in the indictment or the testimony of witnesses. Surely it would have been included, had it occurred, as the most egregious example of Gié's breaching his authority. The tale probably arose out of Anne's voyage to Brittany after Charles's death and Gié's statements that he would not allow that to happen again.

Once the charges had been drawn up, Louis, pressed by Anne, agreed to have the Grand Conseil hear the case, despite his own reluctance to believe that the marshal was guilty. Bonnin, as *procureur général* for that court, was given the case, and he proved to be a relentless prosecutor. In early July 1504 he began to interview witnesses. Most of the captains and lieutenants serving under Gié, including Pontbriand's brother, were interviewed. However, Bonnin could find nothing that supported the charge of treason. When Pontbriand was interviewed, he backed down from a number of allegations but maintained enough to allow the case to proceed. Louise was interviewed on July 17 at Amboise and provided little support for the indictment. She did report on the marshal's opinion that the queen deeply disliked him, which concerned him little, she quoted him as saying, because he expected to have the first place under Francis. The members of the Grand Conseil met with Gié in October at Orléans for a week. He denied doing anything wrong and was able to provide a good explanation for all that he had done or said. The council then recalled most of the earlier witnesses to confront them with Gié's statements. Direct confrontations between him and several hostile witnesses, including Louise and Pontbriand, took place.

In early December Bonnin gave a vehement address before the judges, demanding that the marshal be found guilty of lèse-majesté and condemned to death. Nonetheless, the Grand Conseil, headed by Chancellor Guy de Rochefort, refused to convict. The case was adjourned for three months during which Gié was to be at liberty. Having failed to win a conviction, Gié's foes should have been stymied, but now a far more formidable opponent entered the lists. Queen Anne, whose hostility toward Gié the witnesses mentioned, heard what he was reported to have said about her, and she was furious. She prevailed on Louis to move the case to the Parlement of Toulouse, which operated under the rules of evidence for Roman law; they were far less favorable to defendants. The king justified the move on the grounds that the Grand Conseil was too busy with other matters. Anne went to Brittany to direct the search for witnesses and documents to use against Gié, and she established a special courier service to Toulouse. The zealous Bonnin remained the prosecutor, and he went so far as to argue that the Parlement ought not assign a defense counsel to Gié because of the heinous crimes of which he was accused. The magistrates rejected Bonnin's argument, but the enormous difficulty they had in finding a lawyer to defend the marshal nearly made it true.

During the summer of 1505 the Parlement of Toulouse heard numerous new witnesses. The topics they concentrated on were the relationship between Gié and Louise and the past crimes of the Rohans, Gié's family. Gié asked that the king himself be interviewed, but there is no mention of any royal testimony. Louis was kept informed of the progress of the case, since he issued numerous patents authorizing the various aspects of both the prosecution and the defense.

On February 9, 1506, the Parlement rendered its verdict: Gié was cleared of the most serious charges but convicted of certain excesses and faults, largely in regard to personal use of royal troops. He was removed as guardian for Francis of Angoulême and suspended for five years from his office as marshal. He was enjoined from appearing at court for those five years or even coming within ten leagues of it, and required to repay the government 10,800 *l* for his misuse of royal troops.[11] The Parlement of Toulouse had run up an enormous bill in the case; it came to 35,905 *l*. For example, Bonnin submitted a bill for 744 *l*. Since the queen had been involved as a plaintiff, the bill was passed on to her treasurer. Brantôme quoted Anne as saying that she did not want to see Gié executed because death was a cure for all of one's woes and she wanted him to suffer for a long time.[12]

Gié retired to his Château of Le Verger near Angers, where the king had stayed on his return from Nantes in 1499. The episode gave rise to a jest of the Basoche, the satirists of the era (See below, Chapter 11): "A marshal wanted to mount an ass [*âne*] but she gave him so strong a kick that she booted him out of the court, over the walls, and into the vineyard [*verger*]." He remained at La Verger the rest of his life supervising his estates, but died in 1513 at Paris, where he had a house. It appears that he never had contact with Louis after the king let his appeal for a pardon go unanswered. With Gié disgraced, Cardinal d'Amboise became the sole administrator of the realm, and with the king's health as it was, his power was even greater than simply taking over Gié's clout. Louise was forced to swallow her pride and write a humble apology to Anne for the comments attributed to her, claiming that Pontbriand had made them up.[13]

Anne and Louise were reluctant allies against the marshal because a major issue in the case involved their children—whether Claude and Francis would be married. Hardly had Claude taken her first breath when it was proposed that she be betrothed to her cousin Francis. The queen was fiercely opposed to the idea. Part of her opposition stemmed from a visceral dislike for Louise, probably because Louise did not disguise her ambitions for her son and openly rejoiced in each stillbirth Anne had. After one of them, Louise wrote in her diary: "Anne, queen of France . . . had a son, but he could not retard the exaltation of my Caesar because he was lacking in life."[14]

Perhaps even more a factor in her antagonism to the proposed marriage was her powerful Breton separatism. Should she die without a son, Brittany would go to Claude, and it would revert to its former autonomy. Claude's marriage to the successor to the French throne would compromise that autonomy, as Anne's marriage to two French kings had, while her marriage to a foreign prince would buttress it. Louise also objected to the betrothal, but her reasons are more obscure than Anne's. Both women tacitly agreed to oppose the marriage. On the other hand, Gié, although a Breton, strongly supported the union of Brittany and France and, therefore, urged the betrothal of Claude and Francis. He believed that the marriage was necessary for the future greatness of the French monarchy, to which he had committed his loyalty. During his trial, he admitted to promoting the marriage until the king settled the issue. But there is reason to think that he continued to urge that it take place.

Louis apparently favored the proposed marriage early on, but under the influence of his wife, he began to see his daughter's hand as a diplomatic trump card. Her future inheritance was a valuable prize. If she never had a brother, which was appearing more and more likely since Anne's two pregnancies after Claude's birth had resulted in stillbirths, she would inherit Brittany and the Orléanist lands—Orléans, Blois, Coucy, Asti, and Milan. Louis had not returned his family lands in France to the monarchy but had kept them as his private property. Eager to secure the place of his family, Louis was prepared to ignore the threat that control of those lands by a foreign prince would pose to the next French king.

It did not take long for a most attractive alternative to Francis to be presented—Charles of Austria, the first son of Archduke Philip of Austria and Joanna of Spain. Born in February 1500, he was slightly younger than Claude. As Philip's son, he was future heir to Austria and the Burgundian lands, and since Joanna, as the eldest of Ferdinand and Isabella's daughters, had become their heiress when their only son died just after Charles's birth, he was in line for the Spanish realms. He was a fine prospective match for Claude.

Beyond the matter of their likely inheritances, Louis had other reasons to support the betrothal of the two infants. It was probable that Philip, and Charles after him, would rule lands on both sides of France. Their goodwill would reduce the potential problems of the French monarch. Probably more important in 1501 when the betrothal of Claude and Charles began to be discussed, Louis hoped to get the feudal investiture of the duchy of Milan from Philip's father, Maximilian. Milan was still regarded legally as a fief of the Holy Roman Empire. Maximilian had refused to grant it thus far, but it was expected that a boon that so enhanced his family would change his mind.

Yet, for all that, Louis seems to have been intent on playing a double game with the Habsburgs. On April 30, 1500, he had signed a secret protocol that directed Claude to marry his successor should he die without a son.[15] Despite the secret document, Louis proceeded to deal with Philip for a marriage contract. In June 1501 Philip dispatched an embassy to France with orders to negotiate a marriage contract. After a month of discussions, in which Gié served as the principal French negotiator, a contract was hammered out, which Louis signed on August 10. If both Louis and Anne died without a son, Claude would inherit all of their titles to which the Salic law did not apply. If they had a son, Claude would receive 300,000 *écus*. In either scenario, the first son from the marriage of Claude and Charles would become duke of Brittany, thus ensuring the autonomy of the duchy.[16] The king and queen were reported as being very pleased at an agreement that had the potential of making their daughter a veritable empress of western Europe while still securing for her a good position should God give them a son.

After a round of festivities, Philip's ambassador returned home, accompanied by Cardinal d'Amboise, who went on to Trent, an imperial city, where he met with Maximilian. While pleased that his grandson had been promised a good marriage, the emperor was not happy with his son's handiwork. He felt that Philip should have gained more than he did for the investiture of Milan, and he had good reason to be wary of French marriage contracts. Nonetheless, Maximilian and d'Amboise agreed to a treaty on October 13, 1501, that confirmed the marriage contract. The French agreed to help the Austrians against the Turks and aid Philip in making good his wife's claim to the Spanish thrones. The last point reflected the ill health of Queen Isabella and the consensus among the leaders of Europe that Ferdinand would seize the throne of Castile when she died. Maximilian agreed to invest Louis with the duchy of Milan when the imperial diet next met.[17]

Immediately after this, Louis had an opportunity to meet Archduke Philip. Hearing that he and Joanna were planning to go to Spain, Louis invited them to pass through France and visit him. The invitation stirred up quite a dispute among Philip's advisers. Charles de Croy spoke strongly against his master's placing himself in the power of the French king: "For 400 years those French kings have made war on us Flemings. Do you believe that King Louis does not remember the murder of his grandfather the duke of Orléans? . . . Hatreds are hereditary and King Louis, on this point, resembles his predecessors." De Croy recommended embarking from Calais for England and sailing from there to Spain.[18]

François de Busleyden, archbishop of Besançon and former tutor of the archduke, responded in favor of traversing France. The French, he agreed, are seeking to increase their realm, but in that they are like all others. Louis will not seek revenge for the injuries done to his ancestors; he is not another Louis XI.

> If he were vindictive, would he have said a king of France does not revenge the quarrels of a duke of Orléans? . . . We all know the king of France . . . his magnanimous character, perhaps the best prince of our era. No one hates cheating, craftiness and all hypocrites more than he. We know that he surrounds himself with good men, learned and virtuous. You ask why he is so insistent that the archduke go through France? The answer is simple: it is in hope of cementing more and more the affection between them and secure the archduke's help in obtaining the investiture of Milan.

The archbishop's argument carried the day, and Philip and his party entered France at St-Quentin. They were given a grand entry into Paris on November 20 and entertained at the *hôtel de ville*.[19] Philip attended the Parlement of Paris as a peer of the realm. His party reached Blois on December 7, after having been received "so honorably that it would be impossible to do more" in all the towns it passed through. Louis greeted Philip "as his own brother and entertained him and his wife for five days with jousts, tournaments, banquets, and other good cheer." Meanwhile their ministers ratified the Treaty of Trent. Louis would pay 140,000 *l* for the investiture of Milan and 60,000 *l* more for the territory of the Valtelline north of the duchy. He pledged 50,000 *l* for a crusade against the Turks.[20]

The "summit meeting" between Louis and Philip was a revolutionary idea in the diplomacy of the time. Kings and princes did not place themselves in the power of their rivals in the way that Philip had; previous meetings of this sort took place on the frontiers or in the presence of large forces. The rest of Europe could not decide whether Philip's decision to accept Louis's invitation was an act of profound wisdom or utter folly.

Erasmus, for one, strongly praised the two princes for using words to solve their problems instead of war.[21] Unfortunately for Louis, Philip's father did not share his son's enthusiasm for the French monarch. When the French delegation reached Innsbruck in January 1502, the emperor demanded that Louis come in person to do homage for Milan. As the editor of the diplomatic exchanges between France and the empire wrote, "Such was Maximilian!"[22]

More bad news arrived at the French court with word of the renewed fighting in Naples. The French under the duke of Nemours actually precipitated the fighting, but it led St-Gelais to decry the Spanish as "ingrates for all the good deeds that have been done for the son of their king and queen."[23] As the war in Naples escalated, Philip returned to France. This time he demanded hostages for his security in the realm, unlike his earlier trip when he had refused them.[24] Reaching Lyon in March 1504, he and Louis worked out the Treaty of Lyon, which they signed on April 5. It confirmed the marriage contract of their two children and added to their intended domains the kingdom of Naples. The value of the marriage had increased considerably when Anne's pregnancy in 1501 had resulted in a stillborn son.

As has already been seen, Ferdinand repudiated his son-in-law's handiwork, and the war in southern Italy continued to the final defeat of the French. Philip, who remained in Lyon for several months waiting for the arrival of his sister Margaret on her way to marry the duke of Savoy, had to defend himself to Louis. The king seems to have accepted the archduke's good faith, but the skepticism of his advisers may have been a factor in his reaffirmation in February 1504 of his secret declaration to marry Claude to Francis.[25]

Archduke Philip went to France a third time in late 1504. He clearly enjoyed these visits, for Louis always dealt with him as a major player in the politics of Europe, unlike both his father and father-in-law. He also enjoyed the entertainment at the French court, since the usually frugal Louis did not stint in the expense of entertaining him. This time Philip arrived at the court with the blessing of his father, who finally was ready to grant the investiture of Milan. Maximilian was upset at the clear signs that Ferdinand would grab the throne of Castile after Isabella's death. A new round of negotiations at Blois resulted in three new treaties being signed on September 22, 1504. The first confirmed the investiture of Milan for 200,000 *l* with the duchy going to Charles and Claude if Louis had no son. The second treaty increased the territory Claude and Charles were to receive should Louis have a son—Burgundy, Nevers, Brittany, and Blois in France; Milan, Asti, Genoa, and Naples in Italy. Should the

French king break the marriage contract, Charles was still to receive Burgundy, Milan, and Asti. Louis also granted the revenues of Artois to Philip for his lifetime. The Habsburgs pledged to acknowledge French sovereignty over Burgundy and Flanders if they were responsible for breaking the contract. The third treaty, which was kept secret, committed France and the empire along with the papacy to war on Venice, which Louis had not forgiven for its aid to Spain in the war for Naples.[26]

What does one make of this situation where Louis clearly was double dealing with his good friend Philip? Since the earliest date for the proposed marriage was nine years off, he probably was still hoping for the birth of a son—Anne being twenty-seven at the time—which would undo most of the potential harm to the realm. But even the arrival of a son would have left Claude and her future husband with an enormous inheritance that surely would have caused the next French king, whoever he was, a great deal of difficulty. Nineteenth-century French historians such as Henri Lemonnier, who stridently denounced Louis for his unpatriotic agreement with Philip,[27] failed to realize that it was the motive of dynastic glory and power, which they found so lamentable, that had united Brittany to France, not nationalist fervor. Louis was simply acting with the same motivation in threatening to break up that union.

Early in 1505 Louis sent Georges d'Amboise to Hagenau in Alsace, part of the Holy Roman Empire, to receive the investiture of Milan from Maximilian. Twenty-four archers of the royal guard carried 4,000 écus each in their saddlebags to Hagenau as payment of the sum pledged to Maximilian the year before. On April 7 the cardinal, serving as proxy for his king, swore homage for the duchy, thus acknowledging that it was indeed a fief of the empire. Maximilian added a clause to the investiture that should the marriage contract between Charles and Claude be broken, the investiture was null and void, and Milan would go to Charles.[28]

While d'Amboise was at Hagenau, Louis again fell seriously ill. He had been ill in February, but recovered in time to enjoy the Easter festivities at Blois. Shortly after, a high fever and heavy sweating hit him so hard that he called for his confessor and prepared to die. He fell into delirium and asked for his daughter so he could give her his sword to defend herself against some imaginary enemy, but he gave her a stick. His physicians several times thought he was in his last moments, and the news spread across France. The churches and shrines were filled with people praying for his life, and prayer processions made their way through city streets. Even Pope Julius II led a prayer procession in Rome for his recovery. In mid-May Louis's physicians "were in great doubt about his life."[29]

With his life clearly hanging in the balance, Louis had to give up his hope of yet having a son and face directly the problem of his daughter's marriage and inheritance. The queen, the major advocate of the Austrian marriage, was in constant attendance on her ill husband and "acquitted herself most loyally,"[30] but when she went to Brittany to pray at her special shrines and conduct ducal business, Louis took advantage of her absence to rewrite his will. He included a clause directing that Claude marry Francis of Angoulême and stated that d'Amboise, as papal legate, had absolved him of his oaths sworn in his treaties with Philip. Claude would inherit all of the Orléanist patrimony whether she married Francis or not. Another clause prohibited her from leaving the realm until her marriage. Since his successor was only ten years old, Louis named Anne of Brittany as regent for him with a regency council of Louise of Savoy, d'Amboise, La Trémoille, Rochefort, Robertet, and Engelbert of Cleves, Louis's cousin. The will was signed on May 31, 1505, and countersigned by Robertet and Rochefort.[31] In the months that followed, even as his health improved, Louis obliged his principal captains to swear on the loss of Paradise to uphold his will. While his wife was gone, he went to Amboise to visit Francis and Louise and assigned the prince a new governor, Artus de Gouffier. Anne for her part was so angry over the new disposition that she refused to return from Brittany, going on a grand tour of her duchy, until d'Amboise wrote her a letter begging that she reconcile with her husband. She was gone for about five months, returning in September 1505.[32]

Although Louis had signed two earlier secret documents countermanding Claude's marriage to Charles, after each he had gone on to sign a public contract for a marriage between the two. Lawyers would have had a great time arguing over which held the greater weight. A will, however, was different; it had far higher standing in law and settled the matter. Philip was sent no notice about the will, although rumors surfaced quickly. Two days before the new will was signed, the Venetian ambassador reported its contents to his government.[33]

While Louis was recovering from his illness and spending the late summer of 1505 riding and hunting deer around Tours with Francis, another will upset Philip. After a long illness, Isabella of Castile had died in November 1504. Her will had named her husband as regent of Castile until their grandson Charles was old enough to rule, bypassing the rights of their daughter Joanna and her husband. Joanna's unstable mental condition had become obvious to Isabella and Ferdinand, and they did not want a foreign prince ruling in Spain if she became incompetent. Philip made clear his anger at the will and his intention to make good his wife's rights. Ferdinand, so good at concocting schemes to undo his neighbors, became convinced that Louis and Philip were conspiring against him, since it was so clearly in the best interests of France to divide Castile and Aragon again. They probably were, although there is nothing in the sources to prove it.

Ferdinand's fertile mind quickly hit on a plan that could well turn everything to his advantage: He would make a new marriage to a young French princess. She could give him another son, who would take precedence over Joanna in inheriting Aragon and might be able to get Castile as well. Such a marriage could also neutralize Louis in the looming conflict with Philip. A Spanish monk arrived in secret at the French court to sound out Louis on a possible bride. Louis was receptive, so in August 1505 two members of Ferdinand's council were dispatched to Blois to negotiate a marriage contract.[34]

The only plausible bride was Louis's niece, Germaine de Foix, daughter of his sister Marie and Jean de Foix. There is no evidence that Louis had ever seen his sister after her marriage, but her two children, Germaine and Gaston, were being raised at the court. Germaine was eighteen years old, "a good and beautiful princess even if she has not yet lost her baby fat,"[35] while her husband-to-be was fifty-three. Louis approved of the marriage supposedly because he did not expect Ferdinand to have any more children, on account of the disorder of his life.[36] Germaine did give birth to a son in 1510, but he soon died.

The marriage treaty of October 1505 called for Louis and Ferdinand to be "two souls in one body and enemy of each other's enemies." Germaine received Louis's claims to Naples, Sicily, and the kingdom of Jerusalem. In exchange, he would receive 1 million gold ducats over a ten-year period, which he would have to repay if the marriage was childless or if he tried to reclaim those titles.[37] Louis signed the treaty at Blois on October 12, 1505 and Ferdinand did so four days later at Segovia. In early January the Venetian ambassador at Philip's court reported that he had heard that Germaine de Foix was about to depart for Spain and Philip had given up trying to prevent the marriage. The wedding took place in March.[38]

By late 1505 Philip had every reason to be concerned about the future inheritances of both his wife and son. It was obvious that Louis's providing a bride for Ferdinand was not the act of a staunch friend and signaled a change in policy, while his representative in France made it clear that there was strong opposition to Charles's betrothal to Claude.[39] Gié's trial had removed the most outspoken foe of the marriage, but it also aired the depth of hostility to it. In June 1505 the Venetian ambassador to Philip's court told his government that Philip had received a dispatch from his ambassador in France revealing that "King Louis, on recovering from this last severe illness . . . had become aware that, had he died, his wife and daughter would have been in trouble, because all the princes in France were intriguing against them; and he therefore perceived that his only remedy was to marry his daughter to the Dauphin [Francis]."[40]

Three months later the ambassador reported that if the marriage were broken and Louis gave up the lands promised in the contract, Philip and his father would be content, but they feared that Louis was going to argue that he had not broken the contract but rather the French people had demanded it and no compensation would be necessary. At the same time, Louis sent a letter to Philip declaring that nothing had changed, but soon after, Philip's ambassador in France reported that Louis intended to annul the contract.[41] By early 1506 even d'Amboise, whose papal ambitions were thought to have kept him in support of the Austrian marriage in hope of getting the votes of the imperial cardinals in the next conclave, turned against it. His change of heart was so complete that his seventeenth-century biographer could present him as the principal advocate of the marriage between Claude and Francis.[42]

By early 1506, therefore, the Habsburgs were well aware that the marriage contract was going to be broken. They began to demand the compensation spelled out in it. Louis, searching for a ploy to avoid paying the stiff penalties, came up with the idea of calling a meeting of the Estates-general to request that his daughter marry the successor to the throne and not a foreign prince. Thus, it could be argued that the French people, not the king, were responsible. Some contemporary sources present the convocation of the Estates as having been inspired from below by the people who pressed the king into calling them.[43] Probably more than any other French king, Louis considered public opinion, but the consensus of contemporary authors and modern historians is that the impetus for the Estates came from above as a ploy to break the marriage treaty without paying the heavy price set in it.

Although it appears that the king and his ministers manipulated public opinion into calling for the Estates to meet, they were determined to have the Habsburgs believe that the decision to break the marriage compact had been forced on the king by the people. Accordingly, the reason for the meeting was not revealed in the summons calling on a select number of "*belles et grosses villes*" to send deputies to Tours in May 1506. The letters, sent by the provincial governors or other important officials, only said that the king had important business to discuss with the Estates. For example,

Louise of Savoy, in her capacity as duchess of Angoulême, told that city the king wanted to discuss some matters with the deputies of the principal cities at Tours. On April 23 the city council of Paris met to approve a resolution calling on the king to arrange a marriage between his daughter and the heir to the throne, and it agreed to pay the expenses of the deputies who were going to the meeting.[44]

The deputies apparently did not produce any *cahiers* in preparation for the meeting, which is one of the reasons why some modern historians refuse to designate the meeting an Estates-general.[45] More compelling an argument for that view is the limited attendance at Tours. The selection of deputies was not done by *bailliages*, as was true of those meetings accepted by historians without dispute as Estates-general, although the meeting of 1484 was the first to use that system, which was a real break with the past practice of having the king summon the deputies of all three estates. In 1506 a large number of prominent nobles and clerics was invited to attend, and the larger cities were told to elect delegates. Only some twenty cities were represented; it is not clear whether more were invited. None of the cities were in Provence, Dauphiné, or Brittany, although the last was not yet regarded as an integral part of the realm.[46] There was a much larger number of delegates for the first and second estates, but a complete list cannot be established. According to one account of the meeting, there were present all the princes of blood, a great number of archbishops and bishops, and other lords and officials.[47] Nonetheless, there is no disputing the point that the membership of the third estate in particular was less than was usual for the Estates-general.

On the question of whether the meeting of 1506 should be called an Estates-general, J. Russell Major, the modern authority on the institution, has been ambivalent. In his first study, he called it simply an assembly; later he dubbed it a "limited Estates."[48] In so far as the sixteenth-century authors were concerned, there was little if any question that the meeting was an Estates-general. All contemporary works use that term rather than "Assembly of Notables," a term in use for meetings with very limited representation. The author of a history of the Estates written in 1787 called the convocation of 1506 an Estates, while Francis I's meeting of 1527 was deemed an Assembly of Notables.[49] Certainly Louis's meeting does not meet the norms of the great Estates of 1484 and 1614; it was, however, broader than an Assembly of Notables and, since the deputies were elected in their cities, more representative.

In early May 1506 the deputies began to dribble into Tours, and on May 11 the meeting opened when the deputies from the towns met in the *hôtel de ville* of Tours. They chose a doctor of theology from the University of Paris, Thomas Bricot, as their speaker and requested an audience of the king. Two days later Emperor Maximilian's ambassador reported he had heard that the Estates (his word) were planning to ask the king to break his daughter's marriage contract. On May 14 Louis granted an audience to the entire Third Estate. As its speaker, Bricot made a masterful address to the king.[50] He began by recalling Louis's serious illness of the previous year and "how all his subjects had been sorely grieved, fearing to lose him and calling to mind his singular favors." Bricot went on to describe "how the king kept his kingdom and subjects in a peace so good that no man darst take aught without payment, and the very hens knew that they were safe from violence." Bricot applauded the reduction of the *tailles* by a fourth, the reform of justice, and the appointment of upright judges. For these and other reasons too numerous to mention, stated Bricot, the king ought to be called "Louis the Twelfth, the Father of His People," a title that became irrevocably associated with Louis.[51]

Having so uniquely honored the king, the speaker turned to the real purpose of the meeting: "Sire, may it please Your Highness, we are come here to proffer a request for the general welfare of your kingdom, your humble servants begging that it may please you to give your only daughter to Mister Francis here present, who is France's son." According to a letter that Louis wrote to the city of St-Omer shortly after, the speaker for the Third Estate argued that the marriage of Philip IV's daughter to the king of England was the cause of the Hundred Years War.[52] The contemporary account of the address adds that these and other fair words brought tears to the eyes of the king and all who heard them.

After speaking with Cardinal d'Amboise, the cardinal of Narbonne, and Chancellor Rochefort, Louis directed the chancellor to tell the deputies that he would consider their petition. On the following day the deputies for Burgundy presented their own plea for the marriage. Two days later Louis met with his council and other notables, who argued that the king should agree to the deputies' request. The next day the chancellor reported to the assembly that the king, "whom you have rightly baptized Father of the People because he always has the good and service of his people strongly at heart," had been strongly advised to agree to their request and had decided to sanction a marriage between Claude and Francis.[53] Therefore, the king wished that the ceremony of betrothal be celebrated as quickly as possible, for there was no impediment to its taking place. (The impediment of consanguinity, since Claude and Francis were second cousins, seems to have been ignored.) Rochefort denounced the talk of another match for Claude as just gossip. He added that since nothing is as uncertain as the time of death, the king wanted the deputies present to swear for the cities they represented to accept Francis as their king and lord if Louis died without a son.

Bricot responded for the Third Estate with the phrase *Vox populi, Vox Dei!* Two days later the solemn betrothal of Claude and Francis took place before all those present at the meeting—the princes of blood, the great prelates and nobles, and a representative of each city—who put their signatures on the marriage contract. The cities represented then held assemblies to inform the bourgeoisie about what had transpired and bind them as well to the oath. In Paris the city council met on June 17 to take the oath and ordered a prayer procession in the city for the next Sunday to beg for God's blessing on the marriage. The captains of the six companies of royal guards also swore, "before God with hand on the True Cross at the knee of the Cardinal Legate," to defend the marriage and Francis's right to the throne.[54] The extreme care taken to ensure that the marriage would take place and bind everyone of importance to it reflected not only the king's bad health and the expectation that he would die before the betrothed could wed, but also the likelihood that the queen would try to undo it if Louis died before the wedding. Louis's ambassador told Philip that the barons of France had objected to a marriage between Claude and Charles of Austria because it would have injured the rights of the French crown. He swore that the friendship between Louis and Philip was as strong as ever.[55]

The dream of a Habsburg-Valois family compact was shattered. It gives rise to an intriguing counterfactual question: Could Charles of Austria, wedded to Claude of France, or perhaps a son of theirs, have abrogated the Salic law and become king of France and thereby created a united western European empire? The fact that Louis felt obliged to have the grands of the realm and the representatives of the major cities swear an oath acknowledging Francis as his successor if he did not have a son suggests that the Salic law was not as clearly defined in 1506 as historians have usually assumed. In fact, the Estates of 1506 probably had a role in strengthening it in respect to how the succession passed to cadet lines of the royal family.

The ploy of using the Estates to ratify voiding the marriage treaty with the Habsburgs worked in the sense that Louis felt entirely comfortable with the decision, so much so that he was reported as standing up to Queen Anne, one of the few times in their life together. She was still bitterly opposed to breaking the compact with the Habsburgs. To her protests he replied he intended to mate his mice with rats from his own barn.[56] The betrothal of the heiress to Brittany against the duchess's will indicated that the duchy could no longer carry on its own foreign policy.

Louis sent letters to a number of the cities of the Low Countries to inform them of the decision and the reasons for it, one being that both Charles and Claude were too young to have agreed to the marriage.[57] The king was eager to undercut any sympathy Philip, the prince of the Low Countries, might have garnered from those cities in a war with France over the broken treaty. The Habsburgs did protest loudly, but Philip's death early the next year greatly reduced the potential consequences, and the mercurial Maximilian soon overlooked the insult to his family in order to gain advantages in Italy and the Low Countries through an alliance with Louis.

For the institution of the Estates-general, however, the meeting of 1506 had negative long-term results, despite the complete success of the meeting in achieving its goal. There was a sense of annoyance among the deputies of the cities that they had been called to deal with just that one issue. It can be assumed that they were flattered to have been asked to be involved in a major matter of the realm, but attending the Estates was both a major disruption in the life of the deputies and a large expense. For some, of course, it was an adventure and a break in a humdrum life, and the deputies did receive compensation from their cities, which, however, was less than the cost of the trip and came well after they had returned home.[58] Payment of the deputies was a burden on the constituencies that elected them, and the local people involved were not eager to have meetings of the Estates convoked since it meant a fairly hefty expenditure.

That was especially true in 1506 when the meeting failed to deal with taxation, always before then, the raison d'être of the meetings. Taxes were a perennial problem, while the marriage contract of a king's daughter was a unique concern. The meeting of 1506 was a break in a long-standing tradition of convoking the Estates to approve new taxation, while it failed to establish a new one. Thus, it could not serve as a foundation for the Estates' becoming a permanent institution in French government. When Louis found himself in serious financial trouble late in his reign, he raised taxes without calling the Estates-general, although he made wide use of the provincial estates. Ironically, therefore, the Estates-general of 1506, despite its success in accomplishing what it had been summoned to do, was a factor in the failure of the institution to establish itself as a permanent part of French government.

After the betrothal was ratified at Tours, Louis increased Francis's pension from the 6,000 *l* it had been since 1499 to 20,000 *l*.[59] He also arranged for a grand tournament in Paris. He and the 400 archers of the royal guard paraded in show armor and full arms. A combat of twelve on twelve was one of the events of the first day of the tournament, but the highlight of the festivities was the mock combat of forty light cavalrymen dressed like Albanians and forty like Turks. Several bombards were fired off to simulate even closer the fury of battle, and "the queen and the ladies with her looked on and said that war is a strange thing and marvelous to behold." Two days later twenty prominent nobles again engaged in jousting one on one with sword and lance, "such that each of combatants were covered with honor and pleased the king." After the tournament, Louis and the court went to Blois, where they spent the rest of 1506, which was, so d'Auton says, a year of great peace and prosperity across the realm. It was also a year with beautiful weather both summer and winter. The French people had good reason to believe that God was smiling on their king.

11

The Springtime of the French Renaissance

The tournament given by Louis XII for his daughter's betrothal revealed the continuing hold that medieval culture had on him and his court. France of the early years of Louis's reign was still a medieval world. There had been little evidence of new trends in his joyous entry into Paris in 1499, nor were they apparent in Queen Anne's entry into the city in 1504. The currents of change that had begun to ripple through the economy, the government, and the military were slow to affect the realm of the mind. In particular the ideas of the Italian Renaissance, which were taking root elsewhere in northern Europe, had yet to have much impact in France.

The University of Paris still was the dominant center of French thought, but certainly not to the extent that it had been two centuries earlier. It had lost respect among the French people by supporting the English monarchy after 1420 and playing a major role in the trial of Jeanne d' Arc. For the same reasons the French monarchy no longer gave its virtually unconditional support to "the eldest and dearest daughter of the king," a phrase first used in the reign of Charles V. The student body had declined in size since the mid-fourteenth century because of the Hundred Years War and the competition of numerous new universities both abroad and in France. In the fifteenth century six new French universities had been founded, largely to teach civil law. Paris could not teach civil law because of the papal mandate of 1219, which had been intended to stop students from being lured away from the study of theology, so the great surge in civil law studies of the late fifteenth century passed Paris by. The student bodies of most French universities were quite small in the late fifteenth century. Two or three of them may have been under 100 students, while only Toulouse and Paris were clearly above 1,000.

It is difficult to avoid the conclusion that Louis XII won his easy victory of 1499 over the University of Paris in large part because its reputation then was at one of its lowest levels in history. Nowhere was that more true than in respect to its Faculty of Theology, commonly called the Sorbonne, after the Collège de Sorbonne, a residence for poor theology students, although in this era the colleges of Montaigu and Navarre were more important within the Faculty of Theology. The university did remain the stronghold of scholastic theology, but after Jean Gerson's death in 1429, no Parisian master of theology came close to matching the importance of the dozens of great theologians of the previous 300 years. The Faculty of Theology was then dominated by the Nominalism of William of Ockham (died 1349). It had a brief, brilliant period in the mid-fourteenth century, but by the late 1400s, it had degenerated into the pursuit of increasingly trivial and esoteric questions. That, along with theologians' distaste for the learning of the Italian Renaissance, led the humanists to call them "Théologastres," combining theologian and the Greek word for belly.[1]

One must not conclude from the bitter criticisms of the humanists and the early Protestants that the University of Paris had declined into insignificance or mindless obstructionism to the superior ideas of humanists and reformers. It continued to be called upon to render judgments on the major issues of the day. Louis XII called on it in the midst of his bitter feud with Julius II.[2] In 1514 the celebrated Reuchlin case was brought to the Faculty of Theology. Reuchlin was a German humanist whose study of Judaic works led to charges of error against him. The Paris Faculty decided against him, much to the anger of the humanists, who had taken up Reuchlin's cause. The mutual antagonism between the University of Paris and the humanists, which the Reuchlin affair exacerbated but did not entirely create, has tended to obscure the fact that prior to then the university had a tolerant attitude toward humanism and innovation.

Humanism came early to the university. Guillaume Fichet was a member of the Collège de Sorbonne who became immersed in the works of Italian humanists, especially Petrarch. In 1470 he and another member founded the first printing press in France on the grounds of the college to print humanist works. Lyon had a press by 1478, and by 1500 some twenty French cities had them in operation.[3] Although Lyon had no university, its presses printed more classical scholarship than did those of Paris. Because of its proximity to Italy and the presence of numerous Italians who had taken up residence there, Lyon was a close second to Paris as the center of early humanism in France.

With the creation of the new printing industry came a large group of entrepreneurs and workers, most of whom had to be literate and in close touch with literary and fashion trends in order to be successful. It took some time before printing would have an impact on the intellectual life of

France, but by Louis's reign the influence of the industry is apparent. The king seems to have appreciated the public relations value of the press. Five pamphlets described Louis's coronation, for example, and his first entry into Paris was the subject of several more. The good news from Italy in the first years of the reign was widely broadcasted through printed broadsheets and pamphlets. Of the sixty-five extant broadsheets from Louis's reign, thirty-three have news of the Italian wars.[4]

The principle of royal control of printing became established by means of the royal "privilege to print." The first one was issued in 1498, whether by Charles or Louis is not clear. The privilege usually was issued to control competition and prevent pirate editions, but the device did have the potential, later used, for censoring texts. Louis seems to have had little interest in using it in that manner.[5] He did try to control the number of printers and booksellers in Paris, but it may have been at the request of the university. In his edict of 1513, limiting the number of Parisian booksellers to thirty, Louis made his famous comment that printing was "rather more divine than human."[6] He also eliminated all import duties on books.

It is unknown whether the king had any role in the founding of the two famous presses in Paris early in his reign. In 1503 Josse Badius, a famed humanist scholar from Ghent, set up a print shop to publish classical works. His emblem, showing the inside of a print shop, became a symbol of humanist scholarship. More important, he began to use the style of print created by Aldus Manutius at Venice. Called Roman type, it began to replace the Gothic type in use in France since 1470. Roman type was assured of permanent use in France when Henri Estienne began to use it for his books. Estienne, often regarded as the epitome of Renaissance printers, began to print in Paris in 1504.

Louis took a strong interest in books, although in his era beautifully illuminated manuscripts were much preferred over printed books. He inherited from his grandfather and father a library at Blois of some 200 volumes, to which he had contributed only a few volumes on music before becoming king. Queen Anne added part of her father's library to it. Louis's first substantial addition was the collection of the duke of Milan, which he removed from Pavia in 1500. It consisted of about 1,000 manuscripts, of which seventeen had belonged to Petrarch. Works on antiquity were strongly represented in that collection.[7] From the library that King Federigo of Naples brought with him to France in 1501, Georges d'Amboise obtained ten Greek manuscripts and 218 Latin ones. They later were placed in the royal library. The king purchased 150 Flemish illuminated manuscripts, mostly on religious topics, and he procured the forty Greek manuscripts that the humanist Janus Lascaris had brought to France. Lascaris was the royal librarian for a time, until he was made an ambassador to Venice. After him a royal almoner, François de Refuge, was given the post.[8] Under Louis it appears that the concept of using the royal library as a repository of scholarship for the realm was in effect, since there is evidence that it lent out books at least to privileged patrons. In 1505 the duke of Ferrara had his ambassador request two books, but they already had been lent out. When early in his reign Francis I had the library inventoried, it consisted of 1,626 books and manuscripts, the majority of which Louis had added.[9]

At the beginning of Louis's reign, Robert Gaguin was the teacher of classical rhetoric at Paris; he was a canon lawyer who also taught classical Latin to select students, including Erasmus. Desiderius Erasmus's first published work was a dedicatory poem for Gaguin's *History of France* of 1495. Gaguin's translation into French of Caesar's *Commentaries on the Gallic Wars* was probably his chief contribution to humanism.[10] Gaguin's death in 1502 prevented him from being a significant part of humanism under Louis XII. More prominent were several Italian humanists who came to teach in the University of Paris to promote their humanist agenda.[11] French rule over Milan, an important center of Renaissance culture under il Moro, gave the French a great deal of contact with humanists and artists, many of whom were searching for patrons after Sforza's ouster. By that point in the Renaissance, the Italians had turned to Greek studies, and thus the most noted of those who went to France were both Greek scholars, Janus Lascaris and Girolamo Aleandro. Lascaris, a native Greek, arrived in France in 1496 and frequently served the French government as an ambassador. He was Louis's representative in Venice from 1504 to 1509, where he was an outspoken advocate of a French-led crusade against the Turks. Since the posting took him out of France, it reduced the impact he had on French scholars. When he was in France, he was eager to help those who wanted to learn Greek, such as Jacques Lefèvre d'Etaples and Guillaume Budé. Budé lamented that Lascaris was always at the court and seldom in Paris, but added that Lascaris gladly did what he could to teach him Greek.

Aleandro, who also knew Hebrew, went to France in 1508 through the encouragement of Erasmus and Louis XII, who named him a professor of *belles lettres*, granted him a pension of 500 *écus* in 1508, and gave him letters of naturalization. A year later he was lecturing on Plutarch in Greek at the University of Paris. Already in 1507 a Frenchman, François Tissard, who had studied at the University of Bologna, had been printing books in

Greek and Hebrew; his *Liber Gnomagyricus* was the first Greek book printed in France. He also published a Hebrew grammar in 1508. Aleandro's arrival with a large number of Greek books from Aldus's press in Venice disrupted Tissard's efforts, and apparently he stopped publishing in 1508.[12] In July 1511 Aleandro, now proctor of the German Nation of the University of Paris, gave a public lecture to "such a crowd that . . . two courts of the college could not contain it. And what a distinguished audience! Receivers-general, councillors, rectors . . . the number is estimated at two thousand. Never, either in Italy or France, have I seen a more august or more numerous assembly of educated men."[13] In 1512 he wrote to Erasmus from Paris that the faculty of the university "burdened rather than honored him with offices which he cannot honestly decline." He had been made the rector of the university earlier in the year. He noted that he was not receiving his pension from the king but could hardly expect it "in these hard times."[14] A year later he became secretary to the bishop of Paris and largely gave up teaching Greek, but he had a group of pupils who carried on Greek studies in France. Aleandro had broad influence on Louis XII in church affairs, especially during the conflict with Julius II. Aleandro's later career as a controversialist against Luther revealed a conservatism in theology that may explain the university's ready acceptance of him. Certainly by the time he left it in 1514, the battle lines between the theologians and the humanists were being drawn up.

Erasmus, partially a product of the Paris Faculty of Theology, had much to do with that development, although as a Dutchman rather than a Wallon, he was not well versed in French language and culture. He lived in Paris from 1495 to 1501 and made four short stays between 1504 and 1511. Etienne de Poncher extended patronage to him, as did Archbishop Robert Guibé of Nantes, Anne's protégé.[15] Yet it appears Erasmus did not have extensive contacts with French scholars or the court during his stays in Paris, although his works were avidly read and much appreciated. His first humanist work, the *Adages*, was published in Paris in 1500, the year before he left the city.

Louis XII had a more direct impact on the career of Guillaume Budé, the greatest legal scholar of the Renaissance. Budé came from a well-placed family of royal officials. His career as a student in law at the University of Orléans allegedly was remarkable for the little time he devoted to his studies. Nonetheless, he became interested in ancient learning and taught himself classical Latin and Greek. Meanwhile, he gained a position as a secretary under Charles VIII. When that king died, Budé soon left the court upset "by the scorn in which the grands hold knowledge."[16] While that may well have been an accurate reflection of Louis's reputation in 1498, the fact remains that he heard of Budé's learning and used him on two diplomatic missions to Italy, one of which was to congratulate Julius II on his election in 1503, even though the Venetian ambassador at Rome described Budé as "merely a secretary."[17] Two royal chancellors, Guy de Rochefort and Jean de Ganay, were his patrons, and Ganay received the dedication of his first major work, a commentary on Justinian's *Digest* of Roman law published by Badius in 1508. It was a powerful attack on the study of law in the universities; like scholastic theology, law had emphasized the study of medieval commentaries, not the original text. With it Budé essentially created legal humanism.

Budé spent most of his time at Paris or the court, but legal humanism was centered in the universities where civil law was taught. Toulouse, Orléans, and Valence were the early strongholds of the genre, but these provincial centers of ancient learning began to flourish only after 1515.[18] Louis XII seems not to have appreciated the importance of Budé's work, and Budé later criticized him quite severely for his lack of learning, although it was Georges d'Amboise who took the brunt of Budé's wrath. Budé's criticism in his *De Asse* (1515) of the king who had just died did much to establish the tone found in many modern studies of the sharp contrast between Louis's indifference toward humanism and Francis's beneficence.

There was one group of French humanists, of whom Budé was the foremost, whose interests were largely secular and whose religion rarely intruded into their scholarship. There was another group for whom, like Erasmus, religion was very much the center of their interests. They can properly be called Christian humanists, for they applied to the study of Christian classics the philological principles so profitably used by Budé. The greatest Frenchman among such humanists was Lefèvre d'Etaples. He took a master's degree in arts at the University of Paris and in 1490 was lecturing there. Two years later he traveled to Italy, where he was inspired to work on a critical edition of several of Aristotle's works in Greek and accurate Latin translations of them. After a second trip to Rome in 1500, he turned his attention more to the Christian classics and religious interests. Lefèvre published critical editions of several of the Latin Church fathers in order to go beyond the texts of scholastic theology to the earliest sources of Christianity. Soon he realized that he needed to go directly to the Bible itself. In 1509 he published a critical edition of the Psalms. Even more important was his Latin edition of the Epistles of Paul. He printed the church's official translation by St. Jerome side by side with his own commentary, which owed virtually nothing to scholasticism.

Lefèvre, unlike most humanists then in France, never received patronage from Louis. His principal patron and pupil was Guillaume Briçonnet, son of the prominent royal financial official who had become archbishop of Reims after his wife died. Young Briçonnet rose rapidly in the church, becoming bishop of Lodève at age fifteen and then abbot of the monastery of St-Germain-des-Près at Paris in 1507, where Lefèvre served as the librarian for a decade.

Louis XII was more generous to a group of poets and classicists known as the *Grand Rhétoriqueurs*. More than most literary schools, they had common characteristics: a love of classical Latin, even if their knowledge of it was mediocre; close association with the French court, producing most of their works for various members of it; and an interest in history. The last point probably reflected Louis's own keen interest in ancient history. He was said to have read widely in the histories of ancient times, especially on Philip of Macedonia and Emperor Trajan. A contemporary quoted him as saying that the Greeks had done mediocre deeds in war but had great writers to embellish them; the Romans had done great deeds but wrote of them with dignity; and the French had also been great in war but lacked great writers to tell about it. Louis said he intended to remedy that.[19]

The principal Rhétoriqueurs were Jean Bouchet, André de La Vigne, Jean d'Auton, Jean Marot (father of Clément), Octovien de St-Gelais, and Jean Lemaire de Belges. All but Bouchet were in the service of Queen Anne and dedicated works to her.[20] Marot, for example, wrote a ballad in which the first letters of each line spell out her name and titles. Today none of these authors is very highly regarded for his literary work,[21] except perhaps for Lemaire, but all helped to spread classical Latin in France. All were writers of chronicles of varying value for writing a biography of Louis XII. D'Auton, a Benedictine monk, became the official historiographer for Louis in 1499 and chronicled the Italian wars to 1507. He often inserted poetry into his prose history.

All of the Rhétoriqueurs draw on ancient models for inspiration, both for style and content. Lemaire's *Les Illustrations de Gaule et Singularitez de Troye* was largely responsible for popularizing the myth that Gauls founded Troy (based on the presence of Celts in Galatia) and after the fall of Troy the surviving Trojans fled back to Gaul to create Gallic society and culture.[22] The king of France thus was the descendant of Hector and Aeneas, and as such he had rights not only in Italy and Rome also founded by Trojans, but furthermore to Asia Minor. Consequently, the French king was the natural leader of any crusade. One of Louis's mottos was *Ultius avos Trojae*, "Revenge our Trojan ancestors." Lemaire went on to argue that the Celtic language was the ancestor of Greek, which in turn engendered French. Hoping to flatter Anne of Brittany, he spoke of "your natural Breton tongue, which is the true Trojan language," although she could not speak it.[23]

Today the French poetry of the Rhétoriqueurs is better regarded, not highly regarded, to be sure, than their Latin works; but they themselves and their contemporaries were convinced that their best work was their Latin verse. That was not true of the theater, however, which in Louis's era was still entirely in the vernacular. French drama of the last years of the fifteenth century remained heavily medieval in character. The mystery plays from a century earlier were still being staged by guild confraternities, corporate groups, or entire villages. Charles VIII's reign has been called "the great epoch" for mystery plays of Christ's passion.[24] A successful mystery play had its serious elements, depicting the events from the Bible or the lives of the saints and emphasizing a moral point, and its comic side, injecting farce into the midst of the play. The production of farce was the most noteworthy aspect of French theater in Louis XII's reign, and the best writers of farce were members of the Basoche, the society of the law clerks of the Parlements. The clerks were usually former law students who had not completed their course of study. Well educated and probably somewhat frustrated and bitter, they used rowdy behavior and sharp wit to garner attention. Several other government institutions, including provincial ones, had similar organizations of their clerks involved in producing farces.

The Society of the Basoche had both legal and social aspects. It was organized as a "kingdom" with a king, a chancellor, and other offices elected annually, and it had its own courts that settled disputes between the law clerks and sometimes with outsiders. The Basoche were far better known for their comedies and farces put on for the public, which often included the king, called "*sotties*" (farces performed by *sots*—jesters or fools). Since the writers and performers were minor government functionaries, their topics were usually political, and they often satirized members of the court and even the king and queen. It was the Basoche's satirizing of Anne, especially in the farce "*La Sottie de l'Astrologue*,"[25] that prompted Louis to move against them in 1499. He made it clear that while he could accept satire directed against him, his wife was off limits. "The devil take me! Let them say what they want about me, but respect the women." If they did not, he said, he would hang them all.[26] Yet, for royal entertainment after Anne's entry in 1504, the clerks of the law courts and students of the university put on "many satirical comedies and moral tragedies," which dealt with virtually every topic including the Gié affair.[27]

The sottie most critical of the king was *"Le Monde et Abuz,"* written at Toulouse late in his reign, in which the sots praise the king's vices, especially avarice and miserliness. Another play depicted Louis as seriously ill, attended by physicians with all sorts of medicines for him, none of which works. When someone brings in a vial of liquid gold to give him as a curative, he immediately rises from his bed fully cured.[28] Years later Jean Bouchet, who was at the French court from 1497 to 1507, praised Louis for his liberal attitude toward the Basoche. He stated that the king permitted the *sotties* to be performed because they were a way of informing him of the faults and corruption of his ministers. Perhaps for that reason, Louis subsidized several of the Basoche, giving Gillarot d'Asniôres 15 *l*, for example.[29] During his bitter dispute with Julius II, Louis made use of the greatest of the Basoche, Pierre Gringore, and several other writers of *sotties* as propagandists to rally popular opinion to his side.

The world of science—natural philosophy as it was called in that era—and mathematics remained equally conservative. The flash of innovative thought at Paris in the fourteenth century from several Ockhamist theologians, such as Jean Buridan, had burned out. Teaching the *quadrivium* in the universities involved the use of commentaries on Aristotle and other ancient works. Humanists, especially Lefèvre, made a small contribution, despite concentrating on literature and religious works, by providing critical editions of Aristotle's scientific works and a few other ancient scholars. The one scientific area where some work of note was being done was astronomy, because of its association with astrology. Astrology was the dominant "scientific" discipline of the late Middle Ages, because like any modern science, it was believed to be predictive of the future. The arrival of Arab astrological works in the West in the previous century had provided a great boost to a field that had been largely ignored in the early Middle Ages. As of 1500, no one seems to have been without the services of astrologers, and the kings of France had one as a permanent member of their courts at 200 *l* annual pension. Because astrology depended on interpreting the movements of the heavenly bodies, astronomy was essentially its handmaiden. Work in astronomy was intended to make astrology more accurate.

In medicine, the era was a period of tentative steps toward the use of ancient learning. In 1514 Henri Estienne published a small collection of texts of Galen translated into Latin by an Italian. About the same time, the faculty of medicine at Paris began to teach Galen, at least in a limited fashion. The publication in Paris in the same year of an Italian work on anatomy also indicates new currents in medicine there. Dissections were slowly becoming commonplace by 1515, and they no longer received special note in the records of the medicine faculty.[30] The prominent physician Symphoren Champier of Lyon wrote extensively on medical topics and fostered humanism and especially the study of Plato in his enormous corpus of printed works.

Because he was king, Louis received dedications from authors of all sorts, including humanists. For example, Claude de Seyssel dedicated to him his French translation of Xenophon's *Anabasis,* which Lascaris had translated from Greek to Latin, and he received the dedication of Octovien de St-Gelais's translation of Virgil's *Aeneid* in 1500. But the king's support and enthusiasm for humanism was clearly limited, and he had limited responsibility for the fact that at his death it was well represented in his realm. He was more directly involved in promoting the new style in architecture and art, although the number of building projects he planned was small. The major one was the reconstruction of the Château of Blois. As d'Auton reported for December 1502, "the king went to Blois to stay in his château, which he had made all new and sumptuous, so that it seemed well worthy of a king." The old château was thoroughly medieval in design, intended first of all for defense, not comfort. Louis must have decided immediately upon becoming king to rebuild it, since Gié, ordered in 1499 to conduct Louise of Savoy and her children to Blois, had to take them to Amboise because Blois was uninhabitable due to the construction going on.[31] The reconstruction was finished in 1503.

The remodeled château shows some signs of Italian influence in its construction, such as the patterned use of red and blue bricks and the arabesque decoration, but the most important impact of Italian architecture was in the essential idea that a château need not be a defensive stronghold. By 1500 Italian châteaux were being designed not to protect the occupants but to provide pleasant space for receptions, balls, and gracious living. Louis felt secure enough in his control of the realm and the affection of the nobility to live in a "defortified" place. The great tower of Blois disappeared (it may have been torn down before 1498), and the ditches were replaced by gardens. In 1517 an Italian who visited Blois remarked that "the castle is not a fortress but there are some very fine apartments and some delightful facades."[32] It has been argued that Blois was the prototype of the royal châteaux of the Ancien Régime, which were the centers of life for an absolute monarch secure among his subjects, not the castles of a medieval king worried about rebellious subjects.[33]

Two Italians, Fra Giocondo and Pacello da Mercogliano, largely planned the gardens and fountains at Blois.[34] Giocondo was a Dominican friar, who is best known as an innovative designer of forts intended to counter the greater effectiveness of artillery against traditional medieval structures. He went to France in 1499 at Louis's request as royal architect. Another clearly Italian element of the new château was the equestrian statue of Louis at its entrance. The Italian poets Fausto Andrelini, poet laureate of France who was naturalized in 1502 and received a pension of 180 *l*, and Ludovico Heliano, who later represented Louis at the Imperial Diet in 1510, wrote the verses inscripted at its base. For all the input of Italians into rebuilding the château, the principal architect of the reconstruction probably was not an Italian but a Frenchman, Colin Biart, the royal master mason.[35] Louis spent most winters at Blois and frequent long periods at other times. The town of Blois became the residence of many people associated with the monarchy. Florimond Robertet and Michel Gaillard were prominent royal officers who designed the same type of residence for comfortable living.[36] The nobles, however, continued to insist that their castles be designed first of all for defense.

Both Cardinal d'Amboise and Pierre de Gié rebuilt their châteaux under the influence of new ideas. D'Amboise traveled to Italy often, and he took to Renaissance culture with enthusiasm. He was the sole client of a sculpture studio in Genoa for a time. Fra Giocondo, who left France to return to Italy in 1505 and eventually worked on the new Saint Peter's, is generally credited with the design for d'Amboise's Gaillon, southwest of Rouen.[37] Since the medieval château had been destroyed in 1424, the architect had an open space unfettered by any old structure. Nonetheless, the basic plan is essentially medieval, but as at Blois the decoration and the gardens were clearly Italianate, the latter designed by Pacello. The center of the garden was a great fountain built in Italy, sent by sea to Honfleur and up the Seine. D'Amboise commissioned a Milanese sculptor to do a statue of Louis for Gaillon, which was shipped from Milan to Rouen in February 1509. It depicted Louis in the dress of a Roman officer, the first such representation of a king to be displayed in France. Gaillon had cost the cardinal 153,600 *l* by the time of his death in 1510; he left another 10,000 *l* in his will for the completion of construction, which took another year.[38] Perhaps because of the proximity of Gaillon and the movement of Italian artists and pieces through Rouen, Louis and Anne's formal entry into the city of 1508 showed the impact of classical influence. For example, Apollo and the muses appeared in a skit to offer their services to the king.[39]

Gié's Le Verger, to which he retired after his disgrace in 1506, was rebuilt after he returned from Italy in 1495. Since it was the residence of a great noble, it was more clearly designed for defense. The absence of any new ideas in its defensive works would seem to argue against Fra Giocondo's involvement, despite the tradition that he was. As at Gallion, the interior decoration was highly Italianate. Gié also had an equestrian statue of himself placed over the main gate, like Louis's at Blois. Since such statues were associated with Roman emperors, the hubris this revealed may have been a factor in his later disgrace.[40] Thomas Bohier's Chenonceaux, probably the early Renaissance château most influenced by Italian ideas and certainly the most beautiful, was begun shortly before Louis XII's death. Bohier's wife, Catherine de Briçonnet, is given much of the credit for the beautiful structure.[41]

Fra Giocondo's major known projects in France were both in Paris: the Chambre des comptes, which burned in 1737, destroying not only one of the earliest Renaissance buildings in France but also a huge collection of fiscal records, and the new Pont Notre-Dame. The old bridge collapsed in October 1499, dumping sixty-five houses built on it into the flooded Seine, but only four or five people drowned because there had been plenty of warning. The city government had received money from the king to repair it, but the funds had been used for other projects. As a result, several city officials were so heavily fined that they could not pay and spent the rest of their lives in prison. The dangers of medieval bridges were made clear in the story that the kings would not pass over the Pont St-Cloud over the Seine because it was too risky, while Queen Anne nearly was dumped into a river because the weight of her horses and coach broke the planks of a bridge.[42] Two weeks after the collapse of the Pont Notre-Dame, the city of Paris agreed to rebuild it with stone piers instead of wood as used for the old one.[43] The king agreed to grant Paris the *aides* on fish collected there to finance the bridge. A commission of master masons, including Colin Biart, decided on the basic plan, but soon a heated debate erupted over how high to make the five stone piers and six arches of the new bridge. Fra Giocondo was called in for consultation, and he gained a major role in its design.[44] The first stone was laid on March 28, 1500, with the inscription: *Loys Par la Grace de Dieu Roy de France Douzième De Ce Nom*. The bridge was completed in July 1507 at a cost of about 25,000 *l.* In 1510 the city was still collecting the *aides* on fish to pay for it. After it was completed, the Venetian ambassador called it as fine a structure as any in France.[45]

Despite some innovation in architecture, French buildings remained largely traditional during Louis's reign. In the plastic arts of painting and sculpture, Italian influences were more pronounced. French style in painting prior to 1498 owed more to Flanders, especially to Jan van Eyck, whose style emphasized the detailed realism made possible by the use of oil paint. Flemings, and Frenchman influenced by them, dominated painting in France until Charles's expedition of 1494, when Italian influence became stronger, but such painters as Jean Poyet and Jean Bourdichon, both of Tours, continued to do work in the Flemish style. Each did a *Book of Hours* for Louis and Anne.

In 1499 Jean Perréal, or Jean de Paris, accompanied Louis to Milan and was there in 1501, when he painted a monstrous Milanese baby with two faces for the king.[46] He met Leonardo da Vinci in Milan, who made a notebook entry of his intention to get from Perréal the method of painting in tempera. As *peintre du roi,* Perréal received 240 *l* a year and did various projects for the royal couple, including the design of the tomb for Anne's father. He also organized the royal entries into Lyon and the funeral service for Anne in 1514.[47] He was sent to England to paint the portrait of Louis's third wife, Mary Tudor. The work for which Perréal is best known is his portrait of Louis XII, which he took to England to give Mary.[48] In those few paintings that can be attributed to Perréal with any confidence, Italian influence seems rather limited, largely a better sense of perspective. He has often been identified, although the evidence is slight, with an unknown painter known simply as the Master of Moulins, who did the great triptych in the sacristy of the cathedral of Moulins for Pierre and Anne of Bourbon, with its greater Italian influence.[49]

A handful of Italian painters came to France during Louis's reign. The most important was Andrea Solario, a disciple of da Vinci's from Milan. Charles d'Amboise, the governor of Milan, commissioned Solario to do his portrait after da Vinci refused; he was sufficiently impressed to recommend Solario to his uncle for decorating Gaillon. From 1507 to 1509 he worked at Gaillon and after that at Blois. He did his best known painting, *Madonna with a Green Cushion,* at Blois.[50] Perhaps more influential in introducing Italian techniques to French artists were the finished paintings brought to France. In particular, Louis plundered the château of Pavia of twenty-seven portraits of members of the Visconti and Sforza families and took them to France for his wife.[51] These and other anonymous works brought to France helped to spread Italian influence. Among the most interesting are the frontispieces of a three-volume manuscript of French chronicles. In one Louis is depicted as seated on a throne surrounded by the visages of the nine "good" Roman emperors. According to one art historian, combining a French king and Roman emperors was "an innovation in French iconography."[52]

The Italian influence was most pronounced in sculpture. Charles VIII brought Guido Mazzoni to France in 1495, where he stayed until 1516. Louis XII commissioned him to do two important projects—the tomb of Charles at St-Denis and the equestrian statue of himself at Blois. Mazzoni probably also did the equestrian statue of Gié at Le Verger and the tomb of Commynes. Louis commissioned a monument for his ancestors that was done in Italy and brought to France. Cardinal d'Amboise hired sculptors from Genoa and Milan to decorate Gaillon. Among them were the three Giusti brothers, who worked in France after 1507. Their most important commission was the tomb of Louis and Anne at St-Denis, which Francis I commissioned Giovanni Giusti to do in 1517. It was finished in 1531.[53]

The impact of Italian sculpture works can be found in the productions of Michel Colombe, the greatest French sculptor of the era. Born about 1440, he was producing statues for Louis XI in a completely late-medieval style. Despite his advanced age by 1498, he remained vigorous and open to new—that is, Italian—influence. His major work in the era was the tomb of Francis II of Brittany. It was designed by Perréal, but the sculpture pieces were largely Colombe's work, produced from the marble Anne ordered from Genoa. Italianate influence is most obvious in the statues of the four cardinal virtues set at the corners of the tomb. Both in their dress and the symbols they hold, they are largely Italian. Colombe then did a bas-relief of St. George and the Dragon for Gaillon, which is similar to Donatello's. It is particularly Italianate in the decoration of its borders.

Louis XII's place in the history of the Renaissance in France would stand much higher had he succeeded in persuading Leonardo da Vinci to go to France. The king became familiar with the great artist in 1499 in Milan and asked him to go to France with him, but da Vinci refused because he had too many projects in Milan.[54] In January 1507 the Florentine ambassador reported to his government that the king wanted da Vinci, then at work in Florence, to go to Milan to produce "certain small pictures of Our Lady and others" and perhaps even his portrait. Louis himself wrote to the government of Florence asking that da Vinci be permitted to return to Milan "to make a work of his hand" for the king. He referred to Leonardo as *"peintre du roi."* Leonardo was in Florence because of a lawsuit over an inheritance, for which Louis promised help.[55]

Later that year Leonardo went back to Milan with two madonnas. Was one of them the *Virgin and Child with St. Anne,* one of his best-known works? It is plausible, since Louis might well have commissioned it for his queen.[56] Charles d'Amboise, as governor of Milan, employed him in several engineering and architectural projects, while Florimond Robertet commissioned him to do his *Madonna with a yarn winder.* Georges d'Amboise also tried unsuccessfully to get da Vinci to decorate Gaillon. In 1507, 1510, and 1511, Leonardo, listed as simply "Painter," received 400 *l* each year from the king's treasury in Milan. Whether he did the famous mechanical lion, which was able to take several steps and open its breast to reveal fleur-de-lys for Louis's entry into Milan in 1507, is a disputed point among historians. Some think it was done for Francis I in 1515.[57]

Michelangelo also had received a commission from Louis's courtiers. Early in Louis's reign Gié had asked that he make a statue of David for him similar to the one of Donatello's that he had seen in Florence in 1494. After Michelangelo had finished the great marble *David* in 1504, he agreed to produce a smaller one in bronze for the marshal. By the time it was finished, Gié had been disgraced, and the Florentine government did not wish to waste such a prize on a man without influence. Robertet, however, knew that the statue had been done, and he asked for it several times before it was sent by water to his Château of Bury in 1508. Unfortunately, the statue later disappeared, perhaps during the Wars of Religion, and has never been recovered.[58]

Of all the arts Louis probably appreciated music the most.[59] His father was an accomplished musician as well as a poet, and many of his poems were set to music; his mother was said to have had a band playing at the foot of her bed as she gave birth to Louis. A story has it that the king loved to sing with the choir of the royal chapel, despite completely lacking a voice for singing. The great Flemish composer Josquin Des Prez is supposed to have written a piece entitled *Lutuichi regis Franciae jocesa cantio,* with a very simple part designated *"vox regis"* so that Louis could sing along.[60] While still the duke of Orléans, he commissioned a collection of songs by Josquin and his countryman Jean Ockeghem. Those two were the most noted of the large group of Fleming composers who received patronage from the French monarchy and settled in France. As a group, they contributed greatly to the development of polyphony and counterpoint.

As a music historian has written, the "incredibly productive generation of northern musicians" of the years around 1500 created the High Renaissance in music.[61] Along with Josquin, the best known among those who sang in the royal chapel under Louis were Loyset Compère, Antoine de Févin, and Jean Moutin. The last was more truly in Anne's service, and he composed motets to celebrate the major events of her life, such as her marriage and birth of her children. Josquin, regarded as an important precursor of Palestrina, become the music director of the royal chapel in 1500 after thirteen years in the papal chapel. He is supposed to have written *Memor esto verbi tui,* based on Psalm 118, to remind Louis of his promise to give him a church benefice. Regardless of whether his motive for composing it was so mundane, it is regarded as one of the crowning achievements of his life. After writing a five-voice motet based on Psalm 129 for Louis's funeral, he left France.[62]

In music, the lines of influence went from Flanders through France to Italy. Louis's trips with his chapel singers in tow was one means of bringing Flemish polyphony to Italy. But Italian musicians were not entirely without an impact on the French court. While Louis was in Milan in 1502, he sent back to France "an orchestra of six musicians" who played the sackbut and the oboe, to be paid 120 *l* each a year. They joined two Italian trumpet players already at the court. The king also drew on Italy for organ builders, as did Anne of Brittany, who had a great organ brought from Naples to Amboise. The master organist under Louis was a Master Evard from Tours. Louis and his court also took an interest in popular secular music, in which French poetry was set to music, including some of the pieces from *Rhétoriqueurs.*[63]

As a patron of the arts and learning, Louis played a significant role in the coming of the Renaissance in France, despite being badly overshadowed by the greater accomplishments and reputation of Francis I. Unlike Francis, who was by far the dominant patron of art and learning at his court, Louis shared equal or nearly equal billing with Queen Anne, who as a patron of humanists was more active than he, and several of his officers, especially d'Amboise, Gié, Robertet, Poncher, and Ganay. The last three were part of that large group of bourgeois financiers-turned-royal-officers from Tours who dominated the offices of finance and justice in Louis's reign and who as a group provided broad patronage of new ideas. They probably were necessary to introduce to the very different intellectual atmosphere of France the mental outlook of the merchant-politicians of the Italian city-states who created humanism.[64] Louis XII's more sober personality and frugality compared to Francis I's made it difficult for him to take to Italian culture and learning with the exuberant enthusiasm and lavish spending that his successor did. Louis certainly was more traditional in his tastes, but his reign nonetheless laid a solid foundation on which Francis, the "Father of Arts and Sciences," could build the French Renaissance.

12

Head of the Gallican Church

Closely associated with Renaissance humanism in northern Europe was the call for church reform. As head of the church in France, Louis XII had greater power to effect change in religion than he did in culture, but his attitude toward reform was about the same as it was toward the art and learning of the Italian Renaissance—an interest but limited involvement. It was difficult for Louis to see the pressing need for reform for at least three reasons. One was the completely conventional nature of his religious beliefs. Pilgrimages, relics, and pious practices were very much a part of his usual routine. Another was the interlocking directorate between church and state, in which members of the royal family and families of his close friends and advisers held high posts in the hierarchy. A third was the dominant theory of church governance in France of Louis's era, Gallicanism, which, in one version, proposed that the power and wealth of the church were at the disposal of the monarchy. Although the clergy constituted at most 4 percent of the French population, they controlled about a third of the land of the realm, and one knowledgeable observer (albeit writing in 1563) claimed they received 40 percent of its revenues.

Gallicanism can be defined as the theory that the French church, of which the king was the head, was free from papal control over the administration of its offices and finances, while it accepted the pope's authority in matters of doctrine and discipline. The first clear expression of the concept dated to 1407 when Charles VI proclaimed two cornerstone edicts on the relationship between the French church and the papacy. He declared that the Gallican church had traditionally enjoyed certain liberties from papal authority, in particular, the freedom of France from papal appointive power. Once the Great Schism was resolved and there were no more French popes at Avignon, tensions between France and Rome grew serious. They culminated in the Pragmatic Sanction of Bourges, which was drawn up in 1438 by a national assembly of the French church and promulgated by Charles VII. The Pragmatic Sanction made explicit the

principle of local control over appointments to the French hierarchy. Both
in the manner of its creation and in its content, it was the quintessential
Gallican document, reflecting the ideas that a general council of the
church was superior to the pope and a French national council could leg-
islate for the Gallican church. It expounded the view that the king was
able to call such assemblies and issue their decrees in his authority as head
of the French church.

The Pragmatic Sanction espoused in particular a point of view known as
ecclesiastical Gallicanism, because its crucial clause returned to the French
clergy the power to fill the major benefices (a clerical office with an income
attached) of the French church—the bishoprics and the abbacies of the
major monasteries. The pope still had the right to accept or reject the nominees, since he continued to give them their bulls of office. Royal Gallicanism,
sometimes called *parlementaire* Gallicanism because the Parlement was its outspoken advocate, endorsed the right of the king to fill those benefices. The
Pragmatic Sanction returned the naming of bishops and abbots to the cathedral and monastery chapters, the system that the popes had overturned in the
previous two centuries. The king's rights in the naming of the major churchmen were restricted to the use of "sweet and kind prayers" that the chapters
consider worthy candidates whom he might wish to recommend to them. In
1502 Louis XII successfully waged a extensive campaign to get François de
Castelnau, bishop of St-Pons, elected archbishop of Narbonne, writing to the
pope, the chapter, and several prominent nobles of Languedoc.[1] When the
chancellor came in person to promote the king's choice, as Jean de Ganay did
at Bourges in 1512, there was little question who would be chosen.[2] Last, the
Pragmatic Sanction eliminated papal taxation on French benefices, especially
a tax called the *annates*, the first year's revenues from a benefice when it was
filled. The protection of the wealth of the French church was clearly a major
goal of Gallicanism. The Pragmatic Sanction recognized that the pope could
receive a gift of money from the French clergy but rejected the idea that he
had a right to any funds from France.

By 1498 the Pragmatic Sanction had been in effect for sixty years. Louis
XI had put little stock in its clauses. He rode roughshod over them by
sending names to the chapters and demanding that the clerics elected them.
In numerous cases he simply named the new bishops and abbots, and the
pope presented them with their bulls of office.[3] During the drastic reduction
of royal power marking Charles VIII's early years, the chapters reasserted
their rights. When a more mature Charles sought to regain control, a bitter
confrontation between monarch and churchmen resulted. While ultimate
victory for the king was a foregone conclusion, the chapters fought stub-

bornly, and the decade before 1498 was a period of extraordinary confusion in the episcopate, as numerous sees had two candidates, one elected by the chapter and the other named by the king. In the case of the see of Sarlat, there were three candidates for the vacancy of 1493—two supported by factions in the chapter and a third by the king. Of course, the king's choice eventually won the office. The popes of the era, despite their official position of hostility to the Pragmatic Sanction, which they regarded as a thoroughly schismatic document, usually cooperated with the king by granting the bulls of office to his candidates. Even papal approval, however, did not always end the disputes in the sees. The chapters and their candidates frequently refused to concede, and the disputes continued for years, with violence and force frequently involved. Some were taken to the Parlement, but in one case at least, the disputed see of Pamiers, even a decision by the Parlement failed to settle the case, which dragged on from 1467 to 1498.[4]

When Louis XII reached the throne, his good relations with Alexander VI augured ill for the system of chapter elections. Alexander routinely approved the king's candidates, and the chapters found they could not prevent them from taking office. For example, at Paris in 1503, Etienne de Poncher, the king's choice, quickly won papal approval and easily took control of the see, despite the presence of a well-respected and prominent candidate elected by the chapter. Louis and Alexander settled another long-term problem—papal claims to the right to fill the benefices of Valentinois and Die, formerly a papal enclave in France. The pope recognized royal authority in the counties, which Louis then gave to Cesare Borgia.

The most important concession Alexander gave Louis was granting the office of papal legate in France to Georges d'Amboise in 1501. It gave the king's right-hand man vast power over the French church, but since it was a papal grant, it still preserved the pretense of papal authority in France. The cardinal combined in himself royal and papal rights in the Gallican church, but even that enormous power was not sufficient to overcome the anarchy in the clergy. Among the rights the office gave d'Amboise was that of filling a number of midlevel benefices the Pragmatic Sanction had left in the pope's control. They were an important source of patronage, especially since they were the sort of church office a young nobleman starting a career in the church would have been given. The cardinal now also had the right to judge cases that were appealed to Rome, including disputed chapter elections, and reform monastic orders and universities. It was the first time a French prelate had held so much power, which became even greater when Julius II, immediately after his election in 1503, made d'Amboise's appointment as legate permanent instead of for a specific term, as it had been under Alexander.[5] The most similar situation was Cardinal Wolsey's in England. After d'Amboise's death in 1510, efforts to duplicate his position failed, largely because the prelates named as legates did not have the king's entire confidence. After the Concordat of Bologna was instituted in 1516, the French kings no longer had a need for a "Gallican pope," as d'Amboise has been called.

Not all the French were eager to see d'Amboise become so powerful. Both the Parlement of Paris and the University of Paris protested, using Gallican arguments against his promotion. The former refused to register the papal bill elevating d'Amboise, as it was required to do for all papal bulls affecting the French church. It took a *lettre ðe jussion* from Louis to force the Parlement to register it. Nor did giving the cardinal so much power solve the problems in the church. Disputed episcopal elections continued to occur, and some became violent. The most notorious were the cases of Rodez in 1501 and Poitiers in 1507. In the former, the king sent a letter to the cathedral chapter recommending Charles de Tournon, who was the seventeen-year-old scion of a prominent family. The letter stated that the king "will be content and God well served" if he were elected. The canons, however, refused to read the letter before they made their choice, and they voted fifteen to one for François d'Estaing, a local notable, whom Louis had appointed to the Grand Conseil in 1498. Tournon went to Rome with Louis's blessing to procure an annulment of the chapter election, meanwhile sending men-at-arms to take possession of the bishopric. The affair was taken to the Grand Conseil, which rendered a verdict in favor of d'Estaing. Tournon refused to concede his control of the bishop's revenues and powers, and the matter was settled only in late 1503 when he died.[6]

At Poitiers, upon the death of the incumbent bishop, two factions formed in the cathedral chapter: one supported Claude de Tonnerre, the late bishop's nephew; and the other, Florente d'Allemagne, from a prominent local family. Both candidates had support in the local power institutions—the royal courts, the municipal government, and the nobility. In the evening before the election, one faction seized control of the cathedral, and the other used force to drive it out. A cleric was killed in the episode. Despite this, the chapter proceeded to vote, but after three days of tumult and threats of violence with no results, the local *sénéschal* imposed the king's choice. The loser's party appealed the case all the way to the Grand Conseil in January 1509 before giving up.[7] Violence, albeit on a lesser scale, simony, and corruption were frequent features of the process of electing bishops. So were appeals by the losing parties to the Parlement, the king, and the pope. From 1483 to 1516 at least fifty-five cases of disputed episcopal elections—twenty-two in Louis's reign—and some eighty disputed elections of abbots were heard at the royal or papal courts.[8]

Despite the intent in the Pragmatic Sanction to reduce royal influence in episcopal elections, Louis had good success in seating his choices in episcopal sees, in part because the popes routinely accepted his nominees. In two regions of France, however, royal writ did not run in regard to filling benefices. Both Provence and Brittany did not fall under the Pragmatic Sanction, because they had not been part of the realm in 1438. The pope still appointed their bishops, but in Brittany he needed ducal approval of his choices. In 1505 Anne of Brittany won the concession from Julius II that no bishop would be appointed to a Breton see who was not a native and not residing in the duchy.

Given the haphazard system of episcopal appointments at that time, it is difficult to determine who had the major responsibility for seating the 135 bishops named during Louis's reign. But the fact that nearly 70 percent of those bishops were members of the royal council or their relatives suggests a strong royal influence.[9] Yet such practices as "resignation in favor," by which a prelate could name his successor in his letter of resignation, allowed many prominent noble families to control the sees of their regions, ensuring that family members or clients were given any vacancies. Cardinal d'Amboise's family had kingdomwide influence in that respect; during Louis's reign six family members held bishoprics scattered across France, including the wealthiest see, Rouen. In all, 44 percent of the 135 bishops seated in the period from 1498 to 1514 came from the nobility of the sword. Another 21 percent came from the nobility of the robe, largely from the successful financier families of Tours, who held so many offices under Louis. Only six bishops were clearly commoners by birth, while eighteen were Italians, who were found mostly in Provence.[10] An important source of bishops for the French church was the royal chapel, whose chaplains were far better known to the king than most other clergymen.

The description of Louis's behavior during his illness of 1505 reveals that he was a conventionally pious man for his era. In particular he had a deep devotion to the Holy Eucharist. While ill, he ordered a courier to take his crown to Dijon and bring back in it to Blois the host, famed for its miracles, which Pope Eugene IV had consecrated a half century earlier and given to the duke of Burgundy.[11] When Louis was healthy, he heard Mass at six every morning. During Lent, all unnecessary activity, even his hunting, halted, and the noted preachers of the region around Blois, where the court nearly always was at that time of the year, were brought in to give the lenten sermons. Jean Clerée, Louis's confessor, frequently gave them, often calling for church reform.[12]

The very conventionality of Louis's religion made it difficult for him to see the need for church reform. From the beginning of his reign, he had a bad relationship with the most outspoken of the reformers of the era, Jean Standonck, who had criticized the annulment of his first marriage. Standonck, a native of Flanders, was familiar with the Canons of Windesheim from his homeland and invited them, an offshoot of the Brethren of the Common Life, to establish a house in Paris in the hope of reforming the city's clergy. When he mounted a campaign to be elected archbishop of Reims in order to use that office to direct reform, Louis easily quashed his bid and secured the appointment of his own candidate. Louis also had little to do with Jacques Lefèvre d'Etaples, the noted humanist, but his reputation as an advocate for reform developed only after Louis's death.

With Alexander VI, perhaps the most immoral pope in history, leading the church, there can be little surprise that much of the clergy, both high and low, failed to live up to the standards expected of it. In respect to the prelates, a major problem was the rampant pluralism—the holding of two or more benefices. They would take the incomes from the benefices and find vicars, who often lived in poverty, to do the duties of the offices. In 1515 there were eleven pluralist bishops, not a bad proportion in comparison with later in the century, but, nonetheless, it ensured that eleven sees would not have resident bishops. Pluralism was a greater problem in the monasteries, where the office of abbot of most French religious houses was held "in trust" by the major churchmen. The worst example during Louis's reign was Amanieu d'Albret, the son of Alain d'Albret, who in the course of a twenty-year career as a churchman governed ten sees either as the ordinary bishop or as administrator (but not all at once) and twenty-one monasteries and became a cardinal as well.[13]

There were other reason besides pluralism for the rampant absenteeism. An important factor was the practice of naming royal officials to major benefices as rewards for royal service. Louis's royal council had five bishops who routinely attended its meetings. Several members of the royal chapel were bishops, who were usually with the court. Prelates served as ambassadors and, less frequently, royal governors, as d'Amboise was for Normandy. When Louis made his triumphant entry into Genoa after crushing its revolt in 1507, four cardinals, two archbishops, and six bishops were with him. One of the cardinals, Tristan Salazar, participated in the reduction of Genoa "armed with all weapons and seated on a grand charger holding a great lance."[14] The idea that the upper levels of the church made up a pool of talented or high-ranking men available for the monarchy's use was never challenged in this era.

Still another practice that went unquestioned was the granting of episcopal office to teenage boys if they came from prominent families. To Louis's credit, the number of underage bishops seated in his reign was rather small. One such incidence was the naming of Michel de Bucy as archbishop of Bourges in 1505 at about the age of twenty-one years. The question of whether he was Louis's illegitimate son or that of one of the d'Amboises does not change the facts that he was a bastard and underage. One of Pierre de Gié's sons was named archbishop of Lyon at age twenty-two. In general, however, Louis's reign was not as replete with underage bishops as were those of his predecessors and successors.[15]

More of a problem was the open immorality of many prelates. It is hard to find a vice for which at least several bishops were not notorious, but, as always has been true, sexual misconduct dominated. The prelates had concubines and illegitimate children in large numbers. Brantôme, an abbé himself who loved to relate the misbehavior of the higher clergy, told of one bishop who, "in order to build up his harem," gave pensions to ten-year-old girls so they would be available when they were old enough "Like a hunter who raises puppies for the hunt," he commented.[16] Again it was Amanieu d'Albret who provided the worst example. His many benefices gave him about 40,000 *l* in revenues, which he dissipated in jousting, hunting, and buying jewels. When he died, he had no money left for his three children, of whom his father took custody.[17] When the higher clergy behaved so badly, how could the village curés be expected to be paragons of virtue? Not that every prelate or priest was devoid of virtue by any means, but enough were that reform of the clergy was a major issue of the era.

A major problem in the church was the forging of papal documents granting the income from pensions and indulgences and the collation of benefices. France was full of fake priests and monks as well as real ones, footloose and unattached, who swindled the populace. Even legitimate priests were often extortionists, demanding payment for administering the sacraments and in particular burying the dead. In 1510 the Parisian clergy reportedly raised the fees for funerals so high that the poor had to beg alms to pay for them.[18]

Louis XII can hardly be called a zealous reformer of the clergy, but he did make an effort under the influence of Cardinal d'Amboise. The cardinal exhibited some of the flaws of the high clergy of his era: absenteeism, avarice, grandiosity as revealed in the building of Gaillon, soaring ambition, but not, as far as is known, pluralism or sexual intemperance. There have been those who lamented his failure to win the papacy on the grounds that he would have been an ardent reform pope. Ardent is probably too strong a term for his reforming tendencies, but it is likely that he would have done more to reform the church than did the popes who reigned during his career.[19]

There was a long tradition of calls for church reform, which had gone largely unheeded. The Estates of 1484 had made one of the more powerful such requests, but Charles VIII, distracted by his Italian adventure, paid little attention. A small number of monasteries and convents did reform themselves by returning to the original rule of their founders. Under Louis XII, church reform became less spontaneous and more centrally directed. In early 1502, according to d'Auton, the king devoted two months to the problems of the police of the realm and the reform of the church. Special attention was given to reforming the monastic orders. D'Auton wrote that the monks saw their religious vows as license to do evil and live in dishonor.[20]

The bull creating d'Amboise legate gave him the authority to reform monasteries. He issued an edict in March 1502 requiring the houses of Dominicans and Franciscans in Paris to submit to a formal visitation by a commission of bishops. The commission included Pierre Bonnin, the *procureur général* of the Grand Conseil, who was also bishop of Autun. The Dominicans had 300 to 400 members in Paris, "who failed to observe all the rules of their order and were dissolute in conversation and behavior."[21] They refused to accept the mandate for reform. When d'Amboise and Louis received the commission report, they told the Dominicans that they would use force to drive them out of their house and from Paris if they refused to reform. The friars refused anew and proceeded to fortify their house, aided by many students of the university who at this time sharply opposed Louis. The students brought weapons to the Dominican house, and some 1,200 men in all were in arms there. The archers of the royal guard and the sergeants of the provost of Paris used force to clear the house and drove those who were in it outside the walls of the city.[22]

A third religious institution in Paris that underwent the same process was the Benedictine monastery of St-Germain-des-Près. Again an armed force was needed to force the monks to admit the reform commission. The Benedictines responded by appealing to the Parlement and the papal court. They ultimately lost, but they were able to delay the reform process for several years.[23] Outside of Paris similar episodes took place in the Franciscan houses in Dijon, Amiens, and Tournai and the Dominican houses of St-Maximin in Provence and Figéac in Guyenne. The objections and appeals of the religious orders reached deaf ears at the royal and the papal courts. Both Alexander and Julius supported Louis and d'Amboise. In 1505 Julius explicitly approved of the cardinal's work up to that point and prohibited any appeal by Dominicans and Franciscans until the general chapter of each order had met to direct reform. In 1510, before he died, d'Amboise was seeking papal authority to reform the Carmelite houses in France.

Not every religious institution objected so strongly to proposed reform. In particular the houses of nuns accepted the reimposition of cloister and the regulation of their finances with little objection. The most important case was the convent of Fontevrault where Louis's sister Anne had been abbess. The agreement of 1507 reforming the convent became standard,[24] and in the next few years most houses of nuns had been visited and reformed.

Nonetheless, even with Louis's support d'Amboise's work made little headway in the reform of the French church. It was too piecemeal, religious house by religious house, and the stubborn and skillful opposition of the antireformers took up his time and energy. The situation called for a much broader effort across the entire Gallican church, and that required a national council. The papacy was fiercely hostile to any such meeting, which it regarded as leading to schism, and Louis's Italian ambitions required humoring the pope on such matters. It was only when Louis had clearly broken with Julius II that he called a national council in 1511, and its focus was on the contretemps between pope and French king then going on. Its limited attempts at church reform were tentative and unproductive.[25]

The French kings of the Renaissance era were more than once at the edge of schism with Rome, but heresy was another matter. Their role as head of the Gallican church included an obligation to protect it and drive from the realm those whom the church defined as its enemies. A new king swore to that in his consecration ceremony. The oath had little impact on Louis, because the church of his era was largely free from any organized heretical movements. These were, to be sure, numerous episodes of individual deviation from orthodoxy. For example, a twenty-two-year-old student from Abbeville attending Mass at Sainte-Chapelle in 1502 took the consecrated host, broke it into pieces, and stomped on it. A Dominican of St-Maximin in 1505 broke the head off a statue of Mary. Both were executed, by burning and hanging respectively.[26] Louis issued a harsh decree against blasphemy in March 1511, but its effect is impossible to measure.

In the one case involving organized heresy, Louis's position was ambivalent. Since the fourteenth century anti-Catholic groups had lived in the mountain valleys of Dauphiné. Whether they had direct ties back to Peter Waldo and his Poor Men of Lyon of the twelfth century will probably never be determined, but a similarity in doctrine or perhaps simply the conviction that all dissenters were Waldensians prompted later churchmen to tag them Waldensians. Under Charles VIII, Jean Baile, the archbishop of Embrum, and local nobles, acting with a semblance of papal and royal authority, began a crusade against the Waldensians in 1487. The victims, however, did something no other target of a crusade had ever done: They appealed to the king against the crusaders. As usually happened with appeals to the king, this one was sent to the Parlement of Paris and then to the Grand Conseil, and, as was generally true, it took a very long time to be resolved. In 1498 Louis sent a letter to Alexander VI asking for a formal commission to investigate the affair. Three years later the pope named a four-man commission headed by Laurent Bureau, bishop of Sisteron. He and another member went to Dauphiné to take testimony and decided that the crusaders had indeed illegally seized the property of the accused heretics. Appeals of that decision, jurisdictional disputes between the Grand Conseil and the Parlement of Grenoble, and the death of Bureau in 1504 all served to delay a final resolution. In 1508 the Grand Conseil ordered that the archbishop of Embrum, several of his officials, and some nobles involved in the crusade come to Paris. When they failed to appear, they were declared contumacious, and Louis gave the verdict to the Waldensians. The decision declared that while there was some reason to suspect the orthodoxy of those against whom the crusade had acted, the proper procedures of the law had not been followed. All confiscated property was to be returned.[27]

This episode demonstrated very clearly one aspect of French society in that era—a strong commitment to proper procedure in law, even if those denounced to the law were regarded as heretics. There is no question that Louis XII was deeply committed to that principle, but he had another motive as well. In 1501 a member of commission told the archbishop of Embrum that the king had been given to understand that the people of the region in question "were powerful enough to provide for his needs, when the King should ask, forty or fifty thousand ducats, so the said lord did not intend to lose such subjects."[28] In addition to the taxes they paid, the Waldensians inhabited the approaches to the best passes through the southern Alps into Italy.

Louis proved to be less tolerant toward another group of outsiders—the Jews of Provence. Since Provence had been not part of the realm when Philip IV expelled the Jews from France, a large Jewish community had remained in the province. When Louis XI annexed the region, he, as count of Provence, issued an edict confirming the privileges of the Jews there, which Charles VIII reaffirmed in 1489 for a gift of 3,200 florins. However, popular agitation directed against the Jews in Marseille and

Arles as usurers prompted him to issue an edict expelling them on the pretext that it was for their own protection. In May 1500 Louis reissued the edict, which compelled the Jews of Provence either to convert to Christianity or to leave the realm in three months. The edict emphasized the problem of baptized Jews returning to their former faith and the scandal that the presence of those who did not believe in Christ caused for the people. The implementation of the edict was delayed for a year, clearly in the hope that the threat of expulsion would prompt conversions. Apparently a number of Jews did convert, but many did not, since Louis reissued his edict in July 1501, and it was then enforced. In 1503 the king prevented the converted Jews from taking over the communal property of the former Jewish communities by claiming it for the crown.[29]

Such matters as protection of the Waldensians, expulsion of the Provençal Jews, or the reform of the clergy were all minor issues to Louis XII; his major concern was getting cardinal d'Amboise elected pope. He may have thought that reforming the Gallican church would be easier with a Frenchman as pope, but he could not have been unaware of the enormous benefits that would accrue to the French monarchy with his trusted friend and adviser on St. Peter's throne, especially in respect to his Italian ambitions. Louis was fully committed to getting his friend elected. Guicciardini wrote after the death of Alexander VI that d'Amboise was "in the highest expectations of obtaining the Pontificate by the authority and money and arms of his Master."[30]

When word reached Louis at Mâcon of Alexander's death in August 1503, he and his first minister were ready for the coming conclave. The king had released Ludovico Sforza's brother, Cardinal Ascanio, from captivity two years earlier, and he accompanied d'Amboise to Rome. There is no direct evidence that his release had followed a promise to vote for d'Amboise in the next conclave, but Guicciardini was one of those who believed such a pledge had been asked for.[31] The cardinal of Aragon, a brother of the king of Naples, who was then in exile in France, was sent to Rome with his expenses paid. The French also counted on the support of the very influential Cardinal Giuliano della Rovere, since he had spent ten years in exile in France because of his fierce opposition to Alexander. Louis had been generous to him. When earlier in 1503 rumor said Alexander was dying, Louis had sent the cardinal of Nantes to della Rovere to promote his friend's candidacy.[32] Louis also made a secret agreement with Cesare Borgia, pledging to maintain him in his current possessions in exchange for his support for d'Amboise. Cesare, for his part, held the pledge of the eleven Spanish cardinals to vote for whomever

he designated. On the other hand, there were only three other French cardinals besides d'Amboise. The king had been enraged earlier in 1503
when Alexander had named twelve new cardinals, and none of them had
been French, while five had been Spanish.[33] Guicciardini claimed that
d'Amboise had worked to mollify Louis's anger at Alexander on several
occasions in the hope that the pope would name members of his family as
cardinals and swell the number of votes for him.[34]

As a result of the large number of cardinals Alexander had created in
his reign, largely as a source of revenue since the new cardinals were
expected to give him large gifts, there were thirty-seven cardinals at the
conclave, the largest to that time. The Italians numbered twenty-two, just
short of the two-thirds needed to elect a new pope, but they were badly
divided into factions. The pro-French faction was quite small, including
the only two French cardinals present, d'Amboise and Amanieu d'Albret.

Louis left no stone unturned to make his friend pope. The Venetian
ambassador in Rome reported:

> The representative of the king of France has received an written instruc-
> tion from his master to exhort all the cardinals to consult his pleasure and
> make the cardinal of Rouen Pope. Every possible blandishment,
> promise, and inducement is employed, together with implied threats
> against those who may ignore the request. The message has been com-
> municated to each cardinal individually.[35]

The ambassador went on to say that the Italian cardinals intended to foil
Louis by hurrying the conclave without waiting for the French cardinals,
but he expected that the French king would use his army in the region of
Rome to prevent that from happening. La Trémoille, leading the French
army to Naples, indeed was ordered to halt his march and be in position to
influence the conclave. Meanwhile d'Amboise left Mâcon for Rome on
August 28 "with silver à *largesse*," gentlemen in great number, and 200
archers of the royal guard.[36] He reached Rome late in the evening of
September 10, and was greeted, despite the hour, by a huge crowd shouting "Rouen! Rouen!"

In spite of all that, d'Amboise's bid was doomed to fail. Cesare Borgia
fell ill, preventing him from taking an active part in ensuring that his
clients among the cardinals voted for the French candidate. Without his
direct involvement, the Spanish cardinals followed the directive of
Isabella and Ferdinand, who made it clear they did not want a French
pope. Spanish forces were also moved into the vicinity of Rome. Ascanio
Sforza continued to voice support for d'Amboise while working against

him behind the scenes. He hoped to be elected himself and borrowed over 100,000 ducats "to buy the voice of the Holy Spirit if it could not be heard."[37] Third, della Rovere failed to be as supportive as the French expected. He complained that the French king had promised to make him pope and now was reneging. He added that he was going to look after his own interests and not vote for d'Amboise unless the Frenchman already had enough votes to win, which he did not expect to happen.[38] Before it had become clear to the cardinal of Rouen that della Rovere was working against him, he allowed della Rovere to persuade him to order the French troops to move ten miles away from Rome.

Six days after d'Amboise had reached Rome, the conclave opened in the Vatican Palace with thirty-seven cardinals present. From the first vote or scrutiny, it was clear that there were three strong candidates: d'Amboise, della Rovere, and a Spaniard, Cardinal Carvajal. Sforza did vote for d'Amboise but refused to persuade any of his allies to follow suit. After a week the conclave had reached a stalemate. D'Amboise, like the other leading candidates, looked for a cardinal both for whom he could vote and who was not likely to live very long. As Giustinian reported, "When the Cardinal of Rouen saw that he could not be elected, he thought that if he could not be pope himself, he had better avoid the humiliation of having one elected of whom he disapproved. So . . . he went with the stream and sought the glory of making it appear that the pope was his choice." The pope-makers settled on Cardinal Piccolimini, the nephew of Pius II, who was sixty-four years of age, in poor health, and as neutral a candidate as could be had. He was acclaimed pope on September 22.[39]

While most agreed that the new Pius III was a worthy choice, Louis was enraged that his friend had not been elected. He directed most of his anger at Cesare Borgia: "That son of a whore has prevented Rouen from becoming pope."[40] As has been noted, delaying the French army at Rome for the election was a factor in its eventual defeat in Naples. Thus the campaign to elect d'Amboise pope was disastrous for Louis's interests, all the more so because Pius III died after twenty-six days as pope. He had been elected largely because the other candidates did not expect him to reign long; worn out by the lengthy coronation ceremonies, he greatly exceeded their expectations.

The cardinals had hardly begun to disperse when Pius died, and all were able to return to Rome for the new election. However, della Rovere had already secured the votes needed, whether by promises and persuasion or outright bribery. In the same evening as the conclave opened on October 31, della Rovere was acclaimed pope, the shortest conclave ever under the procedures adopted in the twelfth century and still largely in effect today. He took the name Julius II, more in reference to Julius Caesar, it has been argued, than to his obscure predecessor Julius I. The new pope was sixty years old but in excellent health, and his energy and activity were those of a man much younger. Armed with a powerful will and a fierce temper, he was a formidable opponent, especially since his diplomatic skills matched his determination to dominate.

The French looked favorably on Julius's election, because it was thought the ten years he had spent in France had made him a French partisan. Louis's special envoy who arrived in Rome in April 1505 to render his obedience told Julius that the king had felt great joy and hope when his friend of so many years became pontiff.[41] The pope quickly moved to reassure them by naming d'Amboise's nephew, the bishop of Narbonne, a cardinal. Julius humored d'Amboise by renewing his office of legate and make the title permanent, unlike his previous appointment under Alexander, which had been for a specified term. Julius also gave d'Amboise the legation of Avignon. Again there was resistance in France to d'Amboise's new power. Magistrates of the Parlement of Paris argued that a permanent legate would be a second pope. In April 1504 Louis XII wrote another *lettre de jussion* to the Parlement ordering it to register the papal bull on the matter and threatening to expel the most recalcitrant magistrates. It then did so, despite a last-moment appeal from the rector of the university against it.[42]

Julius II was very accommodating to the French in the first several years of his pontificate, but Cardinal Sforza, who had known him for a long time, had a more accurate assessment of his attitude than did the French. According to Guicciardini, Sforza believed that once Julius was pope, he was likely to be of "the same restless disposition or in a greater degree than he had been in his lower state of fortune" and he might open the way for the Sforza recovery of the duchy of Milan.[43] While Cardinal Sforza never returned to Milan, he was certainly correct about Julius' impact on French rule in Italy. From the moment Julius became pope, he was scheming on how to drive the French out of his homeland. Largely because the papal treasury was empty due to Alexander's extravagance, Julius could not move quickly against the French, but he bided his time and worked to refill his treasury and reestablish his control over the papal states before he confronted the French. Being the shrewd diplomat that he was, he was able even to get the French to cooperate in several of his schemes against other powers in Italy. Soon enough the French and Louis XII would feel the sting of the powerful mind and will of Julius II, *Papa Terribilis*.

13

Back to Italy

The election of Julius II as pope would prove to be a devastating blow to Louis XII's ambitions for French rule in Italy, but its impact would not be felt for several years after 1503. For a time, Julius was cautiously accommodating toward the French. The first target of his fertile mind was Cesare Borgia, whose plans to create his own realm in the papal states threatened to deprive the new pope of a power base from which to drive the foreigners out of Italy. For their part, Louis and d'Amboise were angry with Borgia for his failure to control the outcome of the conclave, and without his father on the papal throne, he was far less valuable an ally. Thus, they made little protest as the new pope moved against Cesare.

Julius quickly demonstrated his shrewdness by persuading Cesare to use his forces against Venice, which was encroaching on papal lands in the Romagna. Thinking that Julius was revealing his support, Cesare agreed. Once Borgia's army was sufficiently worn down, Julius ordered him arrested. He was seized at Ostia where he was about to embark on a galley for Genoa to get the huge sums he had on deposit there. He was taken to Rome in chains. After extensive negotiations, Julius allowed Cesare to go to Naples in exchange for the forts his forces still held. Upon Borgia's arrival, Gonsalvo, on Ferdinand's order, violated the safe conduct he had given Cesare and put him on a ship for Spain, where he arrived in September 1504. Two years later Cesare escaped from his captors and fled to his brother-in-law's kingdom of Navarre, where he died fighting against the Spanish in March 1507. Although Cesare had been Louis's ally, his removal from Italy little bothered the king who regarded Borgia as too fickle to be a true friend. When Cesare, after his escape from the Spanish, asked for the revenues from his French estates, Louis instead confiscated them and stripped him of his French titles. It was probably also the French king who had ordered that the Genoese bankers not turn over Borgia's money. However, it is also possible that Julius had done it, since, as a native of Savona, to the west of Genoa and part of its *contrado,* and kin to the Fregosi, a prominent family, he had broad influence with the Genoese.[1]

For the same reason, when unrest erupted in Genoa in 1506 against French rule, virtually everyone thought that the pope had a hand in fomenting it. The outbreak of violence in Genoa early in 1506 was related to the French takeover of 1499 in that it had given the city's aristocracy the opportunity to regain political power after 150 years out of power. Since then Louis had done nothing to ameliorate the bitter social divisions in the city.[2] A series of street fights between nobles and commoners escalated into a general attack on the nobility and demands for a popular government for the city. When the troubles began, the French governor of Genoa, Philip of Cleves, was in France; his lieutenant, Pierre de Roquebertin, was sympathetic to the popular party. He was accused of accepting a bribe of 10,000 *écus* from it, but that may have been the only way the French could account for his supporting the popular party.[3]

Both factions sought to capture the king's ear by sending delegations to him. He replied in a letter to the popular faction that he was greatly disturbed with the news of quarrels and violence, and he wanted the people of his fair city to live in peace and prosperity. He wrote that he had ordered Cleves to return to his post, and he pledged to provide justice for both sides. Cleves arrived in Genoa in early August 1506 with 1,000 men and immediately erected a gallows in a public square to show how he intended to deal with future disturbances. Unfortunately he failed to live up to his resolve, and after new riots he allowed the popular party to persuade him to expel the nobles from the city. It pushed its advantage further by electing new municipal officials to supervise the French officers. Louis, eager to avoid new trouble and persuaded by Cleves that the right thing had been done, approved of these developments.

As so often has happened in history, the concessions only emboldened the hotheads in the Genoese popular party to push for greater gains. Persuaded that their new power would not be secure as long as the nobles held the *contrado*, popular militia units were sent out to occupy the countryside, with mixed results. The popular leaders decided to concentrate on Monaco, the stronghold of the prominent Genoese noble family, the Grimaldi. The Grimaldi habit of levying illegal tolls on ships passing by Monaco had led to a royal edict against them, and the popular leaders felt that they could conquer the place under the pretext of serving the royal will. Thus in early December 1506, a force of about 4,000 men laid siege to Monaco.

Louis XII was furious when he heard what was happening from the envoys of the Genoese nobles, who offered him a subsidy of 100,000 ducats to use force against the popular party.[4] Julius II told Genoa that his nuncio to France had written that he had never seen the king so angry, to the point that no one dared to say the name of the city in front of him. Louis recalled Cleves and ordered Yves d'Alègre, then in Milan, to go to the relief of Monaco. As d'Alègre assembled 1,000 cavalrymen and 4,000 infantrymen at Asti, the Genoese made a desperate effort to take Monaco before he arrived. On March 10, after a fierce bombardment, they made a general assault on the walls. A stout defense threw them back, and they had to withdraw upon the approach of d'Alègre's army.

This obvious intervention of the French on the side of the Genoese nobility inflamed antagonism inside the city toward the French to a fever pitch. The unfriendly behavior of the French garrison in the city's citadel, which had seized prisoners for ransom and fired its artillery at random into the city, further stirred up the populace. The Genoese put a small French-held fort in the city put under siege. The garrison agreed to surrender on the promise of their lives, but the enraged people massacred them as they came out. Realizing that they had crossed the line to open rebellion, the Genoese assembled on April 10, 1507, and proclaimed the independence of their city and the restoration of the old republic. Paolo da Novi, a dyer by trade and one of the most outspoken leaders of the popular party, was elected doge (duke). By these acts Genoa not only thumbed its collective nose at Louis but also passed under the control of its artisans and workers.[5]

Louis XII was kept well informed of these events. Early on in the crisis he expressed his desire to go in person to restore order and punish the evildoers. Louis left Blois on January 29, 1507, and slowly made his way via Bourges to Lyon and Grenoble, where he celebrated Easter. Taking six days to traverse Provence, he crossed the Alps with Georges d'Amboise. St-Gelais commented that during the journey the king suffered great pain but insisted on riding his charger in arms and armor in order to give "comfort to all his subjects."[6] Hurrying on ahead, d'Amboise met his nephew Charles at Asti, where they reviewed the forces assembled there. They consisted of 1,400 lances and 10,000 Swiss.[7] This army approached Genoa from the northeast, while d'Alègre's forces moved on it from the west. Louis arrived at Asti on April 15, after the main force had already left. With him came "all the gens d'armes of Dauphiné and Savoy and all the princes and great lords of France (except for Francis of Angoulême, second person of France) and a great number of young lords, who, without wages, seeing the king make the trip, sought honor and battle." Last, a fleet of four galleys and eight "galleons" commanded by Prégent de Bidoux headed for Genoa.[8]

Despite the vast array of forces brought against it, Genoa refused to concede. Louis left Asti on April 21 to join the army. D'Auton, who was with him, described how Louis, in full armor, was able to mount his charger without any aid.[9] The king had ordered that no attack on Genoa be made until he was present in person to command it. Upon his arrival three days later, La Palise led a powerful vanguard through the passes just north of Genoa. When their forces failed to halt the French advance, the Genoese asked for negotiations, but as Cardinal d'Amboise rode forward to meet his counterpart, a sharp fight broke out. Each side blamed the other for the battle, which lasted a full day. The Genoese were forced back within the city walls. The city hastily agreed to accept Louis's demand for an unconditional surrender. The new doge and numerous others implicated in the revolt fled, while the population sullenly awaited its fate. Fortunately for the city, Louis only wanted a return to obedience; he had no desire to punish the people except for the leaders of the revolt. Charles d'Amboise entered Genoa on April 27 with a body of hand-picked troops to secure it, while the bulk of the French forces were kept well away to prevent looting. Two days later Louis entered in full armor, carrying a naked sword and accompanied by a party of five cardinals, numerous bishops, and "all the lords of France." When he reach San Tommaso Gate, he struck it with his sword and exclaimed: "Proud Genoa! I have won you with my sword in my hand."[10]

Louis treated Genoa leniently enough for its rebellion. It had to give 200,000 *écus* to the king for an indemnity and 100,000 to pay his army and pledge an additional 40,000 for building another citadel inside its walls. The city was also obliged to fit out three galleys to patrol its coast, and it was forced to give up its weapons, valued at 50,000 ducats. They were given to the footsoldiers in the French army. The king also ordered Genoa to mint a new coin with his arms, titles, and visage on it. The old coin had been in use since the twelfth century. After a formal request for a pardon, Louis granted it but excluded seventy-six archrebels. One of them, Demetrio Giustiniani, was executed on a device similar to the guillotine. Paolo da Novi, the doge of the popular party, was captured on Corsica and brought back for execution. Raoul de Lannoy, the *bailli* of Amiens, was installed as the new governor.[11]

The French were exceptionally pleased with their easy victory over Genoa the Proud, which had always boasted of having never been occupied by an enemy.[12] It had been won with little loss on their part. One source put the French dead for the campaign at 250 men while Genoa was said to have lost more than 3,500. It goes on to say that "it has been over 200 years . . . since any prince has won so great a conquest with so little expense and so little bloodshed."[13] Numerous poets wrote laudatory pieces celebrating Louis's victory; they included d'Auton, Jean Lemaire de Belge,

and Jean Marot, to mention the best known among them. Marot's dedication contains two interesting miniatures showing Louis's victory over
Genoa. Both have the caption: "The king to whom we are subject refrains
from using his stinger." At that time, it was thought that the head of the
hive was male, and political writers frequently compared the kingdom to
the hive. The references to not using his stinger were calls for clemency, or
perhaps references to the clemency given by Louis.[14]

Louis and his courtiers went on to Milan in late May. There they
enjoyed unending banquets, festivals, and tournaments. During one event,
a mock re-creation of the assault on Genoa, the competition got so out of
hand that several men were killed, and Louis himself had to leave his seat
and get between the combatants. Gian Giacomo Trivulzio, whom Louis
had named a marshal of France, gave the grandest banquet, for which the
decorations alone were said to have cost 50,000 ducats.[15] The frugal
French king had cancelled the *crue* on the *taille* that he had levied for use in
the campaign against Genoa because it was over so quickly,[16] but he spent
lavishly in Italy. The money came from the Italians, so he felt no compunc-
tion against spending extravagantly in order to impress them, while they
may not have been aware that it was their money he was dissipating.

The French were convinced that their victory over Genoa made up for
the ignominy of their defeat in Naples and had reestablished France as the
dominant power in Italy and Europe. That seems to have been the view of
Ferdinand of Aragon; certainly it was the interpretation the French gave
to his request for a meeting with Louis. Ferdinand had gone to Naples
with his French bride to tour his new realm in late 1506. The voyage home
by galley hugged the coastline from Naples to Barcelona, as galleys rarely
ventured far out to sea. His route took him past Genoa in June 1507.
Despite the grand time he was having in Milan, Louis was quick to agree
to meet with Ferdinand. He sent his nephew, Gaston de Foix, Ferdinand's
new brother-in-law, to inform him of his agreement. It was de Foix's first
important task for his uncle. The meeting place agreed upon was Savona.

As Ferdinand's fleet passed Genoa, the French fleet joined it. Louis was
waiting at the dock at Savona as Ferdinand's galley came in and boarded
it to welcome his guest. After the royal parties had landed, the two kings
rode side by side into the town with Ferdinand's bride riding behind her
uncle on his horse. At the banquet Louis gave, he invited Gonsalvo de
Cordoba, France's longtime nemesis, who was returning to Spain permanently, to be seated at the table of honor. The chroniclers noted the
exchange of pleasantries and gallantries between the Spanish and the
French captains, who had been bitter adversaries for over ten years. But

the most striking aspect of the meeting was that Louis gave Ferdinand precedence over him in all the ceremonies, contrary to the custom that a king always had the first place in his own domains.

While Louis was lavish in entertaining his guests, the wine cellars being full of choice vintages from Corsica, Languedoc, and Provence,[17] there was also serious business to discuss. Ferdinand, Louis, and d'Amboise closeted themselves for long sessions of negotiations. The presence of the cardinal while Ferdinand worked alone demonstrates how dependent on him Louis had become. A papal legate arrived to participate also. Julius II, who was recorded as saying "I don't believe it!" when told of Louis's quick victory, wanted to urge him to be lenient toward Genoa and disband his army quickly. Clearly the pope was concerned about the rumors that the French king intended to march on Rome, depose him, and place d'Amboise on the papal throne.[18]

The discussions and decisions at Savona were kept secret and have always remained so. Ever since there has been a great deal of speculation over what was decided, but no source gives more than a hint. Presumably the discussions ranged across the affairs of Europe, and it is assumed in particular that the two kings agreed to take arms against Venice. The only certainty, however, is that Ferdinand gave a verbal promise to Louis to send 6,000 troops from Naples if Maximilian went to war with France.[19]

On July 2 Ferdinand returned to sea, and on the following day Louis left Savona. Word had come that Queen Anne was pregnant, and Louis was eager to rejoin her.[20] Nonetheless, the conference of Savona was one of the highlights of Louis's reign, even if historians have usually compared it unfavorably with the meeting between Francis I and Henry VIII in 1519 at the "Field of Gold." Both Ferdinand and Louis were too old to engage in the exuberant wrestling that marked the later meeting, and although Louis spent freely at Savona—40,000 *scudi* according to the Venetians—he could be no match for Francis when it came to spending.[21] There is no evidence that Ferdinand went to Genoese territory to fish in troubled waters; but his presence there underlined the growing commercial relationship between Genoa and Spain. Increasingly deprived of their traditional commercial ties in the eastern Mediterranean, the Genoese sought to replace them, not in France, which could not offer the same opportunities, except perhaps for the bankers in Lyon, but in Spain and its growing empire. By 1528 the ties between Spain and Genoa had become so strong that the dramatic change of alliance of that year should not have surprised anyone.[22]

Louis reached Lyon on July 16 and the next day made a triumphant entry. Among the verses read to the king was one proclaiming that

"Neither Hercules nor Jason had ever made such a conquest."[23] After a month in Lyon, he went on to Blois. His main concern that summer was his relationship with the Habsburgs. Their anger at the breaking of the marriage contract the previous year had been intense, although they probably were more enraged at the French reneging on the lands promised in the contract if it were broken than over the actual ending of the betrothal of Claude and Charles.[24] Prince Philip, however, could not jettison his relationship with Louis entirely because he needed French help in taking control of Castile in the name of his wife. In July 1506 he responded in a friendly manner to a letter, now lost, from Louis. The king apparently had tried to be as conciliatory as possible.[25]

Four days later, however, Philip sent a sharply critical letter to d'Amboise over an issue that had been festering for a long time but with which he now had decided to confront the French—the rebellion of the duke of Gueldres. Charles of Egmont was the duke of Gueldres (Guelderland), a small duchy located just south of where the Rhine makes its westward turn into the Netherlands. It was not a part of the Netherlands that the Burgundian dukes had ruled but was an autonomous unit of the Holy Roman Empire. (Charles V would make it the seventeenth province of the Low Countries in 1543.) Charles of Egmont's hatred of Maximilian was implacable, although it was the emperor's father-in-law, Charles the Bold, who first began the feud by persuading Egmont's unstable grandfather to disinherit his son in 1471 in favor of himself. As a young man, Egmont, a relative of Louis's mother, had fought for Louis in the Breton War; he had been captured in 1487 and held in prison for four years. The two were fast friends and allies ever after. In 1495 he returned to Gueldres with French help and spent the rest of his life causing trouble for the Habsburgs. Louis, for this part, saw Gueldres as helping to form a barrier of allies around France against the Habsburgs.

Over the next ten years French support, albeit limited, for Gueldres was a constant irritant in the French-Habsburg relationship. Philip had insisted on an end to that aid in the Treaty of Blois of 1504. With the duke thus isolated, Philip began to put more pressure on him. When Louis made his abrupt turnabout toward Ferdinand in late 1505, he resumed sending aid to Charles as a way of keeping Philip occupied in the Netherlands and preventing him from going to Castile to take power. In July 1506 Philip complained to d'Amboise that Louis had sent Robert de La Marck with 400 lances to Gueldres.[26] For the rest of Louis's reign, the duke's behavior was a constant irritant between Valois and Habsburg. Charles's zeal to harm Habsburg interests made him a superb ally for

France: He was always willing to strike against them, yet his duchy's small size made him dangerous only if he had French help. The French were in a position to turn him on and off as they pleased.

The French turned Charles back on in the summer of 1506. During the previous winter Philip and Joanna had gone by sea to Spain, as they no longer trusted Louis enough to traverse France. Embarking from Calais, they were caught in a violent storm that nearly sank their ship. After barely making it to the English coast, Philip took advantage of the unexpected turn of events to visit Henry VII and negotiate a treaty with him. Henry pledged to help Philip take power in Castile.[27] The royal couple then proceeded to Spain, where lengthy negotiations over the nature of Philip's authority in Castile were held with Ferdinand. Ferdinand secretly wrote d'Amboise urging him to send more troops to Charles of Gueldres to distract Philip; he promised to help the cardinal win the next papal election. Henry VII in turn promised to send 7,500 troops to aid Philip. In the late summer of 1506 it appeared probable that a general war would erupt with Louis, Ferdinand of Aragon, and Charles of Gueldres on one side and the Habsburgs and Henry on the other.[28]

That was the state of affairs when there occurred one of those sudden deaths that so often dramatically changed the course of history. Just after he had reached an agreement with Ferdinand on his rights in Castile, Philip died at age twenty-eight on September 25, 1506. Of course, poisoning was suspected, and Ferdinand was the prime suspect. He immediately proclaimed himself regent of Castile for his troubled daughter, whose already unstable mental condition was deteriorating badly with the shock of her husband's death. Thus the Spanish realms remained united, to be passed to Charles V. Had Philip lived, it is possible that Ferdinand would have willed Aragon to his second grandson Ferdinand, his favorite, who was being raised there.

Charles of Habsburg became prince of the Low Countries upon his father's death; but since he was only six, Maximilian named his daughter, Margaret, as regent for him. She was the girl whom Charles VIII had jilted to marry Anne of Brittany, and she had survived brief marriages to Ferdinand and Isabella's only son and the duke of Savoy. (Margaret had refused a proposed marriage to Henry VII in 1506.) To say she hated the French may be too strong, but she certainly distrusted them. On several occasions she warned her father, who despite his long experience was quite gullible, about French willingness to deceive. She and Maximilian worked together much better than her brother and father had. Ferdinand of Aragon called her "the person who has the greatest influence with her father."[29] Their voluminous and intimate correspondence is a valuable source for the international politics of the rest of Louis's reign.[30]

Margaret's political ability and the fact that she was regarded as a native by the people of the Netherlands enabled her to deal successfully with most of the problems she inherited, such as the ongoing revolt of Ghent, but a solution to the matter of Gueldres proved to be beyond her. Maximilian failed to provide her with the manpower needed to defeat Charles because he was on his way to Italy for his imperial coronation. Some ten years after his father had died, he had yet to receive the imperial crown from the pope. He felt that he needed the escort of a large army for the trip, although he was able to raise only 12,000 of the 30,000 men he wanted. That size force probably would have been enough to crush Gueldres.

By the time Maximilian marched southward, Louis had smashed the Genoese rebellion. Maximilian would have liked to have knocked Louis down a peg in Italy, which he and the other rulers of Europe had no desire to see under French rule. However, Venice would not allow him to cross its territory with his army but only with a small escort. Because Maximilian refused to leave his army behind, Julius II agreed to let him hold a coronation ceremony at Trent in February 1508. The emperor, determined to punish Venice for its effrontery, sent his forces across Venetian frontier. Unfortunately for him, his army was unequal to the task, and Venice not only drove it out with ease but also occupied several pieces of imperial territory. Although the emperor's correspondence of 1507-8 is filled with complaints about Louis, such as the accusation that the French king had ordered the city of Arras not to recognize him as emperor, in late 1508 he suddenly told Margaret to attend a conference at Cambrai.[31] On October 29 Louis wrote to her expressing his pleasure at the forthcoming meeting and indicated that d'Amboise would attend as his representative.[32]

The next month Margaret, d'Amboise, and the ambassadors of Aragon, England, and the papacy met in Cambrai. Most of the work was done in private sessions between the regent and the cardinal. The problem of Gueldres was finessed by asking its duke up to give a small number of places and submit the rest of his claims to arbitration. The real sticking point was the newly arisen problem of Navarre. Two branches of the d'Albret family were in bitter conflict over that small realm. Jean d'Albret currently held power there, while the claims of the other branch were now being maintained by Louis's nephew Gaston de Foix. D'Amboise showed Margaret written instructions from his king forbidding any agreement that recognized Jean d'Albret's rights. Only after she prepared to leave did d'Amboise back down. The problem of Navarre was to be left unsettled for a year, and Louis pledged that d'Albret would not be disturbed in that time. The agreement also allowed Charles of Habsburg to put off doing homage for the places he held as fiefs from the French monarchy until he was twenty years old and permitted Louis to escape the penalties called for in the broken marriage contract. On December 10, 1508, Margaret and d'Amboise signed the treaty for their sovereigns in the cathedral of Cambrai. Louis swore to the agreement the next March while in Bourges. He sent a letter to Paris requesting the singing of a *Te Deum* to celebrate the treaty.[33]

On December 10, 1508, Louis told the Venetian ambassador: "I see great difficulties ahead."[34] That was the first hint that the real purpose of the conference was the creation of a league directed against Venice consisting of France, the empire, Spain, Hungary, several smaller Italian states, and the papacy. Each of the members was promised a piece of Venetian-controlled land; Louis would recover the eastern part of the duchy of Milan he had conceded to Venice in 1501 for its help then. Venice had earned Louis's enmity by its double dealing in the conflict in Naples. In 1504 he had written a letter to Venice threatening war.[35] He was also eager to win favor with Julius II by challenging Venetian control of towns in the Romagna. French relations with Julius had been touchy since his election. Among the issues was the pope's failure in December 1505 to make cardinals of René de Prie, bishop of Bayeux, and Jean de La Trémoille, archbishop of Auch, both nephews of Georges d'Amboise, as Louis felt he had been promised. The king, still determined to get d'Amboise elected pope, had pressed hard to increase the number of French cardinals. Another issue involved the conflict over who would fill the Milanese benefices of Cardinal Sforza, who had died earlier in 1505. Louis felt that the pope had dismissed him as already dead after his illness of 1505. He told the Florentine ambassador: "All of Italy holds me dead; I will show the Holy Father that I am not."[36]

For these reasons, Louis told the Venetians that while he had great affection for Venice, which was his first ally, he had to protect the church against Venetian ambitions to dominate Italy. Back in 1503, while upbraiding their ambassador for Venice's aid to Ferdinand in the war for Naples, Louis declared that even the thought of breaking with Venice moved him to tears.[37] It was Louis's alleged regard for the church that had led him in late 1506 to agree to help the pope recover Bologna. Julius had forced the issue by taking to the field with an army far too small to be successful. Louis had faced the distasteful choice of allowing the pope to be defeated or going to his aid. The pope still commanded enough respect with Louis to compel him to make the second choice, sending the governor of Milan,

Charles d'Amboise, to Julius's aid. D'Amboise commanded 760 lances, 4,000 footsoldiers, and fifteen pieces of artillery.[38] Julius thanked the king by naming the two French prelates cardinals after he had entered Bologna in November 1506. While the Venetians had not controlled Bologna, they had aided it against Julius, fearing that the towns they controlled in the papal states would be the pope's next targets. Despite his success in Bologna, *Papa Terribilis* was more furious than ever with Venice.

The League of Cambrai had little tangible reason to go to war with Venice, but Venetian arrogance, ambition, and, as much as any thing, refusal to participate in a crusade against the Turks helped to magnify the relatively minor injuries each member of the coalition had endured from the city. Venice always refused to pledge its fleet, the best in Christendom, to any proposed crusade because of its extensive trade concessions in the Ottoman Empire and the vulnerability of its bases in the eastern Mediterranean. This alleged treason to Christendom was deeply resented across Europe.[39]

The pettiness of the French complaints against Venice was revealed in an incident in the summer of 1508. Maximilian's efforts to punish the city for its refusal to let him cross its territory with his army had backfired badly, and he was forced to ask for a truce in June 1508. When the Venetian ambassador in France informed Louis of the truce and its terms, he became highly irate, nearly to tears, that Venice had agreed to the truce without consulting him and had not included his client, the duke of Gueldres.[40] It was certainly because of this hardly justified sense of injury at the hands of Venice that Louis accepted, perhaps even proposed, the terms of the League of Cambrai, which required that he command the French army in person and have it in the field six weeks before his allies would march. Opposition to the treaty appeared in the royal council, led by Etienne de Poncher. As Bayard's biographer wrote: "In short it seems to me, they wanted the French to try their fortune first so that if the king of France got the worst of it, they could turn on him. They wanted to play a schoolboy game of 'If it's good, I'll take it; and if it's bad, I'll leave it.'" Nonetheless, Louis was determined to settle accounts with Venice.[41]

The agreement at Cambrai seems not intended to scare Venice into making concessions, since its details were kept secret from its diplomats. However, it took little effort on their part to realize that something was afoot against their state. In late January 1509 the French ambassador in Venice informed the Senate that he had been recalled.[42] Growing increasingly apprehensive, the Venetian ambassador tried to persuade Louis to give up any designs against his city by pointing out its power and reputation for wisdom. Louis cheerfully responded that he would oppose the

Venetian sages with so many fools that all the wisdom in the world could not resist them. Venice then tried to draw Henry VII into an anti-French alliance by raising the specter of French ambitions for the universal monarchy and the election of d'Amboise as pope. The Venetian ambassador in England argued that it was a possibility greatly to be feared because the king of France and the cardinal were "two in one flesh and would consequently act together, a result never yet witnessed."[43] Henry, however, was dying in early 1509 and could only pledge his friendship to Venice.

As Louis enthusiastically prepared his forces for Italy in early spring of 1509, Pope Julius provided a pretext for the war by demanding Venice withdraw from the Romagna and threatening to excommunicate the whole city if it did not do so in twenty-four days. Even before the time was up, Louis's herald arrived in Venice on April 17 with a declaration of war, proclaiming that Venice had illegally usurped lands that belonged to the papacy, the empire, and the duchy of Milan. A week earlier Louis had left Lyon for Italy accompanied by Cardinal d'Amboise, who was suffering so badly from gout that he had to travel in a litter. They reached Milan on May 1, where they reviewed the army.[44]

Present in unusual strength for a French army were native footsoldiers. Louis had decided to make another effort to establish a regular French infantry corps. The expense of hiring Swiss mercenaries and the frequent difficulty in recruiting them in sufficient numbers dictated a new source of infantry. Gié had drawn up a proposal for creating a native infantry in 1503, and Louis now largely followed it in his edict of January 12, 1509.[45] Its key innovation was giving command of the six infantry companies to respected captains of the *gens d'armes* in the hope that their prestige would raise the always low regard for the infantry and get the cavalry to cooperate much better with it than usual. Furthermore, the respect accorded these captains was seen as fostering discipline and obedience among the lower-class rabble that was recruited for the infantry. The most respected of the captains who agreed to command the infantry was Bayard. Offered a company of 1,000 men, he talked Louis down to 500 on the grounds that he could not control so large a number. His lieutenant in the company was Charles de Bourbon, the future constable, then nineteen years old. Bourbon's presence was evidence of Louis's insistence that officers of the best blood command the infantry. The captains were to see that the men did not pillage the people. They were also ordered to ensure that the muster rolls were not filled with dead or absent men. If a captain gave an inaccurate count to the paymaster, he was to be hanged.[46] The scheme had some success in that the long-despised and poorly led French footsoldier became a permanent part of the French army. Yet Louis and his successors had to continue to hire mercenaries in large numbers, because the long tradition of not arming French commoners made recruiting difficult. In June Louis went ahead and signed a contract with the three Grison Leagues (part of Switzerland not belonging to the Swiss Confederation) for troops, paying each soldier six *l* a month.[47]

Having committed his army to take the field first, Louis immediately moved out of Milan to join his vanguard on the Adda River. The Venetian commander was Count Niccolo of Pitigliano, a typical *condottiere* in his cautious attitude toward large-scale battles and his reluctance to take heavy casualties. The commander of his rearguard, Bartolommeo d'Alviano, was more like a French captain in his zeal to offer battle and give and take heavy casualties. The disagreements between the two reduced the effectiveness of the 22,000-man army Venice had assembled, although a large part of it consisted of militiamen from the cities Venice controlled, whose quality was questionable. Pitigliano refused to attack Louis's force as it crossed the Adda on a bridge made out of boats, passing up the Venetians' best opportunity for victory.

The battle that shortly followed was largely a result of d'Alviano's impetuosity.[48] Disregarding an order to avoid battle and rejoin the Venetian main body, he jumped at the chance to attack d'Amboise's vanguard as it moved past the small village of Agnadello in Cremona on May 14, 1509. In his initial attack, he pushed the French back and disordered their ranks. Had it been only the French vanguard with which he had to deal, he probably would have won, but the French main body, with the king in the midst of his *gens d'armes*, quickly came up. As the cannon thundered, the story goes, someone shouted to Louis, "Sire, take cover!" Louis replied: "No cannon ball can kill a king of France! If you are afraid, stand behind me!" With its far greater numbers, the main force enveloped the Venetians. The Venetian cavalry broke and ran, leaving its infantry to be massacred. D'Alviano was captured; perhaps as many as 10,000 of his men were killed; and thirty pieces of artillery taken.[49] When Louis heard that d'Alviano was a captive, he had the commander brought to him to have his wounds treated by the royal physicians. When Louis asked why he fought while facing such bad odds, d'Alviano reportedly answered that at least he had had the honor of taking on the king of France. He was taken to the castle of Loches in France. Louis ordered that a *Te Deum* be sung at Notre Dame in Paris for the victory.[50]

The Venetian main force was still intact, but with the news of the rout of its rearguard, much of it deserted. Pitigliano retreated with what was left of his dispirited army all the way to the Adriatic. Louis, however, halted his army at the eastern border of the duchy of Milan, having recovered the lands he claimed. Meanwhile an imperial army occupied areas north of Venice including Padua; the pope ousted Venetian garrisons from the disputed towns in the Romagna; and Ferdinand sent his men into the Venetian-held ports in the kingdom of Naples. In order to free itself from the need to spread out its remaining forces in the strongholds left to it, Venice freed all of its mainland subjects from their oaths of loyalty and prepared to defend the city itself.

The terrible behavior of the French and the imperial troops in the areas they occupied soon convinced the locals of the benefits of Venetian rule, and a number of towns quickly returned to Venetian service. Louis, who always in the past had kept a tight discipline on his forces, seems to have given license to his men to misbehave, apparently in the hope of intimidating the Italians. He himself set the example by ordering the hanging of the Venetian commander of Peschiera and his son after his troops had stormed the fortress, despite an offer of 100,000 ducats in ransom. Robert de Floranges, a French captain and author of a lengthy set of memoirs, quoted him as swearing: "I'll never eat or drink again until they are hanged." But as has often happened in history, the terror did the opposite and created a new resolve to resist.[51] That and the failure of the League to push its advantage to final victory left Venice off the hook. Louis had strong opposition to the war from within his court. Queen Anne and La Trémoille were eager to see it end: the queen because she was inherently a pacifist, La Trémoille because he was highly suspicious of the emperor's motive in pushing for Venice's defeat. Anne not only wrote to Louis to urge him to return home, she also sent him poetry by Fausto Andrelini for the same purpose.[52]

Louis was eager to return to France, but he remained in Milan into August 1509 because he was expecting to hold a conference with Maximilian. The emperor had asked for a meeting, which Louis was eager for because he was unsure of Maximilian's intentions toward Venice. While Louis waited in Milan, a Venetian force surprised the imperial garrison in Padua and recovered the city. Maximilian sent a force of about 20,000 men to retake it, and Louis agreed to contribute 500 lances under La Palise.[53] Maximilian, however, neither commanded in person at Padua as he had promised he would nor met with Louis. The French king, furious, growled: "And where is the Emperor? I know where he ought to be. . . . I have made up my mind to leave here on Monday."[54] That Monday was August 6. On his way back to France, Queen Anne and Francis of Angoulême, in residence at the court since 1508, met him at Grenoble. Louis embraced the young prince and exclaimed: "What a fine young gentleman!" He intended to go to St-Denis to give thanks for his victory, but a bad bout of gout persuaded him to return directly to Blois. Ferdinand wrote to the new king of England, Henry VIII, on September 13 that "the King of France has disbanded his army, with the exception of the men-at-arms who form his standing army."[55] Meanwhile Padua withstood the siege by the imperial and French forces.

The French also turned their attention toward damaging the economic interests of Venice. In mid-1510 three French galleys arrived at Alexandria in Egypt to load spices.[56] Encouraged by this sign of French interest in his realm and annoyed by the piracy of the Knights of Rhodes, who were largely French, the soldan of Mamluk Egypt wrote to Louis requesting an ambassador. It took until February 1512 for one to arrive. André Le Roy, a minor royal secretary, and a small party landed at Alexandria and went on to Cairo. Le Roy had good success there, extracting a pledge from the soldan to hand over control of the Holy Places in Jerusalem to French clerics. However, new problems for Louis in Europe and the Ottoman conquest of Egypt diverted this attempt to fashion a French presence in the eastern Mediterranean.[57]

The easy victory over Venice greatly exhilarated Louis. A contemporary source stated that "the king is making very joyous good cheer. He bears himself better than he has done for the past six years, and he seems to be younger by ten years than when he left Grenoble."[58] Yet Louis's desire to return home so quickly is understandable. He was already forty-seven years old and not in good health. The rigors of the campaign surely were tiring to him, and the disruption of what had become a very regular lifestyle since 1505 had to have taxed his energy. Georges d'Amboise was in even worse health, and that perhaps was also a factor in Louis's decision to rush back to France. But many at the time, and historians since, felt that it was a mistake; Robertet in particular felt Louis had blundered.[59] It gave new hope to the Venetians while it undermined the League of Cambrai by removing Louis's influence from the decision making going on in northern Italy. Louis was soon to find that rather than being grateful to him for his major role in securing their gains at the expense of Venice, his allies were eager to cut him cut down to size, gain revenge for all sorts of earlier injuries, real and imagined, and win advantage at his expense.

14

Ministers and Money in the Late Reign

Behind the scenes, as the public events of war and pageantry went on, the business of government continued with a rather different group of advisers around the king. Shortly after Pierre de Gié's disgrace, the Florentine government told its new ambassador to France, Francesco Pandolfini, to cultivate the good will of the queen, the legate, the chancellor, the grand master (Charles d'Amboise, who was at court as much as he was at his post in Milan), and Florimond Robertet.[1] In January 1507 Chancellor Guy de Rochefort was the first of these persons to die, after twelve years in office. Jean de Ganay was promoted to the position. He had been a member of the Parlement of Paris, as his grandfather and father had been. In 1505 he had become first president of the Parlement, the usual stepping-stone to the chancellorship. His promotions owed much to the favor of Anne of Brittany.[2] Antoine Duprat succeeded Ganay as first president. He was also a favorite of the queen since catching her attention in the prosecution of Gié.

It was still Georges d'Amboise who held the most influence over Louis, despite being nearly crippled with gout by 1508. In 1509 Georges wrote his will. He left 2 million *l* to his nephew, Georges II; previously he had won the king's promise to promote him to the see of Rouen after his death. D'Amboise's will included large sums for other relatives and 40,000 *l* to charity. Since his family had not been all that well off and he was the youngest son, while the revenues of the see of Rouen were only in the order of 17,000 *l* a year, he must have accumulated his fortune in royal service.[3] Despite his health problems, which included kidney stones, he remained busy with affairs of church and state, for example, reforming several Franciscan houses in Paris and Rouen. He went to Lyon in the spring of 1510 ahead of the king. When Louis reached the city, d'Amboise was failing fast. Nonetheless, the king went on to hunt in Dauphiné near Grenoble, where on May 25 he received the news of Georges's death at age fifty. According to St-Gelais, he had a very saintly death. The author also wrote that the king wept deeply for him, "and he had reason." Louis also took the time to write immediately to Rome to ask that the see of Rouen be given to the dead man's nephew.[4]

There is no question that the king and the cardinal were essentially partners in governing France for at least the previous five years, and a number of contemporaries and modern historians alike have seen d'Amboise as the senior partner. In 1509 Florentine ambassador Nasi reported that the cardinal had gone to Gaillon and nothing was getting done at court. He wrote shortly before d'Amboise's death that should the cardinal be removed from public life, an incredible confusion would arise in the conduct of affairs. And soon after he died, Nasi reported that those doing business at the French court would have to get used to long delays because d'Amboise had so completely dominated decision making in the royal council that no one would be ready to step forward to take responsibility. Decisions, he said, would be debated endlessly. Machiavelli, who made his third mission to France in August 1510, reached much the same conclusion. He wrote to his government that the cardinal had devoted attention to small matters, which were being neglected. Machiavelli felt that Louis now temporized in making decisions, because he was unaccustomed to working with the details of public business and, being in poor health, he tired of it quickly.[5] In short, even if Louis never said "Let Georges do it!" there is good reason to argue that in the several years before 1510, it was true.

There were several courtiers eager to take d'Amboise's place. Chancellor Ganay expected to step up to his power and influence, but, according to Nasi, he lacked both the ability and energy for so great a position. The Florentine told his government that there were four men who were conducting business: Etienne de Poncher, the bishop of Paris; Raoul de Lannoy, the *bailli* of Amiens, who had served as a financial officer in Naples; Florimond Robertet, Louis's principal secretary; and Imbart de Batarnay, the Sieur de Bouchage. Bouchage had long been close to Louis, but now he moved up greatly in influence. These four along with Ganay made up the Conseil Secret.[6] Robertet was the most powerful of the pretenders to d'Amboise's power, at least in the opinion of Machiavelli and Nasi. Louis himself took on more of the business of being king, even if he did not dispatch it very expeditiously.

In May 1512 Chancellor Jean de Ganay died shortly after returning to Blois from Bourges, where he had urged the cathedral chapter to elect the king's candidate as bishop. Louis left the chancellorship vacant to the end of his reign. Poncher as *garde des sceaux* took over most of the office's duties, but some of its functions were given to Antoine Duprat, first president of Parlement, whom Francis I did name chancellor in 1515. The major beneficiary of Ganay's death was Robertet, whose influence increased accordingly. A contemporary wrote in 1515 that Robertet had governed the whole kingdom after Georges d'Amboise died, since he was the closest to his master and had total charge of the royal offices.[7] La Palise was made a marshal; Artus Gouffier, who had been serving as Francis of Angoulême's governor since 1505, received Charles d'Amboise's position of *grand maistre* when he died in 1511; and his brother Guillaume became admiral. Duprat and the two Gouffiers would become major figures in Francis I's government. By 1511 Louis had largely filled the vacuum in the military created by Gié's removal with his sister's son, Gaston de Foix. Born in 1489, he had come to the court at an early age. Louis soon began to give him important positions and granted him Gié's title of Duke of Nemours in 1507. De Foix had fought well at Genoa in that year, the first episode in a brief but brilliant military career.

In domestic policy, the death of d'Amboise made little difference. Its general direction remained the same as it had been since 1498. The major achievement of the second half of Louis's reign was the redaction and codification of the *coutumes*, the codes of customary feudal law. France of Louis's time was divided into two zones of law: the *pays de droit écrit* in the south, where Roman law had remained in effect throughout the Middle Ages, and the *pays de coutumes* in the center and north, where local custom based on Frankish and feudal law was in effect. In the latter there were some 400 codes of law in place; their writ ranged from towns to small districts to provinces. For example, in the midsize bailliage of Senlis just north of Paris, there were three different *coutumes* in effect. The *coutumes* varied from place to place; some differed only slightly, others, even from neighboring districts, greatly. In a few places the *coutumes* had been written down, thus taking on something of the character of statute law, but in most they depended on the memory of the oldest men of the region. The result was a system of law that necessarily resulted in enormous confusion, protracted litigation, and frequent miscarriages of justice.[8]

It was clearly in the king's interest to have a single code of law across the realm, as part of the process of centralizing that had been going on in fits and starts since 1200. No king of the late Middle Ages had the power or the audacity simply to issue a new code of law for the entire realm. In 1454 Charles VII issued an edict mandating the codifying of the *coutumes*, but little was done in the next thirty years.[9] The Estates-general of 1484 admonished Charles VIII to speed up the process. He took the request to heart and established a procedure: Royal commissions from the appropriate parlements were to visit the *pays de coutumes* in question and establish the text of the local law code through meetings with the local officials, nobles, and other persons of influence, or with the local estates where they existed. The commissions would return to court with the written codes, which the king then officially promulgated.

Charles also decreed that the commissions could make changes in the local *coutumes* to improve them, which provided some opportunity to make them more uniform. Roman law often influenced those changes that were made.

Since Charles set up this procedure only in 1498, its implementation was left to Louis. He proclaimed that the *coutumes* were being redacted so that the Grand Conseil and the parlements could have them when cases came to those courts from their locales. He personally appointed the commissions. Louis required that once the local code had been approved by the local groups, it had to be published in two official copies, one for the local *bailli* and the other for the appropriate parlement.[10]

The pace was greatly accelerated in 1505, and in the next nine years, the *coutumes* of some twenty-five major districts had been redacted. They included the cities of Sens, Chartres, Auxerre, Meaux, Troyes, Orléans, Paris, and La Rochelle and the provinces of Poitou, Maine, Anjou, Auvergne, and Angoumois. One historian has called this work, which continued at a slower pace through the sixteenth century, "a step of the greatest importance in the formation of the law of the Ancien Régime."[11] Certainly it benefited France to have its laws codified, but there was a negative aspect as well: Unwritten customary law allowed for some change, albeit at a very slow pace; a written code of customary law allowed for no change at all. The *coutumes* remained in effect as they had been redacted until the French Revolution. The codification of the *coutumes* resulted in more clearly differentiating French law from both English law, with its national code of common law, and German law, where Roman law was rapidly replacing the German equivalent of the *coutumes*.[12]

Louis had begun his reign with a long edict on law and justice, the Ordinances of Blois. By 1510 it had become clear that the work begun in 1499 was not finished: Many of the earlier ordinances were not being enforced, and other problems had become apparent. After a meeting of the principal officers of justice and other important persons, Louis issued a new edict at Lyon in June 1510, which dealt with a broad range of concerns. The first part mandated a rigorous enforcement of the rules of the Pragmatic Sanction of Bourges regarding papal rights to appointment to French benefices and the *annates*, a reflection of Louis's feud with Julius II. Responding to a problem not considered in 1499 was a requirement that the office of notary be conferred only by the king or the chancellor, while the number of notaries was to be reduced. Complaining about the numerous, inconsistent decrees on appointing *baillis* and *sénéshaux*, Louis ordered that when a vacancy in those offices occurred, a commission made up of the royal officers and six nobles of the district involved were to submit three names to the king, who would select the new officer. Another clause mandated that the language used in the courts of the *pays de droit écrit* be in the vernacular language of the region, not Latin.[13] It was a first step toward Francis I's edict of 1539 mandating French in all the civil courts. The Parlement of Paris refused to register the Ordinances of Lyon until Louis appeared in person in a *lit de justice* in April 1512 to order its registration. The reasons for the magistrates' refusal are not clear, but Quilliet suggests that the new edict was not as well written or thought out as its predecessor, lacking order and unity. He proposes it reflected the illness and death of Cardinal d'Amboise while the edict was being drawn up.[14]

The importance of d'Amboise in inspiring Louis's edicts on administration and justice is strongly suggested by the decline in the number of such edicts after his death. The only significant edict after 1510 was one from the next year that regulated the courts of justice in Brittany. Numerous complaints had reached the king over the interminable length of trials and the corruption of the legal system in that province. He mandated changes designed to speed up the taking of testimony and ensure the integrity of notaries. Persuaded that marriages of minors created a major source of litigation, Louis strongly prohibited them.[15]

Louis continued to tinker with the fiscal system, largely because the wars of his last years required a dramatic increase in revenue. The tax system with its revenue farmers and *baillis* and *élus* provided vast opportunity for corruption and fraud or, as an edict of 1504 put it, "keeping in their hands the taxes imposed on the people and we are not receiving the monies."[16] Louis imposed on anyone found guilty of embezzling royal revenues a fine of a sum four times as large as that taken, but this failed to end the problem, so he issued another, longer edict in 1508. Among its more significant points was a requirement that the fiscal officers take up residence in their jurisdictions within six months of their appointments under penalty of losing the office. Auctions of the *aides* were more carefully regulated, with the requirement that they be publicized for three weeks before the bidding and that farms of the *aides* last for exactly one year. The tax collectors were obliged to forward all money to the treasury by the eighth day after receiving it. Fines and loss of office were mandated for bribe talking. Perhaps the most revealing statement in the edict was Louis's comment: "I have been advised that in many places in the realm great sums of money have been taken from the poor people beyond what I have ordered levied." Accordingly, he ordered that those responsible for collecting the *tailles* take only what he had decreed under penalty of "confiscation of body and goods" for collecting more than that.[17] Special attention was given to the salt tax, the *gabelles*. Not only was there wide corruption among the *gabelleurs*, but there were also serious problems with the salt itself. It often was allowed to sit in the warehouses so long that it deteriorated badly in quality and became unfit for human consumption. When the salt became wet from sitting in damp warehouses—presuming it had arrived reasonably dry—the *gabelleurs* pocketed the extra revenue from its increased weight.

What Louis hoped to achieve was a revenue system where the higher levels of the fiscal bureaucracy carefully supervised the lower levels, with dire penalties for all who failed to do their duty or were corrupt. The officers at the highest level, the receiver-generals and the treasurers, would be the personal appointments of the king, who would serve him well out of love and loyalty and ensure that the entire fiscal system operated to the benefit of the crown. The absence of any further edicts on the fiscal system after 1508 suggests that it worked well enough for Louis, but the wholesale changes under Francis I indicate that it had broken down again in a few years.

If the number of edicts can serve as a valid indicator, the monetary system was a greater problem. France was largely lacking in native sources of gold and silver. There was some silver mining in Burgundy, but it did not meet France's need for bullion. Although native mining of precious metals during Louis's reign may have reached its peak for several centuries, it did not match the increased productivity of the French economy. With more goods chasing nearly the same amount of money, prices fell.[18] The high value of money made counterfeiting and clipping the edges of coins profitable activities. Louis appears to have been determined to maintain the stability of the coinage system. There were at least eight edicts against illegal activities involving the coinage system in Louis's reign. Apparently he did not debase the currency, which many rulers throughout history did when they were in fiscal difficulty. An edict of 1506 reestablished the two French gold coins at the same value as in 1493: the *écu au soleil* pegged at a value of 36 *sols* 3 *deniers* and the *écu à la couronne* at 35 *sols*. The edict set the value of the Venetian gold ducat at 37 *s* 6 *d*.[19] These gold coins were too large to be used in ordinary retail business, and coins made of *billon*, a silver and copper amalgam, were in circulation to meet that need. The most common was the *dixain*, worth 10 *d*. In 1514 Louis ordered the minting of a new silver coin, the *teston*, from *teste* (head), with his visage on it, valued at 10 *s*. It was the first French coin with a royal visage, although the Italians had been using them for some time. Asti and Milan had both minted *testons* for Louis earlier. The French *teston* provided a coin between the *écu* and the *dixain* in value. For its first mint run in 1514, 80,723 pieces were minted, compared to 53,673 *billon* coins and 262,784 gold ones minted in the same year. The minting of *écus* had declined 41 percent since 1500, although the low point in Louis's reign was 1508, when only 169,166 *écus* were minted.[20]

The deflation of prices created by the shortage of bullion was one reason why Louis XII was able to get by on lower tax revenues than did either his predecessor or successor. More significant, however, was his reduction of the expenses of his government, especially his court. For example, in 1510 the *grand écuyer,* Galeas de St-Severin, was told to reduce the number of horsemen in the royal stable from 134 to 120; its size had already been reduced from over 200 men in 1496. Its expenses declined from 70,688 *l* in 1496 to 30,508 *l* in 1510.[21] The expenses of the *argenterie,* which provided plate, clothing, and furnishings for the court, dropped even more sharply, from 136,000 *l* to 30,000 *l* in the same twelve years.[22] The most important reduction in terms of total money involved came in the royal pensions, which totaled 202,000 *l* in 1505; they were pared to 105,000 *l* in 1511. Small wonder that Louis's courtiers complained of his miserliness!

Louis's determination to keep low the tax burden on his people collided with his equally strong will to keep his Italian holdings. The Genoa expedition of 1507 had been financed by reparations demanded from the city, and Louis was able to cancel the *crue* of 500,000 *l* he had imposed prior to crossing the Alps.[23] That act, perhaps more than any other of his, was responsible for his reputation as being concerned for the welfare of the common people. The brief campaign against Venice in 1509 was over before it had cost much. But a year after his return from the Agnadello campaign, Louis found himself deeply involved in a bitter feud with Pope Julius II that would eventually prove to be very expensive.

The pope was able to create a powerful alliance from most of France's neighbors in 1511. In particular England joined the pope's league, which meant that the French fleet became a major priority. Since there were few royal ships, building up a powerful fleet meant impressing private ships into service, which was less expensive than ship construction but still a costly proposition. In 1513, for example, Louis paid 437 *l* 10 *d* to Antoine de Mailly, a Picard nobleman, for a month's service by his ship of seventy tons and crew of seventy men.[24] French shipbuilding in this era seems to have fallen behind that of its Atlantic rivals. While the first gunports may have appeared shortly after 1500 on a French warship of the type known as the parade ship, in general the French appear to have been very slow to pick up on the enormous innovations that had been made in the Iberian fleets. Louis himself seems to have let the Iberian voyages of discovery go unnoticed. There is no hint in any record associated with him of any knowledge of Christopher Columbus's discoveries and the Americas. The only notice of the Portuguese voyages to the East is a mention made by a Venetian ambassador in 1505 that the French court had learned the Portuguese were expecting the caravels from India soon.[25] But there was nothing unusual about the court's lack of interest; it seems to have been true of the French people in general. In 1508 when Louis and Anne made their formal entry into Rouen, a skit was performed in which the world was divided into three parts — Europe, Asia, and Africa. The lack of any mention of the New World, sixteen years after Columbus's first voyage, is surprising for Rouen, which had a strong maritime tradition, especially since there was a fair amount of transatlantic activity by Norman sailors in Louis's reign, largely from Dieppe and Honfleur, to the Grand Banks off Newfoundland.[26]

Louis XII's apparent ignorance of what his seamen were doing in the Atlantic may have prevented him from supporting a larger effort to claim a sphere for France in the New World, and it may explain as well the poor showing of the French fleet in 1512-13. The lack of money, however, was probably just as important a factor. Louis had to find more money for his forces, especially when the war came home to France in 1513. His pinching of *deniers* was a factor in the loss of Italy; he dared not do the same when the kingdom itself was at stake. In July 1512 he took direct control of the large estates of his nephew Gaston de Foix, who had been killed in Italy, in order to take their revenues for the royal treasury. He asked for a *décime* from the clergy the same year, and he ordered the city of Paris to strengthen its defenses, to be funded by the *aides* on wine and fish sold in the city and the *gabelles* on salt.[27] Each confraternity of the city was ordered to provide a sum of money to buy an artillery piece and cover the wages of the men needed for it. On September 4, 1512, Louis requested Paris to grant him a subsidy of 40,000 *l*. After haggling for two months, the city agreed to give him 30,000. Since Paris set the example for the rest of the cities and paid out 10 percent of the total subsidies from the cities, Louis ought to have collected 300,000 *l* in all.[28] However, Louis resorted at this time more to loans than heavier taxes.

Louis's financial position was much bleaker in September 1513. The year before, the "extraordinary for war" had come to 2,777,029 *l*, which was 30 percent higher than the previous year. The Florentine ambassador reported to his government in September 1513 that the cost of the war with England amounted to 400,000 francs a month.[29] Louis's restraint on taxing his people had to go by the board. The *taille*, which had dropped to 1,525,000 *l* in 1509, had to be supplemented by *crues*. In 1512 he had asked for two *crues* of 500,000 *l* each in February and June and one of 400,000 *l* in July 1513. *Décimes* of 320,000 *l* and 300,000 *l* were requested from the clergy in the same years. The king asked the city of Paris for 30,000 *l* again in 1513; after lengthy debate the municipality agreed to grant 20,000 *l*, which meant he should have collected 200,000 *l* from all of the French cities. The *tailles* and *crues* in 1514 came to 2,891,900 *l*, while the total royal revenue for the year was 4,884,900 *l*.[30]

For a war of the magnitude Louis was fighting, that sum was inadequate. On January 27, 1514, he issued a decree in which he laid out the financial catastrophe the monarchy was facing: "For the past three years the other princes and kings have conspired to wage war on our realm, . . . especially the king of England, ancient enemy of the crown of France. We have had to put abroad great armies and navies at great and unestimable expense, mounting to a very great sum."[31] Louis admitted that the treasury was running a deficit of 1,180,000 *l* and more, despite the extraordinary measures of the previous two years to increase his revenues. He reported that he had assembled a great company of good and great persons for advice, and they had recommended that the best expedient in this dangerous situation was the alienation (sale) of revenues of the royal domain and tolls and taxes to a total of 600,000 *l.* The fiscal officers were told to use their consciences to establish a fair price for the rights and properties given up. The properties were to be alienated at 10 percent, so it seems that Louis intended to raise 600,000 *l* by selling properties with annual revenues of 60,000 *l.* The king had perpetual rights of repurchase, but it cannot be determined whether the monarchy ever did buy back those properties. This measure can be seen as the first large-scale *rentes.* Also in 1514 Louis levied a tariff of four *écus* per ton on wine exported from the realm. He later dropped it to one *écu.*[32] Whether Louis left a deficit to his successor, and if he did, how large a one, is difficult to answer. In 1519, when Francis I asked for new taxes from the Norman Estates, they refused to accept his argument that it was because of his predecessor's debts.[33] It does appear that, at the least, Francis had to pay the heavy expenses of Mary Tudor's journey to France in 1514.

Despite the dramatic increase in taxation, Louis did not lose the support of his people. The nobles grumbled about his miserliness, and the fortunes of some of them were adversely affected by the fighting of his last years. For example, the Mailly family had to sell two *seigneuries* in 1514 to a bourgeois of Amiens for 3,200 *l,* because of "their grand and urgent affairs and necessities."[34] Nonetheless, the nobility remained loyal, as did the common people. His entire reign was little troubled by popular unrest. The little that did occur took the form of bread riots at Nîmes in 1505 and Péronne in Picardy in 1512, while the plebeians of several towns rioted over political exclusion. In 1514 there was a tax riot in Agen, but it appears to have been over a local levy to rebuild a bridge, and not royal taxes.[35] In 1513 the war came home to the people of Caen in Normandy, when a force of *landsknechts* on their way to defend the Norman coast stopped in the city for several days. Their rude behavior led to a fight with the townspeople in which the latter gained the upper hand, expelling the soldiers and inflicting heavy casualties.[36] Broad prosperity was the major reason for the lack of serious incidents of popular violence during Louis's reign. The price of wheat remained below the median price of 1.56 *l* per *setier* for Louis's reign during his last six years, dropping below one *livre* in the three years of 1509 to 1511.[37] The king received most of the credit. His image as *Père du Peuple* was little troubled by the large tax increase.

Louis's popularity remained high, despite the great troubles and dangers facing the realm during the last five years of his reign, because of a broad propaganda campaign, which became much more extensive after the feud with Julius II erupted, and the efforts of the king to make himself visible to his subjects. A "progress" was a traditional medieval technique for the monarch to maintain contact with his people. Since the royal person had a mystical quality about him, the best way to inspire loyalty and obedience was for the king to appear in person in the towns and villages, to show himself to his people. Louis always traveled extensively, although frequently the trips were for urgent business, such as war in Italy. Consequently, he spent a great deal of time in Lyon and Grenoble and on the roads between them and Blois and Paris. On a number of occasions, however, the king clearly went on progresses, such as his trip to Rouen and Normandy in 1508, although he never reached the Midi. The best example of Louis's progresses was the one he made in the spring of 1510 from Blois to Lyon through Champagne, where the king had not been since his coronation. St-Gelais reported the reception the king received from the people:

> In all the places where he passed, the nobles and men and women assembled from all parts and ran after him for three or four leagues. And when they could they would touch his mule or robe or anything of his, they kissed their hands and rubbed their faces with great devotion as if they had touched some relic. A gentleman of his escort saw an old plowman who was running as hard as he could. He asked him where he was going. The good man answered him that he was going to see the King. . . . "He is so wise, he maintains justice and makes us live in peace and has removed the pillaging of the *gens d'armes* and governs the best that any king has done. I pray that God will give him good and long life."[38]

St-Gelais said he wanted to put the old peasant's words in writing, because they were so well spoken for a man of the fields. The chronicler added that he would never forget the love and affection the king had from all the people and especially the commoners. The episode demonstrated how well the people responded to a king who was seen as having their interests at heart.

15

Père du Peuple versus Papa Terribilis

A year after his brilliant victory at Agnadello, Louis XII found himself deeply involved in a bitter feud with Pope Julius II that would prove to be disastrous for his claims in Italy and threaten his hold on the French throne. It has been argued that Georges d'Amboise's death had a serious impact on Louis's relationship with the papacy, but whether the cardinal could have kept the king from his confrontation with the pope when his queen could not is difficult to answer. However, d'Amboise probably would have saved Louis from some of his mistakes in the struggle with Julius.

There were several causes for the violent confrontation between pope and king. One was the pope's refusal to grant a cardinal's red hat to several French prelates to whom Louis believed it had been promised. When Julius named twelve new cardinals in early 1510, none was French. Clearly he was determined to prevent the election of a French pope after his death by naming cardinals hostile to France. In turn Louis infuriated Julius by making appointments to church benefices in Milan without papal approval. The pope feared that the French king would march on Rome and throw him off the throne of St. Peter, despite the fact that Louis had twice been in Italy with large forces and had not made any such move. The most important cause, however, was Julius's zeal to free Italy of the barbarians—by whom he meant all non-Italians—starting with the French because they controlled more of Italy than the others. The pope felt he knew how to deal with the French and especially their king because of the time he had spent in France before his election.

Julius's first move was to make peace with Venice. The total defeat of Venice was hardly in the interest of the Italian cause. In late 1509 the city, responding to hints that the pope would consider peace terms, sent a delegation to Rome. In February 1510 an agreement was concluded.[1] Venice conceded virtually every point to Julius, but the cement was removed from the League of Cambrai. Julius had been able through the force of his will to get the mutually suspicious rulers in the League to cooperate, and it quickly fell apart without his direction. Louis, who after twelve years of dealing with the Italians should have known better, was taken by surprise. He lamented that the pope had stuck a dagger in his heart by his peace with Venice. The illness and death of d'Amboise prevented Louis from responding quickly and effectively.[2] Meanwhile, Julius worked diligently toward turning the League of Cambrai against France. He granted Ferdinand of Aragon the investiture of Naples without taking any note of French claims there, while smaller favors went to Maximilian and Henry VIII. However, none of these rulers was yet ready to break with Louis. Nor could the pope foment rebellion in Genoa and Milan, despite his efforts.

Julius had more success with the Swiss. Relations between the cantons and France had been strained, even while the French monarchy employed thousands of Swiss mercenaries. The Bellinzona affair of 1504 was only one of a number of incidents on the Swiss border with Milan, and there were endless disputes over the pay for the Swiss in the French army. Many in France felt that the Swiss were too unreliable, expensive, and barbarian to be good allies, while a large party in Switzerland looked to the Holy Roman Emperor for leadership. Its spokesman was Matthius Schinner, bishop of Sitten. From early in his career Schinner had been a vocal opponent of France. He had supported Ludovico Sforza and been active in the Bellinzona affair. Julius II recognized his value in detaching the Swiss from French service and made him a cardinal and legate to the cantons in 1508. Schinner persuaded the Swiss leaders to demand so high a price for renewing the agreement of 1499 giving France access to Swiss soldiers that Louis broke off negotiations. Louis felt that the new French infantry, which had made a good showing at Agnadello, rendered the Swiss unnecessary. His attitude opened the door to Julius to arrange his own agreement with the cantons in March 1510. It allowed the pope to recruit 6,000 men if the Swiss were not involved in a war and obliged both sides not to join alliances against each other. With Swiss support in hand, Julius could now drop his mask of friendship toward France and show his true feelings.

Convinced that his allies in the League of Cambrai were still true, Louis worked at improving relations with the new English king, who was reported as strongly anti-French. A French delegation headed by Raoul de Lannoy had gone to England in September 1509 and worked out a treaty of friendship in March 1510. It called for the resumption of the annual payment of 50,000 *écus* to England and the payment in full of the sum Louis was in arrears, which amount is not given. Louis had a reputation for bribery and the Venetian ambassador reported that the French had distributed 50,000 *écus* more in bribes to Henry's courtiers. The Venetian had written shortly before this that he believed that the French king had bribed the Spanish ambassador to England, "as he does the whole world." The Spaniard in turn asked Henry whom among his advisers he could trust because he was well aware of how completely Maximilian's courtiers had been bribed to tell everything to the French.[3]

Louis's intentions in the spring of 1510 as he made his way from Blois to Lyon were unclear to everyone except, perhaps, himself. Many foreign observers were convinced that he intended to lead a great army in order to conquer the rest of Italy and impose a French pope, although St-Gelais wrote that Louis went to Lyon to hunt in the mountains of Dauphiné, his favorite hunting grounds.[4] Whether Louis ever intended to cross the Alps that year or not, his troops were in action in northern Italy, taking Legnago but failing in assaults on Treviso and Padua. In midsummer Louis, still in the vicinity of Lyon, received news that Queen Anne's delivery date was imminent. He rushed back to Blois in four or five days, according to St-Gelais, who added that those who could not keep up with the king's pace were left behind. He also noted that Louis was in Anne's room when she gave birth to a daughter who was named Renée. Certainly the birth of a daughter had to be deeply disappointing to both father and mother, but it did give hope that Anne could get pregnant again and produce the son both so badly wanted. Anne de Bourbon and Gian Giacomo Trivulzio stood as Renée's godparents at her baptism.[5] Anne did get pregnant again the following year, but the baby, a male, was stillborn in January 1512.[6]

A second albeit less urgent reason why Louis returned to Blois was his decision to confront Julius II with a national synod of the French clergy.[7] Julius had been active on many fronts challenging Louis. In mid-June he told the Venetians: "These French are trying to reduce me to being nothing but their king's chaplain; but I mean to be pope, as they will find out." A month later he told the French ambassador: "I look upon your king as my personal enemy and do not wish to hear anything more."[8] He then ordered the ambassador out of Rome. Meanwhile Julius had arrested Cardinal de Clermont for attempting to leave Rome without his permission. At the same time he arranged to have 10,000 Swiss assemble on the frontier with Milan. He provided money and encouragement to the Fregosi, his kinsmen, to lead a rebellion in Genoa and in July attempted to attack that city by sea. He had sent a nuncio to Genoa to convince the French naval commander, Prégent de Bidoux, to use his fleet against the North African sea raiders. Thinking he had gone, Julius sent the small papal fleet bolstered by some fifteen Venetian galleys to Genoa. Prégent, however, had gotten word of the pope's scheme and had not sailed. He drove the papal fleet away. In late August it returned, and in a sharp fight Prégent captured four galleys and forced the fleet's permanent retreat.[9] From the French point of view the worst of Julius's actions was his excommunication of Duke Alfonso d'Este of Ferrara, Louis's firmest ally in Italy. It was a serious challenge to Louis's ability to protect his friends. Among the charges laid against Este was that he had plotted to depose Julius and place d'Amboise in the papacy.[10]

Machiavelli, who had gone to France in late June 1510 on his third mission there, has a firsthand account of Louis's response to all these provocations. His task was to persuade Louis to stop pressing Florence to declare against the pope. Machiavelli's reports are very informative on what Louis's attitude toward the pope and Italy was. The statesman felt that after d'Amboise's death, Louis was largely incapable of attending to the details of business and making decisions. One day he was ready to lead an army to Rome and depose Julius; the next he was resolved to stay in France and depose the pope through the structures of the church. Robertet wrote to the French ambassador at Rome that the pope's behavior was causing the king "horrible pain."[11]

On July 30, 1510, Louis convoked an assembly of the French clergy, which was to meet in Orléans two months later. He gave as a reason for the convocation only his desire to communicate with his clergy, but two weeks later he issued a manifesto explaining that he was assembling the clergy in order to get its advice on how to deal with the hostile and provocative policy of the pope. He forbade the clergy from sending money to Rome or seeking benefices from the pope. The papal right to fill a number of benefices in France was voided, and when Louis sent a nomination for the vacancy at Rouen created by d'Amboise's death to Rome for confirmation, he told his court that if the pope refused it, he would seat the new archbishop anyway. The king later transferred the assembly site to Tours, where the deputies of the clergy gathered on September 13. Five archbishops, fifty-five bishops, some fifty theologians and representatives of the universities, and the presidents of four Parlements made up the assembly.[12]

On September 15 Chancellor Ganay formally opened the meeting by presenting a document that a committee of theologians from the University of Paris had been commissioned to draw up.[13] It consisted of a series of questions about papal authority in church and state: Could the pope declare war on a Christian prince when the papal lands or the faith were not under attack? Could the prince defend himself in such an event? In that situation, could the prince withdraw his obedience from the papacy; and if he could, how was the national church to be governed? In a clear reference to the duke of Ferrara, the prelates were asked whether a Christian prince could go to the aid of an ally whom the pope had unjustly attacked. The next day Louis arrived in Tours and presided over the assembly as Ganay addressed it in his name. The chancellor announced that the meeting had three matters before it—the quarrel with the papacy, the disorder in the benefices in the French church, and church reform in general—but the first had priority. He declared that Pope Julius was guilty of perfidy in his handling of the League of Cambrai and urging the king of England to assert his claim to France. The French had intercepted papal letters to Henry VIII in July prompting such action.[14] Other complaints involved the number of foreigners Julius was appointing to French benefices, his heavy financial demands on the French clergy, and his failure to hold to his oath taken at his election to call a general council in two years.[15]

The French clergy quickly concluded that the king ought to ask the pope to convoke a general council and tell him in a spirit of fraternal charity to cease his warmongering. If Julius did not, then the king would be justified in using force against him and withdrawing from obedience. Louis should then appoint a patriarch for the Gallican church and request the emperor to call a general council. The clergy also voted to provide Louis with a *décime* of 300,000 *l*, 60,000 *l* of which were to go for the expenses of the general council. The interesting point about the *décime* of 1510 was that it was directed to the general expenses of the king instead of for a war or a phantom crusade, as all previous ones were. It was an important step in establishing the *décime* as an annual levy on the clergy, as happened under Francis I.

On September 30 the clergy dispersed without having anything further to say on church reform. The gathering agreed to meet again in the spring. The next day the new ambassador from Maximilian presented himself to Louis while he hunted near Tours, killing a wild boar.[16] The ambassador described Louis's anger at the pope, which was reflected in the letter he wrote to Julius demanding a general council. The pope's reply was curt: He did not take orders from princes in regard to the church and would summon a council when his conscience told him to do it. On the diplomatic front Louis's position was being seriously undermined, although he did not realize it for some time. He remained convinced that Ferdinand was still his staunch ally. The wily Aragonese was doing his best to "behave as though the greatest friendship prevailed between king and the king of France," but his diplomats to England, the pope, and the emperor were directed to arrange an anti-French league. Ferdinand's ambassador in England was told to go through Queen Catherine, Ferdinand's daughter, if Henry was not receptive, and if she was not willing to cooperate, to use her confessor to persuade her to influence her husband.[17]

With Ferdinand making clear his eagerness to break with France, Julius became much more aggressive. He ordered his army into action against

Ferrara and occupied several towns in the duchy in early September 1510. A small Spanish force joined the papal army as it prepared to invest Ferrara, although Ferdinand argued that he was simply fulfilling his feudal obligation to his suzerain in Naples. Louis in turn sent Bayard with 3,500 men to help Ferrara. Julius had gone to Bologna to be closer to his army, and Charles d'Amboise, realizing that the Swiss had withdrawn from the frontiers of the duchy of Milan for the winter, marched on Bologna with a potent force. When he appeared before the walls, Julius excommunicated him and his men. The wielding of his spiritual weapons was Julius's major advantage. D'Amboise lost his nerve, withdrew his forces, and began to negotiate. Negotiations went nowhere, but the French lost valuable time.[18]

Respect for the pope as the head of the church and fear of his spiritual power were powerful obstacles for Louis in his struggle with Julius. Ferdinand wrote to his ambassador in England: "Should the King of France really depose the Pope, such an insult to all Christian peoples and to all the princes of Christendom would be even a greater offence than an attack on their dominions, and they would be forced to oppose France with all their might."[19] Julius's sense of the immunity of the pope from attack, along with his impetuous nature, helps to explain why he went in person to command his forces at the siege of Mirandola, regarded as the key to Ferrara. He reached Mirandola in early January 1511, in some of the worst winter weather in memory, and took an active part in the conduct of the siege. He took up quarters so close to the walls that enemy shot hit his rooms several times, once killing two of his servants. When the city agreed to surrender at the end of January, Julius, wearing armor and carrying a weapon, refused to wait for the gate to be opened and entered with his troops through a breach. He was ready to give the city over to sack but was dissuaded by his aides, who emphasized the scandal it would have caused. Guicciardini commented: "The king of France, a secular prince, of an age not yet past its vigor and in a good state of health [a dubious assertion] trained from his youth in handling arms should at present be taking his repose, . . . and on the other side to see the highest priest, vicar of Christ on Earth, old and infirm now involved in person in waging a war stirred up by him against Christians . . . . as leader of soldiers he exposed himself to hardships and perils, retaining nothing of the pontiff but the name and the garb."[20]

The heavy cost of the siege of Mirandola and the bad weather forced a halt to the papal campaign for several months. By the time it resumed, Charles d'Amboise had died and had been replaced as French commander in northern Italy by Gian Giacomo Trivulzio. Trivulzio was much more energetic than his predecessor, who was accused of failing to relieve Mirandola because he had gone back to Milan to visit his mistress.[21] In March 1511 Trivulzio brought his army to Bologna where Julius now was. The pope, unsure of the people's loyalty, retreated to Ravenna. The Bolognese revolted against the papal officers and opened their gates to the French on May 23.[22]

Meanwhile, Louis had recalled the Gallican national synod, which met again at Lyon in April. He invited the clergy of Flanders to attend, but Margaret refused to allow them to go. The convocation at Lyon passed several edicts on church reform and reaffirmed the decrees of the Council of Basil on canonical elections. This convocation agreed to make binding on the French church all decisions of a council called to counter Julius.[23] Louis's scheme of holding a council to depose Julius had received a major boost in December 1510 when five cardinals—two French, two Spaniards, and one Italian—fled to Milan. These five, plus four more, issued in the name of emperor and the king of France the invitation of May 16, 1511, to the princes of Europe to attend a council and send their clergy. The meeting was scheduled to begin on September 1, 1511, in Pisa, which had been under the control of Florence since 1507. Louis had pushed Florence hard into agreeing to hold the council there.

The invitation included a sharp attack on Julius II, whom it accused of causing great scandal in the church. Nonetheless, it also invited him to attend.[24] Placards with the call for the council were placed across Europe; Julius saw one on the cathedral door in Ravenna. He responded by calling his own council for Rome the following spring. Those who attended the French council were threatened with excommunication, and the city where it was held with being put under interdict. In October 1511 Julius became very ill, and most thought he was dying. His illness was the signal for the antipapal faction in Rome, led by the Colonna family, to revolt against "priestly tyranny." Julius's health, however, did a dramatic turnabout, as did his political position in Rome. By the first days of 1512 he was again securely in control of the city.[25]

Louis was eager to ensure that his realm was solidly behind the twofold military and spiritual attack on the pope. To attack the pope in either fashion was terrifying to the people of Christendom, since it posed a very real threat to their eternal salvation. Thus, Charles d'Amboise was reported to have begged papal forgiveness as he lay dying. Julius granted it, but d'Amboise died before he received word. Queen Anne was so opposed to any rupture with the papacy that she refused to allow Cardinal Guibé, archbishop of Nantes, to go to Pisa. Louis retaliated by seizing the cardinal's episcopal revenues, but Julius gave him those from Avignon.[26] Louis was also aware of his people's resistance to more taxes, which were necessary if war with Julius's alliance erupted.

The French people, therefore, had to be convinced of the righteousness of Louis's case against the pope. Royal propaganda to persuade the public was spread through placards, pamphlets, poetry, and plays. One placard carried a caricature of the pope, surrounded by corpses and his flag lying on the ground. The papal throne, over which France is keeping guard, is empty.[27] A group of poets, many in the pay of the king, who included Jean Lemaire de Belges, Jean d'Auton, Guillaume Crétin, and Jean Bouchet, produced poems lambasting Julius and praising Louis as the defender of the church.[28] But plays reached the largest number of people. The Basoche could be called upon to write the kind of satirical play needed, which showed the wisdom of Louis's refusal to censor them earlier in his reign. The best of them, Pierre Gringore, put himself completely to royal service, probably at Louis's request, but there is no evidence he was on Louis's payroll.[29]

The most important of Gringore's attacks against Julius was a *sottie*, "*Le jeu du Prince des sotz.*"[30] It was performed at Les Halles, the main marketplace in Paris, on Mardi Gras in 1512. Highly praised for its drama and eloquence, it made a cutting attack on Julius while adding satirical asides on nearly all elements of society. Louis XII is the one person who escapes unscathed. His goodness and kindness toward his people are strongly portrayed. The war against the pope is fully justified, but Gringore is very aware of the fear of a violent confrontation with the pope. Gringore resolves the paradox of defying the bad pope while loving the head of the church by having Julius appear in disguise in the play, showing that he is a wolf in sheep's skin. A number of serious works also were published to justify Louis's policy. Among them the most powerful was Lemaire de Belges's *Le Traicté de la différence des schismes et des conciles de l'église*, which was printed in May 1511.[31] After giving a long history of both church councils and schisms, Lemaire concluded that the meeting called for Pisa was a true council, and the papacy had created most schisms. The author had strong words in favor of the Pragmatic Sanction of Bourges as vital for the "great good honor and profit of our Christian religion."[32] Julius was accused of planning his own schism through the council he called.

Rome, of course, was not silent in the face of these Gallican salvos. Tommaso di Vio, Cardinal Cajetan of later Reformation controversies, wrote a work in late 1511, condemning councils not called by the pope. The book was sent to the Sorbonne for examination and rebuttal. The theologians of Paris were reluctant to take on the papacy. Louis had to write to the Faculty of Theology on February 19, 1512, insisting that a refutation be produced. The task was given to Jacques Almain, who had just received his doctorate in theology, but he had already had a high reputation as a theologian. He quickly produced *De auctoritate Ecclesiae et Conciliorum generalium* (1512).[33] In it he maintained that the power given to the pope was not absolute; if the pope sinned or erred, the secular authorities had an obligation to oversee the church until he repented. Almain also argued that papal authority did not extend to the civil realm except through the force of moral persuasion. The effectiveness of this propaganda is difficult to ascertain except in so far as the French people accepted the higher taxes without rebelling. There were few defections in France despite the pope's willingness to wield the most powerful spiritual weapons in his arsenal—interdict and excommunication.

The council called for Pisa, however, proved to be a bitter disappointment for Louis. The Florentine government objected strenuously, and the townspeople of Pisa, which had been chosen largely because it was close enough to Rome to annoy Julius, refused to extend any hospitality. Maximilian did not approve of Pisa, as he wanted a site in the imperial lands of north Italy. Louis hoped for prelates to come from the empire, but Margaret of Austria refused to allow any from the Low Countries to go, since only the pope could call a council.[34] The French king had no illusions that the Spanish and English clergy would appear, but many of the French prelates evaded going as well.

After a long delay to assemble a strong French escort for the clergy going to Pisa, the council formally opened on November 1 with only four cardinals, sixteen bishops, and a small group of abbots and theologians.[35] The Pisans, who were about to suffer an interdict for a decision over which they had no control, were decidedly unfriendly. The council members were not allowed to use the cathedral of Pisa or borrow the vestments of the local clergy for their opening Mass. A Spaniard, Cardinal Carajal, was elected president of the council. The members declared theirs to be the only valid council and denounced the one Julius was planning for Rome as schismatic. Before the council could proceed far in its agenda, a violent confrontation between French soldiers of the escort and Pisans revealed the hostility of the townspeople. On November 12 the council leaders agreed to go to Milan, as Louis had promised Machiavelli they would after several face-saving sessions in Pisa. Their reception in Milan, which was French control, was hardly better. The council resumed its business in January with a small increase in attendance. It was largely concerned with issuing decrees against Julius and the council he was organizing.

The success or failure of the Council of Pisa hinged largely on the performance of the French forces in northern Italy. At a time when a blatantly political pope wore the tiara and a general council was used a political weapon against him, it was appropriate that war, "politics by other means," should be the determining factor in its fate. This was an era in which, more than usual, the quality of the commander in the field determined victory or defeat; thus the outcome of the Council of Pisa depended very heavily on the man whom Louis chose to lead the French against Julius II and his allies. Upon Charles d'Amboise's death in February 1511, his replacement as commander was the old *condottiere,* Trivulzio, who had long served the French. His taking command gave the French army a badly needed spark, but the real turnabout came a half year later when Gaston de Foix became governor of Milan and commander of the forces in Italy.[36] Only twenty-two years old, he did not have the experience for those offices, and Louis sent Thomas Bohier, the treasurer of Normandy and a key member of the royal council, to Milan as de Foix's assistant. Presumably his first task was ensuring the good administration of Milan, but apparently Louis intended that he also keep the young general's military expenditures in check.

When Gaston took command in October 1511, the French were spread out across much of northern Italy. The French garrisons in cities like Bologna were threatened by the large force that Julius II was assembling for another attack. In both Milan and Genoa the populace was restless, largely because Louis was intent on keeping the financial burden on the French people low by milking his Italian possessions. As Guicciardini said, Louis was instinctively loathe to spend his money. Pandolfini, the Florentine diplomat now posted at Milan, felt that most of the French problems would be solved with more money, but "the king spends it only with bad humor." He reported that Louis was trying to direct the war without leaving France, which he felt was a very bad idea.[37]

Both problems were present in Louis's dealings with the Swiss in late 1511. The cantons had withdrawn from French service a year earlier and, in response to papal demands, had moved some 16,000 men into the frontier zone with Milan. Still, they were ready to accept French gold, provided the sum was 40,000 *écus* instead of the usual subsidy of 30,000. Louis hated to spend that much money for a force he thought was becoming ineffective because of the use of artillery. His distance from the scene made dealing with the Swiss when two of their envoys were murdered in the duchy of Milan difficult. He failed to appreciate the importance of making quick amends to the Swiss, and the Alps resounded with their bitter complaints. By December 1 they had moved into Milanese territory and occupied the town of Varese north of Milan. Pandolfini reported that the Swiss were only thirty miles from the city and could be in it at any moment, since there was no stronghold between them and Milan. De Foix could only hope for a delaying action against the Swiss until winter weather persuaded them to go home. Fortunately for him, heavy rains delayed the Swiss arrival near Milan until December 14, 1511.

The Milanese did not revolt as the Swiss had expected, and after several days severe logistical problems forced them to retreat to their homeland.[38]

A major diplomatic development two months earlier prevented Louis from remedying the shortages of money and manpower that so badly hindered de Foix's ability to challenge the Swiss. By the end of 1510 Julius and Ferdinand had reached an accommodation. They spent 1511 drawing the other princes of Europe into their anti-French entente. On October 4 an alliance encompassing the papacy, Spain, and Venice was signed that committed its members to defending the papal states and recovering Bologna for the pope.

The special target of Ferdinand's efforts was his son-in-law, Henry VIII. On November 17 their ambassadors signed a treaty directed against France. The two kings proclaimed that they had been planning a crusade against the Muslims when they received the news of the French occupation of Bologna. Ferdinand often used the excuse of preparing for a crusade to justify his military preparations, leading Louis once to remark: "I am the Turk against whom this Crusade is intended."[39] Ferdinand and Henry declared that they were now obliged to defend the church. Since it was difficult for England to send an army to Italy, the English would serve the cause by invading Gascony the next April with the help of a same-size Spanish force. The signatories agreed to oppose the "schismatic" council at Pisa and support the one the pope was convoking. These two treaties created the Holy League. The Swiss were not formally members, but it was expected they would act in concert with it. Maximilian did not join because he was still too angry at Venice, despite very intense diplomatic pressure from the members.[40]

There is no reason to suppose Louis was surprised by the creation of the Holy League. His agents had intercepted letters from Rome to England revealing the diplomatic pressure on Henry.[41] But the new alliance did make a major difference in Louis's strategy. It appears that he had been planning to lead a large army to Italy the next summer to settle finally the question of who would dominate Italy. Now he had to remain in France and keep forces there as well. The new alliance also promised that Louis's enemies would take a much more aggressive stance in Italy. He had to strike quickly before they could assemble their forces for action in the peninsula or for an invasion of France itself. Louis might have to recall forces from Italy the following summer. Therefore, he ordered Gaston de Foix to seek a decisive battle and, if victorious, march on Rome. There he would depose Julius and give administration of the papacy to Cardinal San Severino, the most prominent cardinal at Pisa, until a new pope were elected. Finally he was to go on to occupy Naples. To give legitimacy to the conquests, a legate from the Council of Pisa was to be placed in every town captured.[42]

In early 1512 a papal-Spanish army of about 20,000 men approached
Bologna, where Yves d'Alègre and a small force formed a garrison that
hardly was adequate to the task. In February Gaston feinted in the direction
of the Venetian army assembling near Brescia, suddenly changed direction,
and double-timed his men in snow and ice to Bologna. The enemy's commander did not expect an attack, and Gaston and his men were able to
march into Bologna without resistance. In the meantime, the Venetians
had taken Brescia from its small French garrison, which retreated into the
citadel to wait for relief. As soon as Bologna was secure, Gaston dashed
across the Po to Brescia. His army covered the 120 miles in nine days. When
Gaston arrived before the city, he issued a summons to the municipal leaders to surrender on his pledge of being spared the horrors of a siege and
sack, using "every inducement to the city to surrender."[43] The Venetian
commander intercepted the letter and refused to pass it on to the Brescians.
Thus, at dawn on February 18, Gaston's 12,000 troops began the assault in
a pouring rain. He ordered that his men take off their shoes in order to
improve their footing in the mire, providing the example himself. By
midafternoon the city had been occupied. Gaston's casualties were heavy,
and his men were eager to exact their price in the city. The sack of Brescia
was one of the worst atrocities in a long series that marked Louis's Italian
campaigns. The two groups that made up the French infantry in this era, the
Gascons and the German *landsknechts,* had a reputation for terrible behavior off the battlefield. While de Foix did not intend the sack of Brescia to be
as awful as reported, there was little he could do to halt it. The estimates of
the slain in Brescia start at 8,000 and go up from there.[44]

De Foix did not give his men time to rest after the sack, since Maximilian
was acting less and less like an ally. Gaston knew he had to act quickly before
the emperor joined the Holy League. Leaving Brescia, he headed into the
Romagna, despite atrocious roads. The papal-Spanish army pulled back
toward Ravenna, as it was clearly in the League's interest to delay a battle until
additional forces arrived. Convinced that his foes had to fight for Ravenna, de
Foix quickly laid out siege lines when he reached the city. Four days later the
papal-Spanish army, under the viceroy of Naples, Ramon de Cardona, set up
its camp close by and began digging trenches in the water-logged terrain.

Early the next day (Easter Sunday!) Gaston brought his army out of
camp to give battle.[45] Several of his captains had fought in Naples and presumably told him about Spanish tactics there, which had taken advantage
of the French habit of charging immediately to the attack by fighting from
an entrenched position. Rather than moving directly to the attack, he held
up the assault while his artillery pounded the enemy trenches. For three

hours the guns of both sides punished the opposing lines with heavy casualties. When Gaston moved several guns to enfilade the enemy horsemen, they charged the French lines. Thus the hand-to-hand combat began to the advantage of the French, which they held throughout the battle, despite very hard fighting by their foes. When it was over, at least 10,000 men lay dead on the battlefield, of whom a quarter to a third were French. Among the French dead were several prominent captains, such as Yves d'Alègre, but by far the most devastating loss was the death of the brilliant young general himself. Gaston was killed late in the battle, either as he was rallying the French infantry by leading his company of *gens d'armes* into the enemy line or while pursuing the retreating Spanish infantry.

Regardless of how it happened, de Foix's death meant that, as Pandolfini said, "For the French the victory came to naught because of the death of Monsieur de Foix, who for the virtues he possessed and hope of greater things to come was well loved by all his men."[46] Whether he would have marched on to Rome had he lived is difficult to answer. His army had taken a terrible pounding in its victory, in particular losing a large portion of its horses. It may not have had enough strength left to push on to Rome, although it was able to resupply when Ravenna and several other cities in the region capitulated soon after the battle.

Certainly Julius was terrified that it would march on Rome; he and his cardinals vacillated between making peace with Louis and fleeing the city. When the news of Ravenna reached Milan, the council there quickly voted to depose Julius II, calling on the clergy, princes, universities, and people of Christendom no longer to obey Pope Julius, "because he is a disturber of the peace and an obstinate and daring author of schism."[47] Those harsh words had little effect, because Julius soon began to receive better news from Ravenna. The battered French army was not going to make a quick dash on Rome. La Palise, whom the French captains chose as their commander and who was confirmed by Louis, was not the man to pull off a bold move of the sort Gaston had made in the previous three months. La Palise was slow and cautious. The pope, taking heart, redoubled his efforts to bring the Swiss into the war and recruit a new army.[48]

Back in France, Louis had spent the early spring of 1512 hunting and hawking in the vicinity of Blois, "taking Lady Claude with him as usual." Word of the victory arrived on April 19, but the joy was quickly tempered by the news of the deaths of Gaston and the other captains.[49] Gaston's death was a severe blow to Louis. He went into deep mourning for his nephew, "such that he could not be comforted." "Would to God," he said, "I never had an inch of land in Italy, and my nephew and the other lords were still alive."[50]

According to Floranges, Louis ordered La Palise, who was slowly getting ready to march on Rome, to break up his army and put his *gens d'armes* as garrisons in the cities captured. La Palise objected strongly, arguing futilely that if he could reinforce his army, he would make Louis the prince of all Italy.[51]

With both England and Spain rushing preparations to invade France but with French arms for the moment dominant in Italy, Louis chose to try to negotiate with Julius. Despite all of the assurances of his prelates and theologians, the king harbored deep concerns about what the conflict with the irascible old pope meant for his soul and those of his people. Queen Anne continued to press him to make peace with the papacy to prevent further damage to the church. Louis proposed returning Bologna, Ravenna, and the other towns that his troops held in exchange for the pope's abandoning the anti-French alliance. Under pressure from the cardinals, Julius agreed to receive Louis's envoy but told the Venetian ambassador that he only intended to quiet down the French.[52] Encouraged by the news that the French position was much weaker than could have been imagined right after April 12, Julius redoubled his labors at getting the Swiss and the emperor involved against Louis. By the end of April the pope's spirits had risen to the point that he said he expected soon to go to Paris and place the French crown on the head of the king of England. He had already prepared a secret bull giving Henry the French throne when he invaded the realm.[53]

Julius's renewed optimism came from the news that Cardinal Schinner had persuaded the cantons to invade Milan and La Palise was breaking up the French army. In early May 1512 Maximilian and Venice agreed to a ten-month truce. The emperor further agreed to allow the Swiss to pass through his territory to attack Milan from the northeast, which was less well fortified than the direct route from the north, and he ordered the German *landsknechts* to withdraw from French service. As the Swiss advanced toward Milan, La Palise decided that prudence dictated a hasty retreat to the city. Leaving small garrisons in Bologna and several other cities, he made a dash for Milan. As he moved westward along the Po, the Swiss and the Venetians joined forces behind him and pursued. News from Milan revealed that the city was on the verge of rebellion, and he decided to push on to Asti, which he felt was more secure because it was Louis's hereditary land and strongly fortified. Before he reached Asti, his foes caught up to his army while it was crossing a river. As the panicked French crowded across the bridge, it collapsed under their weight. The large part of the army stranded on the wrong side of the river had to surrender. Bypassing Asti, La Palise and the remainder of his forces straggled across the passes into Dauphiné in late June 1512, barely two months after their glorious victory at Ravenna.

With Milan in revolt, the council members fled to Asti, then to Lyon. On July 20, 1512, what was left of the council agreed in Lyon to grant Louis another *décime* of 300,000 *l* on the clergy and faded away.[54] By the end of 1512 Julius II was completely victorious on the spiritual front. His council, the Fifth Lateran, attracted representation from across Europe except France, although its achievements were very limited.

Julius was victorious on the political front as well. In the summer of 1512 French power in northern Italy collapsed like a house of cards. A papal army moved into the Romagna and accepted the submission of Bologna and the other French-held cities. Genoa rebelled and welcomed the anti-French party back to power. The Swiss moved into Milan and installed Massimiliano Sforza, il Moro's son, as duke, although a French garrison continued to hold out in the citadel, which was also true at Genoa and several other cities. Julius and Cardona agreed to oust the pro-French government in Florence and returned the Medici to power as a Spanish army moved past the city in late August 1512. By then Julius felt confident enough of his position to deprive Louis of his title of king of France. In July the pope proclaimed the deprivation in a meeting of cardinals, although Henry VIII still had to conquer France to win the pope's investiture of the French crown.[55]

Louis's reaction to these events is largely unrecorded. Few of his letters for this period are extant. The two chroniclers closest to him, d'Auton and St-Gelais, had ceased writing by then, and with virtually every government estranged from him, there were no ambassadors at his court to report his words nor any French ambassadors abroad to get dispatches from him. But there were foreigners in France spying for his foes. An Italian wrote that a French nobleman had complained: "It is you Italians who keep the king fixed on Italy. Don't you see that the whole realm is crying about the taxation required by the wars in Italy? It is making the king unpopular with the whole populace, and all the French nobility is being lost there."[56] Nonetheless, no one seems to have defected from Louis. A poem by Jean Bouchet from late 1512, when the threat of an English invasion loomed large, boasted that no other king had ever received such loyal support from his people.[57]

Louis's attention had to be focused on war more than ever in 1512, because the kingdom itself came under attack. On November 17, 1511, two weeks after Louis had paid the semiannual installment of 25,000 *écus* on the pension to the English king, Henry VIII had committed himself to invading Gascony.[58] It had been twenty years since the English had engaged in any large-scale fighting, but all contemporaries agreed that no forces frightened the French as much as did the English. Henry's pledge to join the Spanish in an invasion of Gascony in April 1512 could not be met, but on April 24 an English herald arrived at Blois to present Louis with an ultimatum: Make peace with the pope or face war with England. Robertet told the herald that his king had done nothing to the pope nor had any quarrel with Aragon, so there was no need for England to go to war for them. Seeing no halt to English war preparations, Louis moved to tighten the alliance with Scotland, as French kings always had done when faced with war against England. On May 22 Louis published a treaty that declared, in the event of war with England on the part of one realm, the other would wage war on the English king as well. Louis also declared that he had recognized the rights of Richard De la Pole, the duke of Suffolk and nephew of Edward IV and Richard III, to the English throne. Finally he ordered that all diplomatic mail going to England be opened and read at Boulogne.[59]

The English fleet with 6,000 soldiers aboard finally sailed for Spain in early June.[60] A Spanish fleet met the English to escort the troop transports to Spain, while Lord Howard's warships were free to attack Breton coast. Louis had done little to prepare the French fleet for war, but a concentrated effort quickly began. René de Clermont was named lieutenant general of the fleet. Louis ordered Prégent de Bidoux to bring his galley fleet from the Mediterranean to the Atlantic in the belief that the galleys, especially when the wind was calm, would be effective against the English sailing ships, "which might be easily surrounded by fast rowing galleys, and sunk by gunfire."[61]

Before Prégent's fleet arrived in the Atlantic, a famous encounter occurred off Brest. The English found the French fleet at anchor outside of the harbor there. The French ships were so far from ready for action that they were entertaining some local lords and ladies on board. When the English fleet bore down on them, the smaller French ships slipped into the harbor; but several large ships, including Anne of Brittany's great ship, the *Cordelière*, were unable to get up sail quickly enough. She took the brunt of the English attack. Maneuvering about to finish her off, one of the largest English vessels, the *Regent*, was caught downwind from her. Her crew immediately took advantage of the wind to come into the *Regent* and grapple her. During the combat on the decks, a fire on the *Cordelière* touched off her powder magazine. When it blew up, the two ships, "being grappled together . . . were both consumed by fire at that instant." About 180 of the 800 men on the *Regent* were picked up by other English ships, but only six of the 400 people on board the French ship survived.[62] The English fleet proceeded to land near Brest and burn and plunder before returning to England in September.

Meanwhile, the English army that had landed in northwestern Spain in late June 1512 was not faring well. The Spanish did not provide supplies as promised in the treaty of alliance, nor was their army ready to march on

Bayonne as the English expected to do as soon as they landed. Ferdinand had another use planned for them: the conquest of Haute-Navarre (Navarre south of the crest of the Pyrenees). Control of that region was important to Ferdinand because the routes between northern Aragon and northern Castile passed through it, as did several key passes between France and Spain. The presence of Jean d'Albret on the throne of Navarre meant that a Frenchman controlled these key routes, although the rivalry between the d'Albrets and the de Foix had forced Jean and his predecessor to look to Spain as an ally. The death of Gaston de Foix dramatically changed the situation. His rights to Navarre passed to his sister Germaine, now Ferdinand's wife, and Jean immediately went from being a Spanish ally to a French one. In July 1512 he and Louis signed a treaty of alliance against all foes of each other. It specifically stated that no forces of an enemy would be allowed to cross their territory to attack the other.[63]

A spy quickly informed Ferdinand of the treaty, and he moved rapidly against Navarre, sending his forces across the largely undefended border.[64] The English refused to participate because their orders were to attack France. Jean d'Albret fled across the Pyrenees where he joined the large French army assembled to defend Gascony. Francis of Angoulême, then seventeen years old, was, by virtue of his rank, the titular commander of this army. It was his first military expedition, so François de Dunois, now the duke of Longueville, as his second-in-command, made the decisions.[65] La Palise reached Gascony in August with several thousand veterans of the Italian wars.

By the end of September 1512, the English, who had been idle since their arrival, were eager to return home. Ferdinand agreed to let them go, although he said, "victory would have been so easy with the English army."[66] With the threat of an English attack on Gascony gone, the French advanced into Haute-Navarre with a two-pronged attack under La Palise and Francis. They were in an excellent position to pull off a double envelopment on the Spanish army that had advanced to the crest of the Pyrenees, but the French forces moved too slowly to trap it. The Spanish made it back to Navarre's major city, Pamplona, before the French arrived. A month-long siege in late fall of 1512 failed to take the city, and in early December the French captains had to end the campaign. Straggling across the Pyrenees in winter cost them much of their manpower and artillery. This bungled campaign resulted in the annexation of Haute-Navarre into Castile, where it remained despite several French attempts in the next half century to recover it for the d'Albrets.

At about the same time as the French retreated from Pamplona, Louis received even worse news: Maximilian finally had committed himself formally to the anti-French alliance. On November 19, 1512, a treaty between the emperor and the members of the Holy League was proclaimed at Rome. France would be nearly dismembered: England would take Gascony, Guyenne, and Normandy; Maximilian would recover Picardy and Burgundy; the pope would do with Provence as he pleased; and Dauphiné and Lyon would be divided between pope and emperor. The allied forces would subsist on foraging in France and "do the schismatical French as much harm as possible." The signatories of the treaty were at liberty to go beyond the listed appropriations to destroy or conquer France entirely, "no matter however long the war may last." Julius was optimistic enough about the success of the war against France to include a clause calling for the conquest of the Ottoman Empire after it was over.[67]

However, the situation was not as bleak for Louis as the terms of this treaty suggest. Having gotten a tangible gain out of the year's activities, Ferdinand was ready to abandon his allies and make peace with Louis.[68] Ferdinand never overreached himself. When he made a gain, he always ensured his control of it before looking for anything further. He was also annoyed that the pope had agreed to exclude Venice from the anti-French coalition just because of Maximilian's hostility to the city. Thus, Ferdinand responded positively to hints that Louis wanted to make peace with him. On February 6, 1513, Louis commissioned Odet de Lautrec to investigate terms for a truce or a peace with Ferdinand.[69]

Before that effort had progressed far, Louis had reached an agreement with Venice. Several Venetian gentlemen who had been taken as prisoners of war to France after Agnadello served as diplomatic conduit through which Louis was able to build on Venetian anger at both Maximilian and Julius. On March 26, 1513, Venice and France agreed to a treaty of alliance. The usual problem between the two—the frontier between Milan and Venice—was finessed.[70] Only five days later, Lautrec, acting in the names of Louis, James IV of Scotland, and Charles of Gueldres, and a Spanish bishop with authority to deal for Ferdinand and Maximilian put together a truce for a year's duration. It was effective only "on this side of the Italian mountains."[71] Although Henry refused to be bound by it, the truce did give Louis some breathing space.

The third major development that reduced the pressure on the king of France was the death of Julius II on February 21, 1513. In the last months of his reign Julius had refused to accept ambassadors from Louis unless the king handed over the prelates from the Council of Pisa for punishment, although he did receive a special envoy from Queen Anne.[72] At the conclave for the papal election, the Breton cardinal Guibé was the only French cardinal present among the twenty-five who participated, but the results were well received at the French court. On March 11, after a conclave of a week, Cardinal Giovanni de Medici was elected Pope Leo X. The second son of Lorenzo the Magnificent, at thirty-seven years of age the new pope was one of the youngest in history.[73] The French were euphoric over Leo's elections when the news reached Blois in three days and sixteen hours. A Florentine courier brought the news, and so the ambassador from Florence had the honor of announcing it to the king and queen. They received it "with such obvious pleasure that it was plain no other selection could have been more pleasing to them. . . . The king repeatedly said, 'He is someone to my taste, because he is a good man; from someone good only good can be expected.'"[74] Nonetheless, he was not to be regarded as an automatic friend of France. He belonged to a family that the French had helped to oust from power in Florence, and he had been held captive by French troops for several months after the Battle of Ravenna. However, Leo quickly showed that his more pacific nature allowed him to be more conciliatory to Louis than Julius could ever have been. By April 1513 Louis had every reason to believe that his extremely dangerous situation of the previous year had been relieved and his isolation from the other powers was ending. That meant his thoughts turned again to Milan.

16
Last Acts

Louis XII's fixation on his rights to the duchy of Milan was the central feature of his reign. Several days before he died, he told the Venetian ambassador that he intended to pursue the reconquest of Milan in the spring of 1515. Little wonder that in the spring of 1513, when he was in better health, the king was obsessed with schemes to recover the duchy.

In April 1513 the king went to Paris to meet with his captains and named Louis de La Trémoille as lieutenant-general for Milan. Louis, disappointed in Jacques de La Palise's performance the previous year, sent him to Picardy to guard against an English invasion, although the king did not truly expect Henry VIII to attack that spring. In May La Trémoille led a force of 1,200 *gens d'armes* and 11,000 infantrymen across the Alps. The latter included 500 French arquebusmen, the first time a muster roll explicitly noted them.[1] Massimiliano Sforza, the new duke of Milan, had quickly shown himself to be incompetent, and the heavy taxes needed to pay the Swiss, who had put him in power and kept him there, made him highly unpopular. Many well-placed Milanese contacted Louis to urge a return to French rule.[2] About 4,000 Swiss remained in Milan; many more could rapidly march to Milan should the French attack. However, the quick movement of the French across the Alps caught Sforza and the Swiss by surprise, and La Trémoille captured Asti and Alessandro without resistance. At the same time, a French fleet appeared in the harbor of Genoa, where a French garrison still held out in the citadel. Genoa quickly capitulated. Meanwhile, a Venetian army entered the duchy from the east. Milan seethed with rebellion, and Sforza and the Swiss fled to Novara, regarded as more capable of withstanding a siege, where Louis himself had survived one in 1495. La Trémoille placed his army into siege lines around it, and after eight days his guns opened a breach in the walls. However, he delayed ordering an assault on the breach because sources in Novara informed him that the city was on the verge of surrendering. Meanwhile the Swiss cantons had gathered 4,000 men who were dispatched immediately.

News of the coming of the Swiss relief force persuaded La Trémoille to pull his forces out of the siege lines and move them to a field of his choice for battle.³ Once his men had reached the area, he allowed them to relax for the night, expecting that he would have time the next morning to prepare for battle. The Swiss relief force reached Novara about midnight, but after the captains of the two Swiss bands conferred, they marched out of the city two hours later. Since it was a dark rainy night, the Swiss were nearly on top of the French army before their approach was noticed. As the Swiss crossed the open field in front of the French lines, the French did get their guns firing into the large blocks of infantrymen, but Swiss momentum enabled them to overrun the guns and crash into the French infantry. It fought desperately, but it had no cavalry support because cavalry took longer to prepare for battle. By the time it was ready to fight, the French infantry was being crushed, and the horsemen, from long experience with the Swiss pikeman, were loathe to take them on without infantry support. In two hours perhaps half of the French infantry lay dead or dying, while all but forty of the *gens d'armes* got away, fleeing across the Alps back to Dauphiné. The Swiss had also taken heavy casualties, especially from the French artillery. Novara would be the last battle in which the Swiss tactic of charging in three columns would be victorious.

As the news of the French defeat spread across the region, the places they had occupied fell back into the hands of Sforza, while Genoa again revolted and restored its anti-French doge. Louis had no time to linger on the disaster at Novara; Henry VIII's preparations to invade northern France were well under way by then. In April 1513 Henry had signed a treaty with Maximilian for a joint attack on France.⁴ Louis for his part reaffirmed the "auld alliance" with Scotland. He granted all Scots the right to possess and inherit property and hold benefices in his realm, "for the great services rendered by Scotland." In May Queen Anne sent James IV a letter proclaiming him her knight and bidding him for her sake to "step three feet and strike one blow on English ground." She also sent him a ring, which would be taken off his corpse after the Battle of Flodden Field.⁵

Louis ordered his Atlantic fleet to go to sea early in April to seek out and destroy the English fleet and prevent Henry's crossing. It included Prégent's galleys, which arrived in the Atlantic the previous fall. However, the English under Lord Howard found the French only a few miles out of Brest. The galleys retreated into a small harbor, where they presented a tempting target to Howard. He realized that he could not get at the galleys with his ships, so he transferred a large number of troops to several barges accompanying his fleet and entered the harbor on April 25. Approaching

Prégent's galley, Howard had a grappling line thrown across to it and led a squad of men over to its deck. While the hand-to-hand fighting was going on, his barge broke free and drifted away. Left stranded on the French galley, Howard and his men were pushed into the sea. When Prégent learned the enemy admiral was among the missing, he ordered the sea dragged, and the body was found. Prégent took the whistle of command off Howard's body and sent it to Queen Anne. The death of Howard joined the battle between the *Cordelière* and the *Regent* of the previous year as two of the most famous episodes of sixteenth-century naval warfare.[6]

The death of their admiral did not prevent the English from controlling the Channel, which allowed the English army to cross unchallenged to Calais in early June. In all about 30,000 men were transported to the continent, joining 20,000 mercenaries of several nationalities at Calais. Henry joined them on June 30. The significance of Calais as a secure base from which the English could freely invade northern France was well demonstrated in this campaign. Henry marched out of Calais on July 21, 1513. His target was Thérouanne, a major French fortress to the southeast; it had been built to block any English invasion from the Calais Pale. During the slow march of the English forces to Thérouanne, a large French army under Louis de Piennes shadowed them but did not attack because Louis XII had given Piennes a clear order not to engage the English. The reason for this decision apparently was the fact that the French were unusually weak in cavalry because of the campaign under way in Milan.[7] The English army reached Thérouanne and began to lay siege lines, but since its walls created a large circumference, the southern part was left uninvested. The French were able to bring in food and reinforcements. When Maximilian arrived in the English camp on August 10, the siege was not going well for the English. He insisted that Henry invest the entire town, since there was plenty of manpower. Three days later English units began to move toward the southern approaches to Thérouanne.

Meanwhile, the French had been assembling twenty miles south. Louis was waiting for the cavalry returning from Milan to reach Picardy, but he did not commit all of his manpower there, since the garrison in Thérouanne had reported it had enough provisions to hold out until November. He left 1,000 lances in Dauphiné, which he intended to send back to Milan as soon as the English threat ended. Louis gave the command of his army in Picardy to Francis of Angoulême, although as before he was constrained to take the advice of senior captains. A flareup of gout had delayed Louis's departure from Paris, but on August 14, 1513, he was reported as having reached Amiens. When Louis arrived, he ordered his captains to take provisions into Thérouanne. The early optimism that it could hold out until November had given way to an assessment that it had supplies for only another month. On the morning of August 16, while the French were moving a train of wagons escorted by 6,000 cavalrymen along the road to Thérouanne from the south, Henry personally was leading some 10,000 men, mostly infantry, toward the same road to block it. The two forces ran into each other near the village of Guinegate. Henry had received enough advance notice to deploy his men into battle formation, but the French were taken completely by surprise; they thought all of the English were still to the north.

Under strict orders not to engage the English if they encountered a powerful force,[8] the French captains ordered a retreat, but their forward units had already gotten close enough to the enemy to come under fire from artillery and mounted archers. The fire turned a tactical retreat into headlong flight. A small force of the emperor's cavalry that had accompanied Henry pursued the fleeing French and took 120 high-ranking prisoners, including François de Dunois, Admiral René de Clermont, and Bayard, although the French dead numbered only forty men. The flight of the French horsemen, who dropped lances, armor, and battle standards, was so precipitous that the Battle of Guinegate became better known as "the Battle of the Spurs," because it was said that spurs were the only thing the French used during the episode. It was such a blot on the reputation of the French *gens d'armes* that when they made a strong showing at Marignano two years later, Francis I said they no longer could be called "hares in armor." According to Guicciardini, when word came to Louis that his force had been routed, "Miserably lamenting and bemoaning himself he thought of nothing but flying into Brittany."[9] But the English only thought of taking their valuable prisoners back to camp. The failure to resupply Thérouanne resulted in its surrender a week later. Henry and Maximilian decided to destroy the town, perhaps because they could not agree on who would occupy it. Only the churches were left standing. Thérouanne was never rebuilt, and in 1567 its bishopric was transferred to Boulogne.

Henry and Maximilian then directed their army toward Tournai, which was a French enclave inside the Low Countries. Tournai had been a French outpost beyond France's border for 300 years, but it was not well prepared to withstand a siege by a force as large as the one approaching. There was nothing Louis could do to help the city. Nonetheless, he wrote demanding that it stay loyal and not surrender. The city fathers tried to negotiate with Henry, but he was looking for a military victory, not a diplomatic one, and refused to accept the broad concessions they offered.

The allied forces arrived at the walls and began to bombard them. After six days Tournai agreed to surrender to the emperor, but Henry insisted that it concede to him as its rightful sovereign, the true king of France. On September 21 the city leaders gave up the city to Henry.[10]

The dismal showing of the French army in Picardy was in good part a consequence of the fact that much of the manpower chased from Italy in June could not be used in northern France. It had to stay in Burgundy to counter the Swiss threat to eastern France. Louis's relations with the Swiss continued to deteriorate after Novara because he refused to give up his claim to Milan, while Maximilian pushed hard to get them to commit to an invasion of France. In August 1513 a Swiss force of 20,000 pikemen, along with artillery and 1,000 horsemen the emperor supplied, marched across the Franche-Comté and into Burgundy. La Trémoille, the governor of Burgundy since 1506, commanded the French forces there, but his force was far too small to confront the Swiss. He withdrew his men into Dijon, which the Swiss put under siege in early September. The French forces in the city were no match for the Swiss. It seemed nothing would prevent them from marching on to Paris, "so they can expel the king of the French."[11]

Several Swiss leaders wanted to bypass Dijon and go straight to Paris, which was poorly defended, but most preferred to wait for Maximilian to join them. He, as usual, never appeared. So they settled on a siege of Dijon. La Trémoille's biographer records a speech he gave to its residents to encourage them to fight hard in its defense, since the loyalty of Dijon as the former capital of the Burgundian dukes was still rather suspect. His appeal centered around the peace and prosperity that Louis had given them, unprecedented, so he said, in the history of the duchy, and the contrast with the barbarism and savagery of the Swiss. Despite La Trémoille's efforts, the Swiss opened a breach in its walls on September 13. He immediately asked for negotiations, to which the Swiss leaders, angry at Maximilian, agreed. Their demands were very stiff: Louis XII had to give up all claim to Milan and Asti and order the garrisons in citadels still held by the French to surrender them; he would pay the Swiss 400,000 *écus* and end all unlicensed recruiting in the cantons. La Trémoille had no choice but to accept the terms, since there was no hope of any relief. He agreed to bind the king to the agreement and provided 20,000 *écus* immediately. He also gave up five hostages—three members of the city government of Dijon, his own nephew, and Antoine de Baissey, the *bailli* of Dijon—for the fulfillment of the terms. Upon receiving the hostages, the Swiss pulled out of their siege lines and returned home without waiting for the king's acceptance of the terms. Louis repudiated the treaty as soon as the Swiss had withdrawn, partly because of the amount of money La Trémoille had pledged but even more because it obliged him to give up Milan, "of which he was excessively fond."[12]

The Swiss were furious and declared they would kill their hostages, but it was too late in the season to return to Dijon. As angry as Louis was with La Trémoille for exceeding his authority, the old captain may have saved France. Had the Swiss taken Dijon, they could easily have marched to Paris, and the king of England probably would have joined them.[13] Louis did send the Swiss 50,000 *écus* to keep them from killing the hostages, but it did not assuage the Swiss completely. Instead of returning to Burgundy the next spring, however, they turned to ensuring that Milan would be solidly in their control. As for the hostages, the *bailli* of Dijon soon escaped, and the others were held until August 1514, when they were ransomed for 15,000 *écus*.[14]

As if the bad news from Tournai and Dijon were not enough, word arrived at the French court in mid-September that Louis's ally, James IV of Scotland, had been killed and his army routed on September 9, 1513. In the previous year, Louis and James had agreed to an alliance of mutual aid; the French promised to provide the Scots with 50,000 *écus* and some artillery. James had ignored Henry VIII's efforts to buy him off, being determined to strike a blow for the "auld alliance." On August 11 a Scots herald had delivered James's declaration of war to Henry outside of Thérouanne.[15] Two weeks later the Scots army entered northern England. The earl of Surry gathered the forces of northern England and confronted the Scots at Flodden Field near Berwick. The resulting battle was one of the bloodiest of the era, and when it was over, the Scots king and over 5,000 of his men lay died on the battlefield. The defeat of the Scots also crushed Louis's hope that they would force the English to withdraw from France.

The year 1514 (the new year in the French calendar of that era actually began at Easter) began with another blow to Louis—the death of Queen Anne at age thirty-seven on January 9, 1514 at Blois. She had been active almost to the last minute in negotiations with Ferdinand and Maximilian. In particular she and the king of Aragon, with whom she always felt she could deal, were trying to hammer out a marriage contract for her infant daughter Renée and his second grandson Ferdinand with the duchy of Milan as her dowry. Even as she lay dying, she called for Floranges to ask him to go on a mission to the emperor for her. As he said, "She had a heart marvelously affectionate toward the House of Burgundy."[16]

Anne apparently had never recovered her health after her last pregnancy, which had resulted in a stillborn male child in January 1512, but the immediate cause of death was probably an infection from gallstones.[17] She was in deep pain in her last days, but she prepared for death with serenity and devotion, although her end could hardly have been entirely peaceful, with the future of her duchy uncertain and her daughter committed to a man she distrusted and about to gain a mother-in-law she hated. Nonetheless, in her will she gave the custody of her goods, fortune, and daughters to Louise of Savoy.[18]

Louis, weak with gout, mourned deeply for his Anne, going into seclusion for several days after her death. He was reported as telling his courtiers: "Go make the vault . . . big enough for us both. Before the year is over I'll be with her."[19] He wore black in mourning, which was against tradition for a French king, and insisted that anyone who spoke to him also be dressed in black. He also extended the mourning period beyond the customary forty days. Anne's body was taken to Paris and then buried in St-Denis with "the greatest service and honor a queen of France ever had." The cost of candles alone for the services at Notre-Dame and St-Denis came to 2,050 *l.*[20]

Before she died, Anne had the satisfaction of seeing peace made between her husband and the pope. She had always sharply opposed the rift with the papacy and, as the duchess of Brittany, had refused to take the duchy into schism with the rest of France. Her support for the papacy in the midst of Louis's troubles with it had angered him. He was quoted as telling her: "Madame, don't your confessors tell you that women have no say in the Church?" Anne was weaving a liturgical vestment for Leo X when she died. He wrote a letter of condolence to Louis, praising Anne as a woman "full of virtue and wisdom."[21]

Pope Leo was eager to make peace with Louis, but the political situation at the moment of his accession required that he continue to participate in the Holy League, albeit in a halfhearted manner. He did not celebrate the French defeat at Novara and was quick to accept the submission in June 1513 of two of the cardinals involved in the Council of Pisa. By July pope and king had exchanged envoys, Louis's being Claude de Seyssel, but a successful conclusion to the schism eluded the diplomats as long as Louis refused to repudiate the council. Louis's reluctance to make the humiliating concession that his council had been schismatic delayed a final resolution until Girolamo Aleandro, who had been one of the most outspoken advocates of Louis's calling a council, declared that it had been illegal. In late October the king accepted a statement drawn up at Rome refuting the Council of Pisa and recognizing the Council of the Lateran. In doing so, Louis agreed to its denunciation of the Pragmatic Sanction. At the fourth session of the council, its members had approved Julius's declaration that the Pragmatic Sanction was offensive to God, pernicious to the church, and null and void. Two sessions later the council again had denounced the Pragmatic Sanction specifically and Gallicanism in general.[22]

Thus Louis had taken the first step toward replacing the Pragmatic Sanction. Discussion took place in Rome about its replacement, but Leo's claim that the pope had the power to fill all major French benefices prevented a solution before Louis's death. The pope was far more willing to compromise after Francis I's great victory at Marignano in 1515, which led to the Concordat of Bologna of the next year.[23] Leo accepted a clause in the agreement stating that Louis had never been included in the excommunication Julius II had issued against supporters of the false council. On December 19, 1513, Seyssel presented the signed agreement to the pope, while ten French churchmen who had been at Pisa requested absolution for themselves and their absent colleagues.[24]

Anne's influence over her husband had been a key factor in his making peace with the papacy, and it was her death that provided the opportunity to make peace with England. Only two weeks after she died, Dandolo, the Venetian ambassador, reported that discussion was ongoing about Louis's remarriage; and he named three possible brides: Queen Margaret of Scotland, James IV's widow and Henry VIII's sister, who was twenty-five years old; Princess Mary, Henry's second sister, who was eighteen; and Margaret of Austria, who despite being involved with the French monarchy for over thirty years, was only thirty-four. Dandolo noted that "by the king of France taking any of these ladies, peace might be made."[25]

Although Henry expected to return to war in France in 1514, he was not entirely closed to peace. Ferdinand of Aragon had proven to be less than a steadfast ally. On the pretext that the schism, the cause for the war with France, was over, he had signed a second truce with Louis and was urging Maximilian to do the same. The emperor, as usual, could not pursue a policy to its conclusion. He was ready to negotiate with France, much to the disgust of his daughter, who was always more steadfastly anti-French. She wrote to him in February 1514:

> You, better than any other, can judge the faith and loyalty of the French. The other princes have mountains and the sea between them and their enemies, and are richer than this poor House of Burgundy; so that even if [Louis] now gave up what belongs to us he might within two or three years, on seeing an opening, take it back, and to take to-day and lose again to-morrow were greater shame than

before. They can always find a pretext in the loy salique and other points of this sovereignty which they claim. It is not surprising if [Ferdinand] is the most easily inclined to this peace and advises it, for he has what he demands. You and England have not.[26]

When Henry became aware of Ferdinand's activities, he was furious that after his successes of the previous year, "now when his enemy is at his feet, Ferdinand talks of truce." The Aragonese king wanted peace because he did not want to give Louis any pretext for reconquering Milan or Naples and upsetting the current situation in Italy, where Spanish power was now dominant. He hoped to reinforce the status quo there by encouraging the marriage between Princess Renée and Archduke Ferdinand and even added his eldest granddaughter, Eleanor, to the list of potential brides for Louis.[27]

Leo X had come to recognize the threat that Spanish control of Italy presented to the papacy and turned to helping Louis extract himself from his multiple troubles. The Florentine Pandolfini, back in France again, told Louis that Leo was ready to do all he could to help the French make peace with the Swiss and the English, even use the power of excommunication. By May it was clear that Louis had little to fear from the Swiss for the coming campaigning season.[28] As for the English, Henry's mood made it easy for Dunois, who had been captured at Guinegate and taken to England, to approach him with proposals for peace and marriage. In May a Venetian in London wrote that Henry's expected return to war in France was being delayed because of ongoing negotiations. At the end of May, Thomas Bohier was sent to England to continue the discussions at a higher level. He was described as one "accustomed to handling more difficult matters than the ransom of a duke."[29]

While negotiations for a bride for Louis were going on, the marriage between Claude and Francis also occupied his attention. She had turned fourteen late the previous year, but her mother's opposition may have delayed the wedding until after her death. The Bretons refused to accept Francis as their duke until he had married Claude, and the danger that this would offer the English an opportunity to meddle may have persuaded Louis to proceed with the marriage. Fearing that Francis would do to him what he had done to Charles VIII, Louis had refused to invest him with Brittany until after the wedding. Robertet was reported as strongly advocating that it be done quickly. According to Louis and Anne's marriage contract, Brittany was supposed to go to Renée as the second child, but Louis disregarded that clause. In later life Renée made numerous unsuccessful efforts to secure the duchy.[30]

Only four days before the wedding, Francis was informed that it would take place on May 14, at St-Germain-en-Laye. Although Floranges, his close friend, called it the richest wedding he had ever seen, it could not have been very festive, since everyone was still wearing black in mourning for Queen Anne. Louise of Savoy did not attend; there were no games or tournaments; and the king left the court immediately after to go hunting.[31] Although Claude was hardly the right spouse for a dashing *gallant* like Francis, since she was already quite heavy and, like her mother, had a limp, nonetheless she brought as her dowry the duchy of Brittany, rights to Milan and Asti, over one million *écus* from her mother, and closer ties with her father.

Louis's relationship with Francis's father had been good, but the antagonism between Anne and Louise, and the obvious fact that Francis's ambitions could not be fulfilled unless Louis had the misfortune of not having a son, strained the ties between the king and his successor. Exactly when Louis made the oft-quoted remark "This big boy will spoil everything!" is not clear, but he is supposed to said it to d'Amboise every time some word of Francis's extravagance or misbehavior came to him. Francis's impatience to become king was apparently so obvious that Louis told him a parable to urge him to be patient: When he was a boy, Louis told him, he was on the road with his father (most unlikely since his father died when Louis was an infant) for a long time. Finally they saw the steeples and towers of the city where they were headed, and Louis said to his father, "Our journey is over! We're there!" His father said to him, "Just because you see the towers and steeples, don't think that you have already arrived." Louis is supposed to have told this to Francis when Anne was pregnant with Renée.[32]

In June 1514 a Venetian diplomat reported Louis had said to the Dauphin, a title Francis had used since 1513, that there were four ladies, one of whom he intended to marry so he could have a son and Francis "shall remain the Duke of Brittany."[33] Nonetheless, the king did make an effort to train the young man for his future role. Francis had nominal command of large armies for the past two years, and he became a number of the royal council. He told Dandolo that he would now "speak frankly to the king, as I have not dared to do so far." He engaged himself actively in the business of government, hoping to show Louis that he would make a good king.[34]

In the meantime, the diplomatic efforts between Louis and Henry continued. By June Henry's demands for peace had become known: the concession of Thérouanne, Tournai, and St-Quentin to English sovereignty and a sum of 1,500,000 ducats along with the usual annual pension of 50,000 *écus* in exchange for peace and the hand of one of the king's sisters. Louis was highly indignant at these terms, protesting that he would not pay tribute or yield an inch of his realm.[35] Nonetheless, the negotiations continued with the help of a papal representative. By then Louis was eager to marry again and recapture Milan; both were possible if he made peace with Henry.

Any agreement to concede Thérouanne and Tournai posed a special problem for Louis, since it involved alienating a part of the realm, an act strictly forbidden by the fundamental law of the kingdom. When Louis gave way on the matter, in order to ensure the legality of the concession and to garner support for it, he called a meeting of notables to secure their approval. It met on July 16 and quickly acquiesced in the king's request.[36] On July 29 Louis gave a commission for Dunois and Bohier to sign a treaty of alliance and a marriage contract for Mary Tudor. The treaty required that Louis pay Henry 1,000,000 crowns at the rate of 26,315 crowns twice a year. The sum was described as what was due the English monarchy by old agreements for the ransom of Louis's father in 1444 and between Charles VIII and Henry VII.[37] Louis also agreed to order the "White Rose," Richard De la Pole, out of his realm, but since he had given good service in the recent wars, the king gave him a pension of 10,000 *l* to settle in Metz.

On August 7 representatives of the French and the English kings met to sign the treaty and the marriage contract. Henry agreed to give Mary a dowry of 400,000 crowns, but half of it was to be in the form of jewels and apparel to take to France, while the other half was credited to the sum that Louis had just agreed to pay him. Louis agreed that Mary would receive from him properties worth 700,000 ducats; she would be permitted to keep them for the rest of her life regardless of where she might be living.[38] At the same time, Mary renounced her betrothal to Charles of Austria, made two months earlier. It was the second time Louis had denied Charles a bride, and as Charles's aunt and guardian Margaret had been similarly treated by the French, there is little wonder that he hated them for the rest of his life.[39] On August 13 Mary and Louis's proxy, Dunois, exchanged marriage vows and signed the marriage contract. After that Mary put on night clothes and got into bed, while Dunois, with one leg uncovered, lay on it and touched the princess with his naked foot. The marriage was then declared consummated. At the celebration after, the new queen wore a diamond the size of a pigeon egg called the "Mirror of Naples" that Louis had sent her. Henry had it appraised, and it was valued at 60,000 crowns. Mary wrote to Louis that she had received his letters with pleasure; she promised to "love him as cordially as she could."[40] Although Louis had been quoted as saying after Anne's death that he would never marry again, the diplomatic and dynastic pressures, along with the accounts of Mary's beauty, changed his mind. She was regarded as one of the most beautiful women of her times. At eighteen years of age, she was in full bloom, large-bosomed but slim overall, with red-blond hair and a rosy complexion. She was described as well-educated, an excellent dancer, charming, and affable.[41] In late August Jean Perréal arrived in England to paint her portrait for Louis. When Louis saw the portrait, he said he was "more pleased to have so beautiful a wife than half his state."[42]

As for the princess's reaction to the prospect of marrying a fifty-two-year-old man whom nearly every ambassador's report for the previous year noted as in bed with gout, the evidence is mixed. One report from Rome reported her as weeping "bitterly over her misfortune in being passed from one extreme to another," presumably from the young Charles to the elderly Louis.[43] Louis's portrait that Perréal took her shows a fairly handsome man of middle age, somewhat sober in expression but with no hint of illness. There is no way of knowing how much artistic license was in the painting. Mary gave no sign during her departure from England and arrival in France of any unhappiness. Becoming queen probably was adequate compensation for the age of her spouse.

The peace and Louis's new marriage dramatically changed the diplomatic calculus of western Europe. Louis could now eagerly plan the reconquest of Milan. French garrisons still held several citadels in the region, and they had to be relived soon. The citadel in Genoa in fact surrendered on August 26. Trivulzio and La Trémoille were kept in eastern France with good-size forces in the hope that they could be sent across the Alps, but by the time it was certain that England would not invade again, it was too late to plan a campaign. Louis told numerous people of his intention to go to Milan the next March. In a letter to Charles Brandon, the duke of Suffolk, Henry's favorite, Louis asked for Suffolk's help in getting a loan of 200,000 *écus* from the king for the task.[44] Louis also provided Maximilian with 100,000 *écus* as a loan to aid him in retaking Milan. Far from being upset with the treatment of his grandson Charles, Maximilian was helping his rival.[45]

By September Louis's thoughts turned from Milan to his new bride. He was "marvellously anxious to see her come to France," but her departure took longer than expected.[46] When her party, a veritable army of English notables who included Ann Boleyn, then thirteen years old, reached Dover to board the thirteen ships they needed, bad weather delayed her longer. Finally on October 2, after extracting from her brother a promise to allow her to choose her own husband the next time, Mary went on board. The foul weather came up again while her ship was in the Channel, and it ran aground in Boulogne harbor.[47] An English lord had to carry her ashore through the breakers.

The next day Mary left for Abbeville to meet Louis. Francis of Angoulême and a long list of French nobles met her some miles outside of Abbeville and formed an escort for her triumphal entry. A few miles closer to the town she met her husband, who had been informed of her approach and came out to meet her. It was considered bad etiquette for him to see her before the official reception, but he was so eager to meet her that he feigned being out hawking and coming on her party by accident. An Italian observer thought Louis did this to prove to her he could still ride and hunt. Again ignoring etiquette, which forbade kissing on the lips in public, Louis kissed her on the mouth "as kindly as if he had been five and twenty." The king then quickly returned to Abbeville to await her formal entry. The high rank of both her English and French escorts and the luxury of their apparel bedazzled the observers, but Mary herself clearly stood out in respect to beauty and dress. When she entered Abbeville, she first visited the chief church and then went to Louis's residence, where she met Claude, who was her companion for the rest of the festivities. The evening, while grand entertainments were being held in the residence, a fire broke out in a poor section of town. Because an order had been given that the fire bells were not to be rung that evening to avoid disturbing the king at his fête, the fire burned much of the town.

On October 9 the royal couple dined at the royal residence and attended a ball that lasted until eight at night. Claude then escorted Mary to the wedding chamber "to go and sleep with the king." The following morning Louis "seemed very jovial and gay, and in love. Thrice did he cross the river last night and would have done more, had he chosen."[48] However, Floranges, who related that the king said that he had done marvels, thought it was not true, because he was *"bien malaise."*[49] Floranges's opinion is supported by the fact that Louis's departure later that week for Paris was delayed by a severe attack of gout. Meanwhile, most of the large English contingent left for home with gifts from Louis amounting to 30,000 francs. When Brandon had a royal audience on October 23 at Beauvais, where Louis's gout had again delayed the trip to Paris, he "found the King lying in bed, and the Queen sitting by the bedside."[50]

The royal party reached the vicinity of Paris on November 3, and two days later Mary was crowned at St-Denis. On the next day she made her formal entry into Paris. The city gave her a silver vessel worth 6,000 *l*. Paris and the treasurers-general of France commissioned Pierre Gringore to prepare the event—the first time, it appears, that one person organized an entire royal entry. From his account and those of several other observers, it seems that Mary's entry was more elaborate than Anne's of ten years earlier. Beside the obligatory comparisons to the Virgin Mary, the principal theme was Mary the queen of peace. She was also compared to the queen of Sheba bringing peace as her gift to the new David, the wise and virtuous Louis XII.[51] A week later one of the greatest tournaments of the era began. It had 305 contestants, including fifty English. Francis was responsible for organizing it, and the English suspected that he arranged the jousts to put them at a disadvantage. Nonetheless, they did very well; Louis conceded that their champions, Charles Brandon and the marquis of Dorset, outdid the French. At least one French jouster was killed, and Francis broke a finger. The festivities ended on November 26, when the university sponsored a banquet for Mary.[52]

The expense of all these events involving Louis's marriage was enormous, while Henry VIII was rather miserly in funding his sister's retinue. The French felt that he reneged several times on promises he had made. Louis gave his bride a large number of jewels, including the largest pearl the earl of Worcester had ever seen. While showing the earl the sixty great jewels he intended to give her, Louis joked that he would give them to Mary one at a time, "for which he will have many and divers kisses."[53] The jewels would become a bone of contention after Louis's death, with the French claiming that they were crown jewels, but most wound up in England. Louis also provided large pensions to the most important English lords, such as Wolsey and Brandon, totaling nearly 12,000 *l.*[54]

Despite the age difference, the relationship between Mary and Louis grew warm. She wrote to Henry "how lovingly the King her husband treats her," while Louis wrote to him that Henry "might be sure of his treating her to her own and his satisfaction." Mary asked Dunois and others close to Louis for advice on how to best act in order to content the king, "whereof she was most desirous," and promised to follow their advice because "they were the men the King loved and trusted . . . for she knew well that those the King loved must love her best, and she them."[55] There is no hint that Mary was displeased that her husband was old and gouty, while Louis was utterly taken with Mary's beauty, charm, and eagerness to please. However, the purpose of the marriage was to give Louis a son; it appears that the royal couple tried diligently to procreate. Whether Louis was impotent, as several observers stated, cannot be determined; but only two days after the wedding night at Abbeville where Louis boasted of his virility, Francis of Angoulême happily told Floranges: "Unless I have been badly deceived, it is impossible for the king and queen to have children."[56]

If it was true, the disappointment may well explain why Louis's health, described as considerably better in the weeks around the wedding, grew steadily worse in December 1514. His contemporaries attributed his new health problems to the dramatic change in his lifestyle and diet. From a very regular life with plenty of rest and a diet largely of boiled beef, Louis "for the sake of his wife, changed his whole manner of life." He had retired at six and was now going to bed at midnight, and his diet now included all sorts of rich foods. His physicians warned him about the impact of these changes: If he continued, he would die of his pleasure. The jesters of the Basoche joked that the king of England had sent a *hacquenée* (filly for hire) to the king of France to carry him off quickly and most sweetly to hell or paradise.[57]

Louis and Mary remained in Paris, rather than going to Blois, because she wanted to be there for the Christmas season. On December 24, while reporting that Charles de Bourbon and other captains had come to Paris to plan the next spring's campaign to Milan, Dandolo added that Louis was suffering badly from the gout, which was weakening him. Two days later Louis performed his last official act, signing a letter to Henry VIII praising both Mary and Brandon.[58] By the end of December Dandolo had become convinced that Louis's death was imminent, so he posted a messenger at the Tournelles to bring him immediate word of it. Early on January 1 the messenger told Dandolo that the king was *in extremis* and had received the last sacraments. About this time Louis called Francis in to tell him he was dying. Late on January 1, between the hours of ten and eleven, he died.[59]

Mary, now the *reine blanche,* was immediately whisked away to the Hôtel de Cluny in Paris for the forty days of confinement to determine whether she was pregnant. A son, born up to a year after Louis's death, would have still been his legally and thus the heir to the throne before Francis. Although there were rumors that she was pregnant and that Francis was responsible,[60] she soon told him that she was not, and he proceeded with his *sacre* on January 25.[61] A month later she returned to England with most of the jewels Louis had given her, much to Francis's annoyance. There she prevailed on her brother to honor his promise to allow her to marry whom she pleased—namely, Charles Brandon.[62]

Louis, by dying in Paris rather than in his beloved Blois, made it easier for his successor to organize and expedite his funeral, but Francis hurried them along with unseeming haste.[63] By custom he could not be crowned until his predecessor had been buried, and he was not willing to wait the forty days set by tradition for the obsequies of a king.[64] On January 2 Louis's entrails and heart were removed and buried separately in urns in the Church of the Celestins, the special church of the House of Orléans in Paris, while the rest of the corpse was embalmed and taken to lie in state in the Tournelles for an abbreviated period of ten days. On January 11 the body was removed to

Notre-Dame for a solemn funeral Mass. The twenty-four criers of the city of Paris led the funeral procession through the streets shouting: "The good King Louis, Father of the People, is died! Pray Jesus for his soul!" The following day the body was taken to St-Denis. The solemn procession was marred by a breakdown of the cart carrying the coffin and a dispute between the dead king's servants and the monks of St-Denis over who received the gold cloth that covered the coffin. The monks won.

The coffin remained in the church overnight, and the next morning twenty-five Scots archers carried it down into the dark crypt that served as the final resting place for French royalty. By tradition neither the new king nor the *reine blanche* were present. La Palise, as the grand master of Louis's household, was the master of ceremonies for the interment. He threw his staff of office into the vault and told the other royal officers present to do the same. He then dipped the Royal Banner of France into the tomb, while shouting "The king is dead!" Immediately he pulled it out with the cry: "Long live the king!" The symbolism served to show that the king of France never died.[65]

Francis gave the commission for Louis and Anne's tomb to Gian Justo, who finished it in 1531. Regarded as a superb example of Italianate sculpture, it presents the king and queen praying at the top of the tomb, the *priants*, while underneath are two nearly naked recumbent statues of the dead couple, the *gésants*. The serene and tranquil expressions on the faces of the royal couple are an appropriate representation of the reign of the "Father of the People."

17

Legacy

Louis XII reigned over France for sixteen years less three months, about the median length of time for French kings in the four centuries before 1789. Certainly he was a better king than those who knew him as the duke of Orléans could have imagined. Given both his unpromising youth and serious health problems for much of his reign, his accomplishments and contributions were surprisingly substantial, although they do not put him in the ranks of the most important French kings.

Louis's statement that a king ought not avenge the injuries of a duke underlines one major contribution he made to his realm. If he had tried to exact revenge on Anne of Beaujeu, Louis de La Trémoille, and the others who had opposed him, he probably would have touched off a civil war. Had that happened, his foes, while probably not strong enough to keep him off the throne, would have been able to carry on a protracted struggle and create a constitutional crisis in which the accusation of lèse-majesté and perhaps his parentage would have become issues. The first days of his reign set the tone for one in which only one known episode of injustice to a French subject, the unique case of Pierre de Gié, can be cited.[1]

On the other hand, in Italy Louis often tolerated and even encouraged behavior by his soldiers that he did not permit in France. If forgetting the past was a key to his successful rule at home, he was incapable of doing it in respect to Italy, where he insisted on making good every claim he had to Italian lands. Louis's pursuit of those claims involved him in some extremely dubious decisions and alliances with several of the most Machiavellian characters of his or any era. Beyond precipitating the major military events of his reign, with their high cost in men and money, his Italian policy led to the major episodes of his reign at home—the bungled betrothal of Claude to Charles of Austria and the subsequent Estates of 1506, the schism in the church, and Henry VIII's invasion of Picardy. However, none of these led to long-term changes: France remained "the eldest daughter of the church"; Tournai and Thérouanne were recovered in the next two reigns; and Claude passed to Francis I her inheritance of Brittany and, unfortunately for France, also the claim to Milan and Naples.

In that era of the "gathering-in of the provinces," the permanent attachment of Brittany to the crown was Louis's principal contribution to this process, even if legally it was not completed until the succession of his grandson, Henry II, in 1547. It is true that Louis's succession also brought the Orléanist lands back to the crown, but it is difficult to believe that, with their location in the center of the realm, they could have long remained separatist. In respect to those provinces such as Burgundy and Provence that his predecessors had "gathered in," the enormous affection that their people had for him helped to cement their ties to the monarchy.

This affection for Louis was based in large part on his reduction of the *tailles*. Already before the end of his reign, however, his military setbacks caused the effort to keep taxes low to falter, and Francis I quickly jettisoned it entirely. The new king also moved rapidly to sell judicial offices and change the fiscal administration, so Louis's efforts in those areas were not successful in the long term. Far more durable were his redaction of the law codes and the erection of new parlements.

In regard to the church, Louis XII was too comfortable in the religion of his day to have had much of an impact on reform. His complicity in the abuses in the church was less extensive than that of other kings of the era, but he still accepted them with little thought of correction. His long-range impact on the church came out of his confrontation with Julius II. In accepting the decrees of the Fifth Lateran Council, Louis agreed to its denunciation of the Pragmatic Sanction of Bourges and Gallicanism in general. Thus, Louis made first move toward the replacement of the Pragmatic Sanction, which was achieved two years after his death by Francis I in the Concordat of Bologna.

The failure of the Council of Pisa was also a devastating blow to the theory of Conciliarism. The theory had been predicated on the idea that the Catholic princes, or at least the Holy Roman Emperor, had the right to convoke a council without the consent of the pope. When Maximilian refused to send his clergy to Pisa but did dispatch them to Rome, he signaled his rejection of the theory. It was harmed even more by the failure of the Council of Pisa to accomplish anything at all, and Louis's denunciation of it as a price of reconciliation with the papacy was the final blow. France had always been the mainstay of conciliarism. When it was rejected there, there was little chance that it would take root again elsewhere.

Louis XII's feud with the papacy by no means destroyed Gallicanism, but it was changed substantially. The Pragmatic Sanction had been largely a product of ecclesiastical Gallicanism, which the Concordat of Bologna repudiated. True, there was strong opposition to the Concordat for a time after 1516 from the University of Paris, always a stronghold of the ecclesiastical version, and from the Parlement of Paris, because the magistrates felt it gave away too much to the papacy. Expressions of opposition lingered through the sixteenth century. Nonetheless, the events of 1510-13 allowed royal Gallicanism to emerge victorious and hold sway until 1789. Louis's principal legacy in religion was the image of the quintessential Gallican king who braved papal excommunication to protect the rights and liberties of the French church.

Louis's attitude in appointing bishops and abbots was highly traditional: Rank and privilege merited more of the same. It was largely the same for his government appointments. Military offices and provincial governorships were reserved for the highest-ranking nobles. The high nobility also dominated the royal council, although that dominance declined somewhat toward the end of Louis's reign. However, those advisers who were closest to the king, with the exception of Gié until his disgrace, came from the next levels of society. The d'Amboises were mid-level nobility in 1498, while Florimond Robertet, Etienne de Poncher, and Thomas Bohier were *haute-bourgeoisie*. The latter two were the most influential of that large group of wealthy merchants/bankers from Tours who provided financial and judicial officers for Louis. Although they had already been present in good number before 1498, they came into their own under Louis. By 1515 it was largely accepted that fiscal and judicial offices would be filled by *haute-bourgeois* commoners, not nobles.

That development is part of the evidence cited by a number of historians, including such prominent ones as Roland Mousnier and Roger Doucet, to show that "a great change took place, a change which may be regarded as a transformation of the monarchical system itself." Perhaps the most succinct statement of the idea has come in a recent book by Norman Cantor: The "New monarchies" of 1500, having been scorched by the upheavals of the fourteenth and fifteenth centuries, were more remote from the people they ruled than in 1300. "They were more secretive, self-contained, authoritarian, and disinclined to consult with representative estates and parliaments, even for ceremonial and information-giving purposes."[2] The term "New Monarchy" is used to indicate this point of view, which places the creation of the absolutist state of the Ancien Régime in the early Renaissance era. When it is thought to have happened in France is rather vague; various historians see it as having begun with Louis XI or Charles VIII's expedition to Italy or Francis I. Among the identifying elements of this new style of kingship are said to be the use of Roman law, the creation of a standing royal army, the decline of the Estates-general and other consultative assemblies, and the transfer of power from the nobility to the king in alliance with the bourgeoisie. More broadly, it entailed the building of a more rational and effective government based in part on the model of imperial Rome.

Other historians, in particular J. Russell Major, have challenged the thesis that the French monarchy of the Renaissance era made a dramatic change from feudalism to absolutism. They ask how it was possible for a king to govern absolutely with a bureaucracy of only 8,000 to 12,000 men for 15 million people. They dispute the claim that the nobility lost significant power to the monarchy and the consultative tradition of the late Middle Ages disappeared. While prepared to admit some change, they argue that the style of kingship found in the sixteenth century was neither feudal nor absolutist; rather, it was the "Renaissance monarchy," a style of rule unique to the era.[3]

Where do the two sides see Louis XII fitting into this debate? Doucet did not think highly of Louis or, for that matter, of Charles VIII, but he felt that the few reforms and changes made in their reigns "heralded the appearance of a new system of rule." According to Major, on the other hand, Louis, by respecting the traditions of his realm and privileges of his subjects, handed over to his successor the popular and consultative traditions unimpaired.[4] There can be little argument that Louis practiced a highly consultative form of government. True, the only large assembly he called, in 1506, is subject to debate over whether it ought to be labeled a meeting of the Estates-general. Whatever one calls them, the main purpose of those meetings was approving an increase in taxes. With the *tailles* declining, there was little need for assemblies. Nonetheless, throughout Louis's reign, numerous assemblies of one sort or another took place. They included the assembly of the clergy in 1511, the gatherings of groups of notables at the court, numerous provincial and local assemblies, and meetings of municipal communes. Few people of his era truly wanted meetings of the Estates-general; they were expensive, time-consuming, and not especially useful. More weight was given to the provincial assemblies, which Louis was far more willing to use. They were called to approve taxes on a routine basis, and we know that the Estates of Languedoc, like the Parisian commune, were able to get the levy for the province reduced. Furthermore, local estates consented to both the creation of several provincial parlements and the redaction of the law codes, among the major accomplishments of Louis's reign.

Reflective of Louis's concern that his subjects regard him well was the extensive use of publicity and propaganda. For no king prior to Louis XIV was so strong an effort made to present the king in so favorable a light.[5] It seems to have paid off for Louis in his title "Father of the People" and the absence of any rebellion against him even in the dark days of 1511-13. Louis had many occasions to participate in the grand ceremonies—royal funerals, marriages, and entries—that were used to project the image of the monarchy through the use of royal iconography. A recent study proposes that "such images proliferated to an exceptional degree in the reign of Louis XII," with the results of both obliterating all impressions of the questionable character of the duke of Orléans and elevating royal power to divine status.[6] At the level of the popular "media," the Basoche and other popular writers and pamphleteers turned from critics to boosters, thanks to Louis's decision not to censor them early in his reign. Last, Louis was very fortunate in his many historiographers. Not only did they publish very favorable histories of his reign, but they also included Claude de Seyssel, an intellectual of high quality, who provided a theoretical framework for their praise of Louis's rule.

Nearly all of these publicists, whether literary or artistic, had a common feature—the intermingling, to a greater or lesser extent, of traditional themes and symbols with innovations drawn from the Italian Renaissance era, especially themes drawn from imperial Rome. Thus, the publicity and, in some cases, obvious propaganda combined the advantage of being easily understood by the common folk with the excitement of new ideas. Certainly it is now impossible to gauge accurately the impact of all this activity on the common people, but the overall result seems to have been very favorable to the king.

If Louis's use of consultative assemblies on one hand and the extensive publicity campaign that prefigured Louis XIV's on the other point to no clear answer for the question of whether his reign was feudal or absolutist, so does his relationship with the nobility. Louis had no active policy of reducing its power and autonomy. One powerful nobleman, Pierre de Gié, was broken, but there was no hostile response to the verdict on the part of his fellow magnates. They did not see it as a threat to their class. Louis provided the nobles with wars in which to win glory and honor, always a major consideration in their assessment of a king, and the prosperity of the time allowed them to live well. Louis felt secure enough about his nobles that he could defortify Blois and begin the style of royal buildings found in the absolutist era. There is, however, one discordant note in this image of a contented nobility—the matter of royal pensions. The historians who see Louis as being largely a traditional king regard the vast sums paid out in pensions as a price the monarchy of the Renaissance had to pay for the loyalty of the nobility. However, under Louis they declined from a total of 600,000 *livres* in 1498 to 105,000 *l* in 1511. It appears the decline was largely a result of dropping a good number of noblemen off the pension rolls rather than reducing the pensions of those who stayed on. Yet Louis's nobles did not revolt, although they grumbled, calling him the *roi roturier* (commoner king), a capital insult, since largesse was one of the major attributes of noblesse. Louis supposedly retorted: "I much prefer to make the dandies laugh at my miserliness than make the people weep at my openhandedness," hardly the attitude of an absolutist monarch.[7] Francis I quickly restored the pensions to what they had been in 1498.

Another way of viewing the nature of French kingship in the era of the Renaissance is through the question of centralization. Bernard Guenée has argued that centralization has three different meanings in the context of that era: personal centralization, when fiefs revert to the direct control of the monarch; institutional, when the monarch creates institutions in order to exercise more effectively royal authority; and geographic, when royal power and institutions are concentrated in a capital city (Paris).[8] In regard to the first definition, Louis's reign was not one of the major periods of that sort of centralization, but a number of fiefs did revert to the crown during it. In regard to the other two types, Guenée sees the Renaissance era as a time of institutional centralization but geographical decentralization. Louis's activities as king largely confirm that thesis. He spent little time in Paris, and none of his major advisers and few of his officers came from the city. His creation of the parlements of Normandy and Provence and use of local assemblies rather than the Estates-general furthered the geographic decentralization of royal authority, but they are also the sort of activities Guenée regards as constituting institutional centralization.

Louis himself helps the modern historian very little in respect to the nature of kingly authority, for he makes few comments about it. Those that he did make are mostly about the king's obligation to give justice. Perhaps the best came from the preamble to the Ordinances of 1499: "Since justice is the first and most worthy of the cardinal virtues, also it is the first and most necessary part of all monarchies and realms!"[9] Historians tend to think of royal authority in terms of power; Louis seems to have thought of it first as the obligation to give justice, which places him in harmony with the medieval view of kingship. The number of formal royal officers of justice apparently outnumbered those of revenue collection.

From Louis's historiographers we largely get the simplistic view that kingship was a divine office whose authority came directly from God and thus the king shared in divine authority. The one exception to that was Claude de Seyssel, who pondered the matter at length in his *La grant monarchie de France*, written in 1515. According to him, while the French monarch has received from God absolute power over his realm, his power must be regulated and directed in its proper use by the "bridles" of religion, good laws and ordinances, and the presence of good officers and institutions, especially the Parlement. These bridles prevent him from acting against the well-being of his realm and subjects. For Seyssel, Louis XII came closest to being the ideal king because he ruled most in accord with this theory of royal power. Yet it is not clear whether Seyssel actually believed that Louis did adhere to his description of royal authority so bridled or he was presenting a prescription to Francis I of how to be a good king.[10]

Therefore, Seyssel provides no clear answer to the question of the nature of kingship under Louis XII, although he is used by both sides of the debate. The great difficulties in identifying the style of rule in that era lead not only to the solution put forward by Major—to define the Renaissance monarchy as unique, neither medieval nor absolutist—but to go beyond it to emphasize the enormous variations in the modes of kingship among the kings of the era. Each of its mature kings—Louis XI, Louis XII, Francis I, Henry II, Henry III, and Henry IV (the other three kings spent most of their reigns under the tutelage of others and had no clear styles of rule of their own) differed from one another in their styles of rule more than was true either of the kings of the Middle Ages or of the Ancien Régime. In a period of change, such as the era of the Renaissance, when the traditions of rule were being undercut without being definitively replaced, each king had a great deal of freedom to make of his authority what he willed. Kingship was in large part what the king believed it to be and was capable of making it. The "Renaissance monarchy" thus is a distinctive period in French history, so difficult to define, because each reign was essentially *sui generis*.[11] To look at the problem in that way helps to explain why France was able to go from the consultative, limited monarchy of Louis XII to the more absolutist government of Francis I without pause or rebellion. Both forms had a basis in French law and tradition.

The clear-cut difference between Louis and Francis, however, was largely restricted to domestic policy; it was far less true in regard to Italy. Francis moved immediately to pursue the reconquest of Milan, which Louis had been planning up to the last days of his life. Seyssel regarded Louis's Italian policy as the most negative aspect of his reign because of both its great cost in men and money and its failure. On the other hand, several battles in the Italian wars—Agnadello, Genoa, Ravenna—constituted a major element in the *gloire* of French arms and provided opportunities for several great captains—Bayard, d'Ars, de Foix—to win lasting fame. But in general, the obvious disparity between Louis's success at home and failure abroad is a major theme of modern histories of his reign, although one should never underestimate how much the domestic tranquility in France during his reign depended on the absence from the realm of so many nobles on campaign in Italy.

Louis was not much more fortunate in his progeny. Francis and Claude did have seven children before she died in 1524, including Henry II, who reigned from 1547 to 1559. But the Valois dynasty came to a tragic end when the third of Louis's great-grandsons to reign, Henry III, was assassinated in 1589 without a son. Louis's great-grandsons through Renée, whose daughter, Anne of Ferrara, married François de Guise, played an important albeit indirect role in the events that led to Henry's assassination. Shortly before Henry III's death, a contemporary author urged him to see to it that his people "enjoy the felicity of the reign of the good King Louis XII."[12] Louis left a reputation for being "the Father of the People," not a flourishing dynasty.

For the three centuries after 1515, it was this reputation for ruling France in tranquility, prosperity, and justice that received attention. For the duration of the sixteenth century, Louis's reputation was extremely high. Jean Bodin wrote about Louis in 1583: "Oh, Excellent Prince, worthy of the rule of the entire world, who, relying on the integrity and harmlessness of his life, feared not the maledictions of the wicked."[13] Antoine Mornac, Bodin's lesser-known contemporary, gave Louis the epithet *le roi de bonté*, a term that goes beyond its literal translation of "goodness" to summon up a sense of benevolence, kindness, and solicitude for the poor and the weak.[14] Brantôme, whose grandmother and great-aunt had been ladies-in-waiting for Queen Anne, had this to say about Louis: "When the people of France are overcharged and overwhelmed with taxes, surcharges, and impositions, they always cry: 'If only we could return to the reign of this good king Louis XII, Father of the People.'"[15] By 1600 the story was that Louis would weep when he had to impose a tax.

The *Traicté des finances de France* of 1561 declared that in the seventeen years of his reign, Louis XII had levied no new taxes, lived off of his own desmense, and left his kingdom rich and opulent with treasure in his coffers.[16] A similar view was expressed by René La Barre, whose *Formulaire des esleuz* was published in 1622. He said of Louis XII: "He was a prince who loved his people and contented himself with little more than the income from his own desmense."[17] La Barre, whose discussion of royal finances is generally very intelligent, should have known better about Louis's ability to "live off his own," but the fact that Louis came closer to achieving it than any other king since the outbreak of the Hundred Years War was noted frequently throughout the era of the religious wars. It became almost a doctrine of popular opinion when the Third Estate at the meeting of the Estates-general in 1560 requested that the *taille* be reduced to the amount collected by Louis XII and the monarchy be made to live off its own. The Third Estate wanted to create a commission to examine the current account books of the monarchy and compare them to those of Louis's reign. Its deputies also asked for the enforcement of Louis's edict of 1499 against the sale of judicial offices.[18] After 1561 the call for a return to the fiscal system of Louis's reign was repeated in every type of representative assembly, including the Protestant Synod of 1575, the Estates-generals of 1576 and 1588, and the Estates of the Catholic League in 1593. In short, the reign of Louis XII was the "benchmark for most complaints during the Wars of Religion."[19]

When under Henry IV internal peace and stability were reestablished in France after his conversion to Catholicism, references to Louis XII began to decline. One reason for this is obvious enough: Louis was not an ancestor through whom the Bourbon right to the throne had passed. Additionally, his virtues and the style of government he represented were no longer as valued (which is not to say they were completely devalued) in a monarchy that was moving rapidly toward absolutism. To be sure, Henry IV commented that he was jealous of the title of *Père du peuple*, and the Third Estate repeated the call for a return to the levels of taxation of Louis's reign at the meeting of the Estates of 1614, a call that was made as late as 1671 in a provincial estates.[20] But Louis was less and less cited as an ideal monarch. The memory of "the Father of the People" had faded greatly by the time Pierre de Bayle wrote his *Historical and Critical Dictionary,* in which he devoted only one comment to the king, chastising him for the annulment of his marriage to Jeanne of France.

In the decade before the French Revolution, during the early phases of the revolution itself, and during the Bourbon restoration, when the French were searching for new ideas of kingship, or perhaps the revival of old ones, "the Father of the People" again returned to their consciousness.[21] Louis could serve as a French prototype of the constitutional monarch, as "the forerunner of those who attempted to introduce the principles of liberty, equality, and fraternity into the French political system."[22] Hardly a poor legacy for a man who never expected to rule France until the moment he became king.

▪ APPENDIX: THE MONETARY SYSTEM ▪

The monetary system in use in France around 1500 was highly complicated and confusing. What made it so was the existence of two types of money: a fictitious money of account, for which there were no actual coins; and a real currency, whose coins varied in value constantly compared to the money of account. There were two gold coins in use—the *écu au soleil* and the slightly smaller *écu à la couronne,* which was last minted in 1474. Their values were expressed in terms of the units of *monnaie tournois,* a money of account originally from Tours, consisting of *livre tournois* (*l*), *sol* (*s*), and *denier* (*∂*). There were 20 *s* to the *livre* and 12 *∂* to the *sol,* or 240 *∂* to the *livre.* Accounts were also occasionally expressed in *livre parisis,* whose value was 25 percent higher than the *livre tournois,* and rarely in several other obsolete provincial monies of account. In 1498 Louis set the value of the *écu au soleil* at 1 *l* 15 *s,* but in 1506, probably reflecting a shortage of money in circulation in France and the deflation that was taking place, he reestablished its value at what it had been in 1493—1 *l* 16 *s* 3 *∂*—and the *écu à la couronne* at 1 *l* 15 *s.* The former, larger by 3.6 percent, was by far the more common, and I have assumed that sums expressed in *écus* refer to the *écu au soleil* unless the other is specifically noted. It was the only gold coin minted in the reign of Louis XII; its value rose to 2 *l* in 1519 and to 2 *l* 5 *s* in 1533. In respect to silver coins, the *franc,* a coin worth 1 *l,* was no longer being minted by 1498, but *franc* was often used for *livre.* The principal small coins, made of an amalgam of silver and copper called billon, were the *blanc,* worth 10 *∂,* and also called the *dixain,* and the *grand blanc,* worth 12 *∂* and called the *douzain.* These coins were useful for ordinary retail trade, but for numerous transactions a larger coin was needed. Thus Louis in 1514 ordered the minting of the silver *teston,* worth 10 *s.*

Numerous foreign coins circulated in France, and many accounts were expressed in them. The major foreign coins were the ducat of Venice and Genoa, worth 1 *l* 17 *s* 6 *∂;* the Flemish florin, 1 *l* 4 *s;* the German florin, 1 *l* 7 *∂;* the papal scudi, 2 *l;* and the English gold *noble de Henri,* 3 *l* 14 *s.* Another English coin, the *noble à la rose,* was pegged at 4 *l.* The exchange rate for the pound sterling, also a money of account, was 8 *l* 10 *s* 2 *∂.*[1]

■ ABBREVIATIONS AND SHORT TITLES
USED IN THE NOTES ■

AN Archives Nationales, Paris

Archives curieuses L. Cimber and F. Danjou [Louis Lafaist], eds. *Archives curieuses de l'histoire de France.* 24 vols. Paris, 1834-50.

BN Bibliothèque Nationale, Paris.

Commynes, *Memoirs* S. Kinser and I. Cazeaux, eds. *The Memoirs of Philippe de Commynes.* 2 vols. Columbia, South Carolina, 1969-73.

CSP Milan *Calendar of State Papers and Manuscripts Preserved in Archives in Milan.* Ed. by A. Hinds. 4 vols. Reprint, Nendeln, Liechtenstein, 1967.

CSP Spain *Calendar of Letters, Despatches, and State Papers Relating to Negotiations between England and Spain.* Vols. 1-2. Ed. by R. Tyler. Reprint, Nendeln, Liechtenstein, 1969.

CSP Venice *Calendar of State Papers relating to English Affairs existing in the archives of Venice and Italy.* Vols. 1-2. Ed. by R. Brown. Reprint, Nendeln, Liechtenstein, 1970.

DBF *Dictionnaire de Biographie française.* 17 vols. Paris, 1932-.

Floranges, *Mémoires* Robert de Floranges. *Histoire des choses memorables advenues du reigne de Louis XII et François I* in C. Petitot, *Collection,* Vol. XVI.

Histoire de Bayard J. de Mailles. *La très joyeuse, plaisante et recréative histoire . . . du gentil Seigneur de Bayard.* In C. Petitot, *Collection.* Vol. XV-XVI.

Letters and Papers *Calendar of Letters and Papers of the Reign of Henry VIII.* Ed. by J. Gairdner, 21 vols. Reprint, Vaduz, 1965.

Petitot, *Collection* C. Petitot. *Collection complète des mèmoires relatifs à l'histoire de France.* 130 vols. Paris, 1818-1829.

Procédures politiques R. de Maulde La Claviere. ed. *Procédures politiques de règne de Louis XII.* Paris, 1885.

Vellay, "Histoire" H. Vellay, "Histoire de Louis XII." in BN, Fonds français 2924.

■ NOTES ■

NOTES TO PREFACE

1. B. Chevalier, ed., *La France de la fin du XVe siècle: renouveau et apogée* (Paris, 1985), p. 334.

NOTES TO CHAPTER 1

1. For Charles of Orléans's life and poetry, see A. Champollion-Figeac, *Louis et Charles Ducs d'Orléans* (reprint Geneva, 1980); P. Champion, *Vie de Charles d'Orléans* (Paris, 1889); and S. Spence, *The French Chansons of Charles D'Orléans* (New York, 1986).

2. The child, a daughter, died without children in 1432. R. de Maulde la Clavière, *Histoire de Louis XII: première partie, Louis d'Orléans*, 3 vols. (Paris, 1889-91), I, p. 42. This work provides detailed information on Louis to 1498 but ends there.

3. A. Hinds, ed., *Calendar of State Papers and Manuscripts preserved in archives in Milan* (Reprint, 1967), pp. 353, 359 (an agreement of 1498); and R. H. Brodie, ed., *Letters and Papers, Foreign and Domestic of the Reign of Henry VIII* (Reprint, Vaduz, 1965), I, p. 1325 (for 1514).

4. Maulde admits that the child being Charles's is implausible and thinks the father might have been Louis de Mornac, to whom Mary of Cleves gave several positions. He died in 1472. *Histoire de Louis XII*, I, p. 265-67. Because of Brantôme's comment from a century later, the usual suspect as Louis's father has been a maître d'hôtel of Charles's household, Claude de Rabaudanges, who some years later became Mary of Cleves's second husband. See, for example, J. Michelet, *Histoire de France* (Paris 1978), IV, p. 160; but Michelet failed to get the name of Louis' mother right. B. Quilliet, *Louis XII Père du Peuple* (Paris, 1986), p. 40, argues that Rabaudanges did not yet reside at Blois in late 1461.

5. Report of the ambassador of Milan, in B. de Mandrot, *Dépêches des ambassadeurs milanais en France sous Louis XI et François Sforza*, 4 vols. (Paris, 1916-23), II, p. 135. That Louis XI kept a close watch on Orléans family affairs is shown by his comment to the ambassador in April 1464 (ibid., III, p. 59) that the duchess had not slept with her husband in four months. If true, it raises questions about the paternity of their third child, Anne, because she had to have been conceived during that time and, by inference, about Louis's paternity.

6. For Louis's birth and baptism, see BN, Fonds français 5973, fol. 122; and Maulde, *Histoire de Louis XII*, I, pp. 102-7.

7. Anne became abbess of the convent of Fontevrault in 1478 at fourteen years, young for such a position but not uncommon in that era. She died in September 1491. See B. Palustre, "L'Abbesse Anne d'Orléans et la réforme de l'ordre de Fontevrault," *Revue des questions historiques* 66 (1899), 210-17.

8. CSP Milan, p. 112.

9. For Charles's death, see Mandrot, *Dépêches*, III, 2ff.; for his obsequies, see Maulde, *Histoire de Louis XII*, I, pp. 121-23; for the transition of his bones to Paris, which cost 2,961 *l*, see BN, Fonds français 2881, fol. 198v.

10. On Mary of Cleves, see St-Gelais, *Histoire du roy Louis XII* (Paris, 1615), p. 33; Maulde, "Marie de Clèves, La mère de Louis XII," *Revue historique* 36 (1888), 81-112; and Quilliet, *Louis XII*, p. 57.

11. On the Burgundian court, see J. Huizinga, *The Waning of the Middle Ages* (Garden City, NJ, 1954); and R. Vaughan, *Philip the Good* (New York, 1970), esp. pp. 127-63.

12. Maulde, *Histoire de Louis XII*, I, p. 238. Louis XI told the Milanese ambassador in 1464 that all of the properties of Orléans had been alienated except for the duchy of Orléans itself. Mandrot, *Dépêches*, II, p. 39.

13. Figeac, *Ducs d'Orléans*, II, 362; M. Harsgor, *Recherches sur le personnel du conseil du roi sous Charles VIII et Louis XII*, 4 vols. (Lille, 1980), III, pp. 1273-1312. P. Jacob, *Louis XII et Anne de Bretagne* (Paris, 1882), p. 129.

14. Quoted by J. Marshall, *The Annals of Tennis* (London, 1878), pp. 12, 207. See also W. Wiley, *The Gentlemen of Renaissance France*, (reprint Westport, CT, 1971), pp. 148-51.

15. St-Gelais, *Histoire de roy Louis XII*, p. 33. On hunting and jousting, see *La trèsjoyeuse, plaisante et récréative Hystoire du Seigneur de Bayard* [henceforth *Histoire de Bayard*]; Robert de Floranges, *Histoire des choses memorables advenues du reigne de Louis XII et François Ier*; both in Petitot, *Collection complète des Mémoires relatifs à l'histoire de France* (Paris, 1819-29), E. Charavay, "La Fauconnerie au Moyen Age," *Revue des documents historiques*, I (1873-74), pp. 60-90; and Wiley, *Gentlemen*, pp. 137-44;

16. M. Garnier, *Histoire de France* (Paris, 1768), XIX, p. 159. See also J. Tailhé, *Histoire de Louis XII*, 3 vols. (Paris, 1755), I, p. 5. P. Roederer drew on such accounts of Louis's indocility for his three-act comedy on his education, "Le Fouet de nos pères," in *Comédies historiques* (Paris, 1827).

17. Quilliet, *Louis XII*, pp. 60-61. There is little support for his suggestion that Robert Gaguin, a founder of French humanism, was one of Louis's tutors. St-Gelais stated only that Louis was tutored by the wisest and most virtuous gentlemen that his mother could find. *Histoire de Louis XII*, p. 33.

18. Mandrot, *Dépêches*, II, p. 39. Jeanne has been the subject of numerous biographies and studies. The best researched is Maulde, *Jeanne de France Duchesse d'Orléans et de Berry* (Paris, 1883). Of the many written since her canonization in 1950, the best is J. Drèze, *Raison d'Etat; Raison de Dieu: Politique et Mystique chez Jeanne de France* (Paris, 1991). See also Duc de Levis Mirepoix, *Jeanne de France Princess and Saint*, trans. by C. Muret (Toronto, 1950).

19. Maulde, *Procedures politiques du règne de Louis XII* (Paris, 1885), pp. 915-16. This work is a collection of documents on the two great trials in Louis's reign—the treason trial of Pierre de Gié and the annulment of his marriage with Jeanne. Many of the documents pertinent to the annulment are in Archives Nationales (henceforth AN), KK 553; Maulde published all of them, as far as I could determine.

20. S. Kinser and I. Cazeaux, eds., *The Memoirs of Philippe de Commynes*, 2 vols. (Columbia, South Carolina, 1969-73), II, p. 425.

21. Maulde, *Histoire de Louis XII*, I, p. 32.

22. Depositions of Jallaye and Rabaudanges, in *Procedures politiques*, pp. 999-1002, 1057-61. Even before the arrival of Louis's envoys, Jallaye had been seized at Blois by soldiers, taken to Tours, and threatened with death unless he persuaded the duke to consent to the marriage. Ibid., p. 1002.

23. Maulde, *Jeanne de France*, pp. 86-87; *Procedures politiques*, p. 1118.

24. St-Gelais, *Histoire de Louis XII*, pp. 35-36; Quilliet, *Louis XII*, p. 73. The operative canons were Decretales, Liber IV, Tit. X and XII, in E. Friedberg, *Corpus Iuris Canonici*, 2 vols. (Graz, 1959), II, pp. 694-95, 696-704.

25. Maulde, *Procedures politiques*, pp. 1016-20.

26. Deposition of Pierre Dupuy, in *Procedures politiques*, pp. 984-89.

27. Maulde, *Jeanne de France*, p. 111n.

28. Commynes commented that Louis was "handsome of person, but fond of his pleasures." *Memoirs*, II, p. 453.

29. Deposition of Jean Vigneron, Louis's treasurer, in *Procédures politiques*, p. 1015.

30. St-Gelais, *Histoire de Louis XII*, pp. 30-31.

31. A. Le Ferron, *De Rebus Gestis Gallorum*, 3 vols. (Basel, 1569), I, 39; Harsgor, *Le Personnel*, IV, p. 2269.

32. The imperial ambassador, in noting Bucy's death, stated that he was said to be the bastard son of the king. *Lettres de Louis XII*, III, p. 148. See also St-Gelais, *Histoire de Louis XII*, p. 111; and P. de Brantôme, *Oeuvres complètes*, ed. by L. Lalanne, 11 vols. (Paris, 1864-82), VII, p. 315. Lalanne gives an unattributed note that the mother was a court laundress. However, Maulde, *Les origines de la Revolution française au commencement du XVIe siècle: La veille de la reforme* (Paris, 1889), p. 132, argues that Bucy was a son of one of the d'Amboises, who held an estate by that name. For Bucy's life, see DBF, II, pp. 605-07.

NOTES TO CHAPTER 2

1. Maulde, *Histoire de Louis XII*, II, 38.

2. See a description of Charles by an Italian physician in "Mémoires historiques de Charles VIII," in L. Cimber and F. Danjou [Louis Lafast], eds., *Archives curieuses de l'histoire de France*, 1st series, (Paris, 1834-50), I, pp. 195-96.

3. F. Isambert, *Recueil général des anciennes lois françaises depuis l'an 420 jusqu'à la révolution de 1789*, 29 vols. (Paris, 1821-33) V, p. 421.

4. St-Gelais, for example, was convinced that Charles had to have a regent. *Histoire de Louis XII*, p. 54.

5. N. Valois, *Le conseil du roi et le Grand Conseil pendant la première année du règne de Charles VIII* (Paris, 1883), pp. 7-8.

6. Maulde, *Histoire de Louis XII*, II, 38. Louis had given this oath on the canons of the Mass, the Gospels, his word of honor, and the damnation of his soul.

7. Commynes, *Memoirs*, II, pp. 417-18.

8. Louis XI quoted in J. Bridge, *History of France from the death of Louis XI to 1515*, 5 vols. (Oxford, 1921-36), I, p. 29; Brantôme, *Oeuvres Complètes*, VIII, p. 99. Brantôme did not mean his phrase in a flattering manner. Biographies of Anne include M. Chambert de Lauwe, *Anne de Beaujeu: ou la passion du pouvoir* (Paris, 1980); and J. Markel, *Anne de Beaujeu* (Paris, 1980).

9. The Venetian ambassador wrote in 1487 that "Madame de Beaujeu is very avaricious and does anything for money, regardless of the honor of God or of the Crown." CSP Italy, I, p. 167.

10. "Documents inédits: Mémoires de Jean Foulquart," *Revue de Champagne*, II, pp. 136-39; cited in Bridge, *History of France*, I, p. 31; BN, Fonds français 2831, fol. 66.

11. That is the argument of J.R. Major, *Representative Institutions in Renaissance France, 1421-1559* (Madison, Wisconsin, 1960), p. 64.

12. Maulde, *Jeanne de France*, p. 138.

13. On the relationship between France and Brittany in the fifteenth century, see A. Dupry, *Histoire de la Réunion de la Bretagne à la France*, 2 vols. (Paris, 1880); E. Catta, "Les évêques de Nantes," *Revue historique de l'église Français* 51 (1961), 23-70; and the documents printed in H. Morice, ed. *Mémoires pour servir de preuves à l'histoire ecclésiastique et civile de Bretagne*, 3 vols. (Paris, 1742-46), III, p. 351ff.

14. Bridge, *History of France*, I, p. 13.

15. Chaumart's deposition of 1498 is in *Procédures politiques*, pp. 966-71.

16. On d'Albret, see A. Luchaire, *Alain Le Grand, Sire d'Albret*, (Paris, 1877); on the d'Aydies, see Harsgor, *Recherches*, III, pp. 1325-45.

17. *Ordonnances des roys de France de la troisieme race*, 22 vols. (Paris, 1723-1846), XIX, p. 337; G. Picot, *Le Parlement sous Charles VIII. Le procès criminel d'Olivier Le Daim* (Paris, 1877).

18. See Harsgor, *Recherches*, I, p. 296, for the record of attendance at the royal council in 1483.

19. J. R. Major strongly disagrees with the common opinion of historians that the Orléanist faction pushed for the convocation of the Estates. He argues that the Beaujeus "looked to the deputies of the estates to restore them to the position that Louis XI intended." *Representative Institutions*, p. 66.

20. Jehan Masselin, *Journal des Etats Généraux de France tenus à Tours en 1484*, ed. by A. Bernier (Paris, 1835), p. 81; BN, Fonds nouvelles acquisitions français 1232, fol. 80.

21. *Lettres de Charles VIII*, I, p. 28.

22. P. Viollet, "Election des députés aux Etats généraux réunis à Tours en 1468 et en 1484," *Bibliothèque de l'Ecole des Chartes* 27 (1866), pp. 22-58. According to J. Calmette et al., *Les Premières Grandes Puissances, Histoire du Moyen Age* (Paris, 1939), VII, p. 41, this was the first meeting for which the term "Estates-general" was used.

23. See the discussions in Major, *Representative Institutions*, p. 66; Bridge, *History of France*, I, pp. 64-66; G. Picot, *Histoire des Etats Généraux de 1355 à 1614*, 4 vols. (Reprint, Geneva, 1979), I, pp. 357-58.

24. That is the number established by Major, *Deputies*, pp. 163-65. Other historians generally have higher figures, up to 270.

25. Masselin, *Journal*, pp. 37-65. Rochefort contrasted France with England, where the young king (Edward V) had been murdered and his assassin (Richard III) crowned king. This indicates that the complicity of Richard in his nephew's death was current rumor in France within a year of Edward III's death. See also Bridge, *History of France*, I, p. 66.

26. Masselin, *Journal*, appendix I.

27. BN, Fonds français 2831, fol. 62r-65v.

28. Masselin, *Journal*, pp. 151-53; Bridge, *History of France*, I, p. 72.

29. Masselin, *Journal*, p. 143.

30. Ibid., pp. 595-658.

31. Maulde, *Jeanne de France*, pp. 99-100.

32. BN, Fonds nouvelles acquisitions français 1232, fol. 25.

33. Maulde, *Histoire de Louis XII*, II, p. 123; Bridge, *History of France*, pp. 113-14.

34. BN, Fonds français 15538, fol. 30; *Lettres de Charles VIII*, edited by P. Pélicier, 5 vols. (Paris, 1898-1905), I, pp. 56-66.

35. The following paragraphs are drawn largely from Maulde, *Histoire de Louis XII*, II, pp. 118-146; Bridge, *History of France*, I, pp. 103-29; P. Pélicier, *Essai sur le gouvernement de la dame de Beaujeu* (Paris, 1882), p. 81ff; Y. Labande-Mailfert, *Charles VIII, Le vouloir et la destinée* (Paris, 1986), p. 68ff.

36. Morice, *Mémoires*, III, p. 450.

37. See the documents in ibid., pp. 431-38.

NOTES TO CHAPTER 3

1. Maulde, *Procedures politiques*, p. 970.

2. Ibid., pp. 1036-37, 1050, 1082. The messenger had received 122 *l* for his pay and expenses.

3. Morice, *Mémoires*, III, pp. 489-91.

4. Quilliet, *Louis XII*, p. 101.

5. Morice, *Mémoires*, III, pp. 495, 500-04.

6. *Procedures politiques*, p. 997; Pélicier, ed., *Lettres de Charles VIII*, I, pp. 143-44.

7. Commynes, *Memoirs*, I, pp. 422 and note; S. Cuttler, *The Law of Treason and Treason Trials in Later Medieval France* (Cambridge, 1981), pp. 79-80.

8. BN, Fonds français 15538, fol. 43-45.

9. Brantôme, *The Book of the Ladies*, translated by K. Wormeley (Boston, 1902), pp. 26, 217.

10. BN, Fonds Dupuy 38, fol. 339.

11. St-Gelais, *Histoire de Louis XII*, pp. 56-57; Pélicier, ed., *Lettres de Charles VIII*, I, pp. 187-88.

12. G. de Jaligny, *Histoire de Charles VIII*, edited by T. Godefroy (Paris, 1684), p. 23.

13. Maulde, *Histoire de Louis XII*, II, p. 175; *Procédures politiques*, pp. 995-97.

14. St-Gelais, *Histoire de Louis XII*, pp. 57-60; Bridge, *History of France*, I, pp. 140-42.

15. On the Breton army of that era, see M. Jones, "L'armée bretonne 1449-1491: Structures et carrières" in Chevalier, *La France de la fin du XVe siècle*, pp. 147-65.

16. St-Gelais, *Histoire de Louis XII*, p. 67.

17. Cuttler, *Law of Treason*, p. 235. Charles VIII's summons to the Duc d'Alençon to serve as a judge of Louis's process is in BN, Fonds français 2832, fol. 119-20.

18. Pélicier, ed., *Lettres de Charles VIII*, I, p. 173.

19. St-Gelais, *Histoire de Louis XII*, pp. 61-62.

20. On the battle of St-Aubin, see St-Gelais, *Histoire de Louis XII*, pp. 59-60; J. Bouchet, *Le Panégyric du Chevallier sans reproche ou Mémoires de la Trémoille*, in C. Petitot, *Mémoires complètes*, XIV, pp. 400-9; J. Molinet, *Chroniques*, ed. by G. Doutrepont, 2 vols. (Brussels, 1935), II, pp. 61-62. Jaligny, *Histoire de Charles VIII*, pp. 51-53; Maulde, *Histoire de Louis XII*, II, pp. 222-26.

21. This story first appeared in a 1514 work: A. Bouchard, *Les grandes croniques de Bretaigne*, ed. by H. LeMeignen, (Rennes, 1886). Pélicier, *Essai*, p. 144n, doubts its authenticity; but Maulde, *Histoire de Louis XII*, II, p. 226, accepts it as true. See Pélicier, ed., *Lettres de Charles VIII*, I, pp. 320, 323, II, p. 31, for the king's orders to La Trémoille that "justice be done upon them as traitors without sparing any." But see also Charles's letter mandating that those notables who wanted to submit to him be brought to the court. *Correspondance de Charles VIII avec Louis II de La Trémoille pendant la guerre de Bretagne (1488)* (Paris, 1875), pp. 207-08.

22. Pélicier, ed., *Lettres de Charles VIII*, II, p. 212. Letters to Charles from his commanders in Brittany are in BN, Fonds nouvelles acquisitions français 1232, fol. 80ff.

23. *Ordonnances des roys de France*, XX, pp. 95-98; Morice, *Mémoires*, III, pp. 599-601.

24. CSP Spain, I, pp. 17-18, 21-24, 29-31; see also CSP Venice, I, pp. 173, 178-79.

25. CSP Spain, I, p. 32. For the following paragraphs, see Labande-Mailfert, *Charles VIII*, pp. 94-115; A. Dupry, *Histoire de la Réunion de la Bretagne à la France*, 2 vols. (Paris, 1880), II, pp. 221-22; Pélicier, *Essai*, pp. 84-86; Bridge, *History of France*, I, pp. 173-227.

26. Morice, *Mémoires*, III, pp. 661-62; Molinet, *Chroniques*, II, pp. 234-39.

27. Morice, *Mémoires*, col. pp. 707-708.

28. Pélicier, ed., *Lettres de Charles VIII*, II, p. 188.

29. Pélicier, *Essai*, p. 170.

30. *Procédures politiques*, pp. 888, 998; Maulde, *Histoire de Louis XII*, I, pp. 228-30; St-Gelais, *Histoire de Louis XII*, pp. 60-63.

31. BN, Fonds français 15538, fol. 209-10.

32. *Procédures politiques*, p. 1082.

33. Ibid., p. 1053; Maulde, *Histoire de Louis XII*, II, p. 233n; Maulde, *Jeanne de France*, pp. 216-23.

34. St-Gelais, *Histoire de Louis XII*, p. 71; Tailhé, *Louis XII*, I, p. 60; Quilliet, *Louis XII*, p. 119.

35.   St-Gelais, *Histoire de Louis XII*, pp. 68-69.

36.   Ibid., pp. 69-70.

37.   AN, K 74, fol. 26.

38.   Chambart de Lauwe, *Anne de Beaujeu*, p. 306.

39.   BN, Fonds français 2831, fol. 75. Besides Orléans and Bourbon, seven other nobles signed, including Dunois and d'Amboise.

40.   The definitive biography of Anne is A. Leroux de Lincy, *Vie de la reine Anne de Bretagne*, 4 vols. (Paris, 1860-61). Shorter and more readable is E. Gabory, *Anne de Bretagne, Duchesse et Reine*, (Paris, 1941).

41.   St-Gelais, *Histoire de Louis XII*, p. 74.

NOTES TO CHAPTER 4

1.   St-Gelais, *Histoire de Louis XII*, p. 78. See also Jaligny, *Histoire de Charles VIII*, p. 97.

2.   St-Gelais, *Histoire de Louis XII*, p. 79. See also Jaligny, *Histoire de Charles VIII*, p. 97, for a similar statement.

3.   Commynes, *Memoirs*, II, 439; A. Desjardins et al., eds., *Négociations diplomatiques de la France avec la Toscane*, 6 vols. (Paris, 1859-86), I, p. 227. The Florentine ambassador included Commynes himself as a strong supporter of the expedition.

4.   CSP Venice, I, 184.

5.   In 1510 the income came to 715,000 ducats. AN, J 910, fol. 1ff.

6.   CSP Milan, p. 287. For a contemporary Italian account of how the French came to claim authority in Genoa, see A. Salrago, *Cronaca di Genoa*, ed. by C. Desimoni, in *Atti della Societa Ligure di Storia Patria* 13 (1879), pp. 365-486.

7.   See Sforza's letter of 1492 to his ambassador to England explaining why he could not accept Henry VII's invitation to join in a war against France. CSP Milan, pp. 287-88.

8.   A long letter of 1514 to the English government set out Louis's rights to Milan. AN, J 655.

9.   H. Delaborde, *L'Expédition de Charles VIII en Italie* (Paris, 1888), p. 112.

10.   Labande, *Charles VIII*, p. 220.

11.   Ibid., p. 284. See also Maulde, *Louis XII*, II, pp. 417-21.

12.   Ibid., pp. 236-38; Morice, *Mémoires*, pp. 753-54.

13.   Sums from 200,000 to 400,000 ducats had been proposed in 1464 as a price. Mandrot, ed., *Dépêches*, II, p. 57.

14.   St-Gelais, *Histoire de Louis XII*, p. 80. See also Maulde, *Histoire de Louis XII*, III, pp. 40-42.

15.   A. Spont, "La Marine française sous le règne de Charles VIII," *Revue des questions historiques* 55 (1894), pp. 387-454.

16.   Maulde, *Histoire de Louis XII*, III, p. 61; M. Sanuto, *I Diarii*, 58 vols. (Venice, 1879-1903), I, pp. 86-88. Sanuto, the secretary for the Signory of Venice, kept a record of all the correspondance brought before that body. Like all diplomatic reports, Sanuto's diaries contain much gossip and rumor, but they are invaluable sources for Louis's reign.

17.   For the Battle of Rapello, see St-Gelais, *Histoire de Louis XII*, pp. 81-82; Commynes, *Memoirs*, II, pp. 457-58; Maulde, *Histoire de Louis XII*, III, p. 70; Bridge, *History of France*, II, pp. 130-32.

18.   *Lettres de Charles VIII*, IV, pp. 89-91; St-Gelais, *Histoire de Louis XII*, p. 82. According to P. Desrey, "Relation du voyage du Roy Charles VIII," in *Archives curieuses*, I, p. 211, a courier, "*comme tout éperdu,*" reported to the king that the French had been defeated and Orléans captured. Charles was ready to order a hasty retreat to France when another courier arrived with the accurate news of the French victory.

19. Commynes, *Memoirs*, II, p. 466. See also Desrey, "Relation du voyage," p. 212.

20. Commynes, *Memoirs*, II, pp. 459-60.

21. Ibid., II, p. 459. See Desrey, "Relation du voyage," pp. 213-33, for the details of the route to Rome.

22. *Lettres de Charles VIII*, IV, pp. 142-50; "Le Journal de Burchard," in *Archives curieuses*, I, pp. 279-81. Burchard was the papal chamberlain, whose diary is a detailed account of the events at the papal court and in Rome.

23. The "Vergier d'honneur," a highly detailed account of Charles's expedition in poetry and prose, by André de La Vigne and several other French poets, is in *Archives curieuses*, I, pp. 321-435.

24. St-Gelais, *Histoire de Louis XII*, p. 86; Commynes, *Memoirs*, II pp. 496-98.

25. Delaborde, *Expedition*, pp. 530-34.

26. Commynes, *Memoirs*, II, pp. 496-99; Maulde, *Histoire de Louis XII*, III, pp. 154-55.

27. F. Guicciardini, *History of Italy*, I, trans. by A. Goddard. 10 vols. (London, 1753-56), p. 229.

28. This and several other letters from Louis to Bourbon keeping him informed on what was happening in Italy, are in BN, Nouvelles acquisitions françaises 1232, fol. 289-333.

29. Guicciardini, *History of Italy*, I, pp. 312-14; Commynes *Memoirs*, II, pp. 513-14; St-Gelais, *Histoire de Louis XII*, p. 86.

30. Alessandro Benedetti, *Diary of the Caroline War*, trans. by D. Schullian (New York, 1967), p. 79.

31. Commynes, *Memoirs*, II, p. 526; Guicciardini, *History of Italy*, I, pp. 331-2.

32. Guicciardini, *History of Italy*, I, p. 340. For the Battle of Fornovo, see also Commynes, II, 526-39; Benedetti, *Diary*, pp. 83-105; Delaborde, *Expedition*, pp. 634-46. A. de La Vigne's *Vergier d'honneur* (in *Archives curieuses*, Vol. I [Paris, 1500]), p. 394, says that Charles proved himself "true son of Mars, successor of Caesar, and comrade of Pompey."

33. Guicciardini, *History of Italy*, pp. 266-68; Benedetti, *Diary*, pp. 133-35; Maulde, *Histoire de Louis XII*, III, pp. 271-88.

34. Guicciardini, *History of Italy*, I, p. 356. St-Gelais confirms the story. *Histoire de Louis XII*, pp. 95-96.

35. St-Gelais, *Histoire de Louis XII*, p. 98; Guicciardini, *History of Italy*, II, pp. 32-33; La Vigne, *Vergier d'honneur*, p. 432.

36. Commynes, *Memoirs*, p. 566.

37. St-Gelais, *Histoire de Louis XII*, pp. 97-98. Brantôme said that Louis hosted the ball and danced so gaily that he offended both Anne and Charles. *Oeuvres*, VII, p. 32.

38. P. Lacroix, *Louis XII et Anne de Bretagne* (Paris, 1882), p. 54.

39. St-Gelais, *Histoire de Louis XII*, pp. 100-1; *Procedures politiques*, pp. 716-29, where Charles's will and the royal decision are printed. See also Maulde, *Histoire de Louis XII*, III, pp. 381-83; and Maulde, *Louise de Savoie et François I: Trente ans de jeunesse* (Paris, 1895), which details the relationship between Louis and Louise.

40. Commynes, *Memoirs*, II, pp. 589-90.

41. Labande, *Charles VIII*, p. 472. For Louis's lifestyle upon his return to France, see Maulde, *Histoire de Louis XII*, III, pp. 341-42, 378-80.

42. *Procedures politiques*, p. 910.

43. Ibid., p. 937.

44. Morice, *Mémoires*, III, p. 784; CSP Milan, p. 300.

45. Commynes, *Memoirs*, pp. 574-75; also Guicciardini, *History of Italy*, II, pp. 71-78, who suggests that preparations for the new Italian expedition were much further along.

46. St-Gelais, *Histoire de Louis XII*, pp. 103-5; *Procedures politiques*, p. 1032.

47. E.g., Mirepoix, *Jeanne of France*, pp. 123-27.

48. Commynes, *Memoirs*, II, pp. 590-91. Commynes was absent but returned two days later and heard a first-hand account from Charles's confessor. Other contemporary accounts include Philippe de Velperge's letter of April 8, in L. Pelissier, ed., "Documents sur la prémière année du règne de Louis XII," *Bulletin historique et philogique* (1890), 51; and the Venetian ambassador's, in Sanuto, *Diarii*, I, pp. 21, 38-39. See also L. Caillet, "La mort de Charles VIII," *Revue d'histoire de Lyon* 8 (1909), pp. 468-74; and Maulde, *Histoire de Louis XII*, pp. 398-400

49. Commynes, *Memoirs*, p. 593; Guicciardini, *History of Italy*, II, pp. 194-95; Velperge, in Pelissier, p. 51.

50. "Mémoires de Charles VIII," pp. 162-63.

51. Sanuto, *Diarii*, I, p. 1029. Sforza apparently was proclaiming that Bourbon was the true heir to the throne in order to embroil France in civil war. L. Pélissier, ed., *Lettre de Louis XII à la Seigneurie de Sienne por lui notifier son avènement (1498)* (Montpellier, nd.).

52. N. Machiavelli, "Description of the Affairs of France," *The History of Florence and Other Selections*, ed. by M. Gilmore (New York, 1970), p. 2. The Spanish ambassador to England reported that Henry VII expected to take advantage of anticipated divisions in France over Louis's succession to reconquer what was rightfully his. CSP Spain, I, 156.

53. Commynes, *Memoirs*, II, 593. Velperge wrote the same on April 8: "All the world went to the said duke of Orléans." Pélissier, "Documents," p. 51. Louis told the Venetian ambassador in June that the kingdom rendered obedience to him faster than for any previous king. Sanuto, *Diarii*, I, p. 1029.

54. Chambart, *Anne de Beaujeu*, pp. 356-57; Maulde, *Jeanne de France*, p. 248; Lacroix, *Louis XII*, p. 66.

NOTES TO CHAPTER 5

1. Vellay, "Histoire," fol. 32; dispatch of the Venetian ambassador from Bourges, February 18, 1508; quoted by Maulde, *La Diplomatie au temps de Machiavel*, 3 vols. (Reprint, Geneva, 1970), III, p. 14n. Sanuto, *Diarii*, VII, p. 308, indicated a dispatch from Bourges on that date but did not give a full text.

2. Sanuto, *Diarii*, II, p. 749, IV, pp. 332-33. J.-A. Néret, *Louis XII* (Paris, 1948), pp. 53-54, has a good word portrait of Louis.

3. Desjardins, *Négociations*, II, p. 460.

4. J. Godefroy, ed., *Lettres du Louis XII et du Cardinal d'Amboise*. 4 vols. (Brussels, 1712), preface; quoted by Maulde, *Diplomatie*, III, p. 13n.

5. Desjardins, *Négociations*, II, p. 131.

6. *Procedures politiques*, p. 45.

7. See F. Hackett, *Francis the First* (Garden City, NY, 1935), p. 66, for the suggestion Louis had Graves' disease.

8. Sanuto, *Diarii*, I, p. 1049.

9. A. Le Glay, ed., *Négociations diplomatiques entre la France et l'Autriche*, 2 vols. (Paris, 1845), I, p. lii. Ironically the matter under discussion by the archbishop was a proposed marriage of Louis's daughter to Philip's son, which was the one clear case of double dealing of which Louis was guilty. See below, Chapter 9.

10. A. van Wicquefort, *L'Ambassadeur et ses fonctions*, 3rd ed. (Amsterdam, 1730), I, p. 100. He gives as his source an unnamed Spanish commentary on Commynes, which I have not been able to identify. An alternate version has Ferdinand saying "three times."

11. Commynes, *Memoirs*, II, p. 594; Pélissier, "Documents," p. 52. But by the end of 1498 Louis had dismissed Guillaume Briçonnet, one of the major figures of Charles's court. Sanuto, *Diarii*, I, p. 1013.

12. Bouchet, *Le Panégyric du chevallier*, XIV, p. 430.

13. Quilliet, *Louis XII*, p. 180. The remark does not appear in Bouchet's biography of La Trémoille. In 1501 the archbishop of Besançon cited it as proof that Louis was not vindictive, but he had him saying it to the duke of Lorraine. Le Glay, *Négociations*, I, p. 1*iin.*

14. *Ordonnances des roys*, XXI, p. 27; Chambart, *Anne de Beaujeu*, pp. 375-76. The Parlement balked at this violation of feudal law, and Louis had to send a *lettre de jussion* ordering it to register the edict.

15. Commynes, *Memoirs*, II, p. 594.

16. For this concept, see R. Giesey, *The Royal Funeral Ceremony in Renaissance France* (Geneva, 1960). He argues that Louis made permanent this practice by being the first king to absent himself purposely from the obsequies of his predecessor, following a pattern unintentionally created by the circumstances of the deaths of the four kings prior to Charles.

17. According to St-Gelais the cry was: "Mort est le Roy Charles! Vive le Roy Loys!" *Histoire de Louis XII*, p. 109. Several historians who accept St-Gelais's version argue that the use of the kings' names in the acclamation came from a concern over a possible challenge to Louis's right to the throne; e.g., B. Guenée, *State and Rulers in Late Medieval Europe*, trans. by J. Vale (London, 1985), p. 27. Giesey, *Funeral Ceremony*, p. 139, believes that St-Gelais erred, since two more immediate sources give the phrase without the names.

18. BN, Fonds français 2929, fol. 28.

19. Commynes, *Memoirs*, II, p. 594; St-Gelais, *Histoire de Louis XII*, p. 107.

20. Harsgor, *Personnel*, I, p. 470; R. W. Scheller, "Ensigns of authority: French Royal Symbolism in the age of Louis XII," *Simiolus* 13 (1982), pp. 103-9. He makes a strong case for the novelty of the tomb with its Italianate features.

21. *Ordonnance des roys*, XXI, p. 25. The document provides the names of the members of Parlement. There were two vacancies.

22. See Maulde, *Louise et François*, pp. 259-60, for details about the colors and dress of the four French companies. For the duties and privileges of the Scots archers, see A. MacDonald, *Papers relative to the Royal Guard of Scottish Archers in France* (Edinburgh, 1865), pp. 75-76.

23. The only roll of Louis's household that appears complete is in AN, KK 87, for 1499. A partial roll is in BN, Fonds français 2627, fol. 11ff.

24. Anne's household expenses are published in Leroux, *Anne de Bretagne*, IV, Appendix I. She had 350 persons in her household in 1498.

25. AN, KK 87, fol. 14-23; Harsgor, *Personnel*, II, pp. 874-75.

26. St-Gelais, *Histoire de Louis XII*, p. 175; J. d'Auton, *Chroniques de Louis XII*, edited by R. de Maulde, 4 vols. (Paris, 1889-95), IV, pp. 365, 385-86; BN, Fonds français 2827, fol. 70; M. Piton, "L'Idéal épiscopal selon les prédicateurs française de la fin de XVe siècle," *Revue d'histoire ecclésiastique* 61 (1966), 81*n.*

27. AN, KK 86, fol. 1ff; BN, Fond françois 2926, fol. 55-88; *Ordonnances des rois*, XXI, p. 405; Maulde, *Louise et François*, p. 255.

28. BN, Fonds français 2926 passim; 26107 passim; Lacroix, *Histoire*, I, p. 295; Wiley, *Gentlemen*, p. 141.

29. Brantôme, *La vie des grands captains*, article Montmorency. Victor Hugo used Triboulet as a main character in his *Le roi s'amuse*.

30. D'Auton, *Histoire de Louis XII*, III, pp. 248-49 and note.

31. A letter written by an Italian at Pontaise to a relative in Asti stated: "Never did a king obtain the crown in France so quietly as the present one." CSP Milan, p. 349.

32. R. Jackson, *Vive Le Roi! A History of the French Coronation from Charles V to Charles X* (Chapel Hill, 1984), p. 177, writes that little is known of Louis XII's entry into Reims.

33. For analyses of the French *sacre*, see Jackson, *Vive le Roi;* and Scheller, "French Royal Symbolism," pp. 118-24. The standard source for the details of the ceremony is D. Godefroy, *Le cérémonial français,* 2 vols. (Paris, 1649). It is, however, very limited in what it has on Louis's sacre, so I have drawn heavily on those of Charles VIII and Francis I in the opinion that they were largely the same. "Sacre du rois 1060-1789," AN, K 171, has little on Louis's. See also Molinet, *Chroniques,* III, p. 445.

34. St-Gelais, *Histoire de Louis XII,* p. 126. However, the account of royal alms in AN, KK 77, fol. 124, indicates that eighty silver coins were distributed at Corbeny. Louis touched for scrofula in Pavia and Genoa when he was there in 1500 (d'Auton, III, 34); but in general he did it far less than his successors. See M. Bloch, *The Royal Touch,* trans. J. Anderson (London, 1973), p. 177.

35. Sanuto, *Diarii,* I, p. 1029.

36. For Louis's entry into Paris, see Godefroy, *Le cérémonial français,* I, pp. 238-44; Molinet, *Chroniques,* II, pp. 446-47; B. Guenée and F. Lehoux, *Les entrées royales françaises de 1328 à 1515* (Paris, 1968), pp. 125-38; L. Bryant, *The King and the City in the Parisian Royal Entry Ceremony* (Geneva, 1986), passim; M. Sherman, "The Selling of Louis XII: Propaganda and Popular Culture in Renaissance France, 1498-1515," Ph.D. diss., University of Chicago, 1974, pp. 37-43; and Scheller, "French Royal Symbolism," pp. 101-04.

37. Guenée, *Les entrées,* p. 131.

38. Translated by Scheller, "French Royal Symbolism," p. 103.

39. Molinet, *Chroniques,* II, pp. 446-47; "Sottie nouvelle de l'astrologue" in E. Picot, *Recueil Général des sotties,* 3 vols. (Paris, 1909-12), I, p. 206.

40. Scheller, "French Royal Symbolism," pp. 103-9. He has a third explanation: There was a general inflation in crowns that saw dukes wearing royal crowns instead of ducal coronets, and kings now taking on the imperial crown.

41. *Ordonnances des roys,* XXI, p. 263.

42. BN, Dupuy 412, fol. 123v; cited by P. Contamine, *La France au XIVe et XVe siècles: Hommes, mentalités, guerre et paix* (London, 1981), part 6, p. 425. Boulenger's figure for the dioceses is accurate if one excludes the seven sees of Brittany.

43. E. LeRoy Ladurie, *The French Peasants 1450-1660* (Berkeley, CA, 1987), p. 9, uses the figures of 20 million for 1340, 10 million in 1440, and 20 million again by 1560. The scenario of a drastic decline in population up to 1450 followed by a strong rebound by 1500, is also found in G. Bois, *The Crisis of Feudalism* (Cambridge, 1984); and P. Contamine's introduction to Chevalier, *La France de la fin du XVe siècle,* pp. 1-5.

44. B. Chevalier, *Tours, Ville Royale (1356-1520)* (Louvain, 1975), pp. 521-22; J. Valbelle, *Histoire Journalière* (Aix, 1985), p. 17; H. Vellay, "Histoire de Louis XII," in BN, Fonds français 2924, fol. 49r.

45. *Ordonnances des roys,* XXI, pp. 393-64; M. Baulant, "Les prix des grains à Paris de 1431 à 1788," *Annales ESC* 23 (1968), 520-40. Modern calculations have estimated that the average wage for a day laborer in the era was from 2 *s,* 3 *d* to 2 *s,* 6 *d* a day. At the higher wage, it would take him about twelve days of work to earn enough in 1508 to buy a setier of wheat, which could feed an adult for about four months. Pay for a skilled laborer such as a mason was about twice as high: 4 *s* to 4 *s* 6 *d* a day, or about six days of work for a setier of wheat. Bois, "Le prix du froment à Rouen au XVe siècle," *Annales* 23 (1968), 1262-82. Chevalier, *Tours,* p. 392n. D. Richet, "Croissance et blocages en France du XVe au XVIIIe siècle," *Annales* 23 (1968), pp. 759-87, indicates about ten days of labor per setier of wheat.

46. But see the edict of Cardinal d'Amboise for Normandy, June 1506, forcing all vagabonds to do manual labor. BN, Fonds français 26110, piece 1.

47. The revenues of five estates of the Chabannes family rose 142 percent from 1488 to 1499. Chevalier, *La fin du XVe siècle,* p. 5.

48. Bois, *Crisis,* p. 256.

49. C. de Seyssel, *Histoire de Louis XII* (Paris, 1615), p. 113.

50. N. Tommaseo, *Relations des ambassadeurs Vénitiens sur les affaires de France au XVIe siècle*, 2 vols. (Paris, 1838), I, p. 33.

51. For the populations of other cities, see P. Benedict, ed. *Cities and Social Change in Early Modern France* (London, 1989), p. 9.

52. R. Gascon, *Gran Commerce et vie urbaine au XVIe siècle Lyon et ses marchands*, 2 vols. (Paris, 1971), I, p. 84.

53. *Procédures politiques*, pp. 593-94; Bridge, *History of France*, V, pp. 139-57. The courier probably traded the horses he had exhausted for fresh ones, plus a small sum, rather than purchasing outright new horses. See Maulde, *Diplomatie*, III, pp. 116-17, for more examples of travel time for diplomatic mail.

54. M. Brun, *Recherches historiques sur l'introduction du français dans les provinces du Midi* (Paris, 1923).

55. In that respect I have to disagree with the thesis of C. Beaune, *The Birth of an Ideology: Myths and Symbols of Nation in Late-Medieval France*, trans. by S. Huston (Berkeley, CA, 1991), that there was an early mode of nationalism present among the French by 1500.

NOTES TO CHAPTER 6

1. Morice, *Mémoires*, III, pp. 791-92.

2. Benedetti, *Diary*, p. 113. Benedetti was not entirely sure the story was accurate.

3. St-Gelais, *Histoire de Louis XII*, p. 187.

4. Anne's letter is in BN, Fonds français 2929, fol. 10; and printed in Morice, *Mémoires*, III, p. 194. See also Mirepoix, *Jeanne of France*, p. 133.

5. Bouchet, *Panégyric du Chevalier*, XIV, p. 431. In that era the term "divorce" was used, since it was impossible to end a valid marriage. I will use the modern term "annulment" to signify the judgment that a marriage had been invalid from the first.

6. Morice, *Mémoires*, III, pp. 794-99; *Procédures politiques*, p. 801; Bridge, *History of France*, III, p. 20.

7. *Procédures politiques*, pp. 700, 1106-11; L. von Pastor, *The History of the Popes*, 40 vols. (St. Louis, 1938-53), VI, p. 57.

8. I. Cloulas, *The Borgias* (Toronto, 1989), pp. 150-55.

9. BN, Fonds français 26111, fol. 891; *Ordonnances des roys*, XXI, pp. 114-16; Sanuto, *Diarii*, I, pp. 1059-60.

10. The papal bull is reprinted in *Procédures politiques*, pp. 912-14.

11. Ibid., p. 808n. Between April and August 1498, Louis d'Amboise as a member of the royal council cosigned nearly every royal edict, even more than his brother Georges did. *Ordonnances des roys*, XXI, pp. 825-1115 passim.

12. Harsgor, *Personnel*, IV, p. 2269.

13. *Decretales*, liber IV, tit. I, 21; also IV, 2, 9; in Friedberg, *Corpus Iuris Canonici*, pp. 668-69, 676.

14. *Decretales*, IV, I, 21; in Friedberg, *Corpus Iuris*, pp. 671-72; *Procédures politiques*, p. 955ff.

15. Maulde, *Jeanne de France*, pp. 289-98.

16. *Procédures politiques*, p. 835.

17. Ibid., pp. 871-912.

18. Ibid., p. 918n.

19. See the documents in AN, K 80, fol. 1 ff. Anne of Brittany insisted on keeping copies of the decision and other pertinent documents in her chancellery; thus they are reprinted in Morice, *Mémoires*, III, pp. 808-09.

20. *Ordonnances des roys*, XXI, pp. 141-44. Louis d'Amboise signed *lettres patentes* as a member of the royal council.

21. Words attributed to her by Brantôme.

22. Mirepoix, *Jeanne of France*, p. 188; A. Le Ferron, *De Rebus Gestis Gallorum* (Basel, 1569), Book 3, p. 40; and Drèze, *Raison d'Etat*, p. 118.

23. Maulde, *Jeanne de France*, p. 324 ff; Antoine Redier, *Jeanne de France* (Paris, 1950). Her canonization resulted in the intriguing situation, quite similar to Jeanne d'Arc's, of someone being proclaimed a saint whom an official church tribunal had declared to have been untruthful before it. She was enrolled among the saints who were neither virgins nor martyrs. There still are six houses of her order today.

24. For example, E. Vouter, *Essai Juridique et Historique sur un procès en annulation de marriage au XVe siècle* (Lille, 1931), p. 208.

25. *Procedures politiques*, p. 944n; C. Du Boulay, *Historia Universitatis Parisiensis*, 6 vols. (Paris, 1665-73), V, p. 825. For Standonck's life, see A. Renaudet, *Jean Standonck* (Paris, 1908). When he later was the candidate of the cathedral chapter for the see of Reims, he wrote a letter to Louis asking for his support. Louis showed the letter to his choice, Guillaume Briçonnet, and said: *"Voilà la folie de Standonck."*

26. Alexander's letter presenting Cesare to Louis is in BN, Fonds français 2929, fol. 14. See also Morice, *Mémoires*, III, pp. 890-901.

27. See a description of Cesare's arrival, in Valbelle, *Histoire Journalière*, p. 7. See also Molinet, *Chroniques*, II, pp. 456-67.

28. That Cesare's presence at Chinon was distasteful to the French is clear from St-Gelais's account of his arrival, whom the author calls the pope's nephew. *Histoire de Louis XII*, p. 139. See also Cloulas, *Borgias*, p. 157.

29. Luchaire, *Alain Le Grand*, pp. 32-34. Maulde, *Jeanne de France*, p. 361, accuses Louis of having paid his debt to Alexander "à Louis XI," but the first two candidates were allowed to refuse. It has been argued that Charlotte's father agreed because he wanted to get back in Louis's good graces after betraying him in Brittany. Lacroix, *Histoire*, I, p. 179.

30. The marriage contract is reprinted in *Archives historiques de La Gironde*, III, p. 104.

31. Sanuto, *Diarii*, II, p. 759; Cloulas, *The Borgias*, p. 161. Louise would become Louis de La Trémoille's second wife.

32. BN, Fonds français 2832, fol 102; AN, KK 77, piece 8.

33. L. Pélissier, ed., "Documents sur la première année du règne de Louis XII," *Bulletin historique et philogique* (1890), 110.

34. CSP Venice, I, 573.

35. *Négociations*, II, p. 484. However, that was written in 1510, when Anne was pregnant. None of the letters seems to be extant.

36. Gabory, *Anne de Bretagne*, p. 252.

37. See the documents in AN, K 71, fol. 5; and Morice, *Mémoires*, III, 816ff. Anne's rights were clearly set out in a document Louis signed the day after the wedding. Ibid., pp. 815-18.

38. A. Ledru, *Histoire de la Maison de Mailly*, 2 vols. (Paris, 1893), II, p. 260.

39. Printed in Maulde, *Jeanne de France*, p. 360n.

NOTES TO CHAPTER 7

1. C. de Seyssel, *The Monarchy of France*, trans. J. Hexter et al., (New Haven, Connecticut, 1981), pp. 49-58. Jean Ferrault, a contemporary of Seyssel, gave a more absolutist interpretation of royal power. See J. Poujoul, "Jean Ferrault on the King's Privileges," *Studies in the Renaissance* 5 (1958), 15-26.

2. One of the few times Louis used it was in an order of June 1514 to a royal treasurer to give Sieur Du Bouchage 2,000 *l* above his usual pension, despite the sad state of royal finances then. BN, Fonds français 2928, fol. 9.

3. P. Contamine, *Guerre, Etat et Société à la fin du Moyen Age. Etudes sur les armées des rois de France 1337-1494* (Paris, 1972), pp. 315-17. A very small number of nobles was so poor that they were allowed to serve in the infantry.

4. W. Weary, "Royal Policy and Patronage in Renaissance France: The Monarchy and the House of La Trémoille," Ph.D. diss., Yale University, 1972, p. 76.

5. In Garnier et al., *Histoire de France*, VII, p. 47.

6. AN, JJ 235, fol. 77.

7. J. R. Major, *The Monarchy, the Estates and the Aristocracy in Renaissance France* (London, 1988), XIII, p. 535.

8. BN, Fonds nouvelles acquisitions français 1232, fol. 2, 16.

9. R. Harding, *Anatomy of a Power Elite: The Provincial Governors in Early Modern France* (New Haven, CT, 1978), pp. 8-10, shows that there were several ways in which governorships were created, but the principal reason was for command of frontier forces.

10. *Ordonnances des roys*, I, p. 186; B. Guenée, *Tribunaux et gens de justice dans le bailliage de Senlis à la fin du Moyen Age* (Paris, 1963); R. Doucet, *Les Institutions de la France au XVIe siècle*, 2 vols. (Paris, 1948), I, pp. 251-64; P. Chaunu, and R. Gascon, *Histoire économique et sociale de France*, 3 vols. (Paris, 1977), I, p. 37.

11. Machiavelli, *Description of France*, p. 9.

12. C. Leber, ed., *Collection des meilleurs dissertations . . . à l'histoire de France*, 20 vols. (Paris, 1838), VIII, p. 198.

13. *Ordonnances des roys*, XXI, p. 33.

14. L. Pélissier, ed., *Trois relations sur la situation de la France en 1498 et 1499* (Montpellier, 1894), p. 8; Sanuto, *Diarii*, I, p. 323; Pastor, *History of the Popes*, VI, p. 294n. On d'Amboise's policy, see M. Baudier, *Histoire de l'administration du Cardinal d'Amboise, grand ministre d'Estat de France* (Paris, 1634).

15. BN, Fonds français 23110, fol. 89.

16. Sanuto, *Diarii*, VII, p. 235.

17. Guicciardini, *History of Italy*, IV, pp. 8, 312.

18. I have not found a contemporary source for the saying. It is the opinion of Lacroix, *Histoire*, IV, p. 129, that Louis himself did not use the phrase.

19. In the farce "*Sottie nouvelle de l'astrologue*," in Picot, *Recueil des sotties*, I, pp. 204, 209, 217.

20. For Gié's life, see *Procédures politiques*, pp. xiii-lxxxi.

21. The following paragraphs are drawn largely from N. Valois, *Le Conseil du Roi au XIV, XV, et XVI siècles* (Paris, 1888); Doucet, *Institutions*, I, pp. 130-49, and Bridge, *History of France*, V, pp. 27-34.

22. Seyssel, *The Monarchy of France*, p. 29.

23. Harsgor, *Personnel*, I, passim. Harsgor shows the continuity of the membership of the royal council from Charles to Louis.

24. *Ordonnances des roys*, XXI, pp. 56-57. For example, disputed elections of bishops at Poitiers and Alet were appealed to it. BN, Fonds français 5093, fol. 6, pp. 271-72.

25. N. Valois, *Inventaire des arrêts du Conseil d'état*, 2 vols. (Paris, 1886-93), I, pp. xi-xxxviii; Doucet, *Institutions*, I, pp. 202-6.

26. Registres de ville de Rouen, quoted by A. Floquet, *Histoire du Parlement de Normandie*, 7 vols. (Rouen, 1840-42), I, p. 331.

27.   Lacroix, *Histoire*, I, p. 69.

28.   Report of Contarini, in E. Alberi, *Relazioni degli ambasciatori veneti al Senato*, 1st Series, 6 vols. (Florence, 1839-63), IV, p. 15. He stated that 25,000 to 30,000 men claimed to be students, but only 5,000 were. See also H. Martin, *Histoire de France* (Paris, 1861), p. 309.

29.   *Ordonnances des roys*, XXI, p. 80.

30.   Du Boulay, *Historia Universitatis Parisiensis*, V, pp. 656-832; Vellay, "Histoire," fol. 12v-19v; Sherman, "The Selling of Louis XII," pp. 55-57.

31.   *Ordonnances des roys*, XXI, p. 177.

32.   On the Pragmatic Sanction, see below, Chapter 12.

33.   *Ordonnances des roys*, XXI, pp. 178-80.

34.   G. Botero, *Practical Politics (Ragion di Stato)*, trans. by G. Moore (Chevy Chase, Maryland, 1949), p. 46.

35.   Jean Bodin called it the most laudable of Louis's reforms. *Six Books of the Commonwealth*, ed. by K. McRae (Cambridge, Mass., 1962), p. 136.

36.   BN, Fonds français 2831, fol. 88r-v.

37.   *Ordonnances des roys*, XXI, p. 183; R. Mousnier, *La vénalité des offices sous Henri IV et Louis XIII* (Paris, 1971), p. 35; C. Stocker, "The First Sale of Occies in the Parlement of Paris (1512–1524)," *Sixteenth Century Journal* 9 (1978), pp.4-30, argues Louis had a system of barter for judicial offices.

38.   Botero, *Practical Politics*, p. 51; Lacroix, *Histoire*, I, p. 74. The chancellor had to go to the Parlement to force it to register the edicts creating the new offices.

39.   The following paragraphs on the fiscal system are drawn largely from M. Wolfe, *The Fiscal System of Renaissance France* (New Haven, CT, 1972), esp. pp. 269-303; P. Viollet, *Histoire des institutions politiques et administratives de la France*, 4 vols. (Paris, 1903), III, p. 364ff; Doucet, *Institutions*, I, pp. 188-209; Chaunu, *Histoire économique et sociale*, pp. 35-37.

40.   R. La Barre, *Formulaire des esleuz* (Rouen, 1622), pp. 96-97. See A. Spont, *La taille en Languedoc de 1450 à 1515* (Toulouse, 1890), p. 7, for the estimate of the ordinary revenues. J. Clamageran, *Histoire de l'impôt en France*, 3 vols. (Paris 1867-76), II, pp. 98, 339, estimates it at 250,000 *l* in 1498 and 550,000 *l* in 1523.

41.   Contamine, *France au XIVe et XVe siècles*, part 6.

42.   Spont, *La taille*, p. 7.

43.   *Ordonnances des roys*, XXI, pp. 340-41; La Barre, *Formulaire*, pp. 90-91.

44.   Quoted by Wolfe, *Fiscal System*, p. 335. See also Spont, *La taille*, p. 7; and J.-C. Hocquet, "Qui la Gabelle du sel du roi de France a-t-elle enrichi?" in J.-Ph. Genet, ed., *Genèse de l'état moderne* (Paris, 1987), 209-19.

45.   AN, K73, fol. 46.

46.   Wolfe, *Fiscal System*, pp. 314-16.

47.   See C. Devic, et al. *Histoire générale de Languedoc*, 15 vols. (Toulouse, 1872-92), XI, pp. 163-88, for the details for Languedoc in the era. See also Doucet, *Institutions*, I, p. 348. In Normandy, the *élus* controlled the fiscal system, but the provincial estates met frequently to approve the *tailles*, as in 1509. BN, Fonds français 5093, fol. 272-73.

48.   Spont, *La Taille*, p. 53; BN, Fonds français 25718, fol. 3-78; 26110, fol. 795. Maulde, *Revolution*, p.302n, provides a large list of expenses left unpaid at Charles's death.

49.   BN, Fonds français 25718, fol. 78. The levy of *quinze cens mil francs* was verified by the Norman Estates in 1519 when it complained about Francis I's large tax increases. Maulde, *Revolution*, p. 287n. P. Contamine has calculated that the average day laborer in Normandy had to work 51.2 days to pay his share of the royal levies in 1491. "Guerre, Fiscalité Royale et Economie en France (Deuxième Moitié du XVe siècle)," *Proceedings of the Seventh*

International Economic History Congress, p. 270. In 1506 that number ought to have been reduced by nearly one-third.

50. Louis seems to have examined the expense accounts of his officers, as his signature is on a number of them. E.g., the expenses of the *écurie* for 1498; BN, Fonds français 2926, fol. 88r.

51. BN, Fonds français 2927, fol. 27r-33v, 48r-v; 2930, fol. 88r-91v. D. Potter, *War and Government in the French Provinces: Picardy 1470-1560* (Cambridge, 1993), p. 115, speaks of the proliferation of small pensions under the Beaujeus as a means of gaining support.

52. A roll of the décime "from the time of the late Mons. le legate" is in BN, Fonds Latin 1523, fol. 124-26. It did not include Brittany and several small sees in the Midi. It is doubtful that these sums actually came to as much as 10 percent of the clergy's annual income. In 1509 Louis reimbursed the clergy in December, although a third of the money was to come from a sum that Ferdinand of Aragon owed him. BN, Fonds français 25718, fol. 131. It is improbable that the clergy ever saw that money.

53. AN, KK 86, fol. 1.

NOTES TO CHAPTER 8

1. Sanuto, *Diarii*, II, 749.

2. Technically, Maximilian was not yet the emperor since he had not yet been crowned and would not be until 1509. His proper title was King of the Romans until his coronation, but I shall refer to him as the emperor to avoid confusion.

3. L. Pélissier, "L'Alliance Milano-Allemande à la fin du XVe siècle," *Miscellenea di Storio Italiana* 35 (1898), 337-39, 442-44.

4. Ibid., pp. 368-69, 472-74.

5. Guicciardini, *History of Italy*, III, p. 209.

6. "Procès-verbal de l'hommage fait par Philippe, archiduc de Autriche, comte de Flandres, à Louis XII," in *Archives curieuses*, I, pp. 1-11; Molinet, *Chroniques*, II, pp. 462-65; Scheller, "French Royal Symbolism," pp. 129-31.

7. L. Pélissier, ed., *Recherches dans les archives italiennes: Louis XII et Ludovic Sforza*, 2 vols. (Paris, 1896), I, pp. 139-45.

8. CSP Venice, I, pp. 274-75.

9. CSP Spain, I, p. 188.

10. J. Dumont, *Corps universel diplomatique du droit des gens*, 8 vols. (Amsterdam, 1726-31), III, pp. 397-400; Bridge, *History of France*, III, pp. 47-48.

11. Dumont, *Corps diplomatique*, III, p. 406; Pélissier, *Louis XII et Ludovic Sforza*, I, pp. 145-60; Bridge, *History of France*, III, pp. 53-55; Tailhé, *Louis XII*, I, p. 154.

12. Pélissier, "Documents sur la première année," pp. 51-52.

13. Pélissier, *Louis XII et Ludovic Sforza*, I, pp. 73-82.

14. Sanuto, *Diarii*, III, p. 11.

15. Ibid., II, pp. 1-238, passim; Pélissier, *Louis XII et Ludovic Sforza*, I, pp. 238-84; Bridge, *History of France*, III, pp. 63-68.

16. Pélissier, *Trois relations*, p. 26.

17. Letter of Cesare Guasco, 24 March 1499, in d'Auton, *Chroniques de Louis XII*, I, pp. 329-32. D'Auton, a cleric attached to Queen Anne's court, wrote the official history for Louis's reign to 1508, which is the principal French source for the war in Italy from 1499 to 1504.

18. For the relationship between Genoa and Sforza and Genoa and Louis, see Pélissier, ed., *Documents pour l'histoire de l'établissement de la domination française à Gênes (1498-1500)*. See also P. Coles, "Crisis of a Renaissance Society: Genoa 1488-1507," *Past and Present* 11 (1957), pp. 22-23.

19. F. Lot, *Recherches sur les effectifs des armées françaises des guerres d'Italie aux guerres de Religion 1494-1562* (Paris, 1962), pp. 16-26; C. Oman, *The History of the Art of War in the Sixteenth Century* (Reprint, New York, 1972), pp. 40-42.

20. In 1502 the cost of the lance companies was 416,541 *l.* BN, Fonds français, 2627, fol. 1r-46r.

21. Machiavelli, "Description of the Affairs of France," p. 3.

22. Doucet, *Les Institutions,* II, p. 612; P. Contamine, *Histoire militaire de France,* 3 vols. (Paris, 1992-94), I, p. 249.

23. B. de Monluc, *Commentaires,* edited by P. Courteault (Paris, 1964), pp. 34-35.

24. Botero, *Practical Politics,* p. 177. A large portion of the royal edicts, orders, and quittances on crime (BN, Fonds français 26110-12) from Louis's reign dealt with unruly soldiers.

25. *Procedures politiques,* pp. 87-97. The Swiss cost France 48,000 *l* in an average year. BN, Fonds français 25718, fol. 100.

26. Lot, *Les effectifs des armées,* p. 27. According to BN, Fonds français 2830, fol. 136, the French artillery had 1,430 pieces in 1514, but most were small.

27. Quoted in Pélissier, "Documents sur la première années," p. 6. See also Bridge, *History of France,* III, pp. 80-81.

28. Report of a Milanese ambassador to Ludovico Sforza, quoted in Pélissier, *Louis XII et Ludovic Sforza,* I, p. 382.

29. Ibid., 722; Sanuto, *Diarii,* II, p. 206.

30. Sanuto, *Diarii,* II, 91. Lot calculated the number of lances at 1,460, for a total of 5,840 mounted troops. *Les effectifs des armées,* p. 26.

31. C. Ady, *A History of Milan under the Sforzas* (New York, 1907), 176; J. Hale, *War and Society in Renaissance Europe, 1450-1620* (Baltimore, 1985), p. 62; Sanuto, *Diarii,* II, p. 1112, has 30,000 infantry and 1,200 lances.

32. D'Auton, *Chroniques,* I, p. 10. Trivulzio had a pension of 10,000 *l* from Louis XII, while his lieutenant, Béraud Stuart d'Aubigny, a Scot whose ancestors had served France for several generations, received 4,000 *l.* BN, Fonds français 2928, fol. 12.

33. Pélissier, *Louis XII et Ludovic Sforza,* I, pp. 392-94.

34. Sanuto, *Diarii,* II, p. 590.

35. Ibid., II, p. 998.

36. D'Auton, *Chroniques,* I, pp. 20-21. See also Pélissier, ed., *Louis XII and Ludovic Sforza,* II, pp. 7-8.

37. L. Landucci, *A Florentine Diary from 1450 to 1516,* trans. by A. De Rosen Jervis, (Freeport, NY, 1971), p. 181.

38. D'Auton, *Chroniques,* I, pp. 61-76; St-Gelais, *Histoire de Louis XII,* p. 146; Pélissier, *Louis XII et Ludovic Sforza,* II, pp. 33-38.

39. Pélissier, *Documents,* pp. 122-77.

40. D'Auton, *Chroniques,* I pp. 91-108; St-Gelais, *Histoire de Louis XII,* p. 150; Sanuto, *Diarii,* III, pp. 24-25. Whether Leonardo da Vinci had a role in planning the entry is in dispute. See below, Chapter 11.

41. St-Gelais, *Histoire de Louis XII,* p. 151; Pélissier, *Louis XII et Ludovic Sforza,* II, pp. 227-38.

42. Sanuto, *Diarii,* III, pp. 44-48; Ady, *History of Milan,* p. 178.

43. Jacques Cohory stated that the baby was so named because of a vow that Anne had made to St. Claude, who was invoked in danger of death, but he did not indicate why she took a vow to him. Perhaps it was in reference to her husband being away at war. "De Rebus Gestis Francorum," in BN, Fonds latin 5972, fol. 20r.

44. "Cronicque des faicts et gestes du Roy Loys Douzieme faictz . . . en lan mil cinq cens," in BN, Fonds français 17522, fol. 10r.

45. D'Auton, *Chroniques*, II, pp. 130-40; St-Gelais, *Histoire de Louis XII*, pp. 155-57; Sanuto, *Diarii*, III, pp. 85-103; Pélissier, ed., *Louis XII et Ludovic Sforza*, II, pp. 115-20.

46. Sanuto, *Diarii*, III, pp. 116, 133.

47. Ibid, III, p. 162.

48. Ibid., pp. 202-28; d'Auton, *Chroniques*, I, pp. 256-61, and the letter of La Trémoille to Louis, printed in ibid, pp. 354-59. D'Auton is the principal authority for Ludovico being disguised as a Swiss; those who claim he wore a Franciscan's habit include Vellay, "Histoire," p. 34; Le Ferron, *De Rebus*, p. 53; and Gohory, "De Rebus," fol. 22r.

49. Pélissier, *Louis XII et Ludovic Sforza*, II, p. 200; Sanuto, *Diarii*, III, pp. 320-22. Since the Venetian ambassador is the only one to note the iron cage, Ady, *History of Milan*, p. 184, wonders if the story simply reflected Venetian hatred of Sforza.

50. Vellay, "Histoire," fol. pp. 35r-v.

51. D'Auton, *Chroniques*, I, pp. 198, 288-93.

52. Ibid., pp. 273-74.

53. Letter of provision in BN, Fonds français 5093, fol. 771-80.

54. L. Pélissier, *Lettres inédites sur la conquête du Milanais par Louis XII* (Turin, 1893), p. 6.

55. Vellay, "Histoire," p. 28v; Jean Maire, "Instruction au roi Louis XII," in P. Rouleau, *Jean Maire, Evêque de Condom 1436-1521* (Paris, 1931), p. 72. See also Pélissier, *Louis XII et Ludovic Sforza*, II, pp. 329-41. In 1510 royal revenues from Milan came to 715,700 *l.* AN, J 910, fol. 1ff.

56. Ady, *History of Milan*, p. 194.

NOTES TO CHAPTER 9

1. The instructions to the new Florentine ambassador in 1499, in Desjardins, *Négociations*, II, pp. 15-34, emphasize the necessity of getting French aid for seizing Pisa. Relations between Florence and France during Louis's reign are documented in the diplomatic correspondence edited by Desjardins and the works of Niccolo Machiavelli and Francesco Guicciardini, both Florentine diplomats.

2. Ibid., II, p. 26.

3. The troops' behavior is described in Landucci, *Florentine Diary*, pp. 170-71.

4. See the discussion of the "double Pisan rampart" in C. Duffy, *Siege warfare: the fortress in the early modern world, 1494-1660* (London, 1979), p. 15.

5. Desjardins, *Négociations*, II, pp. 34-41; d'Auton, *Chroniques*, II, pp. 298-317; Sanuto, *Diarii*, III, pp. 533-35; P. Villari, *Life and Times of Niccolo Machiavelli*, 2 vols. (Reprint Westport, CT, 1968), I, pp. 273-75.

6. Quoted by Villari, *Machiavelli*, I, pp. 277-78. Machiavelli's reports are in *Le Opere*, ed. by L. Passerini et al. (Florence, 1873), vol. 3.

7. Louis understood an oration in Italian at Milan in 1507. D'Auton, *Chroniques*, IV, pp. 264-65.

8. Ibid., pp. 278-80.

9. N. Machiavelli, *The Prince* (New York, 1950), p. 14.

10. Dumont, *Corps diplomatique*, IV, pp. 37-38; d'Auton, *Chroniques*, II, pp. 108-36; Guicciardini, *History of Italy*, III, pp. 171-73.

11. Louis's accountants determined in 1502 that Ferdinand's part of the realm produced 89,120 *l* more than his. The total for the realm was 507,198 *l.* BN, Fonds français 2928, fol. 25.

12. CSP Spain, I, pp. 259-61; Dumont, *Corps diplomatique*, III, pp. 44-47.

13. Guicciardini, *History of Italy*, III, p. 30; Machiavelli, *The Prince*, pp. 12-14; W. Prescott, *History of the Reign of Ferdinand and Isabella*, 3 vols. (New York, 1872), III, p. 14. Guicciardini states that Louis had renewed negotiations begun by Charles VIII (p. 29).

14. Sanuto, *Diarii*, III, p. 386; P. Ambri Berselli, "Lettre inédite de Louis XII aux archives d'Etat de Bologne," *Revue historique* 218 (1952), 269-70.

15. St-Gelais, *Histoire de Louis XII*, pp. 162-63; Pastor, *History of the Popes*, VI, pp. 83; K. Setton, *The Papacy and the Levant (1204-1571)*, 4 vols. (Philadelphia, 1976-84), II, p. 514. Il Moro was also accused of inviting the Turks to Italy to aid him.

16. Sanuto, *Diarii*, IV, pp. 76-78; d'Auton, *Chroniques*, II, pp. 55-63; Guicciardini, *History of Italy*, III, pp. 58-60. D'Auton put the number of Capuans killed at 700 to 800; Sanuto said 1,200.

17. BN, Collection Dupuy 160.

18. Anne de Foix was not Louis XII's niece, contrary to numerous historians. For her life, see DBF, II, p. 1331. On her trip to Hungary, see Sanuto, *Diarii*, V, p. 288ff. Anne and Ladislaus also had a daughter, Anne. The double marriage of Anne and her brother to Habsburg siblings secured that family's claim to the throne of Hungary after Louis was killed at Mohacs in 1526.

19. Sanuto, *Diarii*, III, pp. 5-394 passim; Setton, *Papacy and Levant*, II, pp. 517-19.

20. Sanuto, *Diarii*, IV, pp. 71-231 passim; D'Auton, *Chroniques*, II, pp. 151-204; C. La Roncière, *Histoire de la marine française*, 4 vols. (Paris, 1899-1906), III, pp. 39-59.

21. BN, Fonds français 5501, fol. 102-04.

22. For example, Pierre de Gié received a marquisate, a comté, and several other estates. *Procedures politiques*, pp. 684-86.

23. H. Courteault, *Le Dossier "Naples" des Archives Nicolay. Documents pour servir à l'histoire de l'occupation française de Royaume de Naples* (Paris, 1916), pp. 14-17. Nemours's commission is in BN, Fonds français 5501, fol. 97-99.

24. BN, Fonds français 2930, fol. 13; Comte de Castellane, *Le ducat Neapolitain de Louis XII* (Paris, 1901); R. Scheller, "Gallia cisalpina Louis XII and Italy 1499 to 1508," *Simiolus* 15 (1985), 19-20.

25. D'Auton, *Chroniques*, II, pp. 97-98.

26. Ibid., p. 92.

27. St-Gelais, *Histoire de Louis XII*, p. 168; d'Auton, *Chroniques*, II, p. 76.

28. D'Auton, *Chroniques*, III, pp. 77-79, IV, p. 10n. Two recent accounts are M. Croce Bellentoni, *"Intendyo" di Tommasina Spinola e il re de Francia* (Liguria, 1982); and G. Trisolini, *Un manuscrit inedit appartenant à la Bibliothèque nationale de Paris* (Udine, 1971). Trisolini concludes that the love of Louis and Tommasina was platonic, "without a doubt." p. 121.

29. L. Domenichi, *Rimedi d'amore* (1562), cited in d'Auton, *Chroniques*, III, p. 77n.

30. Quilliet, *Louis XII*, p. 283.

31. St-Gelais, *Histoire de Louis XII*, pp. 166-68. In 1503 Louis granted Cesare 20,000 *l.* AN, K 78, fol. 1.

32. Sanuto, *Diarii*, IV, pp. 421-23, 477-78.

33. Ibid., pp. 839-49. See also Spont, "Marine française," pp. 401-06.

34. D'Auton, *Chroniques*, III, pp. 112-21; *Histoire de Bayard*, XV, pp. 228-30.

35. *Histoire de Bayard*, XV, pp. 227-43.

36. Ibid, pp. 244-47; d'Auton, *Chroniques*, III, pp. 127-33; Sanuto, *Diarii*, IV, p. 777.

37. BN, Fonds français 2830, fol. 3; 3087, fol. 105; d'Auton, *Chroniques*, III, pp. 152-57; Desjardins, *Négociations*, II, pp. 75-76; Dumont, *Corps diplomatiques*, IV, pp. 27-28. On Philip's visit to France, see below, chapter 10.

38. For Paris, see *Registres des délibérations du Bureau de l'hôtel de ville de Paris,* edited by P. Guérin et al., 32 vols. (Paris, 1873-1952), I, p. 77.

39. Louis to Nicolay, April 4, 1503 in Courteault, *Le Dossier,* pp. 72-73, 77n.

40. CSP Spain, I, pp. 304-6. Philip had shown Louis a document signed by his in-laws that gave Philip the power to negotiate for them over the marriage of Charles and Claude. It is ambiguous in the authority given him, and they may have been justified in rejecting the concessions he made. AN, K 77, fol. 123.

41. D'Auton, *Chroniques,* III, pp. 168-78; Guicciardini, *History of Italy,* III, pp. 184-92; Oman, *Art of War,* pp. 53-56.

42. Courteault, *Le Dossier,* p. 77.

43. Guérin, *Registres de l'hôtel de ville,* I, pp. 80-84. In November 1503 Louis had to write to the city asking for the 30,000 *l.*

44. *Procédures politiques,* pp. 709-10; BN, Fonds français 25718, fol. 80-89; Bridge, *History of France,* III, p. 181.

45. Louis Gachard, *Collection des voyages des souverains de Pays-Bas,* 4 vols. (Brussels, 1876-82), I, pp. 291-92.

46. Courteault, *Le Dossier,* p. 133.

47. Ibid., p. 118; d'Auton, *Chroniques,* III, p. 254.

48. BN, Collection Dupuy 28, fol. 17.

49. See Chapter 11 for a more detailed account of this conclave and the next one that elected Julius II.

50. St-Gelais, *Histoire de Louis XII,* p. 173; d'Auton, *Chroniques,* III, pp. 205-06.

51. The following paragraphs are based largely on d'Auton, *Chroniques,* III, pp. 255-70, 291-306; Molinet, *Chroniques,* II, pp. 528-33; Sanuto, *Diarii,* V, pp. 205-699; Prescott, *Ferdinand and Isabella,* III, pp. 114-51.

52. The exact sums looted by the French agents in Rome are unknown, but in trials held the next year they were accused of pocketing 1,200,000 *l.* See below, Chapter 9. Some sense of the extent of their crime can be seen in the fact that on May 3, 1503, Louis told Jean Nicolay that he had sent 35,000 *l* to the army. On June 2 the general of finance in Rome wrote to Nicolay that he was forwarding 8,100 *l.* Courteault, *Le Dossier,* pp. 95, 102.

53. For the Battle of the Garigliano, see d'Auton, *Chroniques,* III, pp. 160-80; and Guicciardini, *History of Italy,* III, pp. 274-97.

54. See the lengthy account of d'Ars's adventures in d'Auton, *Chroniques,* III, pp. 318-28.

55. D'Auton, *Chroniques,* III, p. 307.

56. Spont, "Marine française," p. 26. In 1504 Louis did grant Cardinal Guibé 100 *l* in compensation for money he had given the defeated troops in Rome. BN, Fonds français 20978, fol. 131.

57. Landucci, *Florentine Diary,* p. 212; Bridge, *History of France,* III, pp. 201-02.

58. Quilliet, *Louis XII,* p. 292.

59. Ibid., pp. 292-93; d'Auton, *Chroniques,* III, pp. 335-38; Tailhé, *Histoire de Louis XII,* I, p. 376; M. Sherman, "The Selling of Louis XII: Propaganda and Popular Culture in Renaissance France," Ph.D. diss., University of Chiago, 1974, pp. 103-4. D'Auton gives fifteen names and adds that there were others whose names he did not know.

NOTES TO CHAPTER 10

1. In 1501 Louis also had been so ill that for four days he was thought to be at death's door. It had been kept secret. *Procédures politiques,* p. 249.

2. Ibid., passim; d'Auton, *Chroniques*, III, pp. 208-10.

3. *Registres de l'hôtel de ville*, I, pp. 63-67.

4. Ibid., I, 93; d'Auton, *Chroniques*, III, p. 35n; Scheller, "French Royal Symbolism," p. 139.

5. Scheller, "French Royal Symbolism," pp. 139-41.

6. H. Stein, ed., "Le sacre d'Anne de Bretagne et son entrée à Paris," *Mémoires de la Société de l'histoire de Paris et de l'Ile-de-France* 29 (1902), pp. 268-304; Godefroy, *Le Cérémonial français*, I, pp. 687-96. See also Bryant, *Parisian Entry Ceremony*, pp. 93-96; and Scheller, "French Royal Symbolism," p. 141. According to "Le sacre," p. 281, the university students and faculty were not allowed to march because of fear of disorder; they assembled at Notre Dame to greet Anne.

7. D'Auton, *Chroniques*, III, 329; Seyssel, *Louis XII*, p. 105.

8. The enormous amount of extant documentation on the Gié affair is printed in *Procédures politiques*, pp. 1-786; and the introduction provides a good summary of the affair.

9. Ibid., p. 286.

10. "Journal de Louise de Savoie," in Petitot, *Mémoires relatifs*, XVI. See Maulde, *Louise et François*, pp. 111-15, on the relationship between Gié and Louise.

11. In June 1506 he paid half, but there is no evidence he paid the rest. *Procédures politiques*, p. cxx.

12. Ibid., pp. 557-90; Brantôme, *Oeuvres complètes*, III, p. 3.

13. *Procédures politiques*, p. cxxi.

14. "Journal de Louise de Savoie," pp. 390-91.

15. AN, J 951, fol 1. Gié was a witness.

16. BN, Fonds français 2930, fol. 3-6. Louis's signature is placed well above Philip's. See also Le Glay, *Négociations*, I, pp. 24-34. It was proposed in 1505 that Francis marry Philip's daughter Eleanor, who in fact became his second wife in 1530.

17. Dumont, *Corps diplomatique*, IV, pp. 16-17; Sanuto, *Diarii*, V, pp. 152-55.

18. Le Glay, *Négociations*, I, pp. l-lii.

19. *Registres de l'hôtel de ville*, I, p. 62; d'Auton, *Chroniques*, II, p. 206-07.

20. D'Auton, *Chroniques*, II, pp. 208-11; Vellay, "Histoire," fol. 39r-v; St-Gelais, *Histoire de Louis XII*, pp. 164-65.

21. Maulde, *Diplomatie au temps de Machiavel*, I, p. 274; citing Erasmus's dedication to his "Paraphrase of the Epistles to Timothy."

22. Le Glay, *Négociations*, I, pp. 37-49.

23. St-Gelais, *Histoire de Louis XII*, p. 165.

24. Ibid., p. 170; d'Auton *Chroniques*, III, pp. 102-4; Le Glay, *Négociations*, I, pp. 60-61; Guicciardini, *History of Italy*, III, p. 175. The hostages, held at Valenciennes, were prominent nobles, all in their early teens: Gaston de Foix, Charles de Bourbon de Vendôme, and Charles de Bourbon de Montpensier.

25. St-Gelais, *Histoire de Louis XII*, p. 172; AN, J 951, fol. 2.

26. Dumont, *Corps diplomatique*, IV, pp. 55-57.

27. In E. Lavisse, ed., *Histoire de France* (Paris, 1903), V, part 1, p. 68.

28. D'Auton, *Chroniques*, III, p. 358; C. von Höfler, "Die Depeschen der Venetianischen Botschafters Vincenzo Quirino," *Archiv für österreichische Geschichte* 66 (1885), pp. 60-75. Le Glay, *Négociations*, I, p. lxviii, indicates that there is reason to suspect the Habsburgs added the last clause sometime later.

29. St-Gelais, *Histoire de Louis XII*, p. 177; Guicciardini, *History of Italy*, III, p. 361; Gabory, *Anne de Bretagne*, p. 146.

30. St-Gelais, *Histoire de Louis XII*, p. 175; *Lettres de Louis XII*, I, p. 64.

31. BN, Fonds Colbert 1, for Louis's new will; Collection Dupuy 81, for the act creating a regency.

32. BN, Fonds français 2831, fol. 86-89; Fonds Dupuy 85, fol. 20; *Ordonnances des roys* XX, pp. 320-28; d'Auton, *Chroniques*, IV, pp. 10-11, 30-31; Leroux de Lincy, *Vie de la Reine Anne de Bretagne* III, p. 158. Néret, *Louis XII*, p. 124, writes that the relationship between Louis and Anne remained as cold as the winter of 1505-6 was, when wine froze in the cellars.

33. Sanuto, *Diarii*, VI, p. 179.

34. Desjardins, *Négociations*, II, pp. 107-8.

35. Floranges, *Mémoires*, XVI, p. 194. In 1515 a Venetian in Spain described Germaine as "very fat." CSP Venice, II, p. 225.

36. M. Varillas, *Histoire de Louis XII* (Paris, 1688), p. 315.

37. Dumont, *Corps diplomatique*, IV, pp. 72-79. Other documents on Germaine's marriage are in AN, K1639; and Desjardins, *Négociations*, II, pp. 139-43. Louis stopped using the title of King of Naples, Sicily, and Jerusalem after this. It is not clear if he received any of the gold, and if so, whether he or Francis I was asked to repay it.

38. CSP Venice, I, p. 310; BN, Fonds français 4329, fol. 93; Höfler, "Die Depeschen," pp. 151-54.

39. Letter of Maximilian's ambassador in France to the Emperor, in *Lettres de Louis XII*, I, pp. 34-41.

40. CSP Venice, I, p. 301-2.

41. Höfler, "Die Depeschen," pp. 161-63; *Lettres de Louis XII*, I, p. 42.

42. Le Glay, *Négociations*, I, p. 112; Baudier, *Cardinal d'Amboise* p. 139.

43. CSP Venice, I, p. 302; d'Auton, *Chroniques*, IV, p. 58.

44. E. Maugis, *Histoire du Parlement de Paris de' l'avenement des rois Valois à la mort de Henry IV*, 3 vols. (Paris, 1913-16), I, p. 123; Major, *Representative Institutions*, p. 123; *Registres de la ville de Paris*, I, p. 119.

45. Among them Doucet, *Les institutions*, I, pp. 328-29; Lemonnier, *Histoire de France*, V, p. 142; Quilliet, *Louis XII*, p. 326.

46. See the list of cities in Major, *Deputies*, pp. 161-62.

47. "Recit . . . de la remonstrance faict au roy Louis XII," in *Lettres de Louis XII*, I, p. 43.

48. Major, *Deputies*, pp. 161-62; Major, *Representative Institutions*, p. 152.

49. AN, K 1714. Both d'Auton and the Habsburg ambassador used the term "Estates." *Chroniques*, IV, p. 44; Le Glay, *Négociations*, I, pp. 141-45.

50. The address is in "Recit . . . de la remonstrance," in *Lettres de Louis XII*, I, pp. 43-44. I am using Bridges's translation, *History of France*, III, p. 249. See also Quilliet, *Louis XII*, pp. 327-33; Picot, *Histoire des Etats*, I, pp. 552-55.

51. Scheller, "French Royal Symbolism," pp. 95-97, proposes that the Estates used the term *"Père du peuple"* and not *"Pater patriae"* because they regarded themselves as representing the whole people, while the word *patria* then had the sense of "region," as in the French word *pays*.

52. L. Delisle, ed., *Une Lettre de Louis XII aux maire et échevins de St-Omer après les états-généraux en 1506* (St-Omer, 1881). This is the only surviving letter of those sent to a number of cities of the Low Countries.

53. *Lettres de Louis XII*, I, pp. 44-45.

54. *Registres de la ville,* I, pp. 119-20. The oaths of sixteen other cities are in AN, J 951; and the captains, in BN, Fonds Dupuy 85, fol. 20-22. Louis also required the city of Milan and his other possessions in Italy to swear to accept the marriage.

55. Höfler, "Die Despechen," p. 243; Le Glay, *Négociations,* I, p. 142; Le Ferron, *De Rebus,* II, p. 75.

56. Delisle, *Une lettre de Louis XII,* p. 2.

57. On the pay of deputies, see Major, *Deputies,* p. 14.

58. Maulde, *Louise et François,* pp. 105, 148.

59. D'Auton, *Chroniques,* IV, pp. 48-51.

NOTES TO CHAPTER 11

1. H. Bernard-Maître, "Les 'Théologastres' de l'Université de Paris au temps d'Erasme at de Rabelais (1496-1536)," *Bibliothèque d'humanisme et renaissance* 27 (1965), pp. 248-64.

2. See below, Chapter 15.

3. Bridge, *History of France,* V, p. 240.

4. J. Sequin, *L'Information en France, de Louis XII à Henri II* (Geneva, 1961), pp. 56-60.

5. E. Armstrong, *Before Copyright: The French Book-Privilege System 1498-1526* (Cambridge, 1990).

6. *Ordonnances des roys,* XXI, p. 209.

7. Tommaseo, *Relations,* I, p. 29; L. Delisle, *Le cabinet des manuscrits de la bibliothèque Impériale,* 3 vols. (Paris, 1868-81), I, pp. 121-46. Many of the volumes taken from Pavia now at Paris are marked "De Pavye du roy Loys XIIe."

8. BN, Fonds français 1672, fol. 26.

9. L. Pélissier, "Prêt et Perte de Manuscrits de la bibliothèque de Louis XII," *Revue des Bibliothèques* 3 (1893), pp. 361-62; H. Omont, *Anciens inventaires de la Bibliothèque Nationale* (Paris, 1908), I, pp. 1-146; Scheller, "Gallia cisalpina," pp. 14-15.

10. P. Jodogne, "Les Rhétoriqueurs et l'humanisme," in A. Levi, ed., *Humanism in France at the End of the Middle Ages and in the Early Renaissance* (New York, 1970), pp. 150-75.

11. This material on early humanism in France is drawn largely from A. Tilley, *The Dawn of the French Renaissance* (Reprint, New York, 1968); A. Renaudet, *Préréforme et humanisme à Paris pendant les premières guerres d'Italie* (Paris, 1953); and W. Gundersheimer, ed., *French Humanism, 1470-1600* (New York, 1970).

12. P. de Nolhac, "Le Grec à Paris sous Louis XII," *Revue des Etudes grecques* I, (1899), pp. 61-67; E. Jovy, *François Tissard et Jérome Aléandre* (Vitry-Le-François, 1899) .Jovy argues that Louis deserves far more recognition as a patron of humanism; Part II, p. 2.

13. Quoted in Tilley, *Dawn,* p. 265. Some historians feel that Aleandro here was directing sarcasm toward the University of Paris, as would be expected of a friend of Erasmus, but that would be hard to jibe with his accepting high offices in the university.

14. R. Mynors, ed., *Collected Works of Erasmus,* 86 vols. (Toronto, 1975), II, pp. 217-23 The best recent study of Erasmus's years in Paris is R. Schoeck, *Erasmus of Europe: The Making of a Humanist 1467-1500* (Savage, MD, 1990).

15. Letter of Erasmus to Guibé, in Mynors, *Collected Works,* II, pp. 214-15.

16. Quoted in Labande, *Charles VIII,* p. 505.

17. Villari, *Dispacci,* III, p. 485.

18. On Budé, see D. McNeil, *Guillaume Budé and Humanism in the Reign of Francis I* (Geneva, 1975). On Ganay as a patron of humanism, see E. de Ganay, *Un chancelier de France sous Louis XII: Jehan de Ganay* (Paris, 1932).

19. Le Ferron, "De Rebus," fol. 46.

20. For St-Gelais's search for royal patronage, see C. Scollen, "Octovien de Saint-Gelais' translation of the *Aeneid*: poetry or propaganda?" *Bibliothèque d'humanisme et renaissance* 39 (1977), pp. 253-61. On Anne as a patron of art and letters, see Gabory, *Anne de Bretagne*, pp. 157-71.

21. E.g., Tilley, *Dawn*, p. 325: "No School [of French literature] was ever so foolish, so dull, or so pretentious."

22. M. Rothstein, "Jean Lemaire de Belges' *Illustrations de Gaule et Singularitez de Troyes*: Politics and Unity," *Bibliothèque d'Humanisme et Renaissance* 52 (1990), pp. 593-609.

23. A. Jouanna, "La Quête des Origines dans L'Historiographie Française de la fin du XVe siècle et du Début du XVIe," in Chevalier, *La France de la fin du XV siècle*, pp. 302-11; J. Beard, "Letters from the Elysian Fields: A Group of Poems for Louis XII," *Bibliothèque d'humanisme et renaissance* 31 (1969), pp. 27-38. Scheller, "Gallia cisalpina," pp. 5-6. D'Auton wrote an "Epistre de preux Hector transmise au roy Loys XIIe" (1511), in which he claimed Hector as Louis's ancestor.

24. Labande, *Charles VIII*, p. 495.

25. In Picot, *Recueil des sotties*, I, pp. 196-231.

26. Quoted by C. Lenient, *La Satire en France au Moyen Age* (Paris, 1877), p. 371; also Brantôme, *Oeuvres complètes*, VIII, p. 315.

27. D'Auton, *Chroniques*, III, pp. 352-53.

28. Picot, *Recueil des sotties*, II, pp. 68ff. See the discussion in H. Arden, *Fools' Plays: A Study of Satire in the Sottie* (Cambridge, 1980).

29. J. Britnell, *Jean Bouchet* (Edinburgh, 1986); Picot, *Recueil des sotties*, I, p. iv.

30. C. O'Malley, *Andreas Vesalius of Brussels 1514-1564* (Berkeley, CA, 1964), pp. 44-46.

31. D'Auton, *Chroniques*, III, p. 100 and note.

32. A. de Beatis, *Travel Journal*, translated by J. Hale (London, 1979), p. 133.

33. M. Melot, "Politique et architecture: Essai sur Blois et Le Blésois sous Louis XII," *Gazette des beaux-arts* 70 (1967), pp. 317-28.

34. N. Miller, *French Renaissance Fountains* (New York, 1977), pp. 59-61.

35. G. Tournoy-Theon, "Fausto Andrelini et la cour de France," in *Humanisme français au début de la Renaissance* (Paris, 1973), pp. 65-79; Tilley, *Dawn*, pp. 381-94. An eighteenth-century drawing was detailed enough to allow for a replica of the destroyed statue to be made in 1857 and put back in place at Blois.

36. See Harsgor, *Personnel*, IV, pp. 2601-20, on the Italianate features of the houses of Louis's councillors.

37. R. Weiss, "The Castle of Gaillon in 1509-10," *Journal of the Warburg and Courtland Institutes* 16 (1953), pp. 1-12. See also E. Chiral, *Un premier foyer de la Renaissance — Le Château de Gaillon* (Paris, 1952).

38. A. Deville, *Comptes de dépenses de la construction du Château de Gaillon* (Paris, 1850), p. xxi; Scheller, "Gallia cisalpina," p. 56.

39. P. Le Verdier, ed., *L'Entrée de Roi Louis XII . . . à Rouen (1508)* (Rouen, 1900); Scheller, "Gallia cisalpina," pp. 49-50.

40. Scheller, "Gallia cisalpina," pp. 55-56.

41. See G. Huppert, *Les Bourgeois Gentilshommes* (Chicago, 1977), pp. 34-36, on Bohier's patient scheming to acquire the *seigneurie* of Chenonceaux, which he did in 1513.

42. D'Auton, *Chroniques*, III, p. 360; Louise de Savoie, "Journal," p. 391; Lacroix, *Histoire*, II, p. 294. Louis crossed the Seine by barge in 1505 instead of using the Pont St-Cloud.

43. *Registres de l'hôtel de ville*, I, pp. 18ff. A fascinating set of records on the rebuilding of the bridge is in this collection.

44. Contrary to Bridge, *History of France* V, p. 145; and Quilliet, *Louis XII*, p. 372, Louis did not entrust the building of the bridge to Giocondo. He was essentially a consultant. G. Brice, *Description de la ville de Paris* (Paris, 1713), p. 535.

45. *Registres de l'hôtel de ville*, I, p. 155; Tommasseo, *Relations*, II, p. 598.

46. D'Auton, *Chroniques*, II, pp. 102-4. The local clergy blamed the monstrosity on the frequency of the sin of sodomy in Lombardy.

47. *Archives de l'art français*, 2nd series, I, pp. 15-142.

48. Quilliet, *Louis XII*, p. 459.

49. Tilley, *Dawn*, p. 561.

50. Chiral, *Gaillon*, pp. 110-11.

51. J. Adhémar, "Une Galerie des portraits italiens à Amboise en 1500," *Gazette des Beaux Arts* 86 (1975), pp. 98-105.

52. Scheller, "Gallia cisalpina," pp. 26-27.

53. A. de Montaiglon, "La famille des Juste en Italie et en France," *Gazette des Beaux-Arts* (1875), 385 ff; (1876), 552 ff. An Antoine de Juste received 42 *l* in 1510 as a gardener of Blois. BN, Fonds nouvelles acquisitions français 7647, fol. 175-76.

54. M. Cermenati, "Le roi qui voulait importer en France la Cène de Léonard de Vinci," in M. Mignon, ed., *Léonard de Vinci 1519-1919* (Rome, 1919), pp. 8-26.

55. D'Auton, *Chroniques*, IV, p. 293 and note; Desjardins, *Négociations*, I, pp. 210-12; E. Décluze, *Saggio intorno a Leonardo da Vinci con due lettre inedite di Luigi XII* (Sienna, 1844).

56. B. Meyer, "Louis XII, Leonardo and the *Burlington House Cartoon*," *The Art Bulletin* 51 (1975). She finds implausible the argument in J. Wasserman, "The Dating and Patronage of Leonardo's Burlington House Cartoon," *The Art Bulletin* 53 (1971), pp. 312-25, that the Burlington House Carton was a preliminary sketch for the painting.

57. E. McCurdy, *The Mind of Leonardo Da Vinci* (New York, 1928), pp. 101-6. Whether Leonardo had any role in Louis's Milanese entries is also in dispute. Scheller, "Gallia cisalpina," p. 8n.

58. B. Nardini, *Michelangelo His Life and Works*, trans. by I. Quigly (n.p., 1977), pp. 69-71.

59. See d'Auton, *Chroniques*, IV, p. 351n.

60. The story may be apocryphal. An earlier version of the song appears to have been written for Louis XI. E. Clinksdale, "Josquin and Louis XI," *Acta Musicologica* 38 (1966), pp. 67-69. H. Brown, *Music in the Renaissance* (Englewood Cliffs, NJ, 1976), p. 121, suggests that it was the song "*Guillaume s'en va chauffer*," to which the story applied.

61. Brown, *Music in the Renaissance*, p. 117.

62. Ibid., pp. 121-78; P. Chaillon, "Les musiciens de Nord à la cour de Louis XII," in F. Lesure, ed., *La Renaissance dans les provinces de Nord* (Paris, 1956), pp. 63-69; J-M. Vaccaro, "L'Apogée de la Musique Flamande à la Cour de France à la fin du XVe siècle," in *La France de la Fin du XVe siècle*, pp. 253-64; R. Sherr, "The Membership of the Chapels of Louis XII and Anne de Bretagne in the Years Preceding their Deaths," *Journal of Musicology* 6 (1988), pp. 60-81.

63. D'Auton, *Chroniques*, III, 90n, 93; Chaillon, "Les musiciens," pp. 63-64; Brown, *Music in the Renaissance*, p. 147.

64. E. Rice, "The Patrons of French Humanism, 1490-1520," in A. Molho, ed., *Renaissance Studies in Honor of Hans Baron* (Dekalb, IL, 1971), pp. 687-702.

NOTES TO CHAPTER 12

1. There are fourteen letters supporting Castelnau in BN, Fonds nouvelles acquisitions français 499, fol. 1-14. It appears that several letters were never sent, since they lack addressees.

2. Ganay, *Jehan de Ganay*, p. 79. For a good summary of the problems of filling major benefices in this era, see Maulde, *Origines*, pp. 125-34.

3. See P. Ourliac, "The Concordat of 1472: An Essay on the Relations between Louis XI and Sixtus IV," in P. Lewis, ed., *The Recovery of France in the Fifteenth Century* (London, 1971), pp. 102-84.

4. As P. Imbart de La Tour stated: "From 1483 to 1516 the history of [chapter] elections is to give an account of quarrels." *Les Origines de la Réforme*, 4 vols. (Paris, 1905-35), II, p. 219. See also J. Thomas, *Le Concordat de 1516*, 3 vols. (Paris, 1910), I, pp. 200-269; J. Vidal, "Une crise épiscopale à Pamiers 1467-1524," *Revue de l'Histoire de l'Eglise de France* 14 (1928), pp. 305-64; and Harsgor, *Personnel*, IV, pp. 2451-63. Harsgor emphasizes the advantage the royal councillors and their relatives had in the hunt for benefices.

5. For Julius II's bull reappointing d'Amboise, see BN, Collection Dupuy 85, fol. 1-9, which has a description of his powers. See also Imbart de La Tour, *Origines*, II, pp. 183-85.

6. C. Belmon, *Le Bienheureux François d'Estaing, Evêque de Rodez* (Albi, 1924), pp. 68-70. The fact that Louis had favored d'Estaing with an important office yet refused to support him for the bishopric is intriguing, but there is no evidence to explain it.

7. According to Imbart de La Tour, *Origines*, II, pp. 222-23, the chapter elected d'Allemagne; but the record of the appeal to the Grand Conseil has Tonnerre as the winner. BN, Fonds français 5093, fol. 271-72. Tonnerre received the papal bulls for the see.

8. Vidal, "Crise épiscopale," p. 307; Imbart de La Tour, *Origines*, II, p. 235; Ourliac, "Relations between Louis XI and Sixtus IV," pp. 158-83.

9. Harsgor, *Personnel*, IV, pp. 2417-28.

10. M. Edelstein, "Les Origines sociales de l'épiscopat sous Louis XII et François I," *Revue d'histoire moderne et contemporaine* 20 (1978), 239-47; M. Perronet, *Les évêques de l'ancien France*, 2 vols. (Paris, 1978), I, pp. 477-94. Edelstein's count of Louis's bishops also included four princes of blood and eighteen prelates whose social status she could not determine.

11. D'Auton, *Chroniques* IV, pp. 3-9.

12. H. Martin, "Un prédicateur au début de la Renaissance: Jean Clérée O.P. (1455-1507)," *Revue d'Histoire de l'Eglise de France* 77 (1991), pp. 185-206. Queen Anne's confessor is credited with securing the position of king's confessor for Clerée, a fellow Dominican. A fine discussion of preaching in this era can be found in L. Taylor, *Soldiers of Christ: Preaching in Late Medieval and Reformation France* (Oxford, 1992).

13. Imbart de La Tour, *Origines*, II, pp. 278-80; Vidal, "Crise épiscopale," pp. 346-49. At one time or another, d'Albret controlled all of the sees of Foix, Béarn, and Navarre, the areas of southwestern France that his family dominated.

14. D'Auton, *Chroniques*, IV, pp. 121-22; Sanuto, *Diarii*, VII, p. 69.

15. Of the bishops in place in 1516, seven had been eighteen or younger when they were appointed, but it is not clear in whose reign they were seated. Perronet, *Evêques*, I, p. 447.

16. Quoted in Maulde, *Origines*, p. 141. See Maulde's chapter 7 for a wide-ranging examination of the problems in the clergy in Louis's era.

17. Luchaire, *Alain Le Grand*, p. 35.

18. Imbart de la Tour, *Origines*, II, pp. 261-62.

19. A description of his rather limited ideas for church reform are in BN, Fonds français 2961.

20. D'Auton, *Chroniques*, II, pp. 218-20.

21. *Ordonnances des roys*, XXI, pp. 229-30.

22. D'Auton, *Chroniques*, III, pp. 220-22. On the reformed house in Paris, see Piton, "L'Idéal épiscopale," pp. 81-83.

23. D'Auton, *Chroniques*, III, pp. 228-34. D'Auton included the monks' appeal in full. It gives an interesting perspective on the anti-reform position.

24. BN, Fonds latin 5149, fol. 59.

25. See below, Chapter 15.

26. Vellay, "Histoire," fol. 45 r-v; Molinet, *Chroniques*, II, p. 526; Valbelle, *Histoire Journalière*, p. 16.

27. BN, Fonds Latin 3375, fol. 1-2; E. Cameron, *The Reformation of the Heretics: The Waldensians of the Alps, 1480-1580* (Oxford, 1984), pp. 25-61; H. Lea, *A History of the Inquisition of the Middle Ages*, 3 vols., (New York, 1955), II, pp. 60-61.

28. Cameron, *Reformation*, p. 59.

29. Valbelle, *Histoire Journalière*, p. 8; D. Iancu, *Les Juifs en Provence (1475-1501)* (Aix, 1981), pp. 21-30, 179-84. Iancu printed the edicts on pp. 219-23, 290-91.

30. Guicciardini, *History of Italy*, III, p. 238. He and other observers frequently mentioned d'Amboise's ambition to become pope.

31. Ibid.

32. BN, Fonds français 2924, fol. 34.

33. Sources for the two papal elections of 1503 include J. Burchard, *Diarium*, 3 vols. (Paris, 1883-85), II, pp. 245ff; Sanuto, *Diarii*, V, pp. 78ff; Pastor, *History of the Popes*, VI, pp. 185-216.

34. Guicciardini, *History of Italy*, III, pp. 105-06.

35. A. Giustinian, *Dispacci*, ed. by P. Villari, 3 vols. (Florence, 1876), II, pp. 175-77.

36. D'Auton, *Chroniques*, III, p. 202, gives the number as 100 royal archers, but BN, Fonds français 25718, fol. 90, has 200.

37. Guicciardini, *History of Italy*, III, p. 239; D'Auton, *Chroniques*, III, p. 250.

38. Giustinian, *Dispacci*, II, p. 181.

39. Ibid., pp. 200-1; Pastor, *History of the Popes*, VI, p. 195.

40. Giustinian, *Dispacci*, II, p. 181; Sanuto, *Diarii*, V, p. 516.

41. K. Setton, *The Papacy and the Levant 1204-1571*, 4 vols. (Philadelphia, 1976-84), III, p. 35.

42. BN, Fonds Dupuy 85, fol. 3. See also d'Auton, *Chroniques*, III, p. 285; Sanuto, *Diarii*, V, pp. 546-47; and Tailhé, *Histoire de Louis XII*, I, p. 348.

43. Guicciardini, *History of Italy*, III, p. 255.

NOTES TO CHAPTER 13

1. Desjardins, *Négociations*, II, pp. 190-93, 227; Cloulas, *The Borgias*, pp. 253-69; Pastor, *History of the Popes*, VI, pp. 241-45.

2. Detailed contemporary Italian accounts of the troubles in Genoa are E. Pandiani, "Un Anno di Storia Genovese," *Atti della Societa Ligure de storia patria* 37 (1905); and Salrago, *Cronaca di Genua*, pp. 457-492. For the divisions in Genoa, see Coles, "Crisis of a Renaissance Society," pp. 17-47.

3. D'Auton, *Chroniques*, IV, pp. 87-94. D'Auton, who accompanied Louis XII on his expedition of 1507 to Genoa, has the best French account of the revolt. See also Sanuto, *Diarii*, VI, passim; Bridge, *History of France*, III, pp. 266-91; and Coles, "Crisis of a Renaissance Society," pp. 35-41.

4. Desjardins, *Négociations*, II, pp. 206-7.

5. D'Auton, *Chroniques*, IV, pp. 94-143.

6. St-Gelais, *Histoire de Louis XII*, p. 193; Desjardins, *Négociations*, II, pp. 210-11; Louis's itinerary is in AN, KK 88.

7. The member of lances is based on the roll of lance companies in d'Auton, *Chroniques*, IV, pp. 161-62, but the figure assumes that the companies were at full strength, which was rarely true.

8. Ibid., p. 164. It is not clear what d'Auton meant by the term "galleon," but it is a very early use of the word.

9. Ibid., p. 178. Other contemporary sources include the anonymous *La conqueste de Gennes . . . Avec l'entrée du Roy en la dicte ville de Gennes* (Genoa, 1507); in *Archives curieuses*, II, pp. 13-24; "La bataille et assault de Gennes donne par le treschrestien roy de France Loys XII," in BN, Fonds français 7647, fol. 21-27; Sanuto, *Diarii*, VII, pp. 66-68; and Desjardins, *Négociations*, II, pp. 234-48.

10. Pandiani, "Un Anno di Storia Genovese," p. 270. See also Jehan Marot, *Le voyage de Gênes*, ed. by G. Trisolini, (Geneva, 1974); and Scheller, "Gallia cisalpina," pp. 36-41.

11. D'Auton, *Chroniques*, IV, pp. 276, 279-80; Sanuto, *Diarii*, VII, pp. 29, 104. See AN, K 79, fol. 31ff, for a list of the properties confiscated from the rebels.

12. "On dire Gennes la Superbe, pour ce qu'elle ne fust jamais prinse par force, . . . et l'appellant on maintenant Gennes l'Humiliade et non Gennes la Superbe." *La conqueste de Gennes*, p. 24.

13. Ibid., p. 18. See Sherman, "The Selling of Louis XII," pp. 122-23, for a discussion of the French propaganda on the defeat of Genoa.

14. Scheller, "Gallia cisalpina," pp. 39-40.

15. D'Auton, *Chroniques*, IV, pp. 318-19, 368n. See also St-Gelais, *Histoire de Louis XII*, pp. 203-4.

16. BN, Fonds françois 26110, fol. 795; C. de Seyssel, *Les louanges de bon roi Louis XII* (Paris, 1587), p. 106. It was this act as much as any he did that earned Louis his reputation for concern for the common people.

17. D'Auton, *Chroniques*, IV, p. 332.

18. Pastor, *History of the Popes*, VI, pp. 292-93.

19. Maulde, *L'Entrevue de Savone (1507)* (Paris, 1896); d'Auton, *Chroniques*, IV, p. 336.

20. The pregnancy resulted in the birth of a daughter in October, but she soon died. According to the Venetian ambassador, the king and queen bore the disappointment stoically. Sanuto, *Diarii*, VII, p. 165.

21. Ibid., p. 117; Sherman, "Selling of Louis XII," pp. 124-25.

22. Coles, "Crisis of a Renaissance Society," pp. 41-42.

23. L. Bourgeois, *Quand la cour de France vivait à Lyon* (Paris, 1980), p. 17.

24. CSP Spain, I, 399, where Maximilian warned Henry VII to beware of "French foxes."

25. *Lettres de Louis XII*, I, pp. 54-55. See also d'Auton, *Chroniques*, IV, pp. 27-28.

26. *Lettres de Louis XII*, I, pp. 56-60; Höfler, "Die Despechen," pp. 92-94. BN, Fonds français 5013, fol. 153-54, contains a quittance for the pay of French troops in the service of Gueldres.

27. CSP Spain, I, pp. 379-81.

28. Ibid., 64-91; *Lettres de Louis XII*, I, p. 63.

29. CSP Spain, II, p. 27.

30. Much of it is in the four volumes of *Lettres de Louis XII*; the rest is in Le Glay, ed., *Correspondance de l'Empereur Maximilien I et de Marguerite d'Autriche de 1507 à 1519*, 2 vols. (Paris, 1839).

31. Le Glay, *Correspondance*, I, pp. 6-30, 106; Sanuto, *Diarii*, VII, p. 656.

32. *Lettres de Louis XII*, I, pp. 120-21. The mutual safe conducts and d'Amboise's commission are in BN, Fonds françois 5093, fol. 1-3, 77.

33. Le Glay, *Correspondance*, I, pp. 108-9; *Registres de l'hôtel de ville*, I, p. 151.

34. Sanuto, *Diarii*, VII, p. 688.

35. BN, Fonds français 2962.

36. Desjardins, *Négociations*, II, pp. 103-04, 153-54. Rumors of Louis's demise were always rampant. In June 1511 alone, Venice received three such reports. Sanuto, *Diarii*, XII, pp. 227, 230.

37. Sanuto, *Diarii*, V, p. 518. Throughout 1508, the ambassador continually told the Signory how warm the king and the cardinal were to Venice.

38. Pastor, *History of the Popes*, VI, pp. 274-75; d'Auton, *Chroniques*, IV, pp. 70-71. The campaign against Bologna from the papal point of view was described by Paride Grassis, the papal master of ceremonies. *Le due spedizioni militari de Giulio II*, edited by L. Frati (Bologna, 1886).

39. See Landucci, *Florentine Diary*, pp. 231-32, for the glee of the Florentines at Venice's troubles at this time.

40. Sanuto, *Diarii*, VII, p. 554.

41. *Histoire de Bayard*, XV, p. 737.

42. Sanuto, *Diarii*, VII, p. 725. See p. 695 for an interesting account of how the Venetian ambassador unsuccessfully sought to get information from Louis, even following him on a hunt.

43. CSP Italy, I, pp. 334-37; Desjardins, *Négociations*, II, pp. 298-99. See Setton, *The Papacy and the Levant*, III, pp. 51ff, for a lucid description of the complicated diplomacy of the era.

44. Dumont, *Corps diplomatiques*, IV, 116; Sanuto, *Diarii*, VIII, pp. 91-95.

45. BN, Collection Dupuy 85, fol. 26, signed by six captains, including Bayard.

46. *Histoire de Bayard*, pp. 430-32; Lavisse, *Histoire de France*, V part 1, pp. 88-89; Bridge, *History of France*, IV, p. 24.

47. BN, Fonds français 2929, fol. 46-47.

48. For the Battle of Agnadello, see Sanuto, *Diarii*, VIII, pp. 218-70; *Histoire de Bayard*, XV, pp. 267-71; Desjardins, *Négociations*, II, pp. 303-24; and Bridge, IV, pp. 33-36.

49. That is the number given by Louis in his letter to Paris announcing his victory. *Registres de l'hôtel de ville*, I, p. 152.

50. See M. Fogel, *Les cérémonies de l'information dans la France du XVI au XVIII siècles* (Paris, 1989), on the practice of singing Te Deums, which she proposes Louis began at this time.

51. Floranges, *Mémoires*, XVI, p. 177; Machiavelli's reports as summarized in Villari, *Machiavelli*, I, p. 500.

52. Desjardins, *Négociations*, II, pp. 381-89; Lacroix, *Histoire*, III, p. 88.

53. Sanuto, *Diarii*, IX, p. 41.

54. Desjardins, *Négociations*, II, p. 395.

55. CSP Spain, II, pp. 22-24; Maulde, *Louise et François*, p. 289.

56. Sanuto, *Diarii*, XI, pp. 75-76.

57. Setton, *The Papacy and Levant*, III, pp. 27-29.

58. *C'est la tresnoble et tresexcellente victoire du roy nostre sire Loys douziesme . . . sur les venitiens* (n.p., n.d.), quoted by Sherman, "Selling of Louis XII," p. 174. Nonetheless, rumors continued to circulate that Louis had died. Sanuto, IX, pp. 180-84.

59. Desjardins, *Négociations*, II, pp. 381-89.

NOTES TO CHAPTER 14

1. Desjardins, *Négociations*, II, p. 92. Pandolfini was in France off and on for ten years. Louis grew so fond of him that he allowed him to put the fleur-de-lis on his coat of arms. Ibid., p. 89.

2. See BN, Fonds français 5093, fol. 14-15 for Ganay's letter of provision. See also Ganay, *Un chancelier de France*, pp. 16-20.

3. Deville, *Comptes de Gaillon*, p. 482; Jacob, *Histoire*, IV, p. 151.

4. St-Gelais, *Histoire de Louis XII*, pp. 227-28; Sanuto, *Diarii*, IX, p. 412; *Lettres de Louis XII*, I, pp. 233-36; Desjardins, et al., eds., *Négociations*, II, pp. 460-503 passim; Maulde, *Diplomatie*, III, p. 441.

5. Desjardins, *Négociations*, II, pp. 414, 460, 503-4; Machiavelli, *Opere*, VI, pp. 105-6; Villari, *Machiavelli*, I, p. 511.

6. Desjardins, *Négociations*, II, pp. 509, 515. Both Nasi and Machiavelli, "Description of the Affairs of France," p. 12, have the name Boucicault, but there was no one of that name in the French government after the death of Maréchal de Boucicault during Charles VII's reign, whereas Bouchage was active for most of Louis's reign.

7. Ganay, *Un chancelier de France*, p. 79; A. Buisson, *Le Chancelier Antoine Duprat* (Paris, 1935), p. 98; Floranges, *Memoires*, XVI, pp. 263-64. Louis's order to the city of Paris, Ganay's birthplace, to prepare for his funeral is in *Registres de l'hôtel de ville*, I, p. 185.

8. Guenée, *Tribunaux et gens de justice*, chapter 2; Doucet, *Les Institutions*, I, pp. 59-64; Bridge, *History of France*, V, pp. 64-70.

9. *Ordonnances des roys*, XIV, pp. 283-314.

10. The commission to redact the coutumes of Auvergne, given to Antoine Duprat for his native region, is in BN, Fonds français 5093, fol. 227. The cost of publicizing the finished law code came to 267 *l*. Fol. 209.

11. Buisson, *Duprat*, p. 70.

12. J. Dawson, "The Codification of the French Customs," *Michigan Law Review* 38 (1945), 774.

13. *Ordonnances des roys*, XXI, pp. 420-36.

14. Quilliet, *Louis XII*, p. 341.

15. *Ordonnances des roys*, XXI, pp. 443-47.

16. Ibid., p. 387.

17. Ibid., pp. 385-98.

18. According to F. Spooner, *The International Economy and Monetary Movements in France 1493-1725* (Cambridge, MA, 1972), p. 92, using 1471 as a price index of 100, prices rose to 111.5 by 1486, then fell to 106.6 by 1514.

19. *Ordonnances des roys*, XXI, p. 342. In 1488 the écu au soleil had been pegged at 30 *s* 3 *d*.

20. Spooner, *International Economy*, p. 334. The high numbers of gold coins minted reflected the fact that they were far more likely to be clipped. Badly clipped coins were melted down and reminted.

21. *Ordonnances des roys*, XXI, p. 405; AN, KK 86, fol. 1.

22. Spont, *La Taille en Languedoc*, p. 55. The average monthly expenses of the *bouche du roi*, which went for the court's food and drink, rose from 1,017 *l* in 1510 to 2,138 *l* in 1518 under Francis I. BN, Fonds français 25272, fol. 1-18.

23. The edit to levy the *crue*, calling for a second 500,000 if the emperor declared war, is in BN, Fonds français 5093, fol. 247-48.

24. Ledru, *Maison de Mailly*, II, p. 263. The rates were 100 *s* per man and 25 *s* per ton.

25. Sanuto, *Diarii*, VI, p. 208.

26. For the more ambitious voyage of the Norman ship the *Espoir*, in 1503-4 to Brazil, see the journal of its captain published in C. Julien, ed., *Les Français en Amérique pendant la première moitié du XVIe siècle* (Paris, 1946), pp. 25-45. Although it brought back several natives to Honfleur, there is no evidence that Louis was ever made aware of the voyage. For French activities in the Atlantic to 1515, see R. Tomlinson, *The Struggle for Brazil, 1500-1550* (New York, 1970), pp. 46-58.

27. *Ordonnances des roys*, XXI, pp. 477, 489.

28. BN, Fonds nouvelles acquisitions français 7647, fol. 291-301; *Registres de l'hôtel de ville*, I, pp. 191-96.

29. Sanuto, *Diarii*, XVII, p. 27. Not that it would have been much consolation to Louis, but Nasi put Henry's expenses at 600,000 francs a month.

30. BN, Fonds français 5093, fol. 272-73; Collection Dupuy 61, fol. 62; *Registres de l'hôtel de ville*, I, pp. 201-7; Spont, *La taille*, p. 7.

31. *Ordonnances des roys*, XXI, pp. 529-31.

32. Ibid., XXI, pp. 564, 575.

33. Maulde, *Origines*, p. 287n.

34. Ledru, *Maison de Mailly*, II, pp. 265-66.

35. Potter, *War and Government*, p. 25n; H. Heller, *Blood and Iron: Civil Wars in Sixteenth-Century France* (Montreal, 1991), p. 42. According to V. Raytses, "Le Programme de l'insurrection d'Agen en 1514," *Annales de Midi* 93 (1981), pp. 255-77, there is no reason to impute the riot of 1514 to royal taxes. But Raytses's figures (p. 268) do show that the *tailles* in Agen rose from the low of 185 *l* in 1506 to 892 in 1513.

36. Heller, *Blood and Iron*, p. 25. I have to question Heller's acceptance of his source's numbers for the soldiers, 6,000, and their casualties, 300. It seems most improbable that the people of Caen, who surely numbered less than 10,000, could have routed so large a force of soldiers at the cost of only one dead resident.

37. Baulant, "Les prix des grains," p. 538.

38. St-Gelais, *Histoire de Louis XII*, pp. 225-26.

NOTES TO CHAPTER 15

1. In Sanuto, *Diarii*, XIII, pp. 573-94.

2. Guicciardini, *History of Italy*, V, pp. 53-54; Pastor, *History of the Popes*, VI, p. 323.

3. CSP Spain, II, pp. 33-35, 42; Sanuto, *Diarii*, X, pp. 89, 160.

4. Sanuto, *Diarii*, X, p. 313; CSP Spain, II, 46; St-Gelais, *Histoire de Louis XII*, p. 223.

5. St-Gelais, *Histoire de Louis XII*, pp. 229-30. He ended his history at this point.

6. *Lettres de Louis XII*, III, p. 148.

7. See F. Baumgartner, "Louis XII's Gallican Crisis of 1510-13," in *Politics, Ideology and the Law in Early Modern Europe*, ed. by A. Bakos (Rochester, 1994); and I. Cloulas, *Jules II*, (Paris, 1990), pp. 183-250, for a more detailed account of the affair.

8. Quoted in Pastor, *History of the Popes*, VI, pp. 326-27.

9. CSP Venice, II, 33; Sanuto, *Diarii*, XI, pp. 108-439, passim; Pastor, *History of the Popes*, VI, pp. 327-29; La Roncière, *Marine française*, III, pp. 84-88.

10. CSP Venice, II, p. 33.

11. Villari, *Machiavelli*, I, pp. 509-10; Pastor, *History of the Popes*, VI, p. 329; Maulde, *Diplomatie*, III, p. 457.

12. These numbers are given in a letter to Margaret of Austria from her ambassador in France. *Lettres de Louis XII*, II, p. 29. See also Sanuto, *Diarii*, X, pp. 113-297 passim.

13. A record of the proceedings at Tours is in BN, Fonds Latin 1559, fol. 2-10. See also Ganay, *Jehan de Ganay*, p. 6ff.

14. CSP Venice, II, pp. 33-36; CSP Spain, II, p. 53.

15. For W. Ullman, "Julius II and the Schismatic Cardinals," *Studies in Church History*, 9 (1972), 177-93, Julius's failure to fulfill his oath was the strongest justification for the Council of Pisa.

16. *Lettres de Louis XII*, II, p. 48.

17. CSP Spain, II, pp. 46, 52.

18. Sanuto, *Diarii*, XI, p. 250ff; Tailhé, *Histoire de Louis XII*, II, p. 250.

19. CSP Spain, II, p. 52. See also the story in *Histoire de Bayard*, pp. XV, pp. 360-67, where Bayard vehemently opposed the duke of Ferrara's plan to poison Julius, because "God would never forgive so horrible a thing." But note that the duke was willing to contemplate it.

20. *History of Italy*, V, p. 149. For the siege see also Pastor, *History of the Popes*, VI, pp. 340-42; Sanuto, *Diarii*, XI, pp. 712-783, passim. Louis was convinced that Julius was dying and made ready to send an envoy with a large sum of money to Rome for the impending conclave in order to elect Cardinal Briçonnet pope. A. Renaudet, *Le Concile Gallican de Pise-Milan* (Paris, 1922), pp. 160-61.

21. Guicciardini, *History of Italy*, V, p. 173. He argued that d'Amboise was a poor commander and kept his post only because of his uncle.

22. A report to Louis on the capture of Bologna detailed the spoils taken: 1,100 horses and 40 pieces of artillery, including six great guns. BN, Fonds nouvelles acquisitions françaises 7647, fol. 230-32.

23. BN, Fonds latin 1559, fol. 20-26; *Lettres de Louis XII*, II, p. 142. See also Imbart de La Tour, *Origines*, II, pp. 145-46; and O. de La Brosse, *Le Pape et le Concile* (Paris, 1965), pp. 54-66.

24. The invitation to Charles of Habsburg is in *Lettres de Louis XII4*, II, pp. 235-41. See also BN, collection Dupuy 85, fol. 28-29; and Sanuto, *Diarii*, XII, pp. 249-54.

25. Guicciardini, *History of Italy*, V, pp. 248-51; Sanuto, *Diarii*, XI, pp. 203-23; Pastor, *History of the Popes*, VI, pp. 352-54. Landucci, *Florentine Diary*, pp. 254-47, indicates that Florence was under interdict for several months.

26. Sanuto, *Diarii*, XII, p. 56; Gabory, *Anne de Bretagne*, pp. 213-14.

27. Maulde, *Origines*, p. 273.

28. Britnell, *Jean Bouchet*, pp. 160-71; Beard, "Letters from the Elysian Fields," pp. 27-38.

29. Gringore did receive money from the city of Paris on several occasions for his plays and poems. Picot, *Recueil des sotties*, II, p. 111. On Gringore, see the introduction to *Oeuvres complètes*, ed. by C. d'Hericault et al., 2 vols. (Paris, 1858-77); C. Oulmont, *Pierre Gringore* (Paris, 1911); and Sherman, "Selling of Louis XII," pp. 239-72.

30. In Picot, *Recueil des sotties*, II, pp. 132-73.

31. In J. Lemaire de Belges, *Oeuvres*, ed. by J. Stecher (Geneva, 1969), III, pp. 231-359. There is a detailed analysis of the work in J. Britnell, "The Antipapalism of Jean Lemaire de Belges' *Le Traicté de la difference des schismes et des Conciles*," *Sixteenth Century Journal* 24 (1993), 783-800.

32. Ibid., pp. 313-14.

33. Louis's letter is in BN, Fonds latin 16576, fol. 34. The works of Vio and Almain are discussed in O. La Brosse, *Le Pape et le Concile* (Paris, 1965).

34. *Lettres de Louis XII*, II, pp. 421-22.

35. On the Council of Pisa, see Renaudet, *Le Concile Gallican*, (Paris, 1922) especially the "*pièces justificatives*"; and L. Sandret, "Le Concile de Pise," *Revue des questions historiques* 34 (1883), pp. 425-56.

36. Sanuto, *Diarii,* XII, col. 77.

37. Guicciardini, *History of Italy,* V, p. 328; Desjardins, *Négociations,* II, pp. 543-44.

38. *Letters and Papers,* I, p. 495.

39. CSP Spain, II, pp. 523-26; Guicciardini, *History of Italy,* p. 232.

40. CSP Spain, II, pp. 57-59.

41. Ibid., p. 53; CSP Venice, II, p. 50.

42. There is no firsthand source for these orders to de Foix. The most immediate source is a report of the Florentine ambassador in France, which indicated that Louis had ordered de Foix to march to Rome. A letter to the papal legate in Bologna from his secretary in Rome, citing a report from Milan, provides more details. Renaudet, *Concile gallican,* p. 644; Desjardins, *Négociations,* II, pp. 577-78. Guicciardini was convinced of the report's accuracy. *History of Italy,* V, pp. 392-93.

43. *Letters and Papers,* I, p. 516.

44. *Histoire de Bayard,* XVI, pp. 1-15; *Letters and Papers,* I, pp. 516-18. See also Guicciardini, *History of Italy,* V, pp. 398-99; Sanuto, *Diarii,* XIII, pp. 472-525, passim; and Bridge, *History of France,* IV, pp. 130-37.

45. The principal sources for the Battle of Ravenna are *Histoire de Bayard,* XVI, pp. 22-55; Sanuto, *Diarii,* XIV, pp. 123-34, 176-80; Desjardins, *Négociations,* II, pp. 581-86; Guicciardini, *History of Italy,* V, pp. 401-29; *Lettres de Louis XII,* III, pp. 227-32. Modern accounts include Bridge, *History of France,* IV, pp. 142-72; and Oman, *Art of War,* pp. 130-50.

46. Desjardins, *Négociations,* II, p. 586.

47. Quoted by Sandret, "Le Concile de Pise," p. 451.

48. Floranges, *Mémoires,* XVI, pp. 220-21.

49. *Lettres de Louis XII,* III, pp. 197-235; Le Glay, *Négociations,* I, pp. 490-92.

50. Sanuto, *Diarii,* XIV, p. 168.

51. Floranges, *Mémoires,* XVI, p. 222; Quilliet, *Louis XII,* p. 412.

52. Sanuto, *Diarii,* XIV, p. 185.

53. Ibid., 202; Bridge, *History of France,* IV, p. 161.

54. Maulde, *Origines,* p. 325n.

55. BN, Fonds Baluze 14, fol. 159. See also D. Chambers, *Cardinal Bainbridge in the Court of Rome 1509 to 1514* (Oxford, 1965), pp. 38-39.

56. *Lettres de Louis XII,* III, pp. 273-74; Sanuto, *Diarii,* XIV, p. 46.

57. Sherman, "Selling of Louis XII," pp. 304-07.

58. *Letters and Papers,* I, p. 475.

59. Ibid., pp. 540-59; BN, Fonds français 2934, fol. 9.

60. This is the figure Henry gave Cardinal Bainbridge in Rome. Sanuto, *Diarii,* XIV, p. 268.

61. Ibid., p. 583; A. Spont, *Letters and Papers relating to the War with France, 1512-1513* (London, 1897), p. xxiii.

62. The *Cordelière* is often said to have had 1,500 people on board, but that number seems to be impossibly large. The Venetian ambassador in England reported that she carried 400 men, which seems more reasonable. CSP Venice, II, pp. 79-81; Sanuto, *Diarii,* XV, pp. 208-9, 228.

63. *Letters and Papers,* II, p. 590; Dumont, *Corps diplomatique,* IV, p. 69.

64. CSP Spain, II, p. 63-64.

65. The letter patent erecting the comté of Longueville into a duchy is in BN, Fonds français 2926, fol. 20.

66. CSP Spain, p. 73. For the campaign of 1512 in Navarre, see also Guicciardini, *History of Italy*, VI, pp. 88-92 (Guicciardini was in Spain at the time); CSP Venice, II, pp. 79-80; Bridge, *History of France*, IV, pp. 187-92.

67. CSP Spain, II, pp. 79-92. Apparently, neither Ferdinand nor Maximilian ever signed the treaty. See Le Glay, *Négociations*, I, p. 513.

68. Guicciardini, *History of Italy*, VI, pp. 118-22; P. Boissonnade, *Les négociations entre Louis XII et Ferdinand Le Catholique* (Mâcon, 1899), pp. 13-14.

69. CSP Spain, II, p. 93.

70. Sanuto, *Diarii*, XVI, pp. 119-23; Guicciardini, *History of Italy*, VI, pp. 95-96. Guicciardini related that there had been a sharp debate in Louis's council whether to make peace with Venice or the emperor. Robertet carried the day for a peace with Venice by relating a spy's report that Maximilian had recently said the French had injured him seventeen times, and he intended to take revenge for every time.

71. AN, K 1639, fol. 36; CSP Spain, II, pp. 104-5.

72. Sanuto, *Diarii*, XV, p. 557; Guicciardini, *History of Italy*, VI, pp. 108-9.

73. Sanuto, *Diarii*, XVI, pp. 26-29; *Lettres de Louis XII*, IV, pp. 63-97; Chambers, *Cardinal Bainbridge*, pp. 41-45. Bainbridge was the first English cardinal to attend a conclave since 1370.

74. Sanuto, *Diarii*, XVI, pp. 133-34.

NOTES TO CHAPTER 16

1. Floranges, *Mémoires*, XVI, pp. 233-34. Louis's choice for commander in Italy had originally been Charles de Bourbon, but La Trémoille pushed for the command and won it.

2. *Lettres de Louis XII*, IV, p. 248.

3. Sources for the Battle of Novara include Bouchet, *Panégyric du Chevallier*, XV, pp. 463-69; Floranges, *Mémoires*, XVI, pp. 238-47; Sanuto, *Diarii*, XVI, pp. 460-63; Guicciardini, *History of Italy*, VI, pp. 138-60; Oman, *History of the Art of War*, pp. 151-55.

4. CSP Spain, II, pp. 112-15. Ferdinand's and Leo X's ambassadors committed them also to the anti-French alliance, but neither was actively involved.

5. A. Lang, *A History of Scotland*, 5 vols. (Reprint, New York, 1970), I, p. 376.

6. Prégent's report and an English one are in *Letters and Papers*, I, pp. 835, 842-43. La Roncière, *Marine française*, III, pp. 104-10.

7. Sources for the campaign in Picardy included *Histoire de Bayard*, XVI, pp. 72-86; Floranges, *Mémoires*, XVI, 251-60; Sanuto, *Diarii*, XVI, pp. 424-655, XVII, pp. 1-184, passim; *Letters and Papers*, I, pp. 939-1016, passim; and C. Cruickshank, *Henry VIII and the Invasion of France* (New York, 1991).

8. So report *Histoire de Bayard*, XVI, p. 76; and Guicciardini, *History of Italy*, VI, p. 215.

9. Guicciardini, *History of Italy*, VI, p. 217.

10. CSP Venice, II, p. 135; Cruickshank, *Henry VIII*, p. 149.

11. Sanuto, *Diarii*, XVII, pp. 30-32.

12. Dumont, *Corps diplomatique*, IV, p. 175; Bouchet, *Panégyric du chevallier*, XIV, pp. 478-79; Guicciardini, *History of Italy*, VI, p. 222; Tailhé, *Histoire de Louis XII*, III, p. 335.

13. Guicciardini, *History of Italy*, VI, p. 220; *Histoire de Bayard*, XVI, p. 85; and Bouchet, *Panégyric du chevallier*, XIV, pp. 490-92. All agree that La Trémoille probably saved France and the king's anger was unjustified, and he soon repented of it.

14. Floranges, *Mémoires*, XVI, p. 251; Maulde, *Diplomatie*, III, p. 227n.

15. *Letters and Papers*, I, p. 972.

16. CSP Spain, II, pp. 118-92 passim; Desjardins, *Négociations*, II, p. 596; Floranges, *Mémoires*, XVI, p. 261.

17. Sanuto, *Diarii*, XVII, p. 483: "*mal de renele.*"

18. Louise de Savoie, "Journal," XVI, p. 394. Louise added that she had "fulfilled the charge honorably and amiably, as everyone knows." Was she protesting too much?

19. Brantôme, *Oeuvres*, VII, pp. 328-29.

20. Floranges, *Mémoires*, XVI, p. 261; AN, KK 78; *Registres de l'hôtel de ville*, I, pp. 208-10; H. Bloem, "The Processions and Decorations at the Royal Funeral of Anne of Brittany," *Bibliothèque d'humanisme et renaissance* 44 (1992), pp. 131-60. Bloem's article is based largely on a long description of Anne's funeral that Louis commissioned. Thirty-four copies are still extant.

21. Tailhé, *Histoire de Louis XII*, III, p. 258; Gabory, p. 224.

22. The decrees are in La Brosse, *Latran V*, pp. 97-98.

23. Thomas, *Le Concordat de 1516*, I, pp. 289-95.

24. Dumont, *Corps diplomatique*, IV, p. 175; Pastor, *History of the Popes*, VII, pp. 55-72.

25. Sanuto, *Diarii*, XVII, pp. 495-96.

26. *Letters and Papers*, I, p. 1154. She wrote much the same thing again two weeks later. Ibid., p. 1166.

27. Ibid., pp. 1186-97; CSP Spain, I, p. 205. Eleanor became Francis I's second wife in 1530.

28. Desjardins, *Négociations*, II, p. 601; CSP Venice, II, p. 167; *Letters and Papers*, I, p. 1200.

29. *Lettres de Louis*, IV, p. 328; Sanuto, *Diarii*, XVIII, pp. 145, 160, 195.

30. Floranges, *Mémoires*, XVI, p. 263; *Letters and Papers*, I, pp. 1155, 1215. Francis's investiture with Brittany is in *Ordonnances des roys*, XXI, p. 575. Louis declared that the investiture was done without prejudice to Renée's rights, but it is hard to see how that could have been true. In 1576 the Parlement awarded her only child, Anne of Ferrara, several estates as compensation. Gabory, *Anne de Bretagne*, pp. 263-71.

31. Floranges, *Mémoires*, XVI, pp. 263-64; Quilliet, *Louis XII*, p. 434.

32. F. Andrelini, *Les faictz et gestes de tres reverend pere monsieur le legate* (n.p., n.d.). In 1514 Francis's expenses came to over 140,000 *l*, and he had to borrow 10,000 from the royal treasury. Maulde, *Louise et François*, pp. 342-50.

33. *Letters and Papers*, I, p. 1298. Also *Lettres de Louis XII*, IV, p. 300.

34. Harsgor, *Personnel*, I, p. 436; Maulde, *Louise et François*, pp. 356-60.

35. Sanuto, *Diarii*, XVIII, pp. 236-306 passim; Desjardins, *Négociations*, II, pp. 628. Pandolfini's first mention of Mary Tudor as the likely bride dates to July 10. Ibid., p. 638.

36. Desjardins, *Négociations*, II, pp. 640-42. Information on this meeting of notables is very limited.

37. AN, KK 89, fol. 40; *Letters and Papers*, I, p. 1325. The sum Louis agreed to pay varies both in amount and between francs and crowns from source to source. The above is from what seems to be the most authoritative source, but it does require a payout period of nineteen years, which seems implausible.

38. AN, KK 77, piece 8; CSP Milan, p. 439; Dumont, *Corps diplomatiques*, IV, pp. 188-90. W. Richardson, *Mary Tudor: The White Queen* (Seattle, Washington, 1970), p. 84, points out that Mary's income from her French lands after her return to England averaged 6,150 pounds sterling, far less than properties worth 700,000 ducats should have generated.

39. Charles's reaction as related by a Venetian (CSP Venice, II, p. 201):

    It was said that when the Prince of Castile heard that his promised bride had been given to the King of France, he went immediately into his council chamber and said to his councillors, "Well! Am I to have my wife as you promised me?" Whereupon his councillors answered him, "You are young, but the King of France is the first King in

Christendom, and, having no wife, it rests with him to take for his queen any woman he pleases." During this conversation, Duke Charles, looking out of a window, saw a man with a hawk, and calling one of his councillors . . . said to him, "Go buy me that hawk." . . . The Duke put it on his fist. Then, having returned into the council chamber, he commenced plucking the hawk, the councillors meanwhile inquiring, "Sir! what are you doing?" The Duke still continued plucking the bird, and made answer: "Thou askest me why I plucked this hawk; he is young, you see, and has not yet been trained, and because he is young he is held in small account, and because he is young he squeaked not when I plucked him. Thus have you done by me: I am young, you have plucked me at your good pleasure; and because I was young I knew not how to complain; but bear in mind that for the future I shall pluck you."

40. *Letters and Papers*, I, pp. 1343, 1351; Sanuto, *Diarii*, XIX, pp. 167-68.

41. See a selection of descriptions of Mary in Bridge, *History of France*, IV, pp. 250-51.

42. CSP Milan, p. 437. The original apparently no longer exists, but what is thought to be a copy does. Richardson, *White Queen*, pp. 275-79.

43. Ibid., p. 440.

44. CSP Spain, II, pp. 244-46; AN, J 655; Desjardins, *Négociations*, II, pp. 651-53, 659. Richard De la Pole had been the duke of Suffolk, but Henry VIII had given the title to Brandon.

45. Sanuto, *Diarii*, XIX, p. 6; CSP Spain, II, pp. 229-37.

46. There is a vast number of sources for Mary's arrival and marriage. See especially Sanuto, *Diarii*, XIX, pp. 196-230; CSP Venice, II, pp. 194-212; *Letters and Papers*, I, pp. 1388-1420. H. Cocheris, ed., *Entrées de Marye d'Angleterre . . . à Abbeville et à Paris* (Paris, 1859); Floranges, *Mémoires*, XVI, pp. 265-68; A. Champollion-Figeac, ed., *Lettres des rois, reines et autres personnages des cours de France et d'Angleterre*, 2 vols. (Paris, 1847), II, pp. 545-49.

47. The sources do not explain why Calais, a much shorter run across the sea, was not the port of entry, but its use would have certainly offended the French.

48. Sanuto, *Diarii*, XIX, p. 207, quoting a letter from Abbeville to the French ambassador in Venice.

49. Floranges, *Mémoires*, XVI, p. 268.

50. *Letters and Papers*, I, p. 1422. According to Dandolo, the king slept with the queen twice at Beauvais. Sanuto, *Diarii*, XIX, p. 270.

51. *Registres de l'hôtel de ville*, I, pp. 211-19; *Letters and Papers*, I, pp. 1434-39; C. Barkerville, ed., *Pierre Gringore's Pageants for the Entry of Mary Tudor into Paris* (Chicago, 1934); Richardson, *White Queen*, pp. 116-18. Paris paid him and a carpenter 115 *l parisis* for the pageants.

52. "Ce sont les jouxtes faictes a Paris a lentree de la royne Marie," BN, Fonds français p. 5103. See also Maulde, *Louise et François*, pp. 377-81.

53. *Letters and Papers*, I, p. 1403.

54. CSP Spain, II, pp. 242, 246-47.

55. *Letters and Papers*, I, pp. 1446-48; Richardson, *White Queen*, p. 123.

56. Floranges, *Mémoires*, XVI, p. 269.

57. *Histoire de Bayard*, XVI, pp. 88-89; Floranges, *Mémoires*, XVI, p. 271.

58. Sanuto, *Diarii*, XIX, pp. 352, 363; Champollion-Figeac, *Lettres des roys*, pp. 549-50.

59. Sanuto, *Diarii*, XIX, p. 371; Floranges, *Mémoires*, p. 371. H. Hauser, "Sur la date exacte de la mort de Louis XII," *Revue d'histoire moderne* 6 (1903), pp. 177-82, argued that Louis died at 10 P.M., December 31. Bridge, *History of France*, IV, pp. 267-83, examines evidence in great detail and accepts January 1. I find his argument convincing.

60. See the statement of the French ambassador in Venice that Mary was pregnant, Sanuto, *Dairii*, XIX, 372. For the story that Mary and Francis had sexual relations, see Brantôme, *Dames Gallantes*, p. 399. Both Maulde, *Louise et François*, pp. 383-84, and Richardson, *Mary Tudor*, pp. 134-36, argue strongly against its veracity.

61. Floranges, *Mémoires*, XVI, p. 273.

62. Richardson, *White Queen*, p. 144ff, is convinced that Mary was not in love with Suffolk when she married Louis, but fell in love with him while he was with her after Louis's death. Their granddaughter was the tragic Lady Jane Grey.

63. The events following Louis's death and his funeral are described in "Registres en forme de Iournal faict par un domestique de Mons. le Chancelier Du Prat," BN, collection Dupuy 600, fol. 1r-2v; "Obsequies du Roy Loys XII," AN, KK 89; and "L'Obséquies et enterrement du Roy," in *Archives curieuses*, I, pp. 61-70.

64. BN, collection Dupuy 600, fol. 2v. Bloem, in her fine "Royal Funeral of Anne of Brittany," which makes several important points of comparison between Anne's obsequies and Louis's, seems not to be aware that this was the major reason why Anne's were so much longer.

65. Giesey, *Royal Funeral Ceremony*, pp. 112-20. Quilliet, *Louis XII*, p. 416, maintains that Louis, who was considered miserly, spent 52,000 *l* on Charles VIII's funeral, while Francis I, regarded as a spendthrift, spent only 13,000 on Louis. But AN, KK 89, fol. 1, shows the actual expense of Louis's obsequies was at least 27,533 *l*. Among the items were 1,000 *livres* for Masses for the dead and 1,880 *l* in alms.

NOTES TO CHAPTER 17

1. I do not regard Louis's annulment of his marriage from Jeanne as an injustice, as sad as it was for her. He was as much a victim as she was.

2. R. Doucet, in *The New Cambridge Modern History* (London, 1957), I, p. 298; N. Cantor, *Inventing the Middle Ages: The Lives, Works and Ideas of the Great Medievalists of the Twentieth Century* (New York, 1991), p. 268.

3. The best summary of J. R. Major's thesis is in his *Representative Government*, pp. 1-6. See A. Slavin, *The "New Monarchies" and Representative Assemblies Medieval Constitutionalism or Modern Absolutism* (Boston, 1964), for a selection of pieces pro and con on this debate. The number of 12,000 royal officials comes from R. Mousnier, *Les XVIe et XVIIe siècles* (Paris, 1954), p. 99. R. Knecht, *French Renaissance Monarchy: Francis I and Henry II* (London, 1984), p. 15, uses the figure of 5,000 officials with 3,000 subordinates for 1515.

4. Doucet, *Cambridge Modern History*, I, p. 298; Major, *Representative Institutions*, p. 125.

5. Louis's publicity campaign is the subject of Sherman, "The Selling of Louis XII." C. Richard, "Propaganda in the War of the Roses," *History Today* 42 (July 1992), pp. 12-18, makes the useful distinction between publicity as the natural presentation of the iconography of government and propaganda, the deliberate manipulation of information by the government. By those definitions most of what was done for Louis XII was publicity. See also P. Burke, *The Fabrication of Louis XIV* (New Haven, CT, 1992).

6. H. Lloyd, "Louis XII: Medieval King or Renaissance Monarch?" *History Today* 42 (February 1992), p. 23.

7. Quoted by Wolfe, *Fiscal System*, p. 62. As is true for several other *bon mots* attributed to Louis, I have not been able to find a contemporary source for this one.

8. B. Guenée, "Espace et état dans la France du bas Moyen Age," *Annales* 23 (1968), pp. 744-58.

9. *Ordonnances des roys*, XXI, p. 177.

10. For a further discussion, see Sherman, "Selling of Louis XII," pp. 375-79.

11. See remarks in Baumgartner, *Henry II*, pp. 42-43.

12. Louis Le Caron, *Questions diverses . . . de Loys Charondas le Caron* (Paris, 1583), p. 106.

13. Bodin, *Methodus ad facilem historiarum cognitionem* (Lyon, 1583), p. 263.

14. A. Mornac, *Observationes usres fori gallici*, 4 vols. (Paris, 1721), II, p. 46. Mornac, who may have been the great grandson of the Mornac at the Orléanist court when Louis was born, commented some sixty years after his death: "As Louis XII protected uniquely the plebians against the nobles, he was called the commoner king."

15. Brantôme, *Oeuvres complètes*, II, p. 364. Brantôme was extremely favorable to Louis, whom he obviously regarded as the ideal king.

16. *Traicté des finances de France* (Paris, 1561), in *Archives curieuses*, IX, p. 379.

17. La Barre, *Formulaire des esleuz*, p. 96.

18. Major, "The Third Estate at Pontoise 1561," *Speculum* 29 (1954), 474.

19. M. Holt, "Attitudes of the French Nobility at the Estates-General of 1576," *The Sixteenth Century Journal* 18 (1987), p. 499.

20. M. Hayden, *The Estates General of 1614* (Cambridge, 1974), pp. 187-207 passim; Major, *Representative Government*, p. 663.

21. Quillet, *Louis XII*, pp. 448-52. Earlier in the Enlightenment Voltaire penned a paen of praise for "le sage Louis douze." *Oeuvres complètes* (Paris, 1968), II, pp. 524-26. There are thirteen "Eloges de Louis XII" printed from 1778 to 1788 now in the Bibliothèque nationale.

22. Sherman, "The Selling of Louis XII," pp. 13-14.

NOTES TO APPENDIX

1. See the edicts on money in *Ordonnances du roys*, XXI; and Bridge, *History of France*, I, pp. 252-61. For the weight and fineness of the coins, see Spooner, *International Economy*, Appendix A. For the concept of a money of account, see L. Einaudi, "The Theory of Imaginary Money from Charlemagne to the French Revolution," in F. Lane, ed., *Enterprise and Secular Change* (Homewood, IL, 1953), pp. 229-61.

■ BIBLIOGRAPHY ■

The following bibliography is a list of all the primary sources cited in the notes and the principal secondary studies used.

PRIMARY SOURCES

MANUSCRIPTS

Archives Nationales (AN), Paris:
    Fonds J 655, 910, 951
    Fonds JJ 235
    Fonds K 71, 73, 74, 77, 78, 79, 80, 171, 1639, 1714
    Fonds KK 77, 78, 86, 87, 88, 89, 583

Bibliothèque Nationale (BN), Paris:
    Fonds français 1672, 2627, 2827, 2830, 2831, 2832, 2881, 2924, 2926, 2927, 2928, 2929, 2930, 2931, 2932, 2933, 2934, 2961, 2962, 3087, 4329, 5013, 5093, 5103, 5501, 5973, 7647, 15538, 15973, 17522, 20978, 23110, 25272, 25718, 26107, 26110, 26111, 26112
    Collection Baluze 14
    Collection Cinq Cents de Colbert 1
    Collection Dupuy 28, 38, 81, 85, 160, 412, 600
    Fonds Latin 2241, 1523, 1559, 3375, 5149, 5972, 16576
    Fonds nouvelles acquisitions françaises 499, 1232, 1233, 7647

PRINTED WORKS

Alberi, E., ed. *Relazioni degli ambasciatori veneti al Senato.* 1st series. 6 vols. Florence, 1839-1863.

Andrellini, F. *Les faictz et gestes de tres reverend pere monsieur le legate.* N.p., n.d.

Auton, J. d'. *Chroniques de Louis XII.* Edited by R. de Maulde. 4 vols. Paris, 1889-95.

Baschet, A. *La Diplomatie Vénitienne.* Paris, 1862.

Beatis, A. de. *Travel Journal.* Trans. by J. Hale. London, 1979.

Benedetti, A. *Diary of the Caroline War.* Trans. by D. Schullian. New York, 1976.

Boissonnade, P. *Les négociations entre Louis XII et Ferdinand Le Catholique.* Mâcon, 1899.

Botero, G. *Practical Politics (Ragion di Stato).* Trans. by G. Moore. Chevy Chase, Maryland, 1949.

Bouchard, A. *Les grands croniques de Bretaigne.* Edited by H. LeMeignen. Rennes, 1886.

Bouchet, J. *Le Panégyric du Chevallier sans reproche, ou Mémoires de La Trémoille.* In C. Petitot, *Collection complète des mémoires,* Vol. XIV.

Brantôme, P. de. *Oeuvres complètes.* Edited by L. Lalanne. 11 vols. Paris, 1864-82.

Buchard, J. *Diarum.* 3 vols. Paris, 1883-85.

Calendar of Letters and Papers of the Reign of Henry VIII. Edited by J. Gairdner. 21 vols. Reprint, Vaduz, 1965.

Calendar of Letters, Despatches, and State Papers Relating to Negotiations between England and Spain. Edited by R. Tyler. Vol. I. Reprint Nendeln, Liechtenstein, 1969.

Calendar of State Papers and Manuscripts preserved in Archives in Milan. Edited by A. Hinds. 4 vols. Reprint, Nendeln, Liechtenstein, 1967.

Calendar of State Papers Relating to English Affairs Existing in the Archives of Venice and Northern Italy. Edited by R. Brown. Vols. I-II. Reprint, Nendeln, Liechtenstein, 1970.

Champollion-Figeac, A., ed. *Lettres des rois et reines et autres personnages des cours de France et d'Angleterre.* 2 vols. Paris, 1847.

Cimber, L. and Danjou, F. [Louis Lafaist], eds. *Archives curieuses de l'histoire de France.* 1st series, vols. I-II. Paris, 1834-50.

Cocheris, H., ed. *Entrées de Marye d'Angleterre . . . à Abbeville et à Paris.* Paris, 1859.

Conqueste de Gennes . . . Avec l'entrée du Roy en la dicte ville de Gennes. Genoa, 1507.

Delisle, L., ed. *Une Lettre de Louis XII aux maire et échevins de St-Omer après les états-généraux en 1506.* St-Omer, 1881.

Desjardins, A. et al., eds. *Négociations diplomatiques de la France avec la Toscane.* 6 vols. Paris, 1859-86.

Desrey, P. "Relation du voyage du Roy Charles VIII." In *Archives Curieuses,* Vol. I.

Deville, A. *Comptes de dépenses de la construction du Château de Gaillon.* Paris, 1850.

Du Boulay, C. *Historia Universitatis Parisiensis . . . a Carolo Magno ad nostra tempora.* 6 vols. Paris, 1665-73.

Dumont, J. *Corps universel diplomatique du droit des gens.* 8 vols. Amsterdam, 1726-31.

Entrée de très chrestien Roy de France Louys dousiesme de ce nom en la ville de Gennes. N.p., 1508.

Erasmus, D. *Collected Works.* Edited by R. Mynors et al. 86 vols. to date. Toronto, 1974-.

Floranges, R. de. *Histoire des choses mémorables advenues du reigne de Louis XII et François I.* In C. Petitot, *Collection complète des mémoires,* Vol. XVI.

Friedberg, E. *Corpus Iuris Canonici.* 2 vols. Graz, 1959.

Gachard, L. *Collection des voyages des souverains de Pays-Bas.* 4 vols. Brussels, 1876-82.

Gilles, N. *Les chroniques et annales de France . . . jusqu'au Roy Charles huitiesme.* Paris, 1573.

Giustinian, A. *Dispacci.* Edited by P. Villari. 3 vols. Florence, 1876.

Godefroy, D. *Le cérémonial Français.* 2 vols. Paris, 1649.

Godefroy, J., ed. *Lettres du Louis XII et du Cardinal d'Amboise.* 4 vols. Brussels, 1712.

Grassi, P. *Le due spedizioni militari de Guilio II.* Edited by L. Frati. Bologna, 1886.

Gringore, P. *Oeuvres complètes.* Edited by C. d'Héricault et al. 2 vols. Paris, 1858-77.

Guicciardini, F. *History of Italy.* Trans. by A. Goddard. 10 vols. London, 1753-56.

Höfler, C. von. "Die Despeschen der Venetianischen Botschafters Vincenzo Quirino." *Archiv für österreichische Geschichte* 66 (1885), 53-256.

Isambert, F. *Recueil général des anciennes lois françaises depuis l'an 420 jusqu'à la révolution de 1789.* 29 vols. Paris, 1821-33.

Jaligny, G. de. *Histoire de Charles VIII.* Edited by T. Godefroy. Paris, 1684.

Kinser, S., and I. Cazeaux, eds. *The Memoirs of Philippe de Commynes.* 2 vols. Columbia, South Carolina, 1969-73.

La Barre, R. *Formulaire des esleuz.* Rouen, 1622.

Landucci, L. *A Florentine Diary from 1450 to 1516.* Trans. by A. De Rosen Jervis. Freeport, New York, 1971.

La Trémoille, L. de, ed. *Correspondance de Charles VIII . . . avec Louis II de La Trémoille pendant la guerre de Bretagne (1488).* Paris, 1875.

La Vigne, A. de. *Le Vergier d'honneur.* Paris, 1500. In *Archives curieuses,* Vol. I.

Le Ferron, A. *De Rebus Gestis Gallorum.* Basel, 1569.

Le Glay, A., ed. *Correspondance de l'Empereur Maximilian I et de Marguerite d'Autriche de 1507 à 1519.* 2 vols. Paris, 1839.

Le Glay, A., ed. *Négociations diplomatiques entre la France et l'Autriche.* 2 vols. Paris, 1845.

Lemaire de Belges, J. *Oeuvres.* Edited by J. Stecher. Geneva, 1969.

Letters and Papers, Foreign and Domestic of the Reign of Henry VIII. Edited by R. Brodie. Reprint, Vaduz, 1965.

Le Verdier, P., ed. *L'Entrée de Roi Louis XII . . . à Rouen (1508).* Rouen, 1900.

Machiavelli, N. *The History of Florence and Other Selections.* Edited by M. Gilmore. New York, 1970.

Machiavelli, N. *Le Opere.* Edited by L. Passerini et al. Florence, 1873.

Mailles, J. de. *La très joyeuse, plaisante et récréative histoire . . . du gentil Seigneur de Bayart.* In Petitot, *Collection complète des mémoires.* Vol. XV-XVI.

Mandrot, B. de, ed. *Dépêches des ambassadeurs milanais en France sous Louis XI et François Sforza.* 4 vols. Paris, 1916-23.

Masselin, J. *Journal des Etats Généraux de France tenus à Tours en 1484.* Edited by A. Bernier. Paris, 1835.

Maulde La Clavière, R. de, ed. *Procédures politiques du règne de Louis XII.* Paris, 1885.

Molinet, J. *Chroniques.* Edited by G. Doutrepont et al. 2 vols. Brussels, 1935.

Monluc, B. de. *Commentaires.* Edited by Paul Courteault. Paris, 1964.

Morice, H., ed. *Mémoires pour servir de preuves à l'histoire ecclésiastique et civile de Bretagne.* 3 vols. Paris, 1742-46.

Mornac, A. *Observationes usres fori gallici.* 4 vols. Paris, 1721.

Navarette, M., et al. *Coleccion de Documentos Ineditos para la Historia de España*. 5 vols., Madrid, 1842-46.

Ordonnances des roys de France de la troisième race. 22 vols. Paris, 1723-1846.

Pandiani, E. "Un Anno di Storia Genovese." *Atti della Societa Ligure de storia patria* 37 (1905).

Pélicier, P., ed. *Lettres de Charles VIII*. 5 vols. Paris, 1898-1905.

Pélissier, L., ed. *Documents pour l'histoire de l'établissement de la domination française à Gênes (1498-1500)*. Genoa, 1894.

Pélissier, L., ed. "Documents sur la première année du règne de Louis XII." *Bulletin historique et philogique* (1890), 6-110.

Pélissier, L., ed. *Lettre de Louis XII à la Seigneurie de Sienne pour lui notifier son avènement (1498)*. Siena, 1894.

Pélissier, L., ed. *Lettres inédites sur la conquête du Milanais par Louis XII*. Turin, 1893.

Pélissier, L., ed. *Recherches dans les archives italiennes: Louis XII et Ludovic Sforza*. 2 vols. Paris, 1896.

Pélissier, L., ed. *Trois relations sur la situation de la France en 1498 et 1499*. Montpellier, 1894.

Petitot, C. *Collection complète des mémoires relatifs à l'histoire de France*. 130 vols. Paris, 1819-29.

Picot, E. *Recueil général des sotties*. 3 vols. Paris, 1909-12.

Registres des délibérations du Bureau de la ville de Paris. Edited by P. Guérin et al. 32 vols. Paris, 1873-1952.

Renaudet, A. *Le Concile Gallican de Pise-Milan*. Paris, 1922.

Rymer, T. *Foedera, ... Acta publica inter Reges Anglicae*. London, 1749.

St-Gelais, J. de. *Histoire du roy Louis XII*. Edited by T. Godefroy. Paris, 1615.

Sanuto, M. *I Diarii*. 58 vols. Venice, 1879-1903.

Savoie, Louise de. *Journal*. In C. Petitot, *Collection complètes des Mémoires*, Vol. XVI.

Seyssel, C. de. *Histoire de Louis XII*. Paris, 1615.

Seyssel, C. de. *Les Louenges du bon roi Louis XII*. Paris, 1587.

Seyssel, C. de. *The Monarchy of France*. Trans. by J. Hexter et al. New Haven, CT, 1981.

Spont, A. *Letters and Papers relating to the War with France, 1512-1513*. London, 1897.

Stein, H. ed. "Le sacre d'Anne de Bretagne et son entrée à Paris." *Mémoires de la Société de l'histoire de Paris et de l'Ile-de-France* 29 (1902), pp. 268-304.

Tommaseo, N. *Relations des ambassadeurs Vénitiens sur les affaires de France au XVIe siècle*. 2 vols. Paris, 1838.

Valbelle, J. *Histoire Journalière*. Aix, 1985.

Valois, N. *Inventaire des arrêts du Conseil d'état*. 2 vols. Paris, 1886-93.

Vellay, H. *Chronique Abrégée*. In P. Jacob, *Chroniques de Jean d'Auton*. 4 vols. Paris, 1835, IV, pp. 228-36.

SECONDARY STUDIES

BOOKS AND DISSERTATIONS

Ady, C. *A History of Milan under the Sforzas*. New York, 1907.

Baudier, M. *Histoire de l'administration du Cardinal d'Amboise, grand ministre d'Estat de France*. Paris, 1634.

Beaune, C. *The Birth of an Ideology: Myths and Symbols of Nation in Late-Medieval France*. Trans. by S. Huston. Berkeley, CA, 1991.

Bois, G. *The Crisis of Feudalism*. Cambridge, 1984.

Bourgeois, L. *Quand la cour de France vivait à Lyon*. Paris, 1980.

Britnell, J. *Jean Bouchet*. Edinburgh, 1986.

Bridge, J. *A History of France from the Death of Louis XI to 1515*. 5 vols. Oxford, 1921-36.

Brown, H. *Music in the Renaissance*. Englewood Cliffs, NJ, 1976.

Bryant, L. *The King and the City in the Parisian Royal Entry Ceremony*. Geneva, 1986.

Buisson, F. *Le Chancelier Antoine Duprat*. Paris, 1935.

Cameron, E. *The Reformation of the Heretics: The Waldensians of the Alps, 1480-1580*. Oxford, 1984.

Chambers, D. *Cardinal Bainbridge in the Court of Rome, 1509 to 1514*. Oxford, 1965.

Chambert de Lauwe, M. *Anne de Beaujeu: ou la passion du pouvoir*. Paris, 1980.

Chaunu, P., and Gascon, R. *Histoire économique et sociale de France*. 3 vols. Paris, 1977.

Chevalier, B. *Tours, Ville Royale (1356-1520)*. Louvain, 1975.

Chevalier, B., ed. *La France de la fin du XVe siècle: renouveau et apogée*. Paris, 1985.

Chiral, E. *Un premier foyer de la Renaissance—Le Château de Gaillon*. Paris, 1952.

Clamageran, J. *Histoire de l'impôt en France*. 3 vols. Paris, 1867-76.

Cloulas, I. *The Borgias*. Toronto, 1989.

Cloulas, I. *Jules II*. Paris, 1990.

Cloulas, I. *La vie quotidienne dans les châteaux de la Loire au temps de la Renaissance*. Paris, 1983.

Contamine, P. *La France au XIVe et XVe siècles. Hommes, Mentalités, Guerre, Paix*. London, 1981.

Contamine, P., ed. *La France de la fin du XVe siècle*. Paris, 1985.

Contamine, P. *Guerre, Etat et Société à la fin du Moyen Age. Etudes sur les armées des rois de France 1337-1494*. Paris, 1972.

Courteault, H. *Le dossier "Naples" des Archives Nicolay. Documents pour servir à l'histoire de l'occupation française de Royaume de Naples*. Paris, 1916.

Cruickshank, C. *Henry VIII and the Invasion of France*. New York, 1991.

Cuttler, S. *The Law of Treason and Treason Trials in Later Medieval France.* Cambridge, 1981.

Daniel, G. *Histoire de France.* 17 vols. Paris, 1755-57.

Darcy, M. *Louis XII.* Paris, 1935.

Décluze, E. *Saggio intorno a Leonardo da Vinci con due lettre inedite di Luigi XII.* Siena, 1844.

Delaborde, H. *L'expédition de Charles VIII en Italie.* Paris, 1888.

Delisle, L. *Le cabinet des manuscrits de la bibliothèque Impériale.* 3 vols. Paris, 1868-81.

Devic, C., et al. *Histoire générale de Languedoc.* 15 vols. Toulouse, 1872-92.

Dictionnaire de Biographie française. 16 vols. to date. Paris, 1933-.

Doucet, B. *Les Institutions de la France au XVIe Siècle.* 2 vols. Paris, 1948.

Drèze, J. *Raison d'Etat; Raison de Dieu. Politique et Mystique chez Jeanne de France.* Paris, 1991.

Duby, G. *Histoire de la France urbaine.* 4 vols. Paris, 1981.

Duffy, C. *Siege Warfare: The Fortress in the Early Modern World, 1494-1660.* London, 1979.

Dupry, A. *Histoire de la Réunion de la Bretagne à la France.* 2 vols. Paris, 1880.

Ehrenberg, R. *Capital and Finance in the Age of the Renaissance.* New York, 1963.

Febvre, L. *Life in Renaissance France.* Trans. by M. Rothstein. Cambridge, MA, 1977.

Gabory, E. *Anne de Bretagne, Duchesse et Reine.* Paris, 1941.

Ganay, E. de. *Un chancelier de France sous Louis XII: Jehan de Ganay.* Paris, 1932.

Garnier, J., et al. *Histoire de France.* 18 vols. Paris, 1810-21.

Giesey, R. *The Royal Funeral Ceremony in Renaissance France.* Geneva, 1960.

Guenée, B. *Tribunaux et gens de justice dans le baillage de Senlis à la fin du Moyen Age.* Paris, 1963.

Guenée, B., and F. Lehoux. *Les entrées royales françaises de 1328 à 1515.* Paris, 1968.

Gundersheimer, W., ed. *French Humanism 1470-1600.* New York, 1970.

Hackett, F. *Francis the First.* Garden City, New York, 1935.

Harding, R. *Anatomy of a Power Elite: The Provincial Governors in Early Modern France.* New Haven, CT, 1978.

Harsgor, M. *Recherches sur le personnel du conseil du roi sous Charles VIII et Louis XII.* 4 vols. Lille, 1980.

Hauser, H. *Les sources de l'histoire de France au XVIe siècle.* 4 vols. Paris, 1906-15.

Heller, H. *Iron and Blood: Civil Wars in Sixteenth-Century France.* Montreal, 1991.

Iancu, D. *Les Juifs en Provence (1475-1501).* Aix, 1981.

Imbart de La Tour, P. *Les Origines de la Réforme.* 4 vols. Paris, 1905-35.

Jackson, R. *Vive Le Roi! A History of the French Coronation from Charles V to Charles X.* Chapel Hill, NC, 1984.

Kantorowicz, E. *The King's Two Bodies.* Princeton, NJ, 1957.

Kendall, P. *Louis XI, The Universal Spider.* New York, 1971.

Knecht, R. *Francis I.* Cambridge, 1982.

Labande-Mailfert, Y. *Charles VIII, Le vouloir et la destinée.* Paris, 1986.

La Brosse, O. *Le Pape et le Concile.* Paris, 1965.

Lacroix, P. *Louis XII et Anne de Bretagne.* Paris, 1882.

La Roncière, C. de. *Histoire de la Marine française.* 4 vols. Paris, 1899-1906.

Lavisse, E., ed. *Histoire de France.* Vol. V. *Les Guerres d'Italie* by H. Lemonnier. Paris, 1903.

Ledru, A. *Histoire de la Maison de Mailly.* 2 vols. Paris, 1893.

Leroux de Lincy, A. *Vie de la Reine Anne de Bretagne.* 4 vols. Paris, 1860-61.

LeRoy Ladurie, E. *The French Peasants 1450-1660.* Berkeley, CA, 1987.

Levi, A., ed. *Humanism in France at the End of the Middle Ages and in the Early Renaissance.* New York, 1970.

Levis-Mirepoix, Duc de. *Jeanne of France Princess and Saint.* Toronto, 1950.

Lewis, P., ed. *The Recovery of France in the Fifteenth Century.* London, 1971.

Lot, F. *Recherches sur les effectifs des armées françaises des guerres d'Italie aux guerres de Religion 1494-1562.* Paris, 1962.

Luchaire, A. *Alain Le Grand, Sire d'Albret.* Paris, 1877.

Major, J.R. *The Monarchy, the Estates and the Aristocracy in Renaissance France.* London, 1988.

Major, J. R. *Representative Government in Early Modern France.* New Haven, CT, 1980.

Major, J. R. *Representative Institutions in Renaissance France, 1421-1559.* Madison, WI, 1960.

Mandrou, R. *Introduction to Modern France, 1500-1640.* Trans. by R. Hallmark. New York, 1976.

Maugis, E. *Histoire du Parlement de Paris de l'avenement des rois Valois à la mort de Henri IV.* 3 vols. Paris, 1913-16.

Maulde La Clavière, R. de. *La Diplomatie au temps de Machiavel.* 3 vols. Reprint, Geneva, 1970.

Maulde La Clavière, R. de. *L'Entrevue de Savonne (1507).* Paris, 1896.

Maulde La Clavière, R. de. *Histoire de Louis XII. Louis d'Orléans.* 3 vols. Paris, 1889-91.

Maulde La Clavière, R. de. *Jeanne de France, Duchesse d'Orléans et de Berry.* Paris, 1883.

Maulde La Clavière, R. de. *Les origines de la Révolution française au commencement du XVIe siècle.* Paris, 1889.

Maulde La Clavière, R. de. *Louise de Savoie et François Ier: Trente ans de jeunesse.* Paris, 1895.

Michaud, H. *La Grande Chancellerie et les écritures royales au 16e siècle.* Paris, 1967.

Mousnier, R. *La vénalité des offices sous Henri IV et Louis XIII.* Paris, 1971.

Néret, J.-A. *Louis XII.* Paris, 1948.

Oman, C. *The History of the Art of War in the Sixteenth Century.* Reprint, New York, 1972.

Pastor, L. von. *The History of the Popes.* 40 vols. St. Louis, 1938-53.

Picot, G. *Histoire des Etats Généraux de 1355 à 1614.* 4 vols. Reprint, Geneva, 1979.

Prescott, W. *History of the Reign of Ferdinand and Isabella the Catholic.* 3 vols. New York, 1872.

Quilliet, B. *Louis XII Père du Peuple.* Paris, 1986.

Renaudet, A. *Préréforme et humanisme à Paris pendant les premières guerres d'Italie.* Paris, 1953.

Richardson, W. *Mary Tudor, The White Queen.* Seattle, WA, 1970.

Roederer, P. *Mémoire pour servir à une nouvelle histoire de Louis XII.* Paris, 1819.

Rouleau, P. *Jean Maire, Evêque de Condom 1436-1521.* Paris, 1931.

Schnapper, B. *Les Rentes au XVIe siècle.* Paris, 1957.

Sequin, J. *L'Information en France, de Louis XII à Henri II.* Geneva, 1961.

Setton, K. *The Papacy and the Levant 1204-1571.* 4 vols. Philadelphia, 1976-84.

Shennan, J.H. *The Parlement of Paris.* Ithaca, NY, 1968.

Sherman, M. "The Selling of Louis XII: Propaganda and Popular Culture in Renaissance France." Ph.D. Diss., University of Chicago, 1974.

Spont, A. *La taille en Languedoc de 1450 à 1515.* Toulouse, 1890.

Spooner, F. *The International Economy and Monetary Movements in France, 1493-1725.* Cambridge, Massachusetts, 1972.

Tailhé, J. *Histoire de Louis XII.* 3 vols. Paris, 1755.

Thomas, J. *Le Concordat de 1516.* 3 vols. Paris, 1910.

Tilley, A. *The Dawn of the French Renaissance.* Reprint, New York, 1968.

Tomlinson, R. *The Struggle for Brazil, 1500-1550.* New York, 1970.

Valois, N. *Le Conseil du Roi aux XIV, XV, et XVI siècles.* Paris, 1888.

Villari, P. *Life and Times of Niccolo Machiavelli.* 2 vols. Reprint, Westport, CT, 1968.

Weary, W. "Royal Policy and Patronage in Renaissance France: The Monarchy and the House of La Trémoille." Ph.D. Diss., Yale University, 1972.

Wiley, W. *The Gentlemen of Renaissance France.* Reprint, Westport, CT, 1971.

Wolfe, M. *The Fiscal System of Renaissance France.* New Haven, CT, 1972.

ARTICLES

Baulant, M. "Les prix des grains à Paris de 1431 à 1788." *Annales ESC* 23 (1968), 520-40.

Baumgartner, F. "Louis XII's Gallican Crisis of 1510-13." In A. Bakos, ed. *Politics, Ideology and the Law in Early Modern Europe.* Rochester, 1994.

Beard, J. "Letters from the Elysian Fields: A Group of Poems for Louis XII." *Bibliothèque d'humanisme et renaissance* 31 (1969), 27-38.

Bloem, H. "The Processions and Decorations at the Royal Funeral of Anne of Brittany." *Bibliothèque d'humanisme et renaissance* 44 (1992), 131-60.

Caillet, L. "La mort de Charles VIII." *Revue d'histoire de Lyon* 8 (1909), 468-74.

Chaillon, P. "Les musiciens de Nord à la cour de Louis XII. In F. Lesure, ed. *La Renaissance dans les provinces de Nord.* Paris, 1956.

Clinksdale, E. "Josquin and Louis XII." *Acta Musicologica* 38 (1966), 67-69.

Coles, P. "Crisis of a Renaissance Society: Genoa 1488-1507." *Past and Present* 11 (1957).

Dawson, J. "The Codification of the French Customs." *Michigan Law Review* 38 (1945), 765-800.

Guenée, B. "Espace et état dans la France du bas Moyen Age." *Annales ESC* 23 (1968), 744-58.

Hauser, H. "Sur la date exacte de la mort de Louis XII." *Revue d'histoire moderne* 6 (1903), 177-82.

Holt, Mack. "Patterns of Clientele and Economic Opportunity at Court during the Wars of Religion: The Household of François, Duke of Anjou." *French Historical Studies* 13 (1984), 305-322.

Lloyd, H. "Louis XII: Medieval King or Renaissance Monarch?" *History Today* 42 (February 1992), 17-23.

Maulde La Clavière, R. "Marie de Clèves La Mère de Louis XII." *Revue historique* 36 (1888) 81-112.

Melot, M. "Politique et architecture: Essai sur Blois et le Blésois sous Louis XII." *Gazette des beaux-arts* 70 (1967), 317-28.

Palustre, B. "L'Abbesse Anne d'Orléans et la réforme de l'ordre de Fontevrault." *Revue des questions historiques* 66 (1899), 210-17.

Pélissier, L. "L'Alliance Milano-Allemande à la fin du XVe siècle." *Miscellenea di Storio Italiana* 35 (1898), 337-474.

Piton, M. "L'Idéal épiscopal selon les prédicateurs français de la fin de XVe siècle." *Revue d'histoire ecclésiastique* 61 (1966), 81-94.

Rice, E. "The Patrons of French Humanism, 1490-1520." In A. Molho, ed. *Renaissance Studies in Honor of Hans Baron.* Dekalb, Illinois, 1971.

Sandret, L. "Le Concile de Pise." *Revue des questions historiques* 34 (1883), 425-56.

Scheller, R. "Ensigns of Authority: French Royal Symbolism in the Age of Louis XII." *Simiolus* 13 (1982), 75-141.

Scheller, R. "Gallia Cisalpina: Louis XII and Italy 1499-1508." *Simiolus* 15 (1985), 5-63.

Spont, A. "Les galères royales de la Méditerranée 1496-1575." *Revue des questions historiques* 58 (1897), 238-74.

Spont, A. "La Marine française sous le règne de Charles VIII. *Revue des questions historiques* 55 (1894), 387-454.

Vidal, J. "Une crise épiscopale à Pamiers 1467-1524." *Revue de l'histoire de l'église de France* 14 (1928), 305-64.

■ INDEX ■